I0149841

"This colorful anecdotal history of crime in pre-war Los Angeles presents a lively cast of cops, criminals and reformers who, for better or worse, gave us modern Southern California. . . . Fans of both history and noir fiction will revel in the many true-life crime accounts in pre-war Southern California."
    -- *BookLife Review*

A " riveting . . . combination of regional history, true crime, and biography centered around an early twentieth-century detective's ambiguous career. . . . Los Angeles, a gritty, once isolated city, is captured in painstaking detail, including its turn-of-the-century con men, the Tenderloin District, the rise of vice leaders, and criminal cases. . . . a niche history of Los Angeles's turn-of-the-century vice syndicates, detectives, and related ephemera. . ."
    – *Clarion Reviews*

". . . [packed] with lively stories filled with 'goons' and 'coppers.' . . . a fascinating blueprint of the rise of power and corruption in civil service . . . . Extensively researched and annotated"
    – *Blueink Review*

". . . a riveting portrait of early 20th-century LA . . . a well-paced and well-researched account . . . with ample photos, maps, and newspaper clippings. . . . a complex portrait of a brave cop beset with his own demons. . . . An exciting addition to the true-crime history of Depression-era LA."
    – *Kirkus Reviews*

The Acorn: The Munson Bankruptcy Case [Los Angeles Herald Examiner Photo Collection, Los Angeles Public Library]

The Long Winding Road of Harry Raymond:

A Detective's Journey
Down the Mean Streets of Pre-War
Los Angeles

by
Patrick Jenning

Copyright 2020

All rights reserved

July 2024

ISBN 978-1-7367868-1-9 (Hardback)
ISBN 978-1-7367868-0-2 (Paperback)
Library of Congress Control Number: 2021917410

Bay City Press
www.baycitypress.com

NOTE:
All quotations in this book indicating spoken words are directly from printed sources. No dialogue has been invented.

Parts of "The Acorn" were published previously in *Testimony of a Death/Thelma Todd: Mystery, Media and Myth in 1935 Los Angeles* by the same author and Marshall Croddy.

Front Cover: Second and Spring Street, Los Angeles, [Dick Whittington Collection, University of Southern California].

Back Cover: Superimposed on a 1939 photograph of the Los Angeles City Hall and the United States Federal Building and Post Office [Los Angeles Times Photographic Archive, UCLA Library. Copyright Regents of the University of California, UCLA Library] are Earle E. Kynette's' San Quentin booking photograph [San Quentin State Prison Records, 1850–1950. ID #R135, California State Archives, Office of the Secretary of State, Sacramento, California], Clifford Clinton examining Harry Raymond's damaged automobile [UCLA Special Collections], Harry Raymond seated on running track of 1933 touring car [Collection of James Raymond], William Albert Bringhurst San Quentin Booking Photo, Charles Crawford [Family Photo Collection of Linda Burns], Aimee Semple McPherson and Rheba Crawford [Los Angeles Times Photographic Archive, UCLA Library, Copyright Regents of the University of California, UCLA Library] and Harry Raymond [Collection of James Raymond].

ACKNOWLEDGEMENTS

It is unlikely that this book could have been written before the digitalization of historic newspapers and documents now hosted on both governmental and commercial internet sites. Combined with the advanced search capabilities of modern optical character recognition, the digitalized records have enabled me to trace Harry Raymond's footsteps through the seventy-five years of his life. Undoubtedly, some events have been missed, but enough were found to flesh out the remarkable career of this detective.

The papers of Joseph Shaw and Clifford Clinton of the Special Collections Department of the University of California at Los Angeles have also been valuable resources. I also wish to thank the Los Angeles Police Museum, John Duntley, Jim Raymond, Linda Burns, and Lisa Gray for the use of photographs from their personal collections.

However valuable the technological advances were to the completion of this book, the encouragement of family and friends was even more so. I wish to thank my brother Michael, my wife Pam, and two old friends, Marshall Croddy and Julie Robitaille, for their support. I also want to thank two new friends, Jim and Itsu Raymond, for their kindness, generosity and insight into the long career of Jim's detective uncle.

For Pam

Under the laws I'm labeled on the books and licensed as a private detective. Not that I'm proud of that license but I need it, and I've had considerable trouble hanging onto it. My position is not exactly a healthy one. The police don't like me. The crooks don't like me. I'm just a halfway house between the law and crime; sort of working both ends against the middle.

Carrol John Daly, *The Snarl of the Beast*

... of course, he has to swim in the same water we all do.

Robert Towne, *Chinatown*

Contents

10:15 P.M., JANUARY 13, 1938

Detective Harry Raymond rode down the elevator of the Civic Center Building in downtown Los Angeles and crossed to the east side of Broadway. Five feet six and one-half inches tall, he was powerfully built, with hazel eyes and brown hair that the years had thinned, leaving him partially bald. Now in his late fifties, he walked with a cane, limping slightly, his leg still sore from a break sustained in an automobile accident two years before.

It had been a warm winter's day, the kind that made the retired farmers idling on the benches in Pershing Square gloat over their good fortune in escaping the Midwestern cold. Now the night was turning cool, with a gentle breeze drifting in from the ocean. A storm was advancing from the northwest and the first clouds already shrouded a nearly full moon. The diffused moonlight, together with street lamps and storefront neon signs, bathed the city in a soft glow.

Raymond's new Chrysler Royal was parked in a large outdoor lot in the center of the block where a few years before the old Los Angeles City Hall stood. He scanned the lot for suspicious characters and then made his way carefully to the car. The parking attendant kept an eye on it for him. Still, Raymond took a few seconds to check for signs of tampering before he unlocked the door. Tossing his cane before him, he climbed into the driver's seat, turned the switch key, and pressed the starter button. The engine hummed into life.

His home was only a few miles to the east but he took his time getting there. After entering Broadway from the parking lot, he turned left on Second Street and drove through the tunnel before heading south on Figueroa. For a few minutes, he meandered through the downtown streets while studying the headlights in his mirror. Several times, he swung down a side street, pulled to the curb, cut his lights and watched to see if a car stopped behind him.

Shortly before eleven, he reached his house at 955 Orme Avenue, a two-bedroom bungalow he had rented for three years. His driveway was the Hollywood or ribbon type, a pair of concrete strips divided by grass that sloped to a small garage seventy feet from the street. Leaving the motor idling, he unlocked the padlock on the twin barn-style doors and drove the car in slowly, stopping just before the front bumper touched the garage's rear wall. The big Chrysler's passenger side fit snugly against a wooden shelf, where a rolled up bag and some old clothes were piled. Raymond switched off the engine, climbed from the car, and locked the automobile. After closing the garage doors, he locked them with the padlock.

His wife Beulah was asleep in the rear bedroom. For a while, he sat up, smoking and listening to the news on the radio. We can guess what the radio reported that night from the newspapers that day and the next. A US Navy minesweeper had found the wreckage of the Pan American Samoan Clipper off Pago Pago in the middle of the Pacific Ocean. Famous Los Angeles criminal lawyer Jerry Giesler was defending an airport executive who awakened from a drunken sleep in his bedroom, observed his wife fellating his best friend on a piano bench in the front room, and killed them both. The Senate just confirmed President Roosevelt's nomination of Joseph Kennedy as Ambassador to Great Britain. Los Angeles' Superior Court judges were squabbling over the selection of the new grand jury.

After the news, Raymond put out his cigarette and retired to his bedroom in the front of the house to sleep.

12:30 A.M., JANUARY 14, 1938

Across the street, Mary Sakalis awoke to the sound of her husband's voice. He had gone to sleep in the rear bedroom around 7:30 that evening. George Sakalis was a grocery peddler who delivered produce from the back of his truck. He had to be at the Seventh Street Produce Market before dawn and he needed his sleep. Mary got out of bed, glanced at her two sleeping children and went to the other bedroom.

George was leaning into the window that faced the alley on the side of their small, five-room bungalow. She heard him shout in his thick Greek accent that he was going to shoot somebody with a shotgun if they didn't leave him alone and let him sleep. Mary peered over his shoulder at the alley. Three men stood there, part of a group that had moved into the courtyard apartment across the alley shortly after George and Mary and their children moved into their house a few months before. They said they were "radio" men but neighborhood women suspected they were police of some sort and called them "G-Men." Aside from the first few weeks when they busied themselves running wires up telephone poles, the G-Men were usually quiet and kept to themselves. But now they were keeping George awake. The men looked at George for a few seconds. Then they turned and walked through the back door of their apartment.

George closed the window and crossed the hallway to the other bedroom. Mary stayed in the rear bedroom, seated in a chair where she could look out the window. She was still there around 2:30 when George awoke, dressed, and left for work. Mary watched him back his truck down the alley. In the G-Men's apartment, the lights were on. She could hear voices. Unable to sleep, she remained in the chair, listening to the men talking. Around four, she heard whispers and footsteps crunch the gravel of the alley, moving toward the street.

4:15 A.M., JANUARY 14, 1938

Beulah Raymond awakened to the growl of her dog. A month earlier, he had growled and climbed upon the bed to peer through the curtains. She had followed the dog's gaze toward a man a few feet away shining an amber-shaded flashlight up and down the corner of the garage. Harry had not been home so she called the police, but by the time they arrived, the man had vanished. Tonight, the dog was not insistent and Beulah did not look out. After a minute she dropped back to sleep.

Inside 955 Orme, Harry Raymond slept. Beulah Raymond slept. Even the dog slept.

* * *

As for the rest, we can only speculate. About the time Beulah's dog growled, a dark figure slipped down the driveway of 955 Orme Avenue. Somehow, the padlock on the garage door was sprung. We will never know how this was done but it was not a difficult job for hands skilled at such mischief. Perhaps one G-Man himself did the deed, but it may have been a hireling, somebody engaged only to unlock the shackle. The G-Men would know where to find a man with such a talent. If we could compare a list of all picklock thieves in Los Angeles at the time to a list of all departing passengers on trains during the next forty-eight hours, we might be able to guess. In any case, we can assume that, with the padlock removed, there remained a short time—seconds, minutes, or maybe an hour—before the garage doors were opened and the work began. The automobile's hood was center-hinged, allowing one side to open independently of the other. It was easy to expose the driver's side section and wedge the bomb, 6-inches of pipe capped at both ends and filled with smokeless powder, between the engine block and floorboards. Two wires, one black and one white, which extended from a hole in one cap, were quickly twisted around wires of the engine's starter motor. The hood was lowered and the garage door closed quietly. The padlock snapped shut. The dark figure stole across the street to the alley.

What we know is that, in the days that followed, Harry Raymond, already known as "the most feared copper in California," would be celebrated throughout the nation as a tough, defiant man unafraid to take on the powerful political and criminal forces that tried to kill him. The pipe bomb that exploded when he started his automobile that morning drove several hundred pieces of metal into his body, fractured both his ankles, and left him with multiple lacerations, including two puncture wounds in his chest. For days, newspapers across the country ran photographs that showed him stalwartly smoking a cigarette while doctors removed shrapnel from his legs. Before the year was over, his defiance would lead to the indictment of officers in a secret Los Angeles Police squad, the recall of the mayor, the dismissal of twenty-three senior officers in the LAPD, and the migration of many of LA's underworld figures to Las Vegas, where they would create a legal gambling empire. For many, Harry Raymond would go down in Los Angeles history as a true knight in the story of LA's corrupt days, a detective hero like Raymond Chandler's Philip Marlowe. Others, looking back at the years before he pushed his automobile's starter button, would regard him as the kind of cop Marlowe hated: brutal and corrupt.

Albert W Raymond [collection of James Raymond]

Rosella Raymond [collection of James Raymond]

*Harry Raymond 1931 [Author's
personal collection]*

1: THE YOUNG DETECTIVE

Harry Raymond arrived in Los Angeles in 1907, his twenty-sixth year. He was not a tall man. In the coming years, he would often appear, somewhat diminutive but self-confident, in photographs beside much larger policemen. But he was broad-shouldered and strong. "Tough" was an adjective repeatedly applied to him, though physical strength and courage would not be as important to his future success as his keen intelligence and resourcefulness. He was shrewd.[1]

He was born into a railroad family on June 13, 1881, in Nickerson, Kansas. His father, Albert W. Raymond, worked as a boilermaker at Nickerson's extensive Atchison Topeka & Santa Fe Railroad yard. His mother, Rosella, was the daughter of a Union Army veteran and train engineer who had died a few years before in Millington, Illinois, when his locomotive collided with a car filled with hogs that a negligent livestock handler had left on the tracks. After their marriage on November 14, 1878, the young couple had lived with Rosella's widowed mother for two years in Aurora, Illinois, where Harry's older sister, Mary Jennifer was born in 1879.[2]

Nickerson was named after Thomas Nickerson, president of the Atchison, Topeka, and Santa Fe Railroad, which had platted the city in 1872. Were it a few miles further west and a few further north, one could say the small city was in the very center of Kansas, a state in the center of the 48 contiguous states. By April 1881, it had 597 inhabitants and would grow to over twelve hundred four years later. Its rapid growth resulted not only from the AT&SF depot, from which the local harvests were shipped to the hungry cities of the east, but also from an 1,100 feet bridge across the Arkansas River over which the cattle and produce-loaded wagons reached the depot. The bridge allowed Nickerson to lure away business from Hutchinson, its larger neighbor to the southeast, which had neither a bridge nor good roads. Nickerson also had attractions that temperate Hutchinson lacked: saloons. "A more melancholy object we have not lately beheld than a Nickerson saloon, and Nickerson whisky will kill at forty rods," the *Hutchinson Herald* declared in 1881. "It begets, it is said, murder, rape, and abomination."[3]

The Raymond family arrived in Nickerson around the time the *Hutchinson Herald* was bemoaning Nickerson whisky. Employment opportunities at the railroad abounded and not just because of the region's growing commerce. Men were needed to replace those injured or killed in frequent accidents, such as the one that decapitated a Nickerson brakeman in August 1880. A month later Nickerson resident and AT&SF conductor Harry Morgan was murdered after he ordered off the roof of the train coach a rowdy group of New Mexico-bound railroad workers, one of whom pulled a pistol and shot him in the belly. It was a clear case of murder, but because Morgan was tardy in his demise, lingering on for several weeks, his killer's attorney successfully argued that his death was in part due to poor medical care. His murderer was acquitted.[4]

In August 1881, Albert quit his job as foreman of the boilermakers at the Nickerson roundhouse. For a time, the family remained in Nickerson, where Albert helped organize a social club in October 1881. By the following autumn, the family had moved back to Chicago.

In 1885, the Raymonds were living in Argentine, a small city along the Kaw or Kansas River just south of Kansas City, Kansas, where Albert was working once again with the AT&SF. While in the coming twenty years, the Raymonds would follow Albert's career from one western city to another, much of Harry's youth took place in Argentine, a nineteenth-century industrial town whose air stank with a thick, noxious sulfuric odor from the Kansas City Consolidated Smelting and Refining Company's stacks.

On a smaller scale, the town possessed the same elements that young Harry would come to know when he arrived in Los Angeles a few years later. Separated from Kansas City, Kansas, by the river and from Kansas City, Missouri, by a state line, Argentine became notorious for liquor "joints" that defied Kansas' "Prohibitory Law" restricting the sale of alcoholic beverages to licensed druggists for "medical, mechanical or other scientific purposes."[5] Two narrow bridges enabled young men to cross the river to the saloons that lined the streets, where they reveled with smelter workers, many of whom were unmarried immigrants from European cultures more tolerant of liquor use than were most Kansans. Newspapers regularly reported the arrests of joint owners for illegal liquor sales. Allegations that city officials profited from leniency in prosecuting the prohibition laws were also common.

Like Nickerson, Argentine owed its birth to the AT&SF Railroad, which had built a 128-acre yard with a roundhouse and maintenance shops next to the riverbank to serve as the railroad's general terminal facility. South of the yard, between the river and a low ridge of hills, Argentine had grown from a small village of three or four dozen homes to a town of 1,300 inhabitants. In five years, it reached 6,000 residents, including a significant number of carpenters and homebuilders.

Except for a few years in Topeka, where Albert became not only foreman of AT&SF's roundhouse but also a prominent member of the Boilermaker's

Union and a leader in the Kansas chapter of the Ancient Order of United Workmen, the Raymonds remained in Argentine for the next ten years. In early 1896, Albert took a job as foreman of the Union Pacific Railroad's boiler shop in Ellis, a small city in western Kansas. The family remained there until October 1897. On November 24 of that year, when Harry's younger brother James was born, they were living in the Southern Hotel in Kansas City, Missouri. Afterward the family moved to Arkansas City, Kansas, where, in December, Harry's father suffered a grievous injury when hot steam and water blasted a loose boiler plug onto his face, shattering his nose and scalding his neck and one side of his body.

By this time, Harry was seventeen years old. He had completed only the sixth grade, so it is likely that he had already worked as a day laborer for a few years in the railroad yards. In all likelihood, he would have followed in the footsteps of his parent's families, but soon after his seventeenth birthday, he left home and, like many young men, promptly got into trouble. In Emporia, Kansas, he met Albert "Bert" Strout, a young man of twenty-seven with a bad reputation. The two young men bunked together in a hayloft. In late July, Strout burglarized the home of a prominent citizen. A few days later, a sheriff's deputy caught him and another local boy with the stolen goods in hand. After the two young burglars were locked in the city jail, another detective hired a local tramp to pass by the cell window, hoping that Strout would ask him to deliver a message to his other accomplice. The ruse worked; Harry Raymond was identified as the third thief.

Young Harry fled to Kansas City, where the Sheriff caught up with him. Harry had on him some of the items from the burglary, and an Emporia pawnshop owner later claimed that he had sold him others taken from the victim's home. Returned to Emporia, he was clapped in the local jail, where his father visited him the following day. Albert was undoubtedly displeased by Harry's behavior, the more so when newspapers throughout the state reported that Strout and Harry, "two notorious ruffians and bullies," had robbed another inmate of ten cents. The victim, a sixteen-year-old boy, had swallowed a quarter to keep Strout and Raymond from boosting it as well. He claimed the pair had tried to choke the quarter back out of his mouth.[6]

Harry spent over two months in the Emporia jail. On October 10, the court dismissed charges against him after he turned state's evidence against Strout. Released to the custody of his mother, he returned to Arkansas City. Strout was not so fortunate; he spent a year in the state penitentiary.

In the next few years, the Raymonds moved twice more, first to Cheyenne, Wyoming, where Albert worked as a boilermaker in the Union Pacific shops and Harry found work as a day laborer. In December 1902, following a strike of boilermakers in UP shops, Albert joined the Colorado and Wyoming

Railroad, a division of the Colorado Fire and Iron Company, at its mining operation in Sunrise, Wyoming. A group photograph in an album at the University of Wyoming shows Albert seated in the front row of sixteen other men who appear to be managers of the mine. He is looking slightly off camera with an expression of discomfort, perhaps suffering from the kidney and bladder problems that would send him to the company's Minnequa Hospital in Pueblo, Colorado, in early 1903 for an operation that would lead to his death in July of the same year. There is no discernable image of young Harry in the university's album, though it is possible that he is among the tiny figures in the otherwise peopleless images of machinery and scarred hillsides. Possibly, he had left the Raymond household sometimes in the early years of the century. His older sister, Jennie, had already left the household to marry a coworker of her father, John Balderston, a Canadian immigrant.[7]

In any case, Harry's next appearance in public documents comes in August 1903, when he obtained a marriage license to wed Beulah Early of Denver, Colorado. Beulah was the daughter of a notorious Denver lawyer and political figure, Thomas C. Early, the kind of man that Harry would encounter throughout his life, one who lived along the border of the law and most likely crossed over to the side of criminality and violence more than has been recorded.

Early came from a storied southern family. His uncle was Confederate General Jubal Early, a hero of the Shenandoah Valley campaign and an unrepentant promoter of the Lost Cause. T. C. had also fought in his youth for the Confederacy as a Missouri guerrilla. After the war, he had settled in Sedalia, Missouri, attending Missouri State University and working as a reporter, a high school principal and, later, an attorney. In 1876, after he married Adelia Edna Greene of Clinton, Missouri, he moved his family to Leadville, Colorado, where he continued his law career and became active in local Democratic Party politics. In June 1881, Adelia gave birth to their daughter, Beulah.

In 1882, while practicing law in Leadville, Early killed a police officer after an argument over court fees. Although he was eventually exonerated after claiming self-defense, the incident left his reputation in tatters among the newspapers and local citizenry. He moved his family to Denver where he practiced law for the next seventeen years and engaged in mining ventures in the state and beyond. In 1889, his wife Adelia died. Soon afterward, he married Sophia Miller, whose divorce he had secured from her banker husband. The marriage does not seem to have been a happy one. In a year, T. C., complaining of Sophia's extravagance, fled to Ogden, Utah, taking his daughter Beulah with him.

In the coming years, T. C. earned an unsavory reputation as a divorce lawyer, handling the majority of divorces in the County Court and sometimes skirting ethical and legal boundaries. His specialty was obtaining divorces for men who resided in other states from their unsuspecting and unserved wives. He was not alone in this practice. In particular, Chicago-based attorneys were infamous for procuring divorce decrees from remote Colorado courts for men whose wives had refused to end the marriage in their home state. The trick was to hire another woman, an actress of sorts, to stand in for the wife and admit to the charges her husband leveled against her. In 1891, after Denver authorities began to look into two such cases, one involving a Cincinnati police officer and another a wealthy Boston merchant, Early fled the city. In the latter case, neither the defendant wife nor the plaintiff husband had ever set foot in Colorado.

Early somehow escaped from this scandal with his law license intact. A few years later, he was involved in another unseemly matter. In late 1892, an upscale men's clothing store named T. C. Early and Company opened in Boise, Idaho, advertising "Hats, boots, shoes, trunks and traveling bags." The store flourished for several months and then abruptly announced that one of its clerks had purchased it. The move aroused the suspicion of several creditors, who directed local Boise attorneys to obtain writs of attachment against the store's assets. Other creditors followed suit. One firm demanded that the local authorities arrest the store's manager, T. C.'s brother, Wesley H. Manard Early, who went by the transposed initials of H. W. The Boise authorities obtained an incriminating letter, addressed to H. W. Early but delivered by mistake to another man named Early, which outlined a scheme to convert the goods into cash by forwarding them from the Boise store to small towns in Arizona, where they would be sold at rock-bottom prices. To throw the supplier's representatives off track, the goods would ship from Boise through Portland to Los Angeles via steamer and then on to Phoenix.[8]

Wesley Early was clapped into the Boise jail, where he remained for six months while his lawyers argued unsuccessfully for his release amid newspaper reports that he had already committed similar frauds in Kansas City, Missouri, and Chico, California. Thomas C., named by Idaho newspapers as a conspirator in the scheme, denied any involvement. Eventually, Thomas C. settled with the creditors and Wesley H. was released.

T. C. continued his legal career after the Boise debacle but concentrated on promoting mining stocks. Somewhere along the line, he had acquired the title of judge, and it was as *Judge T. C. Early* or the *Honorable T. C. Early* that he was often cited for his political views. By 1901, he had relocated to Wall Street as a New York Produce Exchange member to hustle mining and oil stocks. It was the final act of a life filled with dubious enterprises and deeds.

During 1901 and 1902, his advertisements for shares of oil wells at Spindletop in Beaumont, Texas, appeared frequently in newspapers throughout the nation. While Early claimed that he held no monetary interest in the stocks he brokered and that he sold only on a commission basis, in other ads he offered shares from his own holdings and predicted huge profits for investors. In 1900, his younger brother H. W. joined him in New York City to help hustle stock. A few months before his daughter married Harry Raymond, T. C. died of typhoid fever.[9]

Besides listings in the city directories of Denver and Los Angeles, little evidence exists of Raymond's activities in the five years between his wedding and the beginning of his career as a detective in 1909. How he became a detective is a mystery. Employed as a switchman in Denver in 1904, he appears to be the same Harry J. Raymond who in the 1905 *Denver City Directory* is the proprietor of a restaurant in partnership with Henry Belmont, a man in the middle of a long career in the culinary business. Raymond and Belmont's was the latest incarnation of a restaurant at 712 19th Street, directly across the street from the Denver East High School. It lasted one year. The *Denver City Directory* of the following year contained no listing for the restaurant, Harry Raymond or Henry Belmont.

From probate papers for Thomas Early's estate, we know that Harry and Beulah were in Los Angeles by October 1906. The couple first lived close to Harry's mother, Rosella, in downtown Los Angeles. By 1909, they shared rooms with her at 2024 East Sixth Street. The Los Angeles city directories show that, for a few years, Harry made a living as a salesman, but there is no record of what he sold. However, by the summer of 1909, he worked for the Citizens Detective Agency in the Delta Building at 426 South Spring Street.

The agency had been established on March 1, 1909. In the next months, advertisements for its services appeared in both the *Los Angeles Daily Times* and the *Los Angeles Herald.* Its first manager was a man named Ambrose but within a few months his name disappeared from the ads—apparently, he had resigned to start another agency with a detective named Parker. Harry Raymond's name did not appear in the ad, although in August 1909, he earned a brief mention for his efforts to trace a young girl whose body was eventually discovered in the surf off Hyperion, a suicide.

The Citizens Detective Agency was listed prominently in the business section of the 1910 *Los Angeles City Directory,* though the entry for Harry Raymond described his occupation as "clerk." It is possible that, for a year or two, he served some role with the agency other than actual detective work. On the other hand, he may not have wanted to acknowledge his profession in the directory. Private detectives did not enjoy high esteem with the American public in the early years of the twentieth century and it is arguable that without the literary efforts of Dashiell Hammett, Raymond Chandler and their successors, they would never have become such romantic figures. Larger agencies, such as Burns, Thiel, and Pinkerton, focused on labor issues and dominated the private investigation business. Corporations paid well to uncover employee misbehavior, whether embezzlement, unacceptable off-duty recreational activities, or union affinities, and the large agencies were ready to take their checks. For example, private *spotters* spied on streetcar conductors suspected of pocketing fares and shadowed bank employees to see if they drank on weekends. More lucrative for detective agencies was labor union work. Employers paid them well to infiltrate worker committees, incite violence during disputes, and provide strikebreakers.

Small agencies such as the Citizens Detective Agency played a minor role in the private eye game. While private detectives of big agencies earned the condemnation of the working class and its sympathizers, those of smaller agencies gained their share of disdain by pursuing cheating spouses, small-time embezzlers and grafters. They also had a reputation for using the information they gained in their jobs for blackmail. Hired by one spouse to shadow an errant partner, it was easy to boost one's income by extorting the unfaithful spouse as well. Newspapers often scolded private detectives for these practices. In California, the *Sacramento Record-Union* editorialized repeatedly against the misdeeds of private detectives and advocated for licensing fees to create a fund to recompense innocent persons harmed by them.

Neither large nor small detective agencies focused on criminal activity, which was the police's responsibility. However, Raymond would spend much of his long career ensnaring criminals. In fact, a criminal case made his reputation as a detective in the first place.

The case reflected the special character of the city itself while, at the same time, it harkened back to the time-honored evils of eastern cities. Although unique in many ways, especially climate, Los Angeles was not very different from other American cities of the early twentieth century. A compact little metropolis of just over 100,000 in 1900, it was twice as populous when Raymond arrived, but it is unlikely that its size overwhelmed him. The combined population of the urban area around the two Kansas Cities where Raymond grew up was roughly twice that of Los Angeles in 1900 and half again as large in 1905. Even Denver was more populous than Los Angeles at the time.

While Raymond would live long enough to see Los Angeles dominate its region, other nearby cities that today are part of a continuous urban sprawl in 1905 were distinct towns separated by miles of open land and scattered farms. Although dirt roads and cable cars passed through the narrow canyon of the Arroyo Seco to link Los Angeles to Glendale and Pasadena, only a few homes dotted Glendale, Verdugo and the Eagle Rock Valley to the north. Hollywood, a few years away from becoming the capital of motion pictures, was a quiet suburban community of a few thousand persons at the end of a two-hour streetcar ride along Prospect Avenue (now Hollywood Boulevard). Beyond Hollywood, the Cahuenga Pass provided a narrow wagon road into the San Fernando Valley west of the Los Angeles River, in 1905 a shallow but sometimes dangerous stream. No additional roads would cross the Santa Monica Mountains for decades.

Around the time the Raymonds arrived in Los Angeles, the Cahuenga Pass and most of the few structures within it burned in a fire set by careless campers cooking breakfast under eucalyptus trees. A *Los Angeles Times* reporter who happened to cross the pass at the time marveled at the "swiftness of a wind-driven mountain fire in the drought of a Southern California summer"—words that could have been repeated a thousand times in the coming century. Beyond the pass, in the San Fernando Valley, were the small town of Burbank and a few score dwellings in the area then called Providencia but later Toluca Lake and North Hollywood. West of Hollywood, beyond groves of oranges and lemons, the small platted town of Palms lay along the Santa Monica branch of the Southern Pacific railroad. A mile past Palms to the west was Home Junction, where a rail spur branched north to the National Soldiers Home near the base of Sepulveda Canyon. From there the tracks continued on to their terminus, Santa Monica. Other tracks ran south to distant towns: Watts, Compton, Redondo Beach, San Pedro, and Long Beach. The homes and buildings of Westwood, West LA and Culver City were years in the future.[10]

From a broader perspective, 1905 Southern California was not unlike the rest of the country, a region with a single large metropolis and many smaller independent communities nearby. Yet its isolation made it unique. Historian Carey McWilliams called the region an "Island on the Land," with an ocean to its west, a range of mountains to its north, and another ocean of sand and dust to its east. A quick look at the distances between the 100 major cities in the 1900 census confirms his metaphor. San Francisco, a city over three times the population of Los Angeles at the time, was 381 miles to the north; Oakland across the bay was 371 miles. The next nearest metropolis was Portland, Oregon, at 964 miles. Denver was over a thousand miles away, and Las Vegas, San Diego and Phoenix were too small to matter. No other city with over 38,307 inhabitants, the cutoff point for the 1900 most populous 100 American cities, approached Los Angeles in terms of isolation except New Orleans. Dirt roads crossed the desert but only horse-drawn wagons followed them. As in the gold rush days, ships loaded with passengers docked at San Pedro but most travelers in 1905 came by train.

Unlike Nickerson and Argentine, Los Angeles predated the railroads, but its growth was largely driven by them. The first tracks of the Southern Pacific railroad entered the city from the San Joaquin Valley by way of the Tehachapi Loop in 1876, almost one hundred years after the city was founded. In 1885, the AT&SF reached Los Angeles, descending the Cajon Pass from Barstow via the outlying towns of San Bernardino, Pomona and Whittier. The completion of the AT&SF tracks touched off a furious price war between the railroads. The AT&SF offered fares of $100 from Chicago, a full $25 less than the Southern Pacific. For over a year, the two railroads battled for customers, their competition driving down the price of a round-trip fare to a single dollar in March 1887. The low rates powered a speculative boom in real estate but the boom ended abruptly in late 1887 when local banks tightened their lending requirements. A rapid sell-off and decline in land prices followed, most dramatically in areas outside Los Angeles city limits. Still, the boom had long-lasting effects. As historian Charles Dwight Willard described, it led to the entry of "a speculative and adventurous class" which exercised a disproportionate influence in city affairs.

> Here were 40,000 or 50,000 people suddenly gathered together from all parts of the Union, in utter ignorance of one another's previous history. A great amount of money was passing rapidly from hand to hand, and a great city was in embryo. It was the golden opportunity of the fakir and humbug and the man with the past that he wanted forgotten. . . . The man with whom you were doing business every day might be an ex-convict—or he might be one whom the stripes were destined to ornament some time in the future.[11]

While Willard believed that the experience of the 1880s led many in Los Angeles to exercise more prudence when it came to get-rich-quick schemes, the machinery was still in place for the confidence man. "Fresh fish" poured in from the Midwest—farmers and small businesspersons looking for easier climates and relief from tuberculosis and asthma.

One such "fish" came to Raymond's office at the Citizens Detective Agency in early 1910. Floyd D. Kane had recently arrived in Los Angeles with his ailing wife Ova. The couple, who married six years before, had done well in their hometown of Clare, Michigan. They were popular. Floyd, well regarded as an "obliging" drug store clerk, was endorsed by the local paper as "one of our clean, progressive young men" when he ran for alderman in the small city. Ova was a "tireless worker" in the local Ladies Guild of the

Congregational Church. In 1907, they had moved north to the city of Harbor Springs. Around this time, Ova began to show signs of tuberculosis, the disease that killed her mother when Ova was five years old.[12]

Without telling their friends in Clare, the couple struck out for Southern California in December 1909. Looking for a safe investment to support himself and his wife, Kane responded to a *Los Angeles Times* advertisement for the purchase of a half-interest in a downtown real estate business. When he arrived at 821 South Grand Avenue, he found a bustling, well-furnished office strewn with real estate brochures, salesmen coming and going, and an intense, busy atmosphere. The owner, a well-dressed man named George Clark, waved an expensive cigar as he explained that the real estate market was so hot that he needed a partner to handle the load. He preferred a young, energetic man who could give a good-faith deposit of $320 in order to earn a $125 monthly salary. He did not care if the partner was inexperienced; he could teach him the trade. Clark showed Kane the account books, which demonstrated a healthy profit that could sustain a new partner's pay. He also showed him advertisements that the office had placed for new properties to sell. As Clark and Kane talked, another man came into the office. Clark turned to the man to announce that he had sold his house and received $30 as a down payment. "That's your commission," the man replied. "Keep it."[13]

Kane was eager to buy into the flourishing business, but Clark put him off; he first needed a few days to check Kane's references. The delay had the intended effect of heightening Kane's enthusiasm for the venture. When he returned two days later, Clark informed him that his references had checked out and then wrote a contract bestowing Kane his salaried position for the $320 consideration. A key provision in the contract stipulated that Kane was purchasing his partnership "on his own volition" and absolved his partner from any business reverses that might result.

A few days later, Clark left Kane in charge of the office to pursue urgent business outside the city. After a week, Kane received a telegram from Clark. It informed him that Clark was unable to return and would have to sell the business. At this point, Dolphe M. Greene strolled into the office. Greene told Kane that Clark had also telegraphed him with an offer to sell. Greene said he would step aside should Kane wish to purchase the business, but if the young man declined to do so, then he would buy it himself. In that case, he explained, he would not need a partner. Kane did not have the funds, so Greene took over the business and dismissed him.

Kane was out his full deposit. Had he been able to come up with the additional money to take over full ownership, he would have lost it as well. The real estate office was a fake; the busy clerks were stooges of Greene and Clark and the solicitations for business they ran in the papers were merely part of the fraud. It was a scheme they had worked repeatedly, but not invented. Indeed, the *Los Angeles Times* had warned newcomers of such schemes as early as 1901.

After Kane left, the office was readied for another dupe. Sometimes the phony business was a real estate office, but any business that did not require more investment than some furniture and brochures would do. A much simpler swindle involved fake cigar stores: an inventory of cheap cigars and the swindlers' accomplices posing as steady customers to convince the eager but hapless investor that he was on to a good thing. Greene had run this fraud in Los Angeles for years. A few years before, he had escaped prosecution because police claimed they could not build a case against him. At least once, an investor had sued him in civil court and, on one occasion, the district attorney filed criminal charges only to have them dismissed.

The swindlers relied on two factors to avoid prosecution for their crimes: victims too embarrassed to admit that they were suckers and detectives and prosecutors averse to cases they could not readily prove. Payoffs to the right officials made legal action even less likely. Private detectives, however, needed no more motivation to investigate than the promise of a paycheck and good publicity. Kane visited Raymond's office to tell his story and Raymond, eager to prove himself, took on the case. Although they were reluctant to come forward, he soon had the names of fifteen additional victims. Most were from out of town, many from outside the state.

As Greene and his cohorts had worked the con for seven years, it was possible that the true number of victims mounted into the hundreds. In one case, the fraud led to more dire consequences, as Raymond discovered while his investigation continued with help of LAPD detectives McNamara and Carrol. A few years before, a "timid and weakened tuberculosis sufferer" named Michael McShean had moved to Los Angeles with his invalid sister. Seeing an advertisement for a cigar shop, he contacted Greene who persuaded him to deposit $150 to purchase the cigar stand at Fifth and Ruth Street. After a few days, McShean realized that the customers who frequented the stand while he looked it over were "stallers" whom Greene had hired to boost the sale. Despondent over the loss of most of his savings, McShean returned to his room at the Beulah Rooming house and shot himself in the head. Soon afterward Greene visited the rooming house and reclaimed the keys to the cigar stand. He told McShean's sister that, unless she paid another $150, he would repossess the business. The sister begged Greene to return the original $150 to no avail.[14]

After the story of the Kane swindle broke in local newspapers, Deputy District Attorney Arthur L. Veitch announced that he would file charges against Greene and another of his partners, Harry G. Conner. Clark had already confessed to the fraud. Veitch was meticulous in his trial preparation, believing Greene to be not only cunning but also dangerous. During his earlier career as a hack driver and operator of a laundry wagon, Greene had earned a reputation as a bellicose and violent man. In 1902, he tried to shoot a man whom he believed was having an affair with his estranged wife. After the man fled, Greene turned on his wife. He "beat her shamefully, her head and face being terribly bruised and swollen from his blows" according to the *Los Angeles Times*. When police arrived, they found him continuing to reproach his wife. She begged them to let Greene go, but after they learned of the shooting, the police arrested him for attempted murder. Greene escaped a penitentiary sentence after the district attorney reduced the charges to simple assault. He and his wife divorced a few months later. The following year, he wed another woman, whom he also beat.[15]

Other victims of Greene came forward in the weeks after his initial arrest. Each time police took him into custody. He responded to the mounting charges with contempt. On his second arraignment, he brandished a large roll of bills and asked the judge to use it to spare him the bother of additional court appearances for future charges. The judge declined and told him to handle his own financial affairs. Meanwhile, Clark continued to reveal the mechanics of the frauds in detail.

With the district attorney eager to prosecute him for multiple complaints, Greene's arrogance seemed misplaced. However, he had the means to fight the charges. He employed a bevy of skilled attorneys, including Frank Dominguez, Earl Rogers, Job Harriman, and Frank Dehm, to defend him against three separate indictments.

The first trial began in the courtroom of Justice Williams two weeks after the first newspaper reports of the swindles. It involved a young man named James Guinn, a Columbus, Ohio native, who paid Conner $300 for a half interest in a real estate office. After a few days, Conner told young Guinn he had inherited a newspaper in Bisbee, Arizona, and had sold his interest in the real estate office to D. M. Greene, who gave Guinn "a breezy talk and then disappeared for several days."[16] After learning that Greene had another nearby business, Guinn confronted him. Greene conceded that he did not have time for both businesses and agreed to sell his share to another partner. The new man, George M. Rice, paid Greene $250 for his half. For a few days, Rice and Guinn sat silently in the empty office, eyeing each other suspiciously. Each became convinced that the other was part of a con but when police arrested Greene and Conner, they realized they both were innocent dupes and joined in a complaint against the fraudsters.

Job Harriman and Earl Rogers took the lead in defending Greene and Conner in this case. They got Guinn to admit that the furnishings in the office alone were worth the $300 he had invested. After the jury hung seven to five for acquittal, the judge declared a mistrial. Veitch indicated that he would retry the case after a second case against the swindlers concluded.

On February 17, a second trial began. This time, the complainant was J. H. Umberger, an Oakland rancher who sold his northern California property and moved to Los Angeles with his wife in late 1909. Joining Greene and Conner as defendants was R. E. Ivett, another business opportunity swindler who had operated in Los Angeles for years. Umberger claimed that Ivett had posed as an automobile mechanic with more work than he could handle who was looking for a partner. He gave Umberger two references: Conner and Greene. Satisfied, Umberger shelled out $300 for a part interest in the business. There was no business, however, as Umberger soon learned, just an old barn. Ivett then disappeared for a few days. When he returned, he proclaimed the auto shop was a one man-operation after all and that his wife, who owned the barn, did not want him to use it to repair automobiles. Ivett offered to buy Umberger out for $50. Umberger at first declined the offer, but soon realized that Ivett had him cornered, and accepted. Afterward, realizing that he had been defrauded, he contacted the police, who then asked Raymond to look into the case. Raymond found a witness, Edwin Yates, who revealed that Ivett had bragged that he had "trimmed suckers" five times in the same way.[17]

Despite the damning testimony, Greene was unperturbed, joking with reporters and declaring, "If the man who does not have sense enough to know what he is buying makes a purchase, he is bit." Eager to complete the trial, Judge H. H. Rose convened a night session at 8:00 p.m. on Monday, February 21. After hearing from Yates and additional witnesses that evening, the prosecution and defense rested shortly before midnight. As Judge Rose read instructions to the jury in a quiet monotone, Defense Attorney Rogers repeatedly interrupted him, flustering Rose so completely that the judge threatened him with arrest. At that moment, fate, or perhaps the calendar, or perhaps something else, intervened. Since the following day was Washington's Birthday, a federal holiday, Judge Rose instructed the jurors to convene immediately and hand their sealed verdict to the bailiff the next morning. Shortly after midnight, the jury began its deliberations. After four hours, it reached a verdict and, following the judge's instructions, gave the bailiff the verdict.

Greene, Conner and Ivett were found guilty, but Defense Attorney Rogers and Harriman immediately objected to the procedures under which the verdict was handled. Two days later, a contrite Judge Rose admitted that he had erred in instructing the jury to turn over the sealed verdict to the bailiff; it should have been given to the Clerk of the Court. Rose, worried that a higher court might reverse the verdict, vacated it and scheduled a new trial. "It will not be a hardship on the prosecution," he declared, "As the evidence is fresh and the witnesses are at hand." He set the new trial date for March 21.[18]

Veitch presented his case again in late March. This time, the defense attorneys were more diligent in selecting jurors. In addition, defense attorney Frank Dominguez convinced Judge Rose to exclude Yates' testimony that Ivett bragged about trimming suckers because it also prejudiced the cases against Greene and Conners, whom Ivett had not mentioned in his conversation with Yates. Without this crucial testimony, the prosecution's case weakened considerably. After deliberating a few hours, the jury found all three defendants not guilty.

The retrial of Greene and Conners in the Guinn case also went badly for the prosecutor. Dominguez again represented the defendants. The defense and prosecution struggled to agree on a jury, and the case was tried with ten jurors instead of twelve. The trial took one long day, but the jury reached its decision that night: not guilty.

After two acquittals, the only case left to Deputy District Attorney Veitch was that of Floyd D. Kane, but Veitch figured it was his strongest. However, a few days before the trial began, Kane's wife died, her illness perhaps aggravated by stress from their financial situation and the impending trial. Kane told the judge that he must accompany her body back to her hometown in Michigan and that he would return afterward. In early May, he wired Veitch that he was destitute and could not afford the train fare. He offered to borrow some money to return, but Veitch thought it was too much to ask of the unfortunate man. He dismissed the charges against Greene and Conner.

Greene, Conner, and Ivett were free men. As far as the records show, they remained so. Greene's ads for cigar stands and other cash businesses appeared infrequently for another ten years. By 1923, the *Los Angeles City Directory* listed him as the proprietor of the Greene Apartments at 12 Avenue 24 in Venice. There is no definite record of Conner and Ivett, though a Harry G. Conner took out two building permits in March 1913. Ivett appears to have followed Greene into the real estate business, selling investment properties until he died in October 1912.

Floyd and Ova Kane's wedding photo [Clare Sentinel Oct 28, 1904]

Dolphe Greene [Los Angeles Times May 6, 1908]

2: LA THROUGH THE PEEPHOLE

It is easy to imagine that Raymond watched the trials of Greene and his partners with frustration. Perhaps he considered that the best response to con men was that of one victim, an ex-Confederate soldier named H. B. Gerhardt, who recouped the $500 Greene swindled from him by attacking him with a knife. If young Harry got a lesson in the ways of justice from the Greene case, he got another a few years later when, for the first but not the last time, he was caught up in the serpentine world of Los Angeles vice.

For many years, Los Angeles had segregated gambling, alcohol, and prostitution into a single district known locally as the Tenderloin. The name reflected the fact that the practice was not unique to LA. The original Tenderloin district was in the center of Manhattan Island. How it came by this name is a matter of some dispute. In the 1880s, the term designated the wealthiest districts of New York City, but soon came to be used with areas of the city that were replete with restaurants, nightclubs, and illegal gambling parlors. An editorial in the *New York Sun* in 1913 maintained that a New York Police Captain, "Clubber" Williams, christened the district in 1876. After being assigned leadership of the West 30th Street station, he reflected on the lucrative opportunity for graft now offered him by remarking, "I've been having chuck steak ever since I've been on the force, and now I'm going to have a bit of tenderloin."[2] Soon San Francisco and Philadelphia borrowed the appellation to denote their own vice districts. Other cities found their own nicknames. Washington, DC, had Hooker's Division, named after the troops of General Joe Hooker who camped in the area when Confederate forces threatened the capitol. Chicago had two areas: Little Cheyenne and the Levee District. Many civic leaders approved of segregated vice districts, which allowed prostitutes, gamblers and bartenders to ply their trades while minimizing the exertions of local police and politicians. It was also a moneymaking industry for just about everybody except the customers, whose dollars eventually ended up in the pockets of cops, councilmen, and mayors. The practice was not popular with the clergy and churchgoers, however, nor did social and government reform groups look favorably on the open availability of vice.

It is possible that Harry Raymond first became aware of the controversy over vice districts as a young boy in Argentine, which was to some extent a playground for young males of the two Kansas Cities. The long fight between wets and drys, vice leaders and church figures, politicians happy to restrict prostitution to the Tenderloin areas and crusaders determined to eradicate sin, would shape his career for decades to come. In one of his first cases, in fact, Raymond would go undercover to spy on LA gambling operations at the behest of the *Los Angeles Times*.[3]

In 1910 Los Angeles, the Tenderloin was a triangular section southeast of the historic Plaza and north of the business district. Aliso Street was at the base of the triangle, while Los Angeles Street and Alameda Boulevard formed its other sides. Today, the 101 Freeway slices through much of the old vice district and the names of two infamous alleys, Ferguson and Negro ("Calle del los Negros", where a mob of whites and Hispanics hanged seventeen Chinese men in 1871) have disappeared from maps, obliterated years ago by urban planners. In the nineteenth century, these vanished lanes were the nucleus of violence and degradation in Los Angeles. According to historian James Guinn, in the 1850s, when Los Angeles was a small town of some 5,000 or 6,000 persons, "deaths from violence were almost a daily occurrence" and "Negro Alley" was the "central point from which the wickedness of the city radiated."[4] Saloons, gambling halls and bordellos lined the 500-feet Negro Alley and, in the ensuing decades, opium dens added to the mix. By the 1880s, this area had become infamous for its cribs—small apartments where the most impoverished prostitutes lived and plied their trade. Several hundred of these one-story dwellings filled the properties between Los Angeles and Alameda Boulevard. More lined the eastern side of Alameda from Arcadia Street northeast to the current entrance of Union Station as well as the area now occupied by the station and railroad yards.[5]

Until 1904, Bartolo Ballerino was the "Vice King" of the Tenderloin. Ballerino arrived in California at age nineteen as part of a wave of Chileans who had flocked to the territory after learning of the discovery of gold months before the same news reached the eastern United States. By the time Yankees reached California in 1848, many experienced Chilean miners already occupied many choice claims. Although they generously shared their knowledge with the fledglings from the East Coast, by late 1849 conflicts between the Chileans and Yankees had resulted in riots in San Francisco and small battles in Calaveras County. In the ensuing years, these conflicts subsided and Chileans continued to work in the gold mining counties of California.

Ballerino mined gold in Calaveras County, where a census taker found him in 1852. In 1853, he decamped for Los Angeles. For a couple years, he drove a mule team between the city and the port at San Pedro. By 1855, he had enough capital to go into the cattle business and advertised his eagerness to buy, at reduced prices, cattle that had strayed into the mountains from the region's large rancheros. A year later, he advertised to purchase grapes for his new occupation as a winemaker. He produced 5,000 gallons of wine in 1860 and doubled production in the next two years. He had also married Maria Ampara Salcido, a 24-year-old Mexican immigrant. He was doing well. According to the 1860 Federal Census, he was worth the considerable sum of $1,200.

It is not clear when Ballerino branched into real estate and began to purchase lots in the Tenderloin district. A lawsuit filed against him in 1872 indicates that he acquired a property from Vicente Guerrero in 1861, and a delinquent tax notice of December 22, 1874 reveals that he owned a 100 feet lot on the eastern side of "Negro Alley" that extended to Alameda Street, where it occupied 80 feet of street frontage. In the following years, he purchased properties throughout the city and nearby townships, including a 160-acre tract along what is now Hoover Boulevard in the Pico-Union District.

While Ballerino collected rents for buildings on his Tenderloin property, little direct evidence exists of his involvement with prostitution, liquor, or gambling until the 1880s. The 1880 census found him farming in Ballona Township, over ten miles from downtown Los Angeles' vice district, with his three eldest children working alongside him. A few years later, the *Los Angeles City Directory* listed him as living in Cahuenga, "8 miles northeast of Los Angeles." By the end of the decade, however, he had focused his energy on the crib district, where he owned several properties outright and others in partnership with various investors. An 1884 insurance map shows his cribs, indicated as "female boarding", extending along the west side of Alameda Street. Another map created ten years later shows an expansion of cribs on the east side of the street as well as additional cribs between "Negro Alley" and Alameda. While some structures may date before Ballerino's purchase of the properties, building permits filed with the city during the eighties and nineties, along with accounts in local papers, indicate that he and other Tenderloin district property owners continued to improve the lots. One newspaper described his improvements:[6]

> The property . . . is in the very heart of the tenderloin, and consists of a rookery of one-story shacks divided into small compartments called "cribs." . . . Ballerino improved his new possessions by erecting several rows of cribs and establishing alleyways, electric lights, etc., for the guidance of depraved humanity to the haunts of sin.[7]

The cribs themselves were narrow rooms with few amenities. When not entertaining customers, the prostitutes loitered in their front doors "displaying their charms to as great an expanse" as "the benign laws and humorously tolerant policeman of the day allowed."[8]

Ballerino's involvement in prostitution may not have extended past collecting rents from prostitutes. Aside from a 1902 report in the *Los Angeles Times* that he and another crib owner, former San Francisco political boss Christopher Buckley, required occupants of their cribs to patronize Ballerino's Basket Saloon on Alameda and to stay away from those of competitors, there is little evidence that he managed the women in his cribs. The rents he received from the women, who, according to one expert, "ranked as the lowest order of prostitution in the social scale of prostitution," were considerable. They paid $1.50 to $2.50 per night in advance at a time when an entire house rented for $30 per month. From these proceeds, Ballerino earned between $50,000 and $100,000 per year.[9]

Although newspapers crowned Ballerino the "King" of the vice district, it does not appear that he exercised the devious influence of other vice kings. He seems to have been a figure of some derision in Los Angeles, a litigant in absurd lawsuits, a habitual complainant at the County Board of Supervisors and City Council meetings, an inveterate opponent to street-widenings affecting his properties; a quarrelsome, miserly man. His significant real estate holdings frequently led him into disputes with the County and City of Los Angeles over taxes and his obligations as a property owner. The county sued him when he refused to grant a right-of-way to the extension of 9th Street past Hoover but withdrew its lawsuit when his neighbor to the north allowed an encroachment on her land. He balked at an order to grade Alameda Street opposite his holdings and fought assessments of his properties. He also fought to preserve "Negro Alley," objecting to the city's effort to remove Chinese residents and its plan to extend Los Angeles Street to the Plaza. Twice he tried to turn the tables on the County by seeking public office. He ran for County Assessor in 1875 but lost badly. In 1890, he declared his candidacy for County Treasurer but withdrew as a candidate before the Republican Convention.

While Ballerino rarely got his way, at least publicly, in his disputes with City and County officials over taxes, property rights, or his penchant for illegal construction, he was a leading figure in Los Angeles vice operations for almost twenty years. His kingdom began to fall apart when his wife Maria sued him for divorce in February 1896, alleging that he had entered into an adulterous relationship with one of his tenants. Maria claimed "wild and visionary" schemes possessed him to improve his properties, such as his construction of fishponds. Ballerino dismissed her claims and boasted that he had made money on the fishponds by charging local boys ten cents to swim in them. When the fishponds washed away after a city dam burst during a rainstorm, Ballerino sued the city for damages.[10]

The court awarded Maria $75 per month alimony so she could live apart from her husband during the suit; Bartolo agreed and then failed to pay, earning himself a few days in jail for contempt. Although the court refused to grant Maria a divorce, Ballerino, fearing that she would take her case to higher courts, agreed to deed half his property to her. The Ballerinos then resumed living unhappily together at their homestead on Pico. In 1900, however, Maria filed suit against her husband and his partners in the crib district, demanding a full accounting of the value of his properties and rents. This suit she won. The couple's attorneys seem to have been the big winners, however. To pay the legal fees, the Ballerinos began to divest themselves of their property along Hoover and Pico Boulevards.

The rancorous marital disagreement had split the large Ballerino family into two camps. More trouble was to follow. A year before his wife filed for divorce, the district attorney indicted him on charges of "renting property with the full knowledge that it was to be used for immoral purposes."[11] Horace Bell, who would also represent Ballerino in the divorce case the following year, defended him. Bell managed to get the case dismissed on the grounds that both the mayor and chief of police had failed to demand in writing that Ballerino discontinue renting to prostitutes before the indictment was issued. For some reason, the district attorney took no further action. Ballerino's business was ignored for several years, although he had to defend himself against his former lawyer Bell's suit for unpaid fees. However, in 1903, after Chief of Police Charles Elton told the ever-confrontational prohibitionist Carrie Nation that the cribs were "a necessity," church groups pressured city officials to act.[12] On September 12, 1903, police charged Ballerino once again with renting cribs to prostitutes.

After the case was postponed repeatedly, religious reformers organized a mass protest against the district. Hundreds of church members thronged into the cribs to hand out religious tracts and plead with the women to abandon their lives of sin. Ballerino reacted with fury, calling the church people "a great gang of troublemakers" and threatened to "knock their damned heads off." By Christmas, police had shut down the district and arrested the district's pimps for vagrancy.

In January 1904, Ballerino sued Los Angeles Mayor "Pinky" Snyder to recover the income he had lost when the city closed the district. He also constructed a second story on some of his buildings, asserting that the law could not prevent him from renting to whomever he wanted on the second floor—a novel legal theory that left reporters puzzled. Other crib owners tried another stratagem by dividing the narrow rooms into two and stocking the front room with cigars, tobacco, and chewing gum so that the prostitutes could claim a legitimate trade. Whether either of these tactics worked is no longer clear; Ballerino ultimately lost his criminal case and his lawsuit against Snyder was dismissed. He received 30 days in jail and a $500 fine.[13]

Ballerino's reign as the King of the Crib District was over. Waiting in the wings to seize the crown were two pretenders. The first was Thomas Francis Savage, a San Francisco native born in 1865 to Irish immigrants, longshoreman Richard and his wife Bridgett. His parents had raised a large family on Alta Street on Telegraph Hill, a short walk from that city's Tenderloin district where there was plenty of opportunity for a young man to get into serious trouble. Savage did not disappoint. At age 17, an older man stabbed him in the thigh. A year later, during an altercation another man cut him with a razor, leaving a large scar from his left temple to his chin. While the man who assaulted him would spend three years in Folsom Prison, Savage wore the scar for the rest of his life.

At age sixteen, he took a job as a press operator, an occupation he declared in the years to come whenever queried by census takers or reporters. Moving to Los Angeles in 1888, he worked for the *Los Angeles Tribune* and the *Los Angeles Herald.* When the *Herald* moved its Hoe Printing Press from its current location on Second Street to new press rooms on New High Street, it credited him for managing the process, "a most remarkable and unprecedented mechanical feat."[14] Veteran newspaperman Horace Carr later wrote that Savage had a reputation throughout the country as an expert on presses.

Savage was also a boxing figure in the last years of the nineteenth century. At the time, San Francisco was a major boxing venue and Los Angeles pugilism benefited from its proximity. Newspaper accounts listed him regularly as an assistant or second to fighters at the Southern California Athletic Club and other venues around Los Angeles. Of medium height, 5 ft. 8 inches, he likely fought in the lower weight classes in undercard bouts that did not attract the attention of reporters. In his later years, he returned to the ring as a referee.

While notorious as a hard drinker and frequent street brawler, Savage was known also for his wit and charm. Newspaper reporters loved to mimic in print his Irish patois. One *LA Times* writer conveyed his observations about the gerrymandered local state assembly district in this way:

> "Why," said Tom with rueful appreciation of the tactics, "damn
> if they didn't fix this Assembly district so it begins down here in the
> Ate, hops over into the first, does a back flip clean over the Second

and lands in Hollywood, takes another hop and lands in Soldiers' Home, where they don't read no names on the ballots at all. They jist go down the list and put a stamp for every hole that says Republican next to it. What kind of a show has a Democrat, there?"[15]

He had long been interested in politics, having registered to vote in his native San Francisco as soon as he turned twenty-one. By 1892, he was a leader in the Los Angeles County Democratic Party. He demonstrated his enthusiasm by voting on the same day in both the Second and Eighth Wards, the latter including the Tenderloin and the area immediately to the northeast of 1st and Main, registering from the St. Elmo Hotel in the Second Ward and the Arlington Hotel in the Eighth. He also worked with cohorts in the Tenderloin on a get-out-the-vote effort which involved organizing the Tenderloin's "macs [pimps], hobos and loafers" to vote early and often.[16] In 1894, he obtained a seat on the party's county executive committee. Shortly afterward, he wrested the nomination for City Councilman from the incumbent by means many party members found resonant of the "worst methods of 'boss' politics." In December, he won a plurality of votes in the ward, defeating several prominent saloonkeepers, a Populist Party candidate, and one fellow Democrat running to protest Savage's candidacy.[17]

Soon after his election victory, he was accused of attempting to intimidate a police officer into dropping charges against one of his friends. He explained that he was just trying to help an old friend who might lose his job if the case were pursued. After denying charges that he was friendly to the Eighth Ward pimps, he struck a reformist stance, pledging to clear away Ballerino's cribs on Alameda. Throughout the two years of his term, he repeated his determination to rid the ward of its cribs but always with the prerequisite that another section of the city be set aside as a vice district, as otherwise the prostitutes would scatter across the city. His advocacy for cleaning up the cribs fell flat with reformers, however. Church leaders designated him a man "they could not vote for" a few days before he lost his re-election bid in December 1896. Despite the brevity of his tenure, Savage was remembered as an effective councilman who looked out for the interests of his ward as he advocated improvements in streets and sewers.[18]

Four of his five brothers moved to Los Angeles during the two years of his incumbency. The eldest, Jeremiah, opened a saloon in the Tenderloin district on the corner of Arcadia and Los Angeles, while the other brothers took jobs in the *Herald's* printing departments. By this time, Tom had his own business as a gas and steamfitter, securing some major contracts with local schools to install heating equipment.

After his election loss, Savage journeyed north to the Klondike to look for gold. He did well. In the summer of 1898, he returned to Los Angeles and proclaimed that he had made enough money to "keep me for a while" and planned to re-enter politics.[19] He quickly won election as a delegate to the county Democratic Party, obtaining votes, in the words of a *Los Angeles Times* reporter, "in his own peculiar way." Losers of the election accused him of winning by means "a trifle off color."[20] Two nights later, a reporter described him as wandering about the convention floor "with a chip on his shoulder, looking for trouble."[21] While he ran for office only once more, unsuccessfully, local papers charted his behind-the-scenes, pugnacious maneuvers for other candidates over the course of a dozen years.

Savage's rival for Ballerino's crown was Nick Oswald. Born in Wisconsin in 1869, Oswald moved with his family to Los Angeles around 1890, a few years after Savage arrived from San Francisco. A partner in a grocery market on Jefferson Street in 1895, he branched out on his own to open the South Main Street Market in 1897. In 1899, he opened the Angel City Market at 413 South Broadway. The following year he moved north again, this time landing in the heart of the Tenderloin at 217 Ferguson Alley, where, while living nearby on Commercial Street, he operated a liquor store that soon morphed into a saloon. In 1902, Oswald constructed a "one-story brick store and rooming building" on Los Angeles Street across from the historic Plaza— again, in the Tenderloin—for use by prostitutes. In the same year, after he obtained the liquor license for an establishment at the corner of Los Angeles and Commercial, he hired Savage to run the place.[22]

The relationship between the two vice leaders remained friendly for about three years. Savage continued his political activities and Oswald ran his liquor business, and both continued their involvement in the Tenderloin's core industry—prostitution. When the heat fell on Ballerino's cribs in 1904, it also singed both Savage and Oswald. After the closure of the crib district in late 1903, Oswald took over the New Arlington House, a notorious hotel at the corner of Los Angeles and Commercial Streets. Since the late 1880s, the Arlington had been the scene of numerous thefts, suicides, morphine overdoses and murders, including the assassination of a former Los Angeles Police chief. Oswald and Savage, who reportedly shared a lease on the property that was owned by a "Spanish lady in Fullerton,"[23] converted it into a bordello, superseding the now empty cribs. In 1904, reformers focused their attention on it. Police charged Oswald with "letting apartments to women for the purpose of prostitution" and revoked his license for one of his saloons, The Pantheon.[24]

Relations between the two vice leaders deteriorated over the next few years. The trouble may have begun in 1904, when Savage took over the leases of several saloons in the Tenderloin and, aided by local authorities who charged Oswald with renting rooms to prostitutes, strove to drive Oswald of the bordello business. In late 1905, after Oswald decided to run the New Arlington alone, Savage moved to Santa Monica to run his own saloon. He also abandoned his common-law wife, May Davenport, the New Arlington House manager who had been arrested in 1904 for keeping a disorderly house. May followed him to Santa Monica only to return despondent after a few days. On May 4, she drank a glass of wine mixed with 60 grains of morphine, an undeniably fatal dose. The quick action of her tenants and the police forestalled her death, but only for a few weeks. Her desperate act seems to have affected Savage deeply.[25] Two days after her suicide attempt, the *Los Angeles Times* reported that he was cooperating with a vice investigation headed by the police commissioners.[26] Savage was said to have revealed the names of crooked cops and local politicians. Not trusting the LAPD to investigate its own officers, the commissioners employed the Pinkerton Detective Agency to look into Savage's claims. However, when the Pinkertons realized the case might lead to indictments against some of their own clients among police and governmental officials, they abandoned the case, claiming vice investigations, like divorce cases, were not their normal line of business. As the investigation petered out, police commissioners wondered aloud whether Savage had outsmarted them by seeming to cooperate while he took over the business at the Arlington House. He continued to remain a political force in the Eighth Ward, which, according to the *Los Angeles Times*, he ran on the "Tammany Plan."

> When he was Councilman he was forever inventing the grand jobs for some old duffer who had broken his legs and who never could remember the name of the job he got, but who has sworn by this bright, quick-witted little Irishman ever since.[27]

In 1907, Savage, having regained control from Oswald of both the New Arlington and a second disreputable rooming house in the Eighth Ward named the Belmont, tried to block Oswald's attempt to reopen the crib district, including a few apartments still owned by Ballerino and his wife. Exploiting the annoyance of residents outside the crib district at prostitutes moving into their neighborhoods, Oswald lobbied city officials to re-segregate prostitution in a single locale under his control, out of the sight and mind of the larger community. Savage countered this move by joining with church ministers to keep the vice district closed. Oswald then demanded the closure of Savage's own houses. "If Oswald's crowd can't open, Savage must close," insisted one Oswald ally.[28]

Church leaders and other reformers recognized an opportunity in the dispute. After he thwarted the efforts of Oswald and his "crowd" to reopen Ballerino's cribs, Rev. Wiley J. Philips, a leader of the reform movement, hired a female detective to infiltrate one of Savage's establishments. Along with his associates, Charles Armstrong, Frank Parks and Charles Stack, Savage was charged with renting rooms to prostitutes. However, at his trial, the allies and rivals of the vice leader effected a wall of silence. Several witnesses refused to testify, citing the Fifth Amendment, and the prosecution's star witness, Nick Oswald, played dumb when asked about the ownership and management of Savage's bordellos. As he left the stand, Oswald stopped in front of Savage and offered his hand. The two vice leaders shook hands while the faces of their Tenderloin cronies beamed at the show of camaraderie.

The dramatic courtroom handshake between Savage and Oswald signaled that peace was at hand in the Tenderloin. After the jury split down the middle between acquittal and conviction, the DA decided that there was insufficient evidence for a successful retrial of Savage and his men. Only Parks was convicted and fined $200. Still, reformers and prosecutors kept pressing. Soon, loutish conduct and miscalculation by a city government ally of the segregated district helped end the Tenderloin District's long, soiled saga.

The ally was Police Commissioner Samuel Schenck, a New York state native and former traveling salesman who had come to Los Angeles in 1901 after amassing a small fortune in various Arizona mining operations. In a widely criticized move, Mayor Arthur Cyprian Harper had appointed Schenck to the police commission at the end of 1906. He was known as a player in the city's vice operations, a "gambler and habitual frequenter of saloons" according to the *Los Angeles Herald*. He was likely appointed because political and vice leaders believed him a good fellow who could help make the system work.[29]

His friends claimed that Schenck gave up liquor earlier in 1906. They also claimed his drinking problem made him sensitive to alcoholism among both police officers and his friends, several of whom he had helped quit liquor. If so, he had as of late fallen off the water wagon. His marriage was falling apart. His wife Elsie, a Swedish immigrant and socialite known for her beauty, her athleticism and, like Schenck, her hunting skills, had left him and was about to take their daughter to Catalina Island to live.

On Friday, June 28, 1907, Schenck visited his wife at their luxurious houseboat in Long Beach to celebrate his daughter's fifteenth birthday. His daughter pleaded with her parents to reconcile, but Schenck left the boat and returned to Los Angeles, where he attended a series of amateur matches at the city's premier boxing venue, the Naud Junction on Alameda. Afterward, he took a streetcar to the Alexandria Hotel where he downed a bottle of wine at the hotel's restaurant buffet. Then he began to walk the streets.

Patrolman Edwin M. Barnes was also walking that warm, clear night on his downtown beat. A man who said he was a friend of Schenck approached Barnes to ask for his help. The man explained that the commissioner was drunk and needed somebody to take him home. Why the friend could not do this himself is not clear, but Barnes, who had joined the police force in February of that year, understood his duty. It would not be seemly for a police commissioner to be seen drunk on a crowded downtown street, nor would it look well for him to be observed in the grips of a uniformed patrolman. Barnes called the Central Police Station and requested a plainclothes officer to escort Schenck home only to be told that no officer was available. Barnes was instructed to leave his beat, change to civilian clothes, and conduct the commissioner home himself.

For some reason, Barnes took his time following these orders. Two hours elapsed before he left his rooms at 1002 East 9th Street in search of the drunken police commissioner. He found Schenck lurching along the sidewalk on the corner of Fourth and Spring Streets in front of the Van Nuys Hotel. The theaters had let out and fashionably dressed playgoers crowded the sidewalks. As Barnes approached Schenck, he noticed an attractive young woman in the company of two men pass before the commissioner. The trio had just left a restaurant after attending the Belasco Theater on Main Street. Eyeing the young woman, Schenck leaned over toward Barnes and said in a loud voice, "Ain't she a pretty bird?" Immediately, the younger of the two men, later identified as Kenneth Preuss, excused himself from his company and turned to confront Schenck. What happened next was a matter of dispute. Barnes would claim that he thought Preuss was one of Schenck's acquaintances who had turned to greet him and was shocked when Preuss instead threw a punch at Schenck. Preuss and his friend Bradner Lee maintained that Schenck leered at Preuss for a moment and then struck him in the face. In either case, when Barnes stepped in and separated the two, the furious and intoxicated Schenck ordered the patrolman to arrest Preuss. Barnes took it as an order from a superior and dragged Preuss to a nearby patrol box, where he called for a police wagon. When the wagon arrived, Barnes and Schenck hustled Preuss inside. Meanwhile, Lee took the young woman to a hotel.[30]

The patrol wagon took its time in reaching the central jail. The elder of the pair, Bradner Lee, was already there when it arrived. Preuss was booked on a charge of disturbing the peace and tossed into a jail cell. Lee offered to pay his bail, but Schenck ordered the desk sergeant to mark the booking complaint "No bail." When Lee protested, Schenck had him arrested as well and decreed there would be no bail for either man.

The drunken Schenck then humiliated the men by strutting about the jail and insulting Lee, shouting gleefully, "You thought that you'd play hell, didn't you?" As he chastised the young man, a group of Schenck's friends arrived at the station. He instructed a policeman, Lieutenant George H. H. Williams, to give them a tour of the cells. When the group reached the cell of Preuss and Lee, Schenck derided them in front of his guests, crying, "There's a pair of drunks."[31]

Somebody among Schenck's friends recognized the two men in the cell. Preuss was a prominent and wealthy Angeleno. Lee was a leading attorney who had refused appointment as a Superior Court Judge in 1895 in order to continue practice as a lawyer. He had also chaired the Los Angeles County Republican Party for over a decade. Neither was a man to trifle with. One of the civilians then called Mayor Harper. Aghast, Harper got Schenck on the line and told him to release the prisoners. Schenck had the pair taken out of the cell but ordered them locked up again when Lee and Preuss refused to speak to him. A few minutes later, perhaps with an awareness of his predicament growing, Schenck ordered the two released. He apologized for the incident, told them all charges would be dropped, and suggested that they should also drop the matter. Preuss and Lee made no promises. After they left the station, Schenck followed them down the street and offered to buy them a drink. They refused, retorting acidly that they did not drink.

By the next morning, the entire city knew of Schenck's shameful behavior. After going into hiding amidst calls for his resignation, he resigned his commission on Tuesday, July 2. Not mollified, Lee demanded criminal charges be filed against him and the officers involved. Deputy District Attorney Edward J. Fleming concurred and proclaimed he would prosecute Schenck not only for his loutish behavior the previous Friday but also for any future infractions. The LAPD swiftly punished others involved in the Preuss and Lee incident. Barnes, still probationary, having been on duty less than a year, was removed from the police roll. The patrolman had already earned a reputation for using his position for petty larcenies, such as pocketing eggs and bakery goods from downtown businesses. A week later, the police commission suspended Williams and the desk sergeant, George H. Sparks, for sixty days and four months, respectively.

Prompted by Lee, Deputy District Attorney Edward J Fleming filed charges against Schenck and pursued the case vigorously. The first trial ended with a hung jury. Fleming filed charges again, but Schenck's attorney, his brother Paul, a law partner of Earl Rogers, obtained demurrals and postponements for over a year. By that time, the district attorney's office had lost its enthusiasm for the case. Fleming had quit the office to go into private practice and the case, which was only a misdemeanor, was a low priority item for his former colleagues. When the case was finally tried in December 1908, Schenck was acquitted.

His problems were far from over, however. In October, two editorials in the *Los Angeles Evening Express* alleged that Mayor Harper and the police commissioners protected vice in the city. The paper also claimed that Oswald promised protection to Tenderloin pimps and prostitutes in the mayor's name. Schenck was identified as a key figure in a payoff scheme to protect liquor sales and gambling, allegations the *Los Angeles Herald* echoed in a series of front-page editorials.

According to the newspapers, Schenck and fellow Police Commissioner Nathan Cole Jr. conspired with Mayor Harper, also a member of the commission by virtue of his office, to control the issuance of liquor licenses in the city. The three commissioners organized three related corporations to produce beet sugar in Tulare, California and then sold shares to saloonkeepers and brewers throughout Los Angeles. Schenck had taken the lead in selling the shares. He had done such a good job that the conspirators embarked on a second enterprise known as the Los Angeles-Utah Oil Company, similarly financed by Los Angeles liquor men. The implications were clear. Schenck, Harper, and Cole worked with Police Chief Edward Kern to restrain police from enforcing ordinances against liquor establishments owned by the investors in exchange for investments in the companies. The *Herald* employed private investigators to visit several of the saloons, where they found open gaming tables, upper-floor assignation rooms and underage girls, some as young as fifteen, in the company of wheedling men who plied them with liquor.

Schenck's culpability extended beyond his role as a stock salesman. Assistant DA Fleming claimed that, after Schenck's acquittal for the false imprisonment charges, Schenck took him to lunch at Al Levy's restaurant at Third and Main to show that he had no hard feelings over the prosecution. During the lunch, Schenck told Fleming that he and his associates, the chief of whom was Oswald, were trying to shut down Tom Savage's vice operations and buy his saloon. Savage had demanded a high price, but they were close to settling terms. Once Savage was out of the way, Schenck explained, the Democratic machine would have complete control of the city. "You are ambitious and you could be the next district attorney," he observed. "We will all stand behind you. There is money in this proposition across Commercial Street and you can have yours every month; you can just as well retire independent."[32]

Fleming promised that he would think over Schenck's offer. Instead, after leaving the restaurant, he confronted Police Chief Kern and Mayor Harper. Schenck was Harper's man, after all. Harper had made him police commissioner. Fleming accused the Chief and Mayor of corruptly working with Schenck and others in the city and police administration. The three men argued. Kern and Harper reproached Fleming for acting like a preacher, but Fleming responded that the fact that the bordellos ran openly was proof that officials had been paid off. He declared that, if the mayor and police refused to close the houses, he would use his authority to do it. Harper and Kern realized that they were cornered and agreed to shut down the Tenderloin. Houses run by both Savage and Oswald were promptly closed, only to reopen in the coming weeks.

In December 1907, Fleming himself directed a raid on Savage's hotels. The police arrested Armstrong again and rounded up the Tenderloin prostitutes. Fleming proclaimed that he would lead law enforcement to break up the big houses of the city—those that housed over ten girls—run by men like Savage and Oswald. Having just prosecuted a Deputy County Coroner for beating a prostitute in a drunken rage, Fleming lamented the damage that red-light districts brought to erring politicians and the inevitable graft that flowed from vice bosses to police and politicians. While he had no illusions that prostitution could be outlawed, he wanted to make sure it did not become a large, profitable enterprise that men like Ballerino, Savage and Oswald could use to control elected officials. He did not want to eradicate prostitution, just to "stamp" it out of politics.

One bordello that Fleming targeted was Savage's high priced Arlington Hotel on New High Street, now run by the notorious madam Pearl Morton. The wily Morton tried to dissuade him by threatening to go public with dirt she had on prominent men. When that did not work, she offered him a diamond-studded gold matchbox. Fleming gave it back to her.

While Fleming and his successors focused on closing down prostitution in the Eighth Ward, the struggle between Savage and Oswald shifted to the political arena. In August 1908, another Eighth Ward politician, former Councilman Edward L. Hutchinson, a longtime rival of Savage who had defeated him in 1898 when Savage ran for re-election to the city council, challenged his position on the Eighth Ward's Democratic Council by claiming that Savage no longer lived in the Ward. Despite a spirited defense by attorney Earl Rogers, the party expelled Savage. Meanwhile, Oswald, who had become a Republican Party leader in the Eighth Ward, broadened his influence to the Democratic Party. Just as he appeared to have taken control of the Tenderloin, however, the *Los Angeles Evening Express* ran its allegations against Schenck, Mayor Harper, and Police Commissioner Cole. In a few months, the *Los Angeles Herald* repeated and extended the charges. After two investigations, the grand jury indicted Schenck and the new chief of police,

Thomas Broadhead, who was accused of accepting a $1,000 bribe from Oswald to allow the bordellos to stay open.

Oswald was also indicted, but first the police had to catch him. From middle March until middle April, both private and governmental detectives searched for him. After changing smaller for larger denomination bills at several San Diego locations, including resorts, banks and even the city's Treasury, he was believed to have crossed the border to Tijuana. However, an investigator from the district attorney's office could not find him there. Afterward, he was said to be on his way to San Francisco, but detectives were sure he was in Mexico, just not in Tijuana. Another report had him camping near Tujunga Pass north of Los Angeles, but all the detectives found there were a recently used campsite and a lot of mud. He was not in Gardena either, despite a reported sighting at a train station. Some began to doubt whether authorities were really trying to find him. An offer of reward money—$500 from newspaper publisher Earl and $1000 from the district attorney's office— did not seem to help.

Oswald finally returned to face justice in Los Angeles on April 14 after securing a promise of immunity for his testimony against now former Police Chief Broadhead. He detailed the payoff system he engineered with Chiefs Broadhead and Kern and Mayor Harper to reopen the crib district in 1907. Beyond making money, his primary motive was to get at Savage, he explained. While sensational, Oswald's testimony did not convict Broadhead, who was acquitted after a few weeks of trial. He was not guilty, but he was not innocent. Within a month of his acquittal, the police commission found a reason to remove him from the force. Schenck escaped justice completely. After Broadhead's acquittal, the DA dropped charges against him and Oswald.

While none of the men accused in the scandal ever saw the inside of a jail cell, the crib district closed for good. Ballerino was gone. He had died in the California Hospital in July 1909 just before the Broadhead trial began, two months after he was found unconscious in one of his cribs on Alameda Street. His last years were not good. Estranged from his family, he lived alone in squalor for two years, cooking his own meals and rarely leaving the crib district. He kept several vicious dogs whose penchant for biting passersby landed him in court several times. His attorneys hounded him for years and finally collected. One woman won a lawsuit against him for promising to marry her while concealing that he was still married to Maria. He fought another, his nurse, on a public street. She had stolen his will after learning he intended to remove her considerable inheritance from it. While the declared value of his estate was much less than most Angelenos expected, prompting treasure seekers to search his Tenderloin grounds for money he might have buried on the property, enough remained of Ballerino's estate to generate years of legal dispute.[33]

Thomas Savage's life ended a few years later. Like Ballerino, he had nowhere to go after the crib district closed, so he stayed where he was. Addicted to morphine, he overdosed on January 2, 1915, dying in a squalid room on Commercial Street a few blocks from where Ballerino had expired five years before.

Oswald segued from prostitution to gambling for a few years. Harassed by mortgagees of his Tenderloin property, by 1915 he had moved his family to the city of Marshfield, Oregon, where he opened a butcher shop and made plans to erect a new building. The lure of the old life must have been great in his later years, however. In 1930, he was back in Southern California as part owner, with J. W. Brynes, H. O. Dougherty and Jack Dragna, of the *Montefalcone*, a gambling ship anchored off Seal Beach.[34]

The major casualty in the 1909 vice scandal—besides the Tenderloin district itself—was Mayor Harper. The *Herald's* articles led to a recall attempt against Harper in early 1909. Harper abandoned his candidacy in March to forestall more damaging reports in *The Los Angeles Express*. By doing so, he avoided being the first Los Angeles mayor to be recalled by voters. That honor would go to Frank Shaw thirty years later, largely because of Harry Raymond.

One leader in the recall effort against Harper was a man whose path Raymond soon crossed, Guy Walton Eddie. Eddie had risen through the ranks of the city attorney's office to become city prosecutor in late November 1908. He had aligned himself with the progressive wing of the local Republican Party, the Good Government group, or Goo Goos as they were then called. To some extent, Eddie was a progressive in the Teddy Roosevelt mold. He lambasted the growing concentration of economic and political power "in the hands of a small number of men," urged the federal government to break up local trusts, prosecuted real estate companies that took advantage of naïve buyers, and castigated private utility companies and grocers for overcharging consumers. His forte, however, was attacking vice and immorality as he defined them.[35]

After the closing of the crib district, anti-vice forces in Los Angeles turned their attention to what they regarded as other evils in the city, particularly gambling and the consumption of alcohol. Guy Eddie became one of their leaders. Under District Attorney Woolwine's direction, he began his assault on liquor in 1908 when he took on the California Club, then as now a prestigious Los Angeles social organization, after the club failed to obtain a liquor license as prescribed by a recent law. Between 1909 and late 1912, he criticized and prosecuted a wide variety of offenses that crossed his moral line, charging liquor establishments which violated the city's strict licensing rules, cigar store owners who encouraged patrons to shake dice to win prizes, bettors in the bleachers at baseball games, and theater owners who put on racy plays. He advocated for laws further restricting liquor sales, including one that proscribed restaurants from serving alcohol to customers not eating a substantial meal and another that forbade women from patronizing or working as waitresses in establishments that served liquor.[36]

Although two Los Angeles newspapers, the *Herald* and the *Evening Express,* supported Eddie's crusade, others, particularly the *Record* and *Los Angeles Times,* found his zeal tiresome. In fact, the conservative *Times,* which for several years had grumbled about the high costs of government under the Goo Goos, seemed delighted to report in October 1912 that the prosecutor himself had been arrested on a morals charge.

The complaint against Eddie came from a young woman named Alice Phelps, who told a detective that Eddie made improper advances toward her during a job interview. The detective reported the charges to a humane officer responsible for protecting underage youths in the city. The two enlisted the help of a third man, a private detective working for the city, and the trio set a trap for Eddie. After they drilled peepholes in the door to his office, the three watched while the young woman returned for another interview with the prosecutor. At the proper moment—or improper, if you will—they burst into the room with drawn revolvers and arrested Eddie.

The case was a sensation in the city. Eddie claimed that he was framed and declared that for a long time he had foreseen his enemies would try such a trick. In fact, three years before, there were rumors of a similar charge involving a woman visitor to his office, but the lady in question denied that anything improper occurred. Alice Phelps stuck to her story, however. Eddie retained the services of four leading attorneys associated with him in the Good Government movement—Earl Rogers, Frank Dominguez, Alfred Lee Stephens, and Jerry Giesler. "There are interests which I can't identify in public now because I intend to expose them at a more auspicious moment that would give anything to get me out of my position," Eddie proclaimed.[37]

At a secret session of the Juvenile Court, which had jurisdiction because Phelps was just shy of twenty-one years, Mayor Alexander listened to her testimony carefully. The situation was a bit of a political pickle for him. Eddie was one of his key allies, but the city attorney's office was conducting the prosecution. While the circumstances of the case suggested that Eddie was set up, Eddie's own conduct was not beyond reproach. To make matters worse, within a few days three more women claimed Eddie had "insulted" them in his private quarters.[38]

While Alexander struggled with the Eddie case, two of his assistants were quick to act. It was here that Harry Raymond, who had been a key investigator for the Goo Goos, entered the case, which quickly became a detective vs. detective battle. Raymond discovered that a detective who had helped arrest Eddie, Fred W. Lloyd, attempted to extort money from two men police seized in a gambling raid. He took this information to Mayor Alexander's secretary, George Anderson, who relayed it to Deputy City Attorney F. M. C. Choate. Despite orders from the mayor to maintain a neutral position, both Anderson and Choate worked quietly to help Eddie's defense. The two—and perhaps others more directly involved in Eddie's defense, such as attorney Dominguez—instructed Raymond to set up a sting of Lloyd. Raymond brought two additional detectives and two LAPD patrolman into the operation. Using a marked coin, the detectives had one of the men whom Lloyd arrested in the raid offer him a bribe. Lloyd took the coin and the cops arrested him.

Lloyd was no longer employed by the LAPD, however, his services having been terminated that morning. No longer a public official, he could not be charged with receiving a bribe. The payment of the marked coin was just for his services as a private detective and therefore perfectly legitimate. What was worse, Lloyd had the confidence of the police chief, who upon hearing of his arrest ordered his immediate release. The whole plot then blew up in the plotter's face. Mayor Alexander dismissed Anderson and the city attorney fired Choate. Harry Raymond was indicted for false imprisonment along with Choate and Anderson.

The indictments against Raymond, Choate and Anderson took a backseat to the Eddie trial, which lasted through the final months of 1912 into early 1913. Eddie's lawyers attacked the character of Alice Phelps and the detectives who burst into Eddie's office. They argued that the holes through which the police watched Eddie and Phelps were too small to allow a view of Eddie's chair where he allegedly fondled Phelps and that the prosecutor's office investigators had enlarged them during the trial. They hinted darkly that the entire case against Eddie was a conspiracy to discredit a man fighting the underworld criminals who ran gambling and liquor establishments. Their arguments were strong enough to convince the jury of reasonable doubt. Eddie was acquitted, but Mayor George Alexander refused to give him back his job. His political career finished, he entered private practice and for years was a leading attorney in Los Angeles.

After the acquittal, the prosecutor dismissed all indictments arising from the case, including those against Raymond, Choate and Anderson. Raymond returned to work as a private detective. He was doing well enough to eschew the usual cases offered a private investigator: divorces, collections, and process serving. His name was frequently reported in cases that involved the rich and famous, most notably, those of Ida Morgan, widow of a wealthy gold miner, and Fred Harlow, owner of one of the premier restaurants of Los Angeles, Fred Harlow's Cafe.

The first of these cases began in late November 1913. Ida Morgan, the forty-year-old widow of a wealthy Pasadena capitalist, racehorse owner and miner William Morgan, hired Raymond to apprehend a group of men who had conspired to rob her diamonds. The incident took place at a remote mine in the Mojave Desert near the town—if it could even be called that—of Cima, where Mrs. Ida Morgan was managing the reopening of one of her deceased husband's mines, the Persis. One of the men working at the mine was Ora Budd, a tall, handsome thirty-six year old. Budd was a married man. His wife, Florence, a resident of Long Beach, California, soon learned from other workers at the mine that Mrs. Morgan and Ora were cavorting during luncheons and dinners like young lovers. Morgan had even declared publicly that she would set Ora up in business in San Francisco if he left his wife for her.

Budd's wife Florence hired attorney Louis N. Whealton to file a lawsuit against Morgan for alienation of her husband's affection. In March 1913, on advice of Whealton, Florence, her brother, Everette Burroughs, and a Long Beach detective named Robert E. Fisher took a train to Nipton, where they met Robert Williams of the Persis Mine. The group drove back to the headquarters of the Death Valley Mine near Cima, where they conferred with Robert Lithgow, another Persis employee, who had eavesdropped on Morgan and Ora Budd for over a month, placing his ear to the wall of her sleeping quarters at the Persis mine. After one aborted attempt at surprising the lovers, the Florence and her cohorts broke into Ida Morgan's bedroom. What happened then would be disputed in California courts for years. According to Ida, she was startled from sleep by a half dozen intruders bursting into her room, including Ora Budd, who planted himself on the side of the bed. One of the intruders exploded a flash lamp attached to a camera. The blurry photograph showed Budd seated in pajamas while Ida tried to hide her face. According to Florence Budd and others who accompanied her that night, however, Ida and Ora had been surprised in bed together.

In the confusion, a small bag filled with Ida Morgan's diamonds disappeared. Or so she alleged. While she at first suspected one of Florence Budd's party at having stolen the jewels, she soon came to believe that Ora Budd had taken them. Shortly after the raid on her mining camp boudoir, she contacted Harry Raymond for help. Raymond employed his operatives to search for Budd and others involved in the night raid, many of whom had scattered throughout the western states.

Working with law enforcement officers from San Bernardino County, Raymond issued a wanted poster for Budd. In early December, he was arrested in Salt Lake City, where he was working at a mine under the name of Albert Brodie. After returning Budd from Salt Lake City, Raymond and the San Bernardino authorities jailed him and seven other alleged conspirators, including Florence Budd. With the group in jail, Raymond predicted that Ida's diamonds would soon be found. He declared in a written report that one of the suspects, William Wobig, detailed the plot. "Wobig told me of how the deal was arranged, and that an officer came there to serve papers on Mrs. Morgan and how they laid in wait for an opportunity to catch Mrs. Morgan and Budd; and that Budd told them when the time was ripe to come into the room. This was done by a signal from Budd at a certain time so they could be caught in a compromising position." The raid, Raymond argued, was a "deliberate plot to walk into her room, take the photograph and 'shake' her for a sum of money."[39]

None of the suspects would talk to San Bernardino detectives, however, and without a confession—despite hours of "sweating" by Raymond and other detectives—the San Bernardino DA concluded he had no case against them and dismissed all charges. The drama then shifted back to Florence Budd's alienation of affection lawsuit against Ida Morgan. In July 1914, Florence Budd was awarded a $15,000 judgement despite Morgan's insistence that she had not had a sexual relationship with Ora Budd.

In retrospect, it seems a fair judgement, but it also seems likely that the nighttime raid was a plot, probably one that involved a penitent Budd helping to provide the evidence that would win in court. However, the judgement would never be paid. Soon after she lost the suit, Ida Morgan converted all her assets to cash and left California. In 1918, Florence Budd discovered that Ida had property in Canada, but the Canadian courts refused to seize it until Ida returned from France, where she was serving with the Red Cross. In 1919, Morgan appealed the judgement in California. Three years later, the California Supreme Court reversed the decision, ruling the Superior Court judge had erred in refusing testimony by a witness who claimed he had heard Fisher declare that the night raid on Morgan's bedroom was a frame-up designed to extort money from the widow.

While Florence Budd never received any money from her lawsuit against Ida Morgan, she did at least keep her husband. After filing for divorce in July 1914, the couple made amends, remaining together until Ora's death in 1939.

While the Morgan case strengthened Raymond's reputation as a private investigator, the Harlow robbery threatened to nip his career in the bud. The event came a few months after he sold his interest in the Citizens Detective Agency to B. Workman and Hubert Kittle and took a job with the larger investigative firm of Marston and Miller. Raymond, Thomas Miller, and Fred Harlow had left Harlow's Cafe for nightcaps at Harlow's home in early November 1914. When they opened the front door, they found three masked men pointing revolvers at them. The thieves had already bound and gagged Harlow's maid. Now they took Harlow and the two detectives into a bedroom and ordered them to lie on the bed with their arms to the side and their hats over their faces. At that moment, one bandit's mask slipped and Raymond got a good look at his face. He had a glass eye.

The thieves removed a diamond ring from Miller valued at $900. Harlow lost rings worth $1,200 and $170 in cash. Raymond was out $110 cash and his watch.

In the next few days, Raymond and his LAPD detective friends went through mug shots of known criminals. After three days, they found their man. The thief, Charles Sligh, was a kind of man that Raymond would encounter throughout his career. The son of Captain James May Sligh, a Civil War veteran, prominent Montana physician and political leader, Sligh followed a wayward course for most of his life. After attending the College of Montana from his thirteenth to fifteenth year, he was sentenced to the state reform school in 1896 "for incorrigibility," but pardoned a month later so that he could obtain treatment for his eyes, one of which was blind. For a few years afterward, he seems to have gone straight, completing his education in Phillipsburg, Montana, where he was President of the local high school's literary society. In 1898, he joined the 32nd Michigan Volunteers but did not see any action outside of Florida and Alabama. After his discharge, Sligh returned to his parents' home in Anaconda, Montana, where he earned a solid reputation as one of the town's "most popular young men." In March 1899, he and a friend left for the Montana gold fields. It is likely Sligh began his career in crime shortly afterward. His famous father soon disowned him and his plea for a second pardon from Montana's governor went unrequited. In 1903, he attempted suicide by gas in a San Francisco lodging house, declaiming his "discouragement, bad health, and my unhappy life," but he was rescued before the carbon monoxide could complete its work. Arrested repeatedly in Montana, Oregon, Utah, Washington, California and New York for burglary and robbery, he earned stints at Deer Lodge (Montana), San Quentin (California, under the alias "JC Roberts") Oregon State Penitentiary (Salem), Walla Walla State Penitentiary (Washington), Salt Lake City (Utah),

Rawlins (Wyoming), and most recently, Auburn and Dannemora (New York, as "William R. Francis").[40]

Humiliated by the robbery, Raymond worked hard on the case and spent $1,000 of his own money. His efforts paid off one evening when he spotted Sligh enter the Pantages Theatre on Broadway with a woman. With LAPD Detective Ed King, he instructed the theater manager to restrict the patrons to one exit when the movie finished.

Soon, Charles Sligh emerged with his lady friend. The detectives arrested him and took him to LAPD headquarters. While he refused to talk, his woman companion, who turned out to be his recent bride, told police she believed Sligh's money came from gambling and gave up their address. In their hotel room, the detectives found loot from several recent burglaries. Confronted with the evidence and threatened with the arrest his young wife if he did not cooperate, Sligh confessed not only the Harlow robbery but to a string of crimes in Southern California, including two train robberies. The victims in most of his burglaries were wealthy society women who had indiscreetly reported their latest jewelry acquisitions to society editors of the local newspapers. Sligh kept a list of their possessions and watched the society pages for notices of their absences from their homes.

Sligh also turned in his cohort, Alfred Sells, telling police that Sells brutally murdered an elderly citizen and his wife inside their home in Fruitvale, California. Sells, who had already served three years for manslaughter, at first denied the charges but later confessed to escape the death penalty. He received a life sentence for both the Harlow robbery and the Oakland murders. A few years later, he constructed a dummy figure of himself, complete with the features of his face molded from plaster of paris, as part of an escape attempt. Unfortunately, he could not get past the outer walls. The prison guards found him hiding under a stack of wood. He died at Folsom in 1924 during an operation for ulcers.

The murdered Oakland couple's sons had posted a substantial reward for the apprehension of their murderer. Raymond claimed the reward based on the help he had given to the LAPD, but he had some competition from three other detectives involved in the case, including Miller. Harlow also wanted the money because he heard Sligh finger Sells. Sligh himself thought he deserved the reward for fingering Sells, a claim the Los Angeles Times asserted proved his insanity. Neither Harlow nor Sligh got a dime. The detectives split the money, Raymond getting one quarter. The story should have ended there, but Harlow, angry that he should have gotten something for his trouble, argued with Raymond and Miller in a downtown bar in October 1916. Harlow pulled a pistol and aimed it at Miller. Miller wrested the gun from him, but the hammer smashed his finger. Harlow was charged with

assault with a deadly weapon, but the charges against the prominent
restauranteur were dismissed a month later.

As for Sligh, after serving six years and six months of his ten-year sentence
at Folsom State Prison, he was released in September 1921. He returned to
Montana for the reading of his father's will. He need not have bothered. He
was effectively cut out of the inheritance with a payment of $5.00. In October
1921, a newspaper reported that he had left Anaconda enroute to Tacoma,
Washington, where he had a job in a lumber mill. Two months later, he was
back in Butte, Montana. When the proceeds of his father's will were finally
disbursed in 1927, the check for five dollars found him in the Colorado State
Penitentiary. Following his release, he lived a few years at the National
Soldiers Homes in Dayton, Ohio, and West Los Angeles. Eventually, he
found his way back to Folsom, convicted once more of burglary, where he
died in 1936. He was buried in a soldier's grave in the San Francisco National
Cemetery.

Panoramic view of Hollywood looking west from Laughlin Park, 1905 [California Historical Society, University of Southern California Libraries]

"Orris O. Budd alias Ora Budd Wanted Poster", 1913 [The John Moe Collection, 2003.026.171, Courtesy of the Historical Museum at Fort Missoula Collections]

LOS ANGELES, CALIFORNIA, NOVEMBER 6th, 1913

ARREST THIS MAN FOR GRAND LARCENY

Warrant in Sheriff's Office at San Bernardino, Cal.

$500 $500

Reward Reward

ORRIS O. BUDD alias ORA BUDD

DESCRIPTION.—Orris O. Budd, alias Ora Budd. American; Age 36; Height, about 6 feet 2 inches; Weight, about 170 pounds; Slender Build, Bony Frame; Hair, dark, thick and rather curley, and slightly mixed with grey; Brown Eyes; Sallow complexion; (1) Gold Tooth upper right side. Teeth on upper right side crowded close together; Slender features and prominent Nose. Is an Ice Cream and Candy maker by trade, but has worked at mining for the last 3 or 4 years. Sometimes he wears an Elks pin, was a member of the Elks Lodge at Springfield, Ill. On August 2nd, 1913, at San Bernardino, Cal., a Felony Warrant was issued for this man for Grand Larceny, charging him with the Theft of $2500.00 worth of Diamonds. This Agency will pay $500.00 Reward for the Arrest and Detention of this man until an Officer from the Sheriff's Office of San Bernardino, California, can reach him with the proper papers. We will go any where to get and extradite this man. The above picture was taken about 4 years ago, but is a good picture of him today.

CITIZEN'S DETECTIVE AGENCY
H. J. RAYMOND, Manager

Wire all information to J. C. RALPHS, Sheriff, San Bernardino County, San Bernardino, Cal., or CITIZEN'S DETECTIVE AGENCY. H. J. RAYMOND, Manager, Los Angeles, Cal.

*Ballerino's cribs (outlined) along Alameda in
Sanborn Insurance Map, 1884*

Crib Section of LA [LA Times, 1903]

*Ballerino's cribs (outlined) Alameda in Sanborn
Insurance Map, 1894*

Bartolo Ballerino [courtesy John Duntley]

Tom Savage [Los Angeles Post-Record, Jan 2, 1915]

Nick Oswald [Los Angeles Evening Express, Apr 12, 1909]

Sam Schenck [LA Post-Record, May 10, 1907]

3: VENICE CHIEF

Raymond's work on the Harlow robbery helped land him a job as a special detective reporting to LAPD Assistant Chief George Home. Home, who would use Raymond's skills over the next fifteen years, led a squad formed to combat "eastern crooks" who flooded into Southern California each winter and bunko artists who traveled to LA in the summer to prey on rich Midwestern farmers luxuriating in the warm sun between harvests. The confidence games spanned from sophisticated "large con" conspiracies involving four or more accomplices to simple tricks that played on the gullibility and greed of a convenient dupe.

Home and Raymond also targeted pickpockets, who were as inevitable as flies wherever crowds gathered in the city. Raymond also helped put away a few burglary gangs operating in the city, including one dubbed the "skylight burglars" who, taking advantage of the reassignment of downtown patrolmen to work a dock strike, slipped into jewelry stores through transoms and skylights,. On this case, Raymond worked with a young detective named Guy McAfee, whose name Los Angeles would hear for years to come. The LAPD job lasted until October 1916 when the new chief of police, Claire Snively, reorganized the department and eliminated Raymond's position. Raymond returned to Marston and Miller and quickly became an investigator for the defense in the case against Benton L. Barrett, who was accused of murdering his wife and stepson and disposing of their bodies in a cesspool on his Santa Monica ranch.

Barrett, a prominent Indiana farmer and businessman, had come to Southern California in his sixty-fourth year after the death of his wife of forty years. He had purchased a five-acre farm and walnut grove at the corner of Santa Monica Boulevard and 26th Street. He soon found a new wife through a matrimonial agency, forty-four year old Irene Drake of Venice, who brought along with her a sixteen-year-old son, Raymond Wright. Born Irene L. Rodgers, she had already been married four times, but only told Benton of the first two, the last having been annulled the year before when her current husband's undivorced wife returned from Siskiyou County to accuse him of bigamy. She also had not told him of another man she had met through a matrimonial agency, a Manzanar, California, blacksmith named George

Forbes, with whom she continued to correspond lovingly after her wedding to Barrett.

A cousin of Benton, Charles E. Barrett, had also moved to Los Angeles. Charles, a few years younger than Benton, was also a recent widower who had remarried a much younger woman. He had been prominent in Indiana circles as a criminal defense attorney. Perhaps his occupation had given him a perspective on human behavior that his cousin lacked. In any case, he did not take to the new Mrs. Benton Barrett, surmising that she was faithful only to his cousin's money. She had already milked Benton for several thousand dollars to recover diamonds she had pawned in San Francisco and to disencumber a property in Fort Worth, Texas.

Charles convinced Benton to hire a private detective named Earl McDonald to "shadow" his wife. McDonald quickly discovered that Irene's frequent trips to downtown Los Angeles were not for business, but for pleasure with other men. Working with James S. Rodman, a local entrepreneur whose business schemes crossed the line into fraud on a number of occasions, particularly as he promoted a plan to publish a daily newspaper to rival the *Times* and its half-dozen Los Angeles competitors, McDonald engineered what *Los Angeles Times* described as a "New Twist on Badger Game." Rodman arranged a tryst with Irene at a Los Angeles rooming house while McDonald waited outside with some handpicked "witnesses." Later that night, her husband and his cousin confronted her in a Venice Beach hotel room. To avert the filing of a suit for divorce based on infidelity and the subsequent scandal, she agreed to forfeit her claims on her husband's Santa Monica property. Shortly afterward, Benton published notices in local papers disclaiming any responsibility for Irene's debts.

A few days later, Rodman and McDonald persuaded Benton Barrett to invest $1,500 into one of their schemes, selling a trademark and formula for a perfume named "Cali-fleur." It did not take long for Benton to realize he had been had, and by June, he had filed suit to recover his money. Benton's ill feelings toward Rodman and McDonald led to a temporary reconciliation with his wife, but they did not persuade him to restore her rights to the Santa Monica property. Irene filed lawsuits for reconveyance of her share in the property and a divorce. Benton replied with a cross-complaint for divorce.

The couple continued to live at the Santa Monica farm through the summer of 1916, more or less amiably. In early October, however, his persistent cousin presented Benton with more proof of Irene's perfidy. Charles had convinced George Forbes, who had broken with Irene, to meet with him and Benton at the Santa Monica Pier on Friday, October 13. Forbes, a short, muscular, bald-headed man of 55 years, brought with him Irene's love letters, including one that made her lack of real feelings and interest in her husband unmistakable. After noting that Benton had taken out a life insurance policy payable to her, she predicted optimistically that he would not "last many years at the rate he was going."

"I am paying very dearly for all I will ever get," complained Mrs. Barrett in the letter, "I am putting up with many disagreeable things here, and . . . I am sorry that I ever undertook this job, but I am going to finish it now."[1]

Forbes would later testify that in meeting with Benton Barrett that day, he was "defending an honest man against a dishonest woman. Mrs. Barrett already had four husbands and I seemed to have been marked for number five."[2] It was a thought that must have also gone through the mind of the aged number four husband. Marrying a twice-divorced woman must have tested the tolerance of a religious man who had spent forty years in a conservative marriage. Only recently had he learned of his new wife's short-lived marriage to her third husband. Now he was confronted with undeniable evidence that in her eyes he was just one in a continuing series of lovers and husbands.

Early the following week, the Barretts exchanged legal filings in their dispute over ownership of the Santa Monica property. Benton also directed his attorney to renew his divorce suit and placed a notice in the *Times* declaring he was not responsible for any debts contracted by Irene after October 16. On Tuesday, Benton served his wife with papers for divorce and told her he was moving to a hotel. She responded by threatening him with a knife.

According to Benton, after quarreling with his wife at breakfast, he started a small fire in the northwestern part of his property to burn some rubbish. Afterward, he went into the barn, where his wife and her son suddenly confronted him. "The boy had a pick handle and my wife had a carving knife. I went after them with a piece of iron. We fought in the stalls. We fought. I beat them to death with the club." Afterward, Benton carried the bodies to the fire in a wheelbarrow. He fed the blaze with brush and railroad ties and, after cutting the metal buttons and removing other non-combustible items from the boy's pockets, threw the two bodies into the fire.[3]

For two days, Benton watched the smoldering fire slowly consume the bodies. On Friday evening, he removed the bones from the fire and threw them into a cesspool under an outhouse. The following day, after Santa Monica police investigated the disappearance of Irene and her son following a report from Lillie La Frayne, who lived with the Barretts, he drove to his attorney's office in downtown Los Angeles and confessed to the murders. A few hours later, he repeated the confession to District Attorney Woolwine, who jailed him for murder.

Benton Barrett's story would change over the next few days as police combed his property and presented him with their discoveries. At first, he maintained that he had been attacked by Irene and her son as he tended the rubbish fire and had buried their ashes nearby. Later, he admitted that the confrontation actually took place in the barn and that he had not buried the remaining ashes and bones but had thrown them into the cesspool. He attributed the discrepancies to his poor memory, which was somehow revived through his prayers. Perhaps, he suggested, he was simply insane.

An insanity defense seemed plausible. Benton Barrett mumbled prayers repeatedly during the ensuing legal hearings and seemed puzzled when he tried to recount his actions around the murders. "I think I killed her," he told investigators, "In fact, I seem to remember placing her body in the fire. I think I killed the boy, too, but I don't remember some things." According to his attorney, Lewis D. Collings, Benton would confess to anything suggested to him.[4]

Benton had done a thorough job of disposing the bodies of his victims. Detectives found a small number of human bones and teeth in the cesspool, including parts of two different skulls, but had no way to prove that they belonged to Irene and young Raymond. His attorneys, Earl Rogers and Collings, supplemented by W. Ona Morton and Jerry Giesler, recognized they could make a case that the two alleged victims had slipped out of town as part of a plot to deprive the old man of his fortune, perhaps by sending him to the gallows or inducing him to commit suicide. Their argument that Irene and her son were still alive gained traction from reports that the two had been seen alive after Benton claimed he murdered them.[5]

In early November, Barrett's attorneys employed several detectives, including Harry Raymond, to aid in the investigation. Raymond focused on finding evidence that Barrett's wife and her son were still alive. After running down a report that Irene and her son had fled to San Diego in late October, he learned that a woman matching Irene's appearance had taken a train for Temple, Texas, on October 19, the morning after the alleged murders. When this lead did not pan out, Raymond pursued another sighting of Irene in Phoenix. Again, he was unable to find the woman.

Sympathy for Barrett was widespread among the legal community. District Attorney Woolwine declared Barrett a "lovable old man" after listening to his theories about the afterlife, while the presiding judge of the preliminary Superior Court hearings declared, "I wish it were within my power to discharge the defendant. His wife conspired against this man. I believe her a very designing woman, but that does not justify murder."[6]

After Barrett was indicted for the murder of his wife, he recanted his confessions and pleaded not guilty. While Earl Rogers wanted to continue the search for Irene and her son, he could not convince others on Barrett's legal team to fund the effort. Rogers withdrew from the case in early February and the remainder of the original group followed, except for Morton. Barrett's new legal team pursued a dual strategy, continuing to suggest that Irene and her son were not dead but also that Benton had been insane when he killed them. The strategy worked. After the jurors deadlocked on the charges against him for the murder of his wife, they found him not guilty by reason of insanity. He was committed to Patton State Hospital, where he would remain until his death in 1936 despite occasional claims that his two victims were still alive.

Harry Raymond continued to work as a private detective until late 1917, when a new opportunity opened in Venice, at the time a separate city along the coast west of Los Angeles.

Venice, or "Venice of America" as it was originally named, was the dream city of developer Abbot Kinney, who in 1905 had built a 200 feet pier at the center of a 750 by 900 feet oceanfront tract south of the Santa Monica neighborhood of Ocean Park. A replica of a Spanish galleon, the Ship Café Cabrillo, stretched along part of the pier and served as a hotel and restaurant. Beyond a block-long central business district of ornate three-story buildings fronted by colonnades, Kinney dug a network of seven canals fed by ocean water that flowed through two thirty-six inch pipes over a mile to the south. With another 120-acre tract behind the oceanfront buildings, he had plenty of property for development. He envisioned a seasonal community of wooden and decorated canvas houses along the canals. An improvement society would take care of the gardens and homes while the owners were away during the off-season. The new city would become a permanent Chautauqua site, with artistic exhibits, music, and prominent speakers to enlighten the multitudes. Near the Ship Café, Kinney constructed a large auditorium to serve as a venue for cultural attractions. On the other side of the Café, however, a dance hall pointed to a more prosaic and more likely future. Kinney soon realized that the weekend throngs wanted less edifying entertainment than he had planned. Even when the buildings on the pier closed, they came for the beach, the amusement attractions and the miniature railroad that ran along the streets paralleling the canals. Kinney quickly transformed his cultural mecca into a seaside amusement park that included a roller coaster and Ferris Wheel. To attract older pleasure-seekers, he permitted the sale of liquor.

For several reasons, not the least of which was disagreement about how much Venice should cater to the appetites of young males in pursuit of alcohol, gambling and girls, Venice became a battleground of competing commercial and residential interests. The job of chief of police was a precarious position. Factions divided the city and claims of official misconduct were frequent. The city clerk had been indicted for embezzlement, a former mayor had been accused of bribery, and the city's Board of Trustees had dismissed two police chiefs, the last, Bert Reynolds, after he began a "clean-up" campaign reminiscent of Guy Eddie's a few years before. Reynolds, who earlier ordered the arrest of boys who "fluttered" their eyelids at young women or wore immodest bathing suits, focused on the loose morals of young people and cited pool hall owners who allowed underage youth in their establishments. He also demanded that the city enact ordinances that barred young women from working in concession stands along the boardwalk.[7]

Raymond became the Venice chief of police on November 13, 1917. To some extent, he took up where Reynolds left off, arresting men and women who pretended to be married couples in order to engage in "immoral acts" in apartment buildings and hotels. He and his men raided the boardwalk concession stands, where they seized slot machines that paid off winners with vouchers for merchandise instead of cash.

Alcohol consumption was a more complex problem. The residents of Venice, like those throughout Southern California, battled over liquor. Los Angeles voters had passed the Gandier Ordinance, which restricted over-the-counter sales of liquor to original packages containing less than 14% alcohol, closed all saloons in the city, and prohibited cafés and restaurants from serving liquor after 9:00 p.m. Until nationwide prohibition made liquor sales illegal everywhere, saloons in the outlying cities of Los Angeles County such as Vernon and Venice enjoyed a windfall of sales to thirsty Angelenos. To keep his job, Raymond had to thread his way between Venice's dry and wet forces.

Venice's political battle entangled the new chief as soon as he took office. In late November, Raymond arrested Mrs. May McMahon on charges she had filed a false affidavit accusing Venice Beach Board of Trustee William G. Lutz of illegally selling morphine in Bakersfield. Dispatched to Bakersfield by Bert Reynolds, Raymond's predecessor, to obtain evidence against Lutz, McMahon had posed as a morphine addict named Anna Sullivan when she appeared before a notary public to swear the affidavit. The affidavit was published in a local Venice newspaper days before the election, which Lutz won narrowly. Afterward, Lutz and his allies retaliated against Reynolds, who confessed his part in the scheme and implicated McMahon and her husband. Raymond arrested Mrs. McMahon and confined her for eleven days in a private home before releasing her. In January 1918, both McMahon and her husband sued Raymond and other Venice officials for false imprisonment. The LA County Grand Jury investigated the case, but the jurors were evidently convinced that McMahon's detention had been legal.

A few months later, other claims were lodged against Raymond for false arrest. First, he and other Venice officials faced a $5,200 lawsuit brought by a young man who claimed he was falsely arrested for petty larceny. Raymond and the city prevailed, but a few weeks later, LA County District Attorney Woolwine took another case to the grand jury that involved two young men whom the Venice police arrested as "slackers," a term used for men who failed to register for the draft. "Slacker raids" were common in Venice and other areas where young men congregated. They were normally conducted by quasi-governmental groups, such as the American Protective League, with local police assistance. In this case, the police picked up the young men at their apartment on Sunset Avenue, where they were hosting a small party. The two showed the cops their draft registration cards, but the police arrested them anyway. After they spent two days in the Venice lock-up, they were charged with disturbing the peace. A few weeks later, police arrested one of the young men at his job at a local garage and charged him with draft evasion. Both chose to enter the Army to avoid the slacker charge after paying a $15 fine for disturbing the peace.[8]

A fourth, more serious charge of false imprisonment against Raymond emerged later that summer. In July 1918, James Alexander Johnston, a wealthy Canadian who had lived in California since 1905, derided American soldiers by proclaiming in a beach café that they were only in Europe to parade and salute the American flag. He also asserted that Congress was under the control of Germany. A patriotic group called the Venice Vigilante Committee seized Johnston and brought him to Raymond, who jailed him for violating the Sedition Act of 1918. The charge was not unusual. After the United States entered World War I, thousands of Americans were arrested for "disloyal, profane, scurrilous, or abusive language" directed at the government, the flag or the armed forces. The violation did not even have to be public. Around the time of Johnston's arrest, for example, a court found a Long Beach man guilty of disturbing the peace for "uttering seditious remarks" and stomping on a portrait of President Wilson in his own home.[9]

After three weeks in what Johnston described as an "unlighted and offensive cell," his charges were reduced to disturbing the peace and he was fined $300. Venice cops then took him to the train station in downtown Los Angeles and ordered him to return to Canada. However, instead of returning to Toronto, Johnston headed to the district attorney's office to file a complaint. After it heard the testimony of several witnesses, the Los Angeles County Grand Jury indicted Raymond and Johnston's attorney, Frank Allender, for conspiracy to violate Johnston's liberty. The indictments alleged that Raymond and Allender frightened Johnston with predictions that Department of Justice action under the Sedition Act was likely. Johnston told the grand jury that he not only had paid the $300 fine for disturbing the peace, he was also out Allender's $400 attorney's fee and $1,750 that Raymond and Allender had demanded for his release. He recounted that, one day during his incarceration, Venice police brought him to downtown Los Angeles so he could obtain funds for his release by mortgaging his Los Angeles County property. Afterward, he was returned to his cell. He had gotten out of jail only after he bribed a jail turnkey to smuggle a letter about his plight to the Canadian prime minister, who asked the British consul in Los Angeles to intervene.[10]

Raymond breezily dismissed Johnston's charges, but he fired two jailers for their role in the case. He claimed that Johnston was treated well during his incarceration, though he admitted that he did not think a fine was punishment enough for Johnston's comments and he wanted the Canadian to spend six months in jail. Allender went to greater lengths to address the accusations and explained that Johnston, who had retained him twice before in other cases, asked for his help when Allender visited him in the Venice jail. Allender responded to criticism that he had inadequately defended his client and rushed the case prematurely to a Venice police court by explaining that he feared Federal authorities would file additional charges if given time. Johnston had not only made offensive remarks about American soldiers and Congress but had also falsely claimed that he had fought in the war, had been wounded and poisoned with gas.

In court, Raymond answered the charges flanked by no less than nine high-priced attorneys, including Frank Dominguez, Jerry Giesler, Paul Schenck and Harry Dehm. "We are his friends and intend to see this matter through to the finish," Dominguez declared. District Attorney Woolwine assigned the case to Deputy District Attorney C. W. Fricke. The DA detailed a detective to investigate the case and protect Johnston, who, back from a visit to Toronto, had registered at the Hotel Morris on Fifth Street in downtown Los Angeles. A few days later, Johnston took a brief trip to San Diego. When he returned, the DA's detective, who had also taken a brief vacation, was nowhere to be seen. Outside the hotel, two men accosted Johnston. They threatened him with a Federal prosecution for his disloyal remarks and warned him that Raymond's attorney, Dominguez, would use his power to "trim . . . every cent" he had. When he left the next morning to attend the first day of the trial, he spotted the same two men—"Venice Thugs," he called them—outside the courtroom. He notified the district attorney of the harassment and asked him to speed up the trial. He did not want to remain in the country any longer than necessary.[11]

While he promised to appear in court at 10:00 a.m. the following morning, Johnston instead checked out of his hotel around 9:00 a.m. and left town. The district attorney's office ordered a statewide search amid rumors he had been spirited out of the city. Not found in California, he was reported to be in the Midwest enroute to Toronto. Without his testimony, there was no case against Raymond or Allender. On September 30, on a motion by Deputy DA Fricke, Judge Gavin Craig dismissed the complaints.

Despite the dismissal of charges against him, Raymond was still in trouble. At first, the City of Venice trustees reacted to the indictments with a resolution of confidence in him, but their support waned after another false imprisonment lawsuit was filed in mid-October. One trustee complained that Raymond ran the police department with "dictatorial methods."[12]

On October 21, the trustees fired Raymond. He still had to address the new lawsuit, however, which had been filed by a young salesman, Orville P. Coen, and his wife Violet. The facts of the case appeared in the papers with varying degrees of euphemism and innuendo. The Coens claimed that a prominent middle-aged Rialto orange industry baron, Albert H. Morgan, had met seventeen-year-old Violet in Los Angeles and afterward had shown up at the Coen's home in Venice. Violet accepted his invitation to go on a long ride in the Santa Monica Mountains. On the way, she developed a headache and he gave her a pill that made her drowsy. Afterward, he assaulted her in a secluded canyon. When she returned home, she told her husband about the man's actions. The couple contacted the Venice Police Department, and Violet agreed to induce Morgan to return for another tryst. When he did, he was arrested. Morgan denied that he assaulted the girl and claimed his only interaction with her had taken place when he noticed her "tripping along Windward Avenue" and asked her where she was going. He asserted he was the victim of a blackmail scheme.[13]

Raymond had spent a great deal of effort to develop a case against Morgan, whose money and contacts would make a conviction difficult. When Violet Coen decided to drop the case because of the publicity surrounding it, the angry police chief, suspecting that she and her husband had schemed to blackmail Morgan but lost their nerves, tossed both of them in jail. It was enough to convince them to testify, but before the criminal case against Morgan proceeded, they instituted a $30,000 lawsuit against Raymond for false imprisonment. While Morgan's trial afforded the courtroom reporters some titillation, ("A great part of his testimony is unprintable," reported the *Los Angeles Times*), he was ultimately freed of the charges against him. The Coens' suit, however, bore some fruit, as they were each rewarded $301 in damages.[14]

Fred Harlow's Cafe

St Marks Hotel, Venice, California; Raymond residence in 1918

Abbot Kinney Pier 1907. To the right of the Ship Cafe is the auditorium. To its left is the dance hall. [Library of Congress, Prints & Photographs Division, Detroit Publishing Company Collection]

Charles Sligh, San Quentin, 1915

Alfred Sells, San Quentin, 1909

4: AUTO CLUB DETECTIVE

After losing his job in Venice, Raymond returned to the LAPD as a special officer reporting directly to George Home, who had risen to chief of police in July 1919. Raymond worked on a variety of cases but focused on suppressing illegal gambling and combating radical unionists in the International Workers of the World. A few days before Christmas, Home dispatched him to meet with a mob of ex-servicemen planning to assault the IWW headquarters in downtown Los Angeles. Raymond was able to convince them to allow authorities, including the LAPD under Home's leadership and the American Legion under young ex-serviceman Buron Fitts, to deal with the IWW.

Despite his successes, Raymond's appointment soon came under attack by reform groups and one of the many local newspapers, *The Los Angeles Post-Record.* Home had reinstated a number of cops who had resigned during the war to their former ranks and salaries. His actions violated regulations requiring former officers to reapply through the Civil Service Commission. Among those rehired were about a dozen officers who had been dismissed for misconduct. The reinstatement of these officers incensed reformers, including the *Record* and officials of the United Church Brotherhoods of Los Angeles. There was no reason for Raymond to be caught in the controversy—he had voluntarily resigned his position with the LAPD in 1916 and had not been a regular officer anyway—but the attacks on him reflected how gravely the Venice false imprisonment scandals had tainted his reputation. The *Record* signaled him out along with Hubert 'Brute' Kittle, whom the newspaper described as Raymond's "sidekick," and future gambling baron Guy McAfee. Kittle, a former champion motorcycle racer, railroad fireman, and daredevil aviator who in a few years would add bank robbery to his curriculum vitae before ending his wild ride through life with a capsule of cyanide, earned the newspaper's scorn for his brutality toward suspects. He had also recently gone on a drunk in the detective bureau, which ended after he discharged several bullets into the floor while cursing his coverage in the local papers. McAfee earned the *Record's* censure for repeated gambling infractions within police headquarters. Raymond was blasted for his Venice tenure of "incompetency, corruption, and brutality," and for the low morale that resulted when he was placed in charge of sworn officers in the LAPD. A few months later, when a satirical review entitled "The Follies of Los Angeles" opened at the Philharmonic Auditorium, "Harry Raymond of Venice" was held up for particular derision.[1]

In order to relieve pressure on Home, Raymond resigned his position in February 1920 and announced that he planned to open a new detective agency. Home still needed him, however, and a few weeks after his resignation, Raymond helped the LAPD crack a ring of young bandits and burglars. He also worked with detectives in the Automobile Club of Southern California Auto Theft Squad, which he joined full-time in September 1920.

Formed in December 1914 to combat the alarming increase in automobile thefts, the squad worked with detectives from the Sheriff's department and the LAPD. Automobile theft had become a significant problem in Los Angeles about the time that Raymond arrived in the city. In the century's first decade, joyriding young men committed most thefts, but within a few years, a criminal industry had developed that would last until the present day. By 1914, Los Angeles was the center of an auto theft ring that resold parts stripped from stolen automobiles nationwide and used the remnant chassis to build delivery trucks and roadsters. To address this growing problem, entrepreneurs developed theft prevention devices, such as Earl E. Chapman's Auto Theft Signal, which clamped onto the vehicle's tire and wheel rim and required several hours to remove without the key. The Automobile Club's response was manifold. Its anti-theft squad placed ads in local papers with details of the stolen vehicles and created an alert system to notify detectives positioned in fast cars and motorcycles on prominent roads in Southern California whenever thefts occurred. Other detectives concentrated on deterring thefts of accessories from parked automobiles. The club also printed newspaper articles advising owners how to deter thieves and wrote legislation to track vehicle titles and punish perpetrators. After Harry Raymond joined the squad, a special squad of the Club's auto theft unit equipped itself with shotguns to use on raids of suspected strip shops.

The Automobile Club's detective squad was a resounding success, recovering up to 70% of the automobiles stolen in 1917 and receiving national attention. The squad's accomplishments helped expand the Club's membership and keep down auto insurance rates. In 1919, the Club's directors added two detectives from the LAPD, Harry Hickok and Jesse Erven, whom they called the "best automotive investigators on the coast." Chief of Police Butler and then Chief of Detectives Home, while regretting the loss of the two detectives' services, predicted that they would be a great asset to the Club and its efforts to stem auto thefts.[2]

Catching auto thieves sometimes led the detectives to bigger game. Raymond was with the squad six months when he made his first big collar. While riding with Hickok and Erven, he spied a new Buick that had been reported stolen in San Francisco. The thieves had neglected to change the license plate. One waited behind the steering column of the automobile while his companion, a tall, lanky lad, talked on a pay phone nearby. The driver, a seventeen-year-old youth named James Reynolds, had fallen in with the young man in the phone booth in San Francisco. The two had boosted the automobile and ridden it south, stopping other vehicles to rob their drivers and passengers of valuables, which they pawned in downtown Los Angeles.

While Reynolds was a nascent hoodlum of little account, the other man seemed familiar to Raymond, who looked through circulars in the LAPD's Identification Bureau after taking the two young men to the downtown jail. He turned out to be nineteen year-old Sam Purpera, who was wanted in Cleveland for slaying two business executives. Fresh out of prison, Purpera had slammed a stolen automobile into a car carrying Wilfred C. Sly, President of the W. W. Sly Manufacturing Company and George K. Fanner, the company's superintendent, on a wooden bridge near the factory. Suspecting a holdup, Sly leveled a revolver at Purpera and accused him of deliberately causing the collision. Purpera pretended to be a careless teenager mortified at having wrecked his father's automobile. Sly fell for the ruse, pocketed his gun and started gathering names and addresses of witnesses. A few seconds later, a second car filled with four men arrived from the opposite direction. One man, pretending to survey the damage to Sly's car, reached inside the automobile and pulled out the payroll satchel. When Fanner objected, Purpera and the other men drew their guns. Purpera shot Sly in the belly, then shot him again as he writhed on the ground. When Fanner tried to escape, Purpera shot him as well.

The four other gangsters piled in their car, leaving Purpera with the wrecked stolen vehicle. When they drove away without him, he lit off through the backyards of neighboring homes.

Within a few days, police identified the other gang members, whom they arrested but had to release for lack of evidence. Purpera had already left town on a long escape odyssey that took him to Boston, Philadelphia, Chicago, El Paso, and Juarez before he wound up in California. After the Auto Club detectives arrested him, he denied any part in the killing. However, when confronted by Cleveland authorities with the evidence against him, including eyewitnesses who identified him from his mug shots as Sly's killer, he confessed. He was returned to Cleveland, where, after fingering one of the fellow gangsters who deserted him at the wooden bridge, he was tried, convicted and executed for murder a year later. Two of his partners in crime followed him to the electric chair, including the one whom he had identified.

Praise for the Automobile Club detectives for Purpera's capture came from across the nation. The three detectives each received $1,700 as part of the reward, enough to buy a new car in 1921. Raymond may well have used the money—and a bit more—to purchase the automobile he made famous in Los Angeles, a seven-passenger Case that he fitted with a large front bumper protruding almost a foot beyond the sides of the car. Christened the "leaping tuna," the automobile was involved in over 100 accidents during his three years with the Auto Club squad. Repeatedly, Raymond used its massive bumper either to smash into fleeing vehicles or to hook their left front wheel and then slam on the "leaping tuna's" brakes to stop the fugitive.[3]

At least once, the leaping tuna was not enough to stop a car thief and Raymond used his gun instead. On March 4, 1923, he and two other auto club detectives were on their way to police headquarters with two suspected car thieves when Raymond noticed a reported stolen vehicle parked along South Figueroa Boulevard. A man sat in the automobile. Raymond ordered the man out of his car. Instead, the man started the automobile and sped toward Raymond, who leaped out of the way and pulled his revolver. As the car passed him, he fired several shots. The car careened down the street and smashed into the curb. The driver, a known car thief, was pronounced dead on arrival at the Georgia Receiving Hospital.

Raymond's exploits over the next few years helped restore his reputation following his dismissal from Venice. Just days after the Purpera arrest, he and his fellow detectives made another big bust. On March 14, Raymond found a stolen automobile that five bandits used the night before in an aborted robbery of a downtown drugstore. When the proprietor attempted to take the gun from one robber, they dragged him outside and shot him in the stomach. The robbers fled as he staggered back inside. A short time later, they robbed another drugstore a few miles away.

A few days later, Raymond and Hickok spotted a recently stolen car as they drove along Broadway in downtown LA. After they followed the car for a few blocks, it picked up speed and weaved in and out of traffic. A rapid chase ensued. Raymond cut off the fleeing vehicle at Seventh Street while Hickok jumped onto the running board of the other car. The three occupants reached for their revolvers, but the detectives knocked the weapons out of their hands before they could fire.

At police headquarters, the trio confessed to the drugstore robbery and a string of other robberies during the last few months. They also fingered their cohorts. Police arrested their leader, William Seagoe, at his apartment on

Grand. He and the shooter of the druggist, Julius Galliher, were old friends who met as juvenile delinquents committed to the Whittier State School in 1912. Both earned long sentences to San Quentin.

Raymond's reputation continued to rise through the 1920s. While newspapers noted his exploits in recovering automobiles, his involvement in some of the decade's most infamous criminal cases made him famous. The first began on the night of Tuesday, December 6, 1921. Two police officers, William L. Brett, 38, and Harry Clester, 30, were patrolling the Boyle Heights area east of Los Angeles in a Ford touring car. Both Brett and Clester were from the Midwest, Kansas and Indiana, respectively. They had joined the LAPD about the same time a few years back and become good friends. Both had two children—Brett's oldest, George, was a cabin boy on the coastal steamer *Harvard*. Both lived in the district they patrolled, a good neighborhood, working-class and diverse, with a growing immigrant population and many stable Jewish families. They were practically neighbors; only the broad green field of a cemetery separated their small cottages.

It was a mild evening, fine weather for an open car. Detective William Reed accompanied them. Over the previous weekend, there had been what the *Los Angeles Times* called a "saturnalia of violent crimes" that included four burglaries and seven highway robberies, and the three cops were on edge. Violent crime was up overall that year and although there were calls to add more officers, the city's budget was tight and opposition to tax increases was widespread. As the trio made their way through the dark streets of the hilly district, they had in their minds the killing of Detective John J. Fitzgerald earlier in the year. Fitzgerald's killer, "Little Phil" Alguin, was on the loose and in hiding, perhaps in Mexico, but maybe much closer. He had threatened to kill any police officer who looked for him. Despite the threats, Brett was persistent in chasing leads about Alguin's whereabouts.[4]

Around 10:00, while driving east on Fourth Street, Clester noticed that an automobile appeared to be tailing them. Reed suggested they find out what the other vehicle wanted. Brett pulled to the side. The car passed them slowly and turned at the next corner. The officers watched for a few seconds and then decided there was nothing to it. They continued down Fourth to Lorena and then drove south to Stephenson Avenue (now Whittier Boulevard), where they dropped Reed off.

After stopping for a meal at the Hollenbeck Park Boat House, Brett and Clester drove east on Fourth Street. It was now 10:30. At the corner of First and Indiana, the easternmost boundary of the Boyle Heights Division, they reported to the substation on a call box, then drove south on Indiana. Turning west on Stephenson, they shined a spotlight on the closed and darkened businesses along the avenue, looking for anything amiss. Near the junction of Lorena and Stephenson, where an hour before they had dropped off Reed, the officers spotted a large Ford touring car idling in front of a furniture store. Its top was down and the heads of five men were visible, two in the front seat and three in the back. One of its headlights was out. They passed the car, drove a half block and made a U-turn. The other automobile pulled away from the curb and turned left onto Lorena Avenue, a broad street with two lanes in both directions, heading north. The cops followed.

Brett sped up behind the vehicle and then stepped hard on the gas pedal. As they drew alongside the other automobile, Clester leaned out the passenger side window, badge in hand, and ordered the other driver to pull over. To make sure he complied, Brett veered the police car over to the right and pinned the Ford against the curb.

Clester leapt to the ground and demanded the driver's license while Brett crossed in front of the police vehicle to the front of the other car. What were they up to, Clester demanded? Why were five men driving around a quiet neighborhood in the middle of the night? The driver did not seem to have a good answer and the men did not look like the kind you wanted to talk with on a dark street late at night. Mounting the driver's side running board, Clester straddled the rear door with his right leg and ordered the driver to follow his directions to the station. They would sort things out there.

The driver pulled away from the curb while Brett followed in the police car. They had traveled about two and one-half blocks when suddenly there was a commotion in the rear seat of the automobile. Somebody cried, "I'm not going any further!" The car braked, throwing Clester off balance. A man in the back seat brandished a pistol. Clester shouted, "Don't do that!" and pulled out his service revolver. But before he could fire, another man wrestled the gun from him. A second man then grabbed the pistol and fired. Three shots struck Clester on the wrist, the chest and the forehead. He swayed on the rear door for a few seconds, and then somebody pushed him into the street. The man with the pistol jumped from the car and ran along the sidewalk. Brett leapt from his car and fired at the vehicle but the running man came from his flank and shot him twice, once in the head and once in the chest. Brett collapsed, then lifted himself on his elbow and fired back at the fleeing man.[5]

The Ford took off down the street, running over Clester's prostrate body. A block away, it picked up the running man as he emerged from a side street, revolver in his hand, then turned west on Fourth Street toward downtown Los Angeles.

After a minute, the residents of the neighborhood swarmed into the street where the two officers lay dying.

At the time, Harry and Beulah Raymond lived in an apartment at 2323 West Eleventh Street, not far from 16th and Flower, where the Police Relief Association was having its annual dance that evening at the Golberg-Bosely Hall. It is likely that they were in the ballroom when the band suddenly stopped at 11:30 and Police Lieutenant Howard I. Nicholson, head of the Relief Association, informed the 2,000 guests of the shooting. The dance floor cleared immediately. In a few minutes, officers from the Boyle Heights substation and other police stations throughout the city rushed to Lorena Avenue. Off-duty cops also abandoned their wives and sweethearts and hurried to their stations to begin what became the biggest manhunt to date in the city's history.

The involvement of an automobile in the crime made the skills of the Automobile Club's Theft Bureau detectives critical to the investigation, especially as it was possible that the car was stolen. While that night Raymond was unable to match the witnesses' descriptions of the vehicle to a stolen vehicle report, he kept on the case. The next morning, when he and Erven studied the scene, they noticed shards of glass unlike the broken glass on the police vehicle. They soon determined that the glass came from a light reflector not commonly in use on the Pacific Coast.

During the next few days, police officers throughout the city tried to match the broken glass at automotive supply stores. It was the only good clue. Although residents in the neighborhood came forth to testify, none could provide any details to identify the killers. However, several thought Brett wounded the man who ran from the vehicle. On that possibility, police followed a blood trail that led into an immigrant district near the cross streets of North Broadway and Sunset Boulevard. After they found no wounded gunman, they gave up the search. Still, the possibility that one of the killers was wounded gave the police something to go on.

With no strong leads, the police cast a wide net over the highways in and out of Los Angeles while Federal authorities kept a close watch on automobiles crossing to Mexico. Shortly before dawn the next morning, two patrol cops pursued a suspicious car, exchanging shots with the occupants until the fleeing car plunged into a ditch near Culver City and the suspects escaped on foot. In the following days, several crooks and some innocents were ensnared in the manhunt. Two armed men walking along the highway toward San Diego, another two driving a car with a broken headlamp in Glendale and a man wanted on a warrant discovered working in the Imperial Valley found themselves jailed under suspicion of murder. In a few cases, the suspects admitted to other crimes they had committed at the time of the Brett and Clester killings to prove their innocence of the officers' deaths. Other police detectives traveled to San Bernardino to investigate an abandoned automobile with bloodstained seats. While there, they arrested a pair of young hoodlums who had stolen an automobile in Venice and used it to rob a tobacco shop.

The slaying of two policemen, headline news in the city's newspapers, also became a political issue as advocates for expanding the LAPD seized on the tragedy. Previously, anti-tax groups had blocked efforts to increase the number of patrolmen on the force, but the morning after the murders, Mayor George E. Cryer convinced the city council to add 200 officers.

Early on, detectives focused on "Little Phil" Alguin's gang, which operated in the area of the killing. Detectives theorized that Alguin's gang might have ambushed Brett and Clester. The theory got legs after Detective Reed told the coroner's jury of the strange automobile that appeared to follow Brett and Clester's patrol car earlier in the evening.

Despite the massive effort, the killers' trail grew cold. Raymond's discovery of the broken reflector glass had not produced a solid lead. With 1,500 police officers searching for the killers, it was time for Raymond to go back to his day job.

On Friday, December 16, ten days after the murders, Raymond and fellow detectives Hickok and Erven, both of whom had rejoined the LAPD, drove to a house at 330 10th Street in Hermosa Beach. Earlier in the week, they had received a telegram from Tulsa, Oklahoma. Police there suspected that Ralph Waldo Pontius, whom a Federal grand jury had indicted for violating the Dyer Act forbidding the interstate transportation of stolen vehicles, had fled to Southern California. Raymond traced Pontius to the Hermosa Beach cottage, which he had rented under the surname of Pearson.

Pontius told them he was the former chief of police of Dodge City, Kansas but actually, he had only been a traffic cop for a few months the previous summer. As a young man in Larned, Kansas, he traded horses, ran skating rinks and billiard halls, played baseball and finally served as a minor league umpire between 1913 and 1921. In 1921, he became a fence for automobile thieves, reselling the vehicles with phony papers. By the time insurance investigators caught up with him at the end of the summer, he had left town. Dodge City authorities began a nationwide search for him.

Pontius denied everything when Raymond confronted him. The thirteen cars that he had sold he claimed to have purchased legally. The detectives did not care if he were innocent or guilty. He was a fugitive with a price on his head and his crime involved their mission of protecting the automobiles of those affluent enough to own them. They took him into custody and drove him to Central Jail.

Something about Pontius must have aroused Raymond's suspicion. He seemed more than just an auto thief. Maybe the firearms he observed in the

Hermosa Beach cottage did the trick. The detectives grilled Pontius at the Central Jail. Although reluctant to talk, Pontius said enough to make them want to hear more. After a while, he spoke of a woman named Mary White. Maybe she could tell the cops whatever it was they were looking for.

Raymond and Erven drove to the address Pontius gave them and waited. Around 11:00 p.m. Tuesday, December 20, Mary White returned. After expressing an interest in the $10,000 award offered for the apprehension of the killers of Clester and Brett, she began to talk. What she told them led Raymond, Hickok and Erven to suspect that they had stumbled upon the murderers of the two policemen. Pontius' girlfriend, Rhea Simpson, whom they arrested at her apartment on Olive and Sixth and jailed at the University Police Station, furnished leads to additional suspects. Around six o'clock the following morning, they arrested a man named William Thompson at a rooming house at 518 South Grand. After leaving two uniformed cops in Thompson's room in case additional suspects should show up, the three detectives took Thompson to Central Jail. An hour later, the detectives held shotguns pointed at a second suspect, William Albert Bringhurst, at another boarding house on Georgia Street.

After Bringhurst was safely in the Central Jail, Raymond and his fellow detectives rushed to San Diego, where, according to the suspects in custody, the other gangsters had fled. However, when they reached San Diego, they learned that the two other suspects, identified as Cal Richards and Jesse Windle, had returned to Los Angeles. By this time, a third gangster, James Wheaton, had made the mistake of knocking on Thompson's door. Two cops with sawed-off shotguns answered.

When he got back to Los Angeles, Raymond had Rhea Simpson transferred to the Central Jail, where she and Pontius began to talk. The story they told corroborated what Raymond already heard from Mary White. In addition, Simpson gave them Cal Richards's real name—Calvin Rowell. On Thursday, December 22, Rowell showed up at Thompson's room on Grand Street. Two LAPD detectives and their shotguns greeted him.

Both Wheaton and Rowell quickly confessed to the killings. Bringhurst promised to talk if he were guaranteed that his wife would receive the benefits of a life insurance policy were he to hang. However, after police found a smuggled file in his cell and theorized that he planned to use it to escape they were in no mood to make a deal. Thompson remained mum.

Over the next few days, Raymond worked with the LAPD to develop the case against the men they now held. The small criminal gang had operated in Los Angeles for months, led by Bringhurst and Thompson, two ex-cons from Utah who met twelve years earlier while employed at the Highland Bay Smelter in Murray, Utah. Both Bringhurst and Thompson came from prominent Mormon families (Bringhurst, the great nephew of William Bringhurst, leader of the first white settlers of Las Vegas, Nevada, had attended the University of Utah). In the spring of 1910, they committed a series of burglaries and robberies that culminated in a holdup at the Clift House Gambling Room in Salt Lake City. Utah authorities suspected the two in several additional crimes, including an attempted bank robbery and the street-corner strangulation of an elderly Salt Lake City man.

The two had fallen out after Bringhurst, the first to be identified and caught, protested his innocence and blamed Thompson for the Clift House crime, but they made up in Utah State Prison. The warden remembered Bringhurst as "a nervy fighter who will tackle anything" and Thompson as "criminally cunning." Both, he recalled, were frequently in fights with other inmates.[6]

Although Utah sentenced both to long prison sentences (twelve for Bringhurst and twenty for Thompson), neither served his full sentence. Paroled in 1912, Bringhurst returned to prison two years later for violating his parole. Released in 1916, by 1918 he had moved to Long Beach, where he worked in a shipyard.

Despite escaping briefly in 1914, Thompson also had his sentence commuted. He left prison on June 29, 1917, but was re-incarcerated after he robbed a store two years later. By late 1921, he was out of prison and living in a boarding house in downtown Los Angeles. By this date, his friend Bringhurst had moved from Long Beach to Los Angeles and was trying to make a living as a real estate salesman but not doing well. In April 1921, police arrested him after he tried to pawn two watches that had been stolen from a conductor and motorman of the local streetcar company three years before. Although he may have been involved in additional criminal activity since 1918, when he and Thompson reconnected in 1921, he moved further along his old path.

The three other members of the gang were James Wheaton, Calvin Rowell, and Jesse Windle. Wheaton had met Thompson in Utah State Prison in 1918 while serving time for forgery. Rowell and Windle were both friends of Pontius. Windle, who had been a small-time bootlegger in Oklahoma, and Rowell were auto mechanics, and it is likely they helped Pontius steal automobiles in Oklahoma and were doing the same in Los Angeles.

On Tuesday night, December 6, the group, minus Pontius, met in downtown Los Angeles. They cased several businesses to burglarize in Hollywood and East Los Angeles in Rowell's late model Ford Touring car. None seemed a safe target, however. They were about to disband around 11:00 p.m. but Bringhurst was adamant that he needed to get some money to buy Christmas presents for his two children. They continued looking.

Shortly afterward, Thompson noticed Britt and Clester's car behind them. It was at that point that they turned north on Lorena Avenue. As Thompson had already declared that he "could not afford" to go to jail and would tie up any police that bothered them, the fates of the two officers and the gangsters were sealed once the patrolmen turned onto Lorena to follow.

After the arrests of Bringhurst, Thompson, Wheaton and Rowell, one suspect remained free: Jesse Windle, alias Jesse Walters. Raymond and the LAPD detectives searched for him at Pontius' Hermosa Beach house, but all they found was a smoldering fireplace. Assuming Windle was on the run and driving east toward his home state of Oklahoma, they used a technique they had employed in tracking auto thieves, "the telegraphic barrage," which involved two hundred telegrams sent to sheriffs throughout the southwest to ask them to be on the lookout for the fleeing suspect. The Automobile Club detectives did not invent the term—it had been use before to describe an organized campaign of telegrams sent to congressmen—but they were the first to use the telegraph to combat auto theft. It was an effective tool in the empty desert landscape of the far west, with its paucity of roads, paved or otherwise.[7]

The telegrams described Windle as "five feet, seven inches tall, smooth shaven, florid complexion, light brown eyes, brown hair. When last seen he was wearing a blue serge coat and brown trousers and was driving a Ford coupe bearing the state license plate 633-881." It was ample information to ensure the fugitive would not go far, but it needed to be sent, received and read before he got away.[8]

On the day before Christmas, at Beal's Well twelve miles northeast of Niland in the Imperial Valley, Mack Harris was guarding a prisoner road gang that had been sent out to repair the dirt road to the city of Blythe on the Colorado River. Harris was a Texas native who owned a homestead farm northwest of Niland. He had been the town's blacksmith but recently had become Niland's constable, a first step in a long career in law enforcement.

Niland sat near the southeastern bank of the Salton Sea along the Southern Pacific railroad, which ran from Yuma through the Coachella Valley and San Gorgonio Pass to Los Angeles. Promoters had dubbed it the "inevitable city" in newspaper advertisements in Los Angeles, San Diego, and other cities throughout California, claiming its location at the northeastern entrance to the flourishing agricultural lands of the Imperial Valley ensured its growth. The city's principal booster, the California Land and Water Company, marketed lots through daily lectures at its headquarters on Spring Street in downtown Los Angeles and arranged weekend train excursions to the site. By 1921, however, the dream of a prosperous city was already going bust. One of its chief promoters, William F. Carlson, a former San Diego City mayor, had been convicted of mail fraud after he failed to honor his guarantee that the lots he sold would appreciate 25% in one year. Ambitious plans for commercial buildings, including a large hotel, had gone up in smoke—literally in the case of the hotel, which burned to the ground a short time before its scheduled completion when a campfire started by tramps got out of control. Nine months later, an entire block containing the local post office, a clothier, a poolroom and a drugstore went up in flames as well. By 1921, the only new structure in Niland impressive enough for the *Los Angeles Times* to feature in a rotogravure page of Imperial Valley points of interest was a v-shaped commercial building housing the First National Bank, an institution that would stumble through the early 1920s and fail completely in 1924. In another century, the bank's building, vacant after years of serving as a recycling center, would be all that remained of the original boomtown. In 1921, however, hope for the future still inspired local boosters, who saw the town's salvation in the prospect of paved highways along the tracks to Los Angeles and through gaps in the Chocolate Mountains to Blythe and the fertile Palo Verde Valley on the Colorado River.[9]

It was on the Niland-Blythe road that Harris' prison road gang toiled that morning when a Ford Roadster drove up and a man got out. He had one hand in his pocket and kept an eye on Harris' revolver. He was looking for a place to eat, he said, a curiously optimistic desire in that desolate terrain. Constable Harris offered to let him eat lunch with the road gang but the man said he was in a hurry to find the road to Needles. He returned to his car and peeled off toward the north. Suspicious, Harris made a note of the automobile's license plate number. Two days later, on Monday morning December 26, Harris received Raymond's telegram, complete with a description of Windle and the vehicle in which he had fled, including its plate number. Realizing that he had let a cop killer get by him, Harris contacted Raymond, who sent out another telegraphic barrage to notify all sheriffs in Nevada, Utah, New Mexico and Arizona to be on the alert for the fugitive.

The men who received the telegrams were not unlike their counterparts of fifty years before, when automobiles were only a dream of eastern tinkerers and trains crept over the barren land from one water tower to the next. They were as raw and pitiless as the terrain they watched over. Many had tracked desperate men on horseback over the back roads and trails to dilapidated huts in the forlorn canyons of their territories. All had come across travelers who had miscalculated, underestimating the parching desert sun or overestimating their own resiliency, and died miserably from heat stroke or dehydration. While Windle did not have to worry about the summer sun, the inhumane land he was passing through could kill him in a dozen other ways should his car break down. He had spent Christmas day following dirt roads, some former stagecoach routes, through the jagged mountain ridges and broad desert plains of the California desert east of the Salton Sea, passing forsaken mining camps and abandoned wells as he headed toward the Colorado River. Along the way, he found an abandoned car and swapped the license plates on his automobile for a pair from Texas. He reached Needles early Monday morning, half-famished, and crossed the Colorado River into Arizona, heading north. Outside the gold-mining town of Oatman, he ran out of gas and had to walk to town to fetch a gallon of gasoline. When he returned to the filling station in the Ford a short time later, the local constable, Deputy Sheriff William Mackay, was at the station. Mackay looked inside the coupe and spotted a rifle, shotgun, and two pistols in the rear seat.

Around 5:30 that evening, MacKay received a call from Sheriff William P. Mahoney of Kingman, Arizona, who had received Raymond's telegram. Mackay told the sheriff of Windle's visit. By that time, Windle was on the road north again. Mahoney dispatched his deputies to watch for the Ford with Texas plates. However, Windle skirted Kingman during the night of Monday, December 26. After he got stuck in the mud near Truxton, 35 miles northeast of Kingman, he was reported driving fast through Peach Springs around 10:30 the following morning.

Heavy rains made the roads nearly impassible, so Sheriff Mahoney and his deputy, John Harris, took an eastern-bound train to get ahead of the fugitive. At Seligman, they were joined by another deputy and a railroad officer. They also received a telegram from a railroad officer on board an earlier eastbound train. He had spotted an abandoned Ford coupe about seven miles west of the town of Ash Fork on the roadway paralleling the tracks.

Mahoney ordered the conductor to stop the train near the abandoned car. He and his deputies then hiked back to the vehicle. It had Texas plates. The deputies disabled the starter motor and trudged eastward down the railway. After a mile and one half, they came across the railroad section house at Pinaveta. Two men were standing outside. One was the railroad section boss, W. P. McNeil. The other was Windle. Inside, McNeil's wife was cooking breakfast. Seeing the lawmen approaching, Windle darted inside the house.

Mahoney identified himself to McNeil and asked to see the man who owned the vehicle abandoned down the road. "He's in the house," McNeil responded. "My wife is there, too."

"Get him out," Mahoney demanded.[10]

McNeil went inside while the sheriff and his deputies waited. Windle came to the front door, looked them over, and then went back into the house. A minute passed. Suddenly four shots rang out. McNeil's wife rushed from the house in terror. Mahoney and one of his deputies approached the house carefully. Inside, Windle lay dying, three self-inflicted bullets in his belly. A gold watch he claimed to be a gift from his wife had deflected a fourth from striking his heart.

Mortally wounded, Windle lingered on for a day, long enough to claim that he was not the man who shot the LA policemen and to blame the others, particularly Thompson and Rowell, for the deed. He died in a hospital in Kingman on December 28. Raymond and the LAPD detectives arrived too late to take a written statement.

With Windle dead and the other gang members behind bars, the city's attention focused on the prosecution of the killers. Rowell and Wheaton stood trial first. Their defense attorneys tried to keep their confessions from the jury, charging that they were coerced and naming Raymond and his fellow detectives as the ones who performed the third degree. The tactic did not work. The two were convicted and sentenced to consecutive life terms. Bringhurst and Thompson were tried separately. Both were condemned to death.

Wheaton and Rowell entered San Quentin in December 1923 along with Bringhurst and Thompson. Wheaton was transferred to Folsom within a week of his arrival. He died July 7, 1925, at the Stockton Insane Asylum. Rowell applied for parole repeatedly, once after he ratted on several fellow prisoners who planned a prison break. Transferred to Folsom in 1932, he died there in 1936.

Pontius returned to Muskogee, Oklahoma after the murder trials, where he was briefly lodged in the city jail before he posted bond. For the rest of the summer, he resumed his career as a minor league umpire but, in December, Tulsa authorities arrested him for auto thefts he committed in 1921. Pontius confessed his crimes, which included interstate transportation of stolen vehicles. Sentenced to Leavenworth Prison for two and one-half years in 1923, he was re-indicted for aiding another prisoner's attempted escape. After prison, he found work as a farm hand in Florida, but, by 1949, he was back in prison, convicted of defrauding a New York state farmer of $3,500 in a confidence game. He died in 1959.

On April 21, 1924, Bringhurst and Thompson were hanged in San Quentin.

Raymond was heralded for his work in the Brett-Clester murders. LAPD Chief Everington presented him and his fellow Auto Club detectives with diamond-set gold badges purchased by a consortium of civic groups. The three detectives had already donated the $10,000 reward for the capture of the murderers to the two officers' widows. The *Los Angeles Times* even named Raymond as a possible replacement for Police Chief James W. Everington when the latter came under criticism in April 1922. After his disastrous tenure in Venice, his star had risen a great way. He was also well respected by the LAPD's rank and file, who presented him with a gold watch in appreciation for his work as chairman of the Square Club, an internal LAPD organization.

He complemented his work in apprehending the murderers of Brett and Clester by helping to capture another notorious cop killer, "Little Phil" Alguin. Alguin had served two previous prison sentences for burglary and had been on the run since June 1921 after shooting Detective John J. Fitzgerald as the latter emerged onto the porch of a house that police had just raided. Raymond and other detectives from the Automobile Club had aided in the pursuit of Alguin, but the gunman fled into Mexico, leaving in his wake letters threatening any police officers who hunted him. His capture was a major goal of the LAPD. Police Chief Louis D. Oaks, who followed Everington in the job, traveled repeatedly to Juarez to check out rumors Alguin was hiding there, but Mexican authorities thwarted his attempts each time.

Raymond's involvement in the case began in late November 1922, when he arrested Herbert Uribe and his wife Catherine, a former Broadway stage star, in Pasadena, for possession of a stolen automobile. The Auto Club detectives had been working with Juarez authorities to break up a vehicle theft ring operating in Southern California and northern Mexico. Herbert was held along with his brother Fernando, but police decided that his wife was not involved in the crime and released her. Afterward, Catherine contacted her husband's relatives, who were prominent citizens of Juarez, hoping to find Alguin and exchange him for her husband and brother-in-law's freedom. When her early efforts failed, she attempted to locate Clara Phillips, who had escaped the Los Angeles Jail after her conviction for murder in the hammer bludgeoning of her husband's mistress. Catherine was unable to find Phillips, but her efforts to persuade Mexican authorities to trade Alguin for the Uribe brothers paid off. They captured Alguin and returned him to Los Angeles, where he was convicted of Fitzgerald's murder and sentenced to San Quentin.

Raymond also played a large role in the hunt for the murderers of Sam McGee. Accompanied by two guards, McGee was driving a bank-owned automobile west on East Fourth Street near the intersection with Wall Street when a small touring car with three men pulled up alongside. Without warning, one of the touring car's occupants leveled a sawed-off shotgun at the bank car. The guards held up their hands, but McGee ducked beneath the automobile door. When he looked up again, the shotgun exploded in his face. The trio then fired their revolvers on the other bank guards. The bank vehicle smashed into the curb. One bandit leapt out of the touring car and grabbed a mailbag filled with over $200,000 in Liberty Bonds, stocks, and corporate securities. McGee, conscious when the police arrived minutes later, died on the way to the hospital.

As they did in the Brett-Clester killings, police once again took advantage of the city's isolation by telegraphing all outlying law enforcement agencies in Southern California to blockade roads and railroads leading from the city. The following day, police found the stolen automobile the killers had used. As the bandits had not been apprehended fleeing the city, the police believed they were holed up somewhere within the metropolis.

The trail was cold, however. On March 20, what was evidently the same trio forced an automobile with the receipts of a downtown department store chain off the road at Fourth Street and Beaudry. Once again, the driver faced a sawed-off shotgun and two men armed with revolvers, but this time no shots were fired. The trio got away with the victim's automobile and $6,000 in cash in canvas bags, which they threw into a vacant field at Wilshire and Norton before they disappeared.

The following day, Raymond and Jesse Erven located the bandit's car, a stolen vehicle, on Ingraham Street just west of Witmer Street, not far from the site of the robbery. Whether Raymond was working the case for Home is not clear, but, in the ensuing months, he used his contacts in the criminal underworld of bunko artists and fences in search of the stolen bonds. After a few months, he found some in the possession of Frank Bernard, alias Frank Grant. Bernard was acting as a fence for a group of Latino men and women on Aliso Street, one of LA's poorest streets near the old Tenderloin district. Raymond befriended the group, none of whom seemed to match witness descriptions of the robbers, hoping to trace the bonds back to the killers of McGee. For several weeks, he socialized with the group and even traveled with them to Madera, California, to visit one member who had bought a pool hall with his share of the bonds. In the end, he was convinced that, although they had the loot from the robbery, they had no connection with the original crime itself. On June 21, he and LAPD officers lowered the hammer. Eight suspects were arrested in Los Angeles and Madera, including two local businessmen enlisted to peddle the bonds.

One suspect, Salvador Martinez, admitted that he had found the bonds and, uncertain as to how to negotiate them, had spread them among his friends. Martinez explained that he came across the missing mailbag under a culvert on Pico Boulevard. After a couple of trips back to the culvert to retrieve more bonds, he threw the bag with the remaining bonds into the creek. Police proceeded to the location where Martinez said he had abandoned the bag, but the reeds were so dense that they could not find it. Finally, almost two months after the arrest of the Latino group, a search party found the bag sunken in the mud underneath some boards. It had disintegrated in the water and oil from nearby Wilshire oil fields, but some of the paper was recoverable. The detectives worked into the night with coal oil to separate the bonds from the grime. The $75,000 they recovered was much less than the amount stolen, but, from the standpoint of the bank and its insurers, it was better than nothing.

The police theorized that the robbers and killers of Sam McGee stashed the mailbag in the culvert and intended to return to it when the heat died down. For some reason, they had not done so—at least not before Martinez found it and hid it again. Nobody was ever charged with the crime.

In February 1924, following months of laudatory articles for his exploits with the "Leaping Tuna" in capturing auto thieves, the *Los Angeles Times* reported Raymond was leaving the Automobile Club to start his own detective agency. A month later, the paper reported that he had abandoned his plans for a private agency to become chief of detectives in the district attorney's office, reporting to DA Asa Keyes. The position gave him "general supervision of all criminal investigations" in Los Angeles County. Despite his title and broad authority, other department detectives reported directly to the deputy DAs heading the various units within the DA's office. Still, it was an impressive position and one that brought him into direct contact with diverse aspects of law enforcement in Los Angeles.[11]

His new job involved a variety of cases, ranging from embezzlement to illegal gambling, extortion, bunko operations—including a "business chance" fraud reminiscent of the cases that he began his career with in 1910—and the dynamiting of LA Water and Power's aqueduct in the Owens Valley. He also helped investigate one of the era's great tragedies, the burning of the Hope Development Home, where twenty-two mentally challenged young women died in May 1924. The home had taken over the former Hotel Del Rey on a Playa Del Rey lagoon a few years after Los Angeles authorities closed the hotel, once a popular vacation spot, after charging it had become a bordello. A few weeks after the tragedy, an inmate confessed that she started the fire.[12]

Pleased with Raymond's performance, Keyes consolidated the department's detectives under him after Raymond returned from a trip to Chicago and New York, where he observed operations in the detective squads of the DAs of those cities. Raymond had the authority to assign detectives to cases as he chose. He also got a bigger office to conduct his business. Not long after his promotion, however, rumors circulated that he was involved in an internal departmental feud over the arrest and pending prosecution of a prominent Long Beach cafeteria owner on sexual misconduct charges. In early September, one of his subordinates, Detective John Dymond, had resigned because of the case. After Raymond demanded authority to fire several others, Keyes returned from his annual vacation to address the internal turmoil in his department.

The Long Beach cafeteria owner, Albert J. Nicholson, 50 years old, had been arrested in August 1924 and charged with committing an "unnatural act" upon a young woman named Florette Duvall. Nicholson had lunched with Duvall and another couple at the Café Montmartre in Hollywood before the group returned to Duvall's house on Mariposa Avenue. After the other couple left for the grocery store to purchase some food for the weekend, Duvall and Nicholson became involved in what he termed "affectionate demonstrations." At that moment, the husband of his former wife, Charles J. Cornellison, and a private detective burst out of a closet. Two deputy sheriffs who had watched the action through a window also entered the room. When Nicholson offered each deputy $100 to forget what they had seen, they added attempted bribery to the charges against him.[13]

It was an obvious variation of the badger game. The motive behind it became clear when Cornellison admitted that he hired the private detective, Larry Belgar, after Nicholson threatened his wife. Nicholson and his former wife had quarreled over the property settlement in their divorce and things had gotten ugly. Nicholson, who was known to harass young women, was an easy target. He was also wealthy and knew how to fight back. He declared the whole business a frame-up, demanded a grand jury investigation and hired the Burns Detective Agency.

George Pross, the local Burns Agency manager, worked with Detective Dymond and Deputy DA Costello on Nicholson's behalf. The three spirited away Duvall, who had signed a statement implicating Nicholson and was under subpoena to testify at his preliminary hearing, after telling her she was under arrest. For three days, Burn's operatives moved her from Los Angeles to Santa Barbara and finally to San Francisco while a female Burns operative watched over her. After she demanded to be returned home, she was brought back to Los Angeles, where she made a new statement about Nicholson's actions that contradicted her former statement. Duvall then complained to Harry Raymond, who was following leads to find other young women whom Nicholson might have mistreated, about her treatment by Dymond.

Duvall's treatment and the entry into the case of G. W. Price, a local Ku Klux Klan leader, elevated it from a simple badger game arising from a divorce squabble into a possibly serious act of malfeasance by members of the DA's office. Dymond, a notorious anti-labor detective who had once been an International Workers of the World leader and a saboteur before he turned on the IWW in 1920 to testify against other members, was a Klansman. So was Pross. Price conferred with Dymond and other DA staff members. Deputy District Attorney Buron Fitts declared that the Klan was interested in "an angle in the Nicholson case" but did not identify the nature of this interest, stating only that Price was not a witness and had no information about the case.[14]

On Nicholson's request, the grand jury conducted an inquiry but declined to issue any indictments. Keyes also decided not to pursue charges against Nicholson, citing the grand jury's inaction and claiming that prosecuting Nicholson would be "wasting the county's money and the time of the courts." Incensed, Cornellison took the matter to the California Attorney General a week later, denouncing the shadowy role the KKK played and arguing that Keyes failure to move the case forward amounted to misconduct. It was all for naught, however. The Attorney General refused to get involved.[15]

Raymond's tenure as the chief of detectives for the district attorney ended about the same time as the Nicholson case. In early October 1924, he submitted his resignation. A month before, on September 5, DA Keyes had asked his entire staff to resign as part of an ongoing reorganization of the DA's office spurred by the backbiting and internal dissension within the department. Keyes claimed that he had not asked Raymond to resign but that the detective had done so on his own volition after declaring that he intended to resume his career as a private detective. One way or the other, Raymond was once more out of a job, but he was still one of the best detectives in Los Angeles and the West Coast. There was always enough crime for a good man.

Sam Purpera

Jess Windle

Jess Windle

Poster for Arrest of
Ralph W. Pontius
1921

1912

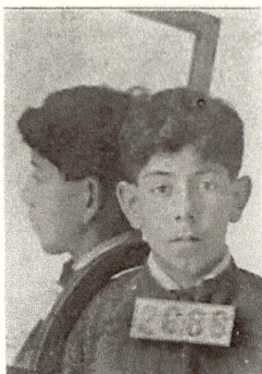 

1921

1933

Lifetime Partners in Crime

Julius Galliher   *William Seagoe*

Department of Corrections, Whittier Reformatory, San Quentin Prison, Folsom Prison.
California State Archives, Office of the Secretary of State, Sacramento, California.

William Brett (Photo courtesy of the Los Angeles Police Museum)

Harry Clester (Photo courtesy of the Los Angeles Police Museum)

William Bringhurst, San Quentin, 1922

William Thompson San Quentin Prison 1922

Calvin Rowell, San Quentin, 1923

James Wheaton San Quentin Prison 1923

5: THE PLOT AGAINST AMERICA'S SWEETHEART

After leaving the district attorney's office, Raymond remained a private investigator until the summer of 1927. However, he was available when detective friends in the LAPD called. In December 1924, he and LAPD Detective Lieutenant Jack Trainor were on patrol on the three hundred block of Fremont Street to the west of Bunker Hill when they spotted a man passed out in the street. After Trainor stopped the car and determined the man was drunk, Raymond went to a nearby house to use the phone to call a police wagon. When he returned he found two men confronting Trainor. The men, who were both intoxicated, had pulled up in an automobile seconds before and concluded that Trainor was robbing their friend, the unconscious drunk. One of them, an off-duty cop, stuck a pistol in Trainor's ribs and pulled the trigger. The gun misfired. His friend then grabbed the pistol and aimed at Trainor. The latter leapt behind a telephone pole where he returned fire, aiming low. Two bullets caromed off the ground, but one struck the shooter in his leg. From behind, Raymond rushed to overpower him while Trainor covered him with his gun.

The incident only became public because of the gunplay, but it indicated that Raymond was again working for the police. It was in the capacity of a temporary hireling that he became a key player in one of the years' most sensational cases, the conspiracy to kidnap Mary Pickford. Pickford, born Gladys Louis Smith in Toronto in 1892, was the most famous actress of the silent screen. She had been a child stage actress from January 1900 until 1909 when she signed a contract with Biograph Pictures for $10 per day. By 1915, she was making $2,000 per week and married to actor Owen Moore. Her marriage did not last, but her fame and fortune grew over the next ten years. After divorcing Moore, she married actor Douglas Fairbanks. The couple founded the Pickford-Fairbanks Studio and bought and remodeled a sprawling Beverly Hills mansion, "Pickfair," that was soon famous for its gatherings of film society. Los Angeles newspapers reported her activities closely throughout the twenties, making her an easy target for kidnappers.

The plot to kidnap Pickford began in the winter of 1922-3, more than two years before the police discovered it. Its architect was Charles Zachary Stevens, a former streetcar conductor who served as a Second Lieutenant at the Air Services Depot in Garden City, New York during World War I and became a purchasing agent for the International Petroleum Company. Stevens first began talking about kidnapping a film star with his roommate John Harney. They considered another screen star, Pola Negri, but doubted she was sufficiently wealthy to be a good target. Then they considered child start Jackie Coogan but rejected him because he was a ward of the court. Harney testified that the conversations, usually fueled by liquor, continued for about a year.

In November 1923, Stevens began scheming with Hollywood gas station operator Adrian James Wood, and truck driver Arthur Holcomb. The targets now were either Pickford or the grandchildren of oil magnate Edwin Doheny. The three men drank together a few months and worked out a rough plot. As Wood recounted to police:

> They'd use notes. Get the [kidnapped] party and get them [sic] settled at some place at some house and use notes in some way to communicate and give a letter telling them to come to some place to find a note. That would direct them to come on to some other place to find another note, and so on. At the same time they were supposed to have this money with them.[1]

The men continued to talk, but they took no definite action until spring of 1925. At that point, not having settled on a target, they began to monitor the activities of both Pickford and the Doheny children. In watching the Doheny grandchildren, however, they were careless. Doheny himself noticed them and called the police.

Chief of Detectives George Home once again called on Raymond. With LAPD Detective George Mayer, Raymond staked out the Doheny mansion for a week. Finally, Stevens and Holcomb drove up and parked outside the mansion. After a few minutes, the two suspects drove to the Pickford-Fairbanks studios, picking up Adrian Wood on the way. There they watched as studio employees left for the day.

It soon became clear to the detectives that the suspects were plotting a kidnapping for ransom. There had been few cases of the crime in Los Angeles to that date. The most notorious occurred a few years before when a pair of inept kidnappers abducted a wealthy young wife named Gladys Witherell and negotiated her ransom over a course of several days. After they overheard a phone call between one kidnapper and Witherell's husband, telephone operators alerted police, who arrested the kidnapper as he emerged from a pay phone at the Union Depot in downtown Los Angeles. The police sweated him until he confessed and told them his partner was holding Witherell at a sheep ranch in Corona. Police stormed the ranch and freed Witherell before the second kidnapper knew what had happened.

While kidnapping was rare in the city, Los Angeles had enough oil magnates and rich cinema stars to keep the potential for the crime alive in the minds of local police. Home and Raymond must have recognized that both the Doheny family and Pickford were at serious risk. The problem was how to thwart the crime without endangering the victims. Were the would-be kidnappers forewarned, they might resurrect their plans later, perhaps somewhere else with a different target. The kidnappers of Witherell had admitted they had plotted against other persons before selecting Witherell.

The detectives continued to trail the three suspects. One day they observed Stevens talking with his ex-roommate, John Harney. Somehow, the detectives persuaded Harney to cooperate. He told them where the plotters met, a room at the Hayward Hotel in downtown Los Angeles. Raymond rented an adjoining room, removed part of the wall in the conspirators' room, and replaced it with wallpaper. He also drilled some peepholes in the wall and placed a mattress on the floor next to the door where he and his fellow detectives could listen in comfort. Then he brought in an LAPD stenographer who recorded the conversation in the next room while listening through a stethoscope. While Raymond and the other detectives listened, Stevens, Holcomb, Wood, and a fourth man, Louis Alvarez Geck, plotted the kidnapping for several nights. Stevens later testified that the conspiracy was just "drunken talk," a claim that *LA Record* reporter Sadie Mossler endorsed by calling the Hayward Hotel parties "lots of lurid conversations, which sounded like wild flights of imagination." The man supplying the liquor for the drunken talk was Geck, an ex-con working as a police informant for Home.[2]

How Geck managed to slink his way into the conspirator's confidence is not clear. Stevens and his wife Pauline had known him since 1917 when they all lived in New Mexico. Pauline had been Geck's nurse after he was injured in a motorcycle accident. In fact, Charles Stevens loaned Geck $500 [the equivalent of almost $7,000 in 2020 dollars] that Geck acknowledged in a letter postmarked from Tampico, Mexico, in 1922. Geck never repaid the loan.

Sometimes alone and sometimes with Geck or Holcomb, Stevens continued to case both the Doheny mansion and the Pickford-Fairbanks Studios. The detectives kept an eye on the group but did not intervene. Once, Raymond and George Mayer followed the conspirators to a house in Tujunga

Canyon where they planned to confine Pickford. The detectives hid in the bushes outside the house, eavesdropping on the conversation inside.

Meanwhile, Home conferred with District Attorney Asa Keyes about the legal requirements for a conviction. A charge of felony criminal conspiracy required three stringent elements. There had to be "an agreement about the objective of the conspiracy," "a specific intent to achieve that objective," and "an overt act in furtherance of the agreement." With a town full of clever lawyers, before making an arrest the detectives had to make sure they had a case. Otherwise, defense attorneys would be able to argue that the alleged conspiracy was nothing more than idle talk and fantasy, not real and dangerous. However, waiting too long might endanger Pickford's life.[3]

In the last days of May, the conspirators discussed disguising themselves as Shriners, whose annual convention was to start in LA the next week. They reasoned that the frolicking Shriners, dressed in fez hats and robes, driving an automobile decorated with the Shriner's colors of red, green, and gold, should not alarm Pickford were she to notice them following her. By this time, however, Pickford and her husband had been warned of the plot, as had Doheny, who summoned guards from his New Mexico oil operations. Fairbanks was carrying a pistol and Pickford now knew the men by sight, having observed them three times in front of the studio.

On May 30, the day the plotters planned to abduct Pickford, the police acted. Raymond and Mayer seized Stevens and Holcomb as they sat in their automobile outside the Pickford-Fairbanks Studio and afterward drove to Alhambra to arrest Wood. With the suspects booked on criminal conspiracy charges, the action now shifted to the courts. The lawyers were now in charge.

As Keyes had explained to Home, the case centered on what an imaginative *Los Angeles Times* reporter dubbed "Old Man Overt Act." It soon became clear that the defense's main argument would be that no overt act occurred and that the whole "plot" was just a bunch of guys talking. The prosecution would point to several "overt acts": the surveillance of the Doheny children and Mary Pickford, the rental of a house to be used to confine Pickford, and Wood's purchase of a pistol for capturing the actress. These acts were "in furtherance of the agreement" to kidnap and hold Pickford for ransom. Proofs of the intention behind them were the confessions of Wood and Stevens and the corroborating testimony of witnesses Geck and Harney.[4]

Raymond's actions during the investigation became a key focus of the defense, which attacked the confessions he obtained from the suspects, alleging that he had beaten Stevens and Holcomb. Defense Attorney Hahn claimed that Stevens suffered three broken ribs. Holcomb testified,

I was brought down to Chief Home's office and Harry Raymond

said to me, "Fat, we want a statement out of you and we want to get it free and voluntarily." Then he said, "what were you doing at the studio." I said, "We went there with Louie to see a friend of his about a job." Then he struck me in the nose. I threw up my hand to protect my face and [Detective] Mayer stopped me. Mayer then took me to the wash bowl and washed the blood from my face and coat using water and paper. Then George Home came in. He looked at Raymond and smiled. Then he went out and bought me some cigarettes.[5]

Afterward, Holcomb stated that he confessed after Raymond warned him he would "stump hell out of me every day until I did." The following day, DA McCartney introduced evidence that on the day of Steven's arrest Raymond had an injured hand and so could not have beaten the two suspects. The evidence included a newspaper photograph of Raymond with a bandaged right hand that had been taken on May 30, the day before Stevens and Holcomb's arrests. In addition, a masseur at the downtown YMCA testified that Raymond injured his hand while breaking his fall after slipping on a bar of soap in the gymnasium shower.[6]

The final defense argument centered on Geck—"Geck, the Spider" as Hahn called him to the delight of local newspapers. In 1912, Geck had been convicted in Los Angeles as an accomplice to murder and spent four years at San Quentin. The son of a wealthy New Mexican, from whom he stole $500 before bolting to Los Angeles with a girl, Geck had robbed a grocery store on October 1, 1910, with Joseph Condolero. The storeowner begged for his life, but Condolero ended it with a blow from an ax. While Condolero busied himself with a tin box containing the store's receipts, Geck nonchalantly sold a loaf of bread to a customer and bowed as she left. Condolero died six months later, a rebel hero of the Battle of Casas Grande during the Mexican revolution, but the LAPD caught up with Geck in August 1912. Arrested in El Paso, he was extradited to Los Angeles in the company of then Detective George Home.[7]

The defense argued that Geck was the principal in the kidnap plan and that he had persuaded the conspirators to go along. It was true that he furnished both the room at the Hayward Hotel and the booze to keep the conversation going. While Detective Chief Home declared Geck, a "100 percent American," the defense charged that Home and Raymond used Geck to entrap the defendants to bolster their own reputations as detectives.[8]

On the witness stand, Geck did neither himself nor the detectives much good. He admitted that he had long been friends with Stevens and Holcomb and had palled around with them for a few years in Tampico. When asked why he had betrayed them, he declared that he was not their keeper and they had to look out for themselves. His performance was not the kind to endear him to a jury but then that was not the point. He had the endorsement of the LAPD and the assurance that he was working for the right side.

Critical to the prosecution were the testimonies of Mary Pickford and Douglas Fairbanks. The latter testified that he carried a revolver to defend his wife after police warned him a plot was afoot. He also said he spotted the conspirators hanging around the entrance to the Pickford-Fairbanks Studio three times. His wife's testimony proved even more important, not because she had anything relevant to say about the conspiracy, but because she was who she was. When she appeared to testify, movie fans crowded the courthouse and the chambers of adjoining courts emptied. One errant juror, escaping the boredom of her assignment in a nearby manslaughter case, led other women jurors out a skylight eight stores above Broadway into the courtroom, shook hands with Pickford, and gushed afterward, "She's the sweetest thing!" Mary returned the favor, exclaiming, "It is wonderful to feel that they are so interested. It makes you thrill—inside. You know, we live in another world, apart, and so much enthusiasm is encouraging."[9] Coupled with the testimony of the police stenographer, who read Holcomb's statement in the Hayward Hotel that he would shoot America's Sweetheart should she resist, her appearance was damning for the defense. That Holcomb had already been implicated in a gangland shooting did not help the defendants' cases, as it was hard to argue that they were just a bunch of guys talking if you considered that at least one of them had taken part in a string of strong-arm robberies.

In his instructions to the jurors, the judge made it clear that their decision must be based on the role Geck played in the conspiracy. If they believed he initiated the plot, they should acquit the defendants. If they determined the whole episode was a scheme by Raymond and Home to advance their careers at the expense of some hapless, loose-tongued men, then a conviction would be "repugnant to justice." However, the court explained, when a conspiracy is in progress, police officers may employ extraordinary means to prevent it.[10]

The jury took little time in convicting Stevens and Holcomb but took four ballots to acquit Wood on the same charges. The case against the younger man was weak. He was driving a truck in Alhambra when the Pickford kidnapping was to take place and the gun he supposedly bought for the kidnapping was in a trunk in his house. Several jurors afterward told Wood that he narrowly escaped imprisonment and warned him to watch with whom he associated in the future. Wood took the advice to heart. Marrying in 1927, he served in the US Army during World War 2 and died in 1953 in a hunting accident in Anchorage, Alaska. He was buried in St. Anthony, Idaho with a military headstone.

Stevens also received a military headstone a year later. He died after working for many years at a turkey farm in Santa Susanna after serving a little over five years of his ten-to-life sentence. He had reunited with his wife Pauline. In 1935, the Pickford case was far enough in the past that a *Los Angeles Times* columnist could write about Stevens shooting a gray fox in Santa Susanna as if the shooter had never been involved in the infamous kidnapping plot. The third man in the plot, Claud Holcomb, was paroled a few days after Stevens, having spent over six years at San Quentin. He died in 1936.

As for Geck, "the Spider" or otherwise, he returned to El Paso after the Pickford affair. On February 25, 1929, he attempted to smuggle 48 pints of liquor across the US/Mexican border. Arrested for violating the Volstead Act, he spent a year in the Federal Prison in Leavenworth, Kansas. By 1935, he was back in Los Angeles where he stayed until 1942, working off and on as a wholesale produce buyer, and living for a time at the YMCA. In the late 1950s, he returned to El Paso where he died in 1966.

Charles Zachary Stevens at the time of his trial {Los Angeles Times Photographic Archive, UCLA Library. Copyright Regents of the University of California, UCLA Library}

Louis Geck, San Quentin, 1912

*Douglas Fairbanks and Mary Pickford [Harris and Ewing
photograph collection, Library of Congress]*

6: NINETEEN TWENTY-SEVEN

After the Pickford kidnapping plot, Raymond worked variously as a private detective, a special officer for the LAPD, and an investigator for the Automobile Club. In April 1927, he was reported to have joined a special LAPD robbery squad probing a series of bank and jewelry robberies. A month later, a short report in the *Los Angeles Times* indicated that Raymond was also working for the Automobile Club. He may have also found occasional work with the many private detective agencies throughout the city and county. While the *Los Angeles City Directory* in 1926 and 1927 listed him as a detective, there is no corresponding listing of a business in his name.

By 1927, he had been a detective in various guises for twenty years. During that time, the city's population had grown from around three hundred thousand to well over a million. Los Angeles County had seen a nearly four-fold increase from slightly under a half million to approximately two million. The municipality had extended from the old downtown into the valleys and coastal plain, where planners laid out the streets that would soon be known as the "West Side" amidst the empty lots and bean fields. Raymond and his wife followed this geographic expansion, renting houses and apartments in areas into which the city had stretched during the first three decades of the twentieth century, including the MacArthur Park area and Hollywood.

Although George Home, his primary contact and employer within the police department, had retired, Raymond continued to work off and on for the LAPD. In the summer of 1927, he joined the department's auto theft unit. Whether he was officially on the LAPD's payroll at the time is not clear. Most observers claimed that, while he worked closely with police detectives throughout the years, especially in auto theft, he was never a sworn officer. Still, he was familiar with the department's culture, including the rife dishonesty and corruption of many officers within the force.[11]

Raymond would be linked with some of the LAPD's dishonorable acts for the remainder of his career. While some of these derogatory claims are not credible, others are repeated enough times to suggest there is truth behind them. One of these charges was that he played a part in the death of a notorious 1920s liquor hijacker, Harry Owen Thomas, whom the police had nicknamed "MileAway" because whenever accused of a crime he retorted that he was a mile away when it occurred. Thomas' real name was Fred Thomas Owen. He was a Missouri native but had spent much of his life in Wellington, Kansas, where his mother moved her family after her husband's death in 1895. While one former neighbor would claim that he had been a "good boy" until he left Kansas, there is a faint trace of a criminal past in the Kansas newspapers. In 1920, one Fred T. Owen was arrested after he stole a truck in Kansas City, Missouri. Whether the suspect was the same man who would become one of Los Angeles' most notorious criminals of the 1920s is not clear, nor is it certain that MileAway Thomas was the Fred Owen who registered for the World War 1 draft from the Missouri State Penitentiary in 1917.[12]

When MileAway arrived in LA is not certain either, but he seems to be the Harry Thomas who was charged along with two accomplices for auto theft in 1922, an event that may have first brought him to Raymond's attention. The trio specialized in expensive automobiles. Police caught them red-handed with seven, including two from a resident member of the exclusive California Club. Evidently, the arrests and subsequent term in the county jail cured Thomas of his auto theft habit, for the crime does not appear again in his rather substantial curriculum vitae of the next five years. In March 1925, a patrolman caught him and a cohort, Paul Parker, burglarizing a home at 12742 Ventura Boulevard. Thomas stuck a gun in the cop's ribs, but two officers arrived immediately to arrest the two thieves. In October of the same year, Thomas and Parker were arrested again with two other men, Charles Finch and Robert Rankin, for stealing a private stash of liquor from an automobile broker's garage at 1193 South Windsor Boulevard. They were caught in the act by the man's wife. After threatening her with pistols, they escaped with 140 cases of whiskey and an overcoat. Since under prohibition laws the whiskey was illegal and therefore had no legal value, the court dismissed charges for its theft but held Rankin for stealing the overcoat.

A month later, Thomas got into a fistfight with a smalltime bootlegger named Paul Mitchell at Mitchell's apartment near McArthur Park. Mitchell objected to Thomas' influence over his younger brother Marion, a budding nineteen-year-old thief who had lately joined Thomas' gang. Thomas got the better of the older brother, dishing out a black eye and some facial lacerations. That evening, as Thomas, his wife, and the younger Mitchell climbed into Thomas' car outside his Hollywood apartment, the brother rushed up with a 22-caliber rifle and fired three shots. The bullets crashed through the windshield. One struck Marion in the head, killing him instantly. While Paul Mitchell claimed that he fired at the automobile's tires to frighten Thomas, police alleged he had targeted Thomas. In either case, he was a poor shot and a worse driver, for in his haste to flee the scene he crashed his automobile.

Police found the .22 inside. Arraigned on manslaughter charges, Mitchell's case was dismissed after the police were unable to locate Thomas and his wife to testify.

In May 1926, Thomas was arrested twice more. The first was on suspicion of robbery. After police booked him, they recognized him as the Harry Thomas of the Mitchell case. They also suspected him in the recent murder of bootlegger/hijacker Eddie Hannon. Later that month they arrested him on a hit-and-run charge arising from an automobile accident in downtown LA the previous January. True to form, he convinced the detectives that he was miles away in San Francisco at the time of both events.

In August, Thomas was named as a target of the LAPD "rousting" campaign against local rumrunners. Recently appointed Police Chief James Davis directed cops to jail known violators of prohibition laws on vagrancy charges even though he knew that lawyers would quickly obtain the scofflaws' release and the charges would not stick. Davis hoped that continuous harassment would induce the men to find lawful means of employment or move elsewhere. Although the court dismissed a vagrancy case against Thomas after his attorney proved that he had $100,000 in the bank, nothing prevented police from arresting him again on the same charge.[13]

With the heat on him Thomas should have taken a long vacation somewhere miles away from Los Angeles as other Southern California bootleggers, including Tony Cornero and Milton B. "Farmer" Page, had done already. The public had grown weary of gun battles between bootleggers and the police were under pressure to act. It was just a matter of time before he was caught red-handed, without an alibi. Still, he persisted. In late December, the LAPD dry squad arrested one of his girlfriends, an attractive young woman named Betty Carroll, in his apartment for possession of five gallons of liquor. Thomas was not home at the time and Carroll took the rap for the booze, claiming she had received it as collateral for a loan.

Five weeks later, late on a foggy Tuesday evening, Luther H. Green, a wealthy stockbroker, returned to his home at 1053 Bonnie Brae Avenue to find men carrying cases from his cellar to a large Packard touring car parked along the adjacent street. Green stopped his car in the street and ran through the front door into his house. Upstairs, his eighteen-year-old son was in his second-floor bedroom. Talking excitedly about thieves downstairs, Greene snatched a small caliber rifle from the closet and rushed down the stairs onto the porch. The boy followed, but before he reached the porch, he heard a burst of gunshots. On the short lawn at the front of the house, his father lay dying, shot through the heart. The bandits piled into the touring car, which roared off into the dense fog.

Cops arriving at the scene quickly determined what had happened. In the cellar, they found a large quantity of liquor that Green had accumulated before prohibition and maintained with a government permit. They also found liquor bottles in the rear of the garage. The cops theorized that the burglars were a hijacking gang that somehow learned of Green's private stock. When Green challenged them from his front lawn, he faced criminals skilled in the use of firearms. His own rifle had jammed.

Green's death saddened and angered the city's business elites. The Los Angeles Stock Exchange closed to allow members to attend his funeral and offered a $5,000 reward for the arrest and conviction of his killer. Police rounded up local bootleggers and hijackers for interrogation. One they focused on was MileAway Thomas. A squad of detectives raided his apartment, where they found one of his girlfriends but not the elusive gangster himself. The girl told them enough to sanction warrants for Thomas and five members of his gang, including Betty Carroll. Two gang members surrendered voluntarily, but ten days passed before police captured Thomas and Carroll. Thomas was arraigned for the murder, but, within a few days, he and others in his gang walked free. LAPD Captain of Detectives James Bean admitted during a preliminary hearing that he did not have the evidence to prove Thomas and his gang murdered Green. Witnesses to the shooting were unable to identify Thomas, who had colored his gray hair brown to hamper their efforts.

Released from jail, Thomas did not do the smart thing, which was to leave town. The public was outraged, and law enforcement personnel in the LAPD and DA's office were frustrated and embarrassed by his ability to get away with his crimes, including murder. The LAPD decided to take action.

Although Thomas laid low for a time, by April he was looking for more booze. He got a tip about a stash of liquor in a garage in the rear of 1408 West 35th Street. On the evening of Thursday, April 21, he climbed over a wooden fence and pried open the garage door lock. As he entered the garage, he directed a flashlight to its corner where it fell on the faces of three LAPD officers, patrolman Ellis Bowers, Detective Charlie Hoy, and Detective Richard "Dick" Lucas. Lucas called for MileAway to throw up his hands. Instead, Thomas went for his gun. He got off one shot. The cops responded with much heavier firepower: a shotgun, a machine gun, and a revolver. Thomas was hit six times, three in the chest, two in the side, and one in the hand. He staggered out of the garage down the driveway and into the street, where he collapsed in the arms of a uniformed cop. On the way to the hospital in a police ambulance, Lucas told him he was dying. MileAway shrugged off the news. "Everybody has to fall sometime," he said. He died a few minutes later.[14]

A few days later, a crowd numbered in the hundreds attended services for Thomas in a downtown funeral home. He was buried in Forest Lawn beneath a flat reddish brown marker inscribed, "Sweetheart and Pal."[15]

The detectives had staked out the garage for three nights. They initially told reporters they first visited the property to investigate a complaint of prowlers lodged by the resident. Inside the garage, which the resident claimed was rented out to another party, they found an expensive automobile, bottles, and sacks. They concluded that the garage was being used as a hiding place by an unknown bootlegger. At least, that was one story. Another was that an informant had alerted the detectives that Thomas planned to raid the garage. Most likely, both stories were partially true: the police discovered the bootlegging evidence in the garage and conceived a simple plan to lure Thomas to it and so to put an end to his depredations.

While it was clear that the police had laid a trap for Thomas, a coroner's jury justified the killing, observing that Thomas entered the garage with criminal intent, failed to obey the officers' demand that he surrender, and instead responded by shooting at them. Chief Davis praised the detectives for doing their duty and warned the police would "meet gunmen on their own ground." "Here is my answer to the people who don't like the way Thomas, a known killer, hijacker and disturbing element, died," Davis snapped, "I have given all my officers instructions to kill without mercy any criminal caught committing a felony. I want criminals brought in dead, not alive. I will reprimand any officer who shows any mercy to a criminal." Newspaper commentary also condoned the tactics, focusing on Thomas' criminal behavior. The *Los Angeles Times* declared Thomas' death the working of an "informal justice" which catches up with the "most immune of criminals." The *Oakland Tribune* called him a "thug, a common, blunted and stunted outcast."[16]

It is hard to argue with either newspaper editorial about the character of MileAway Thomas. Still, the detectives likely foresaw the result of the three-night stakeout in the garage. Thomas was known to be quick to go for his gun. They could count on him to trigger his own execution. The trick was to get him to the garage. For that, according to Betty Carroll, they used an "ex-copper" to provide the phony tip about the liquor stock. When Carroll cautioned Thomas about this shadowy figure, he dismissed her concern, stating that the former policeman was "all right."[17]

Thomas' attorney, S. S. Hahn, claimed that the cop was Dick Lucas, the man who wielded the machine gun in the garage that night. However, Lucas was a cop when Thomas died, not an "ex-copper." A more likely suspect—and one whom ten years later Earle Kynette would name on the witness stand—was Harry Raymond. Repeating rumors that floated among reporters and cops for years, Kynette claimed that Raymond "put 'Mile-Away' Thomas on the spot so that Dick Lucas could riddle him with machine gun bullets."[18]

Kynette's assertions were plausible. Raymond's central skill as a detective was his knowledge of the underworld, both the identity and the methods of criminals. His expertise could only have been acquired through close and continuous interactions with the era's hoodlums, hijackers, gamblers, and con artists. He often worked for the police but also for less respectable individuals. He was even rumored to have worked for vice leader Charlie Crawford for a time, perhaps watching for competitors hoping to muscle or worm their way into the LA vice market. He may have also been a man who could offer a tip as to where a bootlegger kept his hoard–either to the cops or to a hijacker.

Shortly after the Thomas killing, Raymond became embroiled in the scandal surrounding the arrest of Councilman Carl Ingvald Jacobson. Jacobson was an immigrant who had been born in Oslo, Norway, on March 12, 1877. When he was five, his father immigrated to the United States, leaving his wife and two children in Norway. A year later, his father paid for his family's transatlantic passage and purchased land in western Wisconsin. The Jacobson farm was a "rough, stony and grub-covered land," but the Jacobsons turned it into a thriving home by hard work and frugal living. They imparted to Carl their sober values but not their eagerness for working the land. After attending college in St. Paul, Minnesota, Carl worked for the Chicago-Northwestern Railroad as a laborer. By 1910, married with a three-year-old daughter, he was living in Los Angeles and working as an engineer for the Southern Pacific Railroad. He remained with the railroad until the mid-twenties, when he ventured into real estate before he became a councilman.[19]

For nearly two years, Jacobson had represented LA's 13th District, a working class community in the city's northeast section bordering Alhambra. He had been appointed to the seat after the downfall of Joseph Fitzpatrick, a tall Irishman who served for many years as secretary of the local Fraternal Order of Eagles. "Big Fitz," as his friends called him, had barely beaten Jacobson in the election that spring, winning a plurality of 3,722 (37.8%) to Jacobson's 3,710 out of 9,837 votes cast despite the fact that Jacobson was a write-in candidate. (After Jacobson demanded a recount, the margin between the two candidates stood at nine votes in favor of Fitzpatrick). Unfortunately, as he himself remarked ruefully, the "job was too big" for Big Fitz. He did not understand the city council game well enough. Although there were plenty of rumors of councilmen on the take before, none was so clumsy as to be caught. That distinction fell to Fitzpatrick along with his fellow newcomer Councilman Charles Downs less than two months after they took their seats. After raising objections to a construction project during a council meeting, the pair agreed to let a young wheeler-dealer named Jack Murphy solicit a bribe from the interested firm. Instead of paying up, the company contacted the head of the city council, who brought in District Attorney Asa Keyes. Keyes furnished the construction company with $2,000 in marked bills and before the day was up Big Fitz and Downs, caught red-handed, were in the city jail. Fitzpatrick confessed to his crime readily, but Downs, a construction contractor who most likely had been on the giving side of graft before being elected, claimed the $1,000 he received was merely a campaign donation. Somewhere along the line, Fitzpatrick decided he was not guilty after all, claiming he and Downs were victims of a frame-up, but both ended up in San Quentin. Murphy, the young go-between, went free.[20]

After Fitzpatrick's arrest, Jacobson was appointed to the vacant seat. "I stand for the Constitution of the United States, for the American flag and for the observance of our laws," the new councilman declared. "Therefore I am not a dangerous man, and I shall strive to serve my city and my district in the public interest and for the public good."[21] Whether he was a dangerous man depended on one's business, as the city would soon learn.

Jacobson pursued the normal goals of a city councilman, arguing for street improvements, for additional streetcar lines to serve his constituents, and even for a special railroad service to the Imperial Valley to bring cheaper produce to Los Angeles markets. He tried to shift the location of the future Union Terminal from the Plaza area to the junction of North Broadway and Dayton Avenue (now Figueroa Boulevard). In December 1925, he convinced the Council to limit the number of babies a nurse could take care of at one time in the local hospitals from the California maximum of fifteen to seven, and two months later advocated for large pay increases for city employees. None of these positions made him a dangerous man, although he was a lone voice in several debates. What got him in trouble was his insistence on "the observation of our laws." As it soon developed, he meant vice laws, including those against gambling, prostitution, and liquor. To some extent, he took up the mantle dropped years ago by Guy Eddie. Other public figures, particularly church leaders such as Gustave Briegleb and Robert Shuler, regularly denounced Los Angeles public officials for their failure to reign in vice, but Jacobson was the most vocal elected official to do so since Eddie's downfall. When it came to vice infractions, regarded by many if not most of their constituents as victimless crimes, most local politicians preferred to go along to get along.[22]

With the allegations of police corruption in the headlines, Jacobson embarked on his personal campaign against vice operations and police misconduct in the final days of 1925. The catalyst for his crusade was the LAPD's reduction of charges against Albert Marco, a known pimp and bootlegger, from felony assault with a deadly weapon to misdemeanor disturbing the peace. In 1906, Marco a short, heavy-set, pugnacious immigrant from Trieste had arrived in New York City, where he had earned his living as a hat maker for five years before moving to Los Angeles. While he continued to list his occupation as a hat maker, his ownership of a Scripps-Booth automobile suggests he was involved in more lucrative pursuits, some of which likely brought him to the attention of other underworld figures such as Charles Crawford.[23]

Earlier in the year, Marco was a prime witness in the killing of gangster Al Joseph by Milton "Farmer" Page, Los Angeles' most notorious gambler of the period, in a downtown bar on Sixth Street. His more recent misadventure had occurred in late December. Marco had threatened an LAPD cops' civilian friend with a revolver before the officer subdued him. The victim had accompanied his friend to investigate a report of a fight between two men at a bungalow on South Westlake Avenue. They found a group of men but no sign of trouble. As the cop and his friend started to leave, Marco accused the civilian of calling in the report of a disturbance. The situation quickly got out of hand, the civilian striking Marco, who then pulled his gun. The cop disarmed Marco and took him to the police station for booking on assault with a deadly weapon. However, at the police station, two senior officers intervened and the charges were dropped. While the two officers claimed that they lacked witnesses to charge Marco with the more serious crime, other reports circulated that friends of Marco had interceded, threatening the arresting officer's job if he charged the felony. Marco was not just an ordinary pimp or bootlegger; he was wealthy and well connected. In fact, the IRS was after him for failing to pay over $150,000 in taxes on three year's income of over $500,000.

Jacobson introduced a resolution in the City Council requiring Chief of Police Robert Lee Heath to explain why the charges against Marco were reduced and why he was issued a permit to carry a gun in the first place. Jacobson also harangued the police, the mayor, and other political figures who he claimed protected illegal gambling in the city. It was the beginning of an eighteen-month anti-vice campaign. While religious leaders had declaimed against protected vice in Los Angeles for years, Jacobson's council seat provided a powerful platform, often to the discomfort of his fellow council members who preferred to leave the matter to the police commissioners. However, by choosing Marco as the focus of his indignation he had not only taken on a dangerous opponent but also Marco's supporters in Los Angeles' criminal underworld.

Jacobson's tirades included charges against the LAPD's upper hierarchy, particularly the police commissioners. In August 1926, he proposed that the commissioners be elected by the voters rather than appointed by the mayor and approved by the Council. This attempt to weaken the power of the mayor, then George E. Cryer, was a direct threat to Cryer's political operative Kent Kane Parrot, who was widely viewed as the real political power in Los Angeles. Parrot's control extended deep into the LAPD and underworld. He was a dangerous man.

Parrot had arrived in Los Angeles a few years after Raymond with his wife, the future novelist Mary Alsop. Born in Kennebunkport, Maine, in 1883, he was the youngest child of a Unitarian Clergyman. When he was a young boy, his father moved his family to Boston where Parrot attended public schools. Despite their father's profession, he and his four brothers were a rough lot: bossy, opinionated, and in trouble with the law enough that the local police considered them a gang of thugs, the "Pro Brothers." Bullied as a boy, Parrot grew into a big man who soon turned the tables on his older siblings.[24]

In 1901, he entered Philips Exeter Academy in New Hampshire where three of his brothers had studied before. After graduating from Phillips Exeter, he worked briefly for the Home Life Insurance Company of Brooklyn, New York. Two of his older brothers, William Joseph Jr. and Louis Howard, were in the insurance business and it was not surprising that young Kent considered following their lead. Parrot's vision may have been broadened by the example of another of his brothers, Charles Francis, who had immigrated to Australia, as well as by the two months he spent in the south with a classmate, John Gaston Troy, the son of a prominent attorney in Montgomery, Alabama. The two youths took an excursion to Belize and New Orleans the following autumn.

It is not clear whether Parrot spent any real time in the insurance business. His heart was in the forests of Maine, where he had developed into an expert woodsman and dreamed of making a fortune by mining feldspar. He also loved automobiles. At some point, Parrot quit insurance to become what he grandiosely called a "gas-engine consultant" —but which really meant that he bought and sold used cars.[25]

On Oct 21, 1905, he married Mary Alsop, a third cousin, in Brooklyn, New York, despite the objections of her father, who was unimpressed by Parrot's prospects and complained that "getting a straight answer out of [Parrot] . . . is like pulling teeth."[26] The couple soon departed for Quebec, where they spent the winter "roughing it" in a small cabin on a remote lake island. To Mary's surprise, Parrot revealed that he had bigger ambitions than camping, selling cars or insurance. He told her he wanted to get a law degree and go into politics. Her initial skepticism dropped away when she reflected on his "invincible" skill at chess and his determination and self-confidence.[27]

Following the birth of their first child, Mary O'Hara Parrot, the couple moved to Los Angeles in 1908, taking rooms at a family hotel at 671 S. Coronado in the then fashionable neighborhood west of McArthur Park. It was a propitious time to arrive in Los Angeles for an ambitious young man. Construction of the Los Angeles Aqueduct to supplement the scant water supply of the city with Owens River water had just begun. Work on the Panama Canal, which cut the cost and length of ocean transportation from Europe and the eastern seaboard, would be completed in 1914, a year after the first waters from the Owens River flowed into the San Fernando Valley. The Southern Pacific Railroad would build the first wharf of the Port of Los Angeles in 1912. To the natural advantages of the region, a fine climate, rich soil, and billions of barrels of oil underground, were added the man-made improvements of abundant freshwater, a deep-sea port, and access to the world's markets.

Parrot began studies toward a degree in law at the University of Southern California after transferring some units from Dartmouth. He made a strong impression at USC; *Stare Decisis*, the law school's yearbook, printed a poem entitled, "Senior Sonnet" with a quatrain dedicated to Parrot:

> Who is this boy with frame so large
> And head so very small
> Why that's timid little Parrot
> With his wholesale stock of gall.[28]

Parrot was big—6' 2" and well over 200 pounds. It was later reported that he starred in football while at USC, but there is no documentary evidence to support this assertion. He was not listed as a player for the Methodists, later to become the Trojans, in the yearbooks published while he attended the school, nor is he on rosters for the team that appeared in the local newspapers. Similarly, he is not on the rosters of USC's freshman or prep squads or the Law School's team, the Lawyers.

After joining the state bar shortly before graduating in January 1910 with a Bachelor of Laws Degree, Parrot formed a law firm with another USC Law graduate, Frederick Cole Fairbanks. By 1910, he and Fairbanks joined with two other USC graduates, Frank M. Porter, Dean of the USC Law School, and Vincent Morgan to form the firm of Porter, Morgan and Parrot. Parrot allied himself with Republican Progressives of the Teddy Roosevelt stripe, helping to organize the Billiken Club before he graduated. The club's membership, comprised of "disciples of the Grand Old Party, free and independent of push or pull, [who] . . . represent the young manhood" of Los Angeles, swelled to over 400 members. Parrot organized 100 members to journey to New York City to greet ex-President Roosevelt as he returned from his post-presidency world tour. The following year, he joined his mentor, Judge Gavin Craig, to establish the Metropolitan Club, a forum for political discussions and an elegant venue for local clubs.

Parrot's entry into political life did not go unnoticed by his alma mater. The 1911 *Stare Decisis* included a piece by "Scotty" the elevator boy, who noted the emergence of a USC clique in local politics:

> Course there's Judge [Gavin] Craig, who even made the Goo-Goos take to cover. Did these young students support the judge? Does Polly want a cracker?
>
> . . .
>
> The King-Pin guys of the whole bunch are Doherty and Parrott [sic], who are the political bosses. Meyer Lissener [a Goo-Goo leader] ain't got nothin' on 'em. Some of these days they'll probably manage Benedict's campaign for governor, if they don't get caught in the City Council shavin' the garbage contract."[29]

Parrot would never run for political office, preferring to work behind the scenes to promote the political fortune of his associates. In 1914, he managed the campaign of his USC friend and law partner, Vincent Morgan, who was running for district attorney. The *Los Angeles Times* quoted the 31-year-old Parrot as boasting that he was a "great political manipulator" who could "fix newspapers for Morgan." Parrot's stewardship was not enough to move his inexperienced friend past the primary in August 1914, however. The district attorney's office was claimed by another USC graduate, Thomas Woolwine.[30]

After graduating from USC, Parrot and his wife had moved to a small house at 2302 Juliet Street. They soon became active figures in the city's social scene, joining the Los Angeles Country Club on Frank Porter's recommendation. Mary Parrot was an avid and skilled golfer. Kent Kane also golfed but was less interested in the challenge of the sport than in its social rewards. The *Los Angeles Times* chided him as the "Apollo-like personage, K. Parrot, lackadaisical, careless, indifferent, who probably can golf, but mostly doesn't." The Parrots were often noted at social gatherings during the early 'teens, but, as the decade advanced, Mary often was unaccompanied. In 1917, six years after their second child, Kent Kane Jr., was born, the couple separated—according to Alsop, because of Parrot's infidelity. Parrot moved to 2674 Ellendale. Alsop moved with her children to a small town north of Santa Cruz and waited for the divorce decree to become final.[31]

In the summer of 1916, Parrot became a key figure in the battle between conservative and liberal factions in Los Angeles. The skirmish developed when church leaders tried to outlaw dancing in restaurants and cafés in the city. San Francisco had banned dancing in its central district in 1910. Other cities, including Detroit, Chicago, Buffalo, and Seattle, soon followed suit. Los Angeles' police commission prohibited dancing in public places on July 30, 1915, at the urging of a city councilwoman. Church leaders supported the ban, arguing especially against the "promiscuous" nature of the fox trot and the danger to public morals of dancing when combined with the consumption of liquor.[32] Parrot managed the campaign to enact an ordinance allowing dancing in "reputable hotels and restaurants under rigid supervision." Both women's clubs and the *Los Angeles Times*, which objected to the strict dancing ban as harmful to business, backed the proposed ordinance. The church and prohibitionist factions prevailed, however, after mustering a large turnout. It was a harbinger of prohibitionist victories to come.[33]

In early 1921, Parrot successfully managed Cryer's campaign for mayor against incumbent Meredith Snyder with the support of the *Los Angeles Times* and church groups angered over Snyder's failure to eradicate gambling and other vices in the city. After the election, Cryer considered rewarding Parrot with the position of city prosecutor, but the current officeholder declined to resign. Cryer then moved to appoint Parrot to the Board of Public Service Commissioners, which oversaw the city's water and hydroelectric power departments. The *Times* editorialized against the appointment, charging that Parrot was a politician and not a man "of business training and experience and standing in the community for integrity." The City Council rejected his appointment. Parrot had already clashed with railroad representatives before the Harbor Commission and the council members viewed him as an intimidating figure, one who might abuse power. If so, his opponents' rejections backfired as, unfettered by a single office's duties and constraints, Parrot broadened his power in the Cryer administration. Both the *Times* and *Record* deemed him the city boss and the power behind Cryer's throne. As the *Times* complained, after the City Council refused to place Parrot and his ally, H. H. Kinney, on the Public Service and Harbor boards, Parrot slipped close associates onto the same boards.[34]

Parrot's office in Room 504 of the Western Mutual Life Building at 321 West Third, a block from city hall, afforded him ready access to the mayor's office. He visited daily, often sitting in the "Mayor's chair with his feet on the Mayor's desk" while he interviewed candidates for city positions, focusing not on their qualifications but on their political affiliations. Parrot, along with Kinney and Cryer, demanded loyalty to the mayor and his administration foremost and warned prospective officeholders to avoid organizations that poked their noses into governmental activities such as the letting of leases and contracts. Parrot was often condemned for his rough, underhanded tactics, particularly in trying to gain control over the Harbor and Police Commissions.

In 1923, Police Chief Oaks accused him of "dictatorial and threatening" behavior and complained that he interfered with the Police Department.[35]

The *Los Angeles Times* supported Cryer for re-election in 1923, but, by 1925, the paper was disenchanted with both the mayor and Parrot. The "city's affairs have fallen into the hands of politicians who have made the Mayor's office a tool for personal self-seeking," the paper declared, "We have had enough of Kent K. Parrot and the rest of the city hall kitchen cabinet . . . the real bosses of Los Angeles." Although it supported Cryer in his third bid for re-election in 1925, the *Los Angeles Record* also denounced Parrot's influence over the city. In a moment of high journalistic drama, the *Times* reprinted in facsimile the *Record*'s front-page article on its own City section front page and followed up the next day with an editorial entitled "Shall We Re-elect Kent Parrot?" To the question posed by the *Record* about what Parrot, unpaid and without governmental office, received in exchange for the long hours he spent manipulating governmental boards and managing the mayor, the *Times* declared,[36]

> The *Record* quotes Mr. Parrot as saying "I get a lot of fun out of it."
>
> . . .
>
> Probably Mr. Parrot does "get a lot of fun out of it" when he can go to the office of Mayor of this city, close the office door, put his feet on the Mayor's desk, and cajole, persuade or virtually force the city's chief executive to do his bidding.[37]

However, the *Times* observed, that was not all to it. *The Record* had quoted the observation of an anonymous insider:

> Parrot is a lawyer. Lawyers get fees for seeing that certain things come about. Parrot takes cases and promises nothing. But he gets results.[38]

As the city was to learn a few years later when Federal officials charged Parrot with failing to pay over $75,000 in income taxes in 1926 through 1928—in addition to whatever he did pay—the twenties were very good for Kent Kane Parrot, even without a real government job. As reporter Charles Garrigues observed a few years later, "The Attorney's fee . . . is one of the safest and simplest method of soliciting and paying a bribe."[39]

Despite the *Times'* opposition, Cryer was re-elected in 1925 for a four-year term. Parrot continued to maneuver behind the scenes. In April 1927, with his own election looming, Jacobson charged that Parrot intimidated City Hall civil service employees into working for his candidates. It was not the first time that Jacobson had named Parrot as a malevolent force at City Hall from his council seat. In response, Parrot targeted Jacobson in the 1927 election, but his efforts to remove from office the annoying councilman failed badly. Jacobson won a majority on the first ballot, avoiding a runoff. In the following months, he continued to denounce vice activities, prostitution, liquor, and gambling even when it meant attacking organizers of a fund-raiser for Spanish-American war veterans. He also kept Marco in his cross hairs, introducing a resolution in the city council to congratulate Federal prohibition agents who had arrested Marco on July 28 at his bar at 130 South Spring Street. Marco had threatened to have them fired and boasted, "he knew plenty of officials around town."[40]

Jacobson also feuded with the President of the police commission, Isadore Birnbaum. In mid-July 1927, Birnbaum resigned his position, charging that he had lost the support of the mayor who, he said, was now taking dictation from Jacobson and reformist minister Robert Shuler. Jacobson announced Birnbaum's resignation to the Council with a "broad smile." He was on a roll. In the past few months, Birnbaum had resigned and Marco was on his way to jail. Efforts of the Parrot/Cryer faction to unseat him had failed miserably. Indeed, Parrot failed almost completely in electing favorable candidates in the prior election. Cryer's comment to Birnbaum that he was inclined to "let the opposition . . . name the Police Commission" indicated that the mayor felt somewhat defeated and that Jacobson and Shuler were ascendant. It was a high point in Jacobson's political career, one that a tragedian would have recognized.[41]

As a train engineer with the Southern Pacific, Jacobson spent considerable time in Indio, California, a desert community in the Coachella Valley between Los Angeles and Yuma. The railroad had founded Indio in the mid-1870s as a water stop where locomotives' steam engines could be refilled with water from artesian wells. By 1920, 1,200 persons lived in the town, including those employed by the Southern Pacific in its service facilities. Jacobson must have known many of them, including Frank Cox, who began working in the freight car repair shop in March 1918. Cox was unmarried, a fact that earned him a furlough in June 1918 and a short stint in the army from September to December. After his discharge, he returned to Indio. By the time he transferred to Los Angeles a year later, he had married an Oklahoma girl named Sue Michael.

His wife was the youngest of the nine Michael siblings, four of whom were living in Indio between 1917 and 1919, including an older brother, Ransom, and two sisters, Ida and Katherine. They were a close-knit group. By 1920, all had departed for Los Angeles where they lived either in the same house or within a few blocks of each other. Ransom worked for the railroad, and both sisters were married to railroad men. Ida, the oldest sister, had married Leslie Russell in 1913. Katherine, or Callie, the second youngest Michael sibling, had married Victor S. Grimes, in May 1917.

Jacobson knew the family. He later recounted that one of their nephews, an orphan, lived with him for a short period. Callie, he claimed, he knew casually. After she departed Indio, he did not meet her again until July 1927, when she attended a meeting of property owners in the Rose Hill district of his council area. He was surprised to learn that she owned a home in his district. After leaving Indio, she had lived with her husband and daughter on a farm on Ventura Boulevard in what would become the suburb of Tarzana. In 1922, they bought a house at 4372 Beagle Street in LA's Omaha Heights neighborhood. It was a small home, just over 500 square feet, with one bedroom, one bath, and a kitchen, to which a dining room had been added in 1926. Like other homeowners in the area, the council's recent decision to assess homeowners for paving Beagle Street concerned Grimes. She and her husband had separated. The house was the only significant piece of common property involved in the divorce proceedings.

Grimes asked Jacobson's opinion on whether to pay the assessment, which she believed was more than her house was worth. Jacobson agreed to meet with her to discuss the matter further. He stopped by her home briefly on Monday, August 1. Finding Grimes' daughter was home, he had suggested that Grimes send the girl to the store so they could talk alone, but Grimes declined to do so, and he left after a half hour. On Friday evening, August 5, Grimes telephoned Jacobson's home to arrange a second meeting. She first suggested they meet at a Westside apartment, but Jacobson explained that he had another meeting with residents of his district that evening and proposed that he stop by afterward. Around 9 p.m., he arrived at her home. What happened next will forever remain in dispute; like so many other incidents in what we call non-fiction, no witness to the event can be trusted. A few facts seem to be clear, however. First, Grimes greeted him with a bottle of whiskey and two glasses. The councilman declared he had not had a drink in thirty years and would not take one now. Jacobson said they talked about the house and its value, and then Grimes asked him to look at her bedroom. "The lights went out and shortly thereafter . . . [police] officers . . . turned on the flashlight and grabbed me," he claimed. The police told a different story. Jacobson and Grimes had enjoyed a little more time together, enough, after a few preliminary caresses in the main room, for them to retire to the bedroom, where Jacobson began disrobing and Grimes undressed completely. They found the councilman in his pantaloons. He still had on his shirt and tie.[42]

While Jacobson maintained that the police must have been in the small apartment all along, the officers declared they watched the two would-be lovers through a window and rushed in when they observed them engage sexually. In 1927 Los Angeles, such behavior could be criminal. Jacobson was charged with violating ordinance 49.354 (NS) of the Los Angeles Municipal code, the resorting ordinance, which prohibited two adults not married to each other from occupying the same room together. For reasons never made clear, Grimes was arrested for a different crime, that of being a "dissolute person."[43]

The arrest of a priggish councilman caught literally with his pants down was a matter of great interest and amusement to the newspapers and its readers. Many Angelenos may have recalled that in the preceding days, Jacobson had accused a war veterans' organization of conducting illegal gambling at a charity event organized to fund a trip to a convention in Detroit. Even after being told that winners received only script to purchase merchandise at the event, the councilman had persisted with his charges. His self-righteous demeanor seemed to have dropped off along with his pants.

Although Jacobson was contrite, he realized that he had been set up. He declared that he was the victim of a "frame-up" and that he was "trapped at that house." "A dirty, outrageous frame-up," echoed his attorney, M. O. Graves. The charge resonated with his allies in the anti-vice community, particularly pastor Robert Shuler, who held a series of meetings at his Trinity Methodist Church to support Jacobson. Jacobson also received "a continuous stream of telephone calls" and telegrams from his friends and supporters in the days after his arrest. One newspaper, the *Hollywood Daily Citizen*, which was becoming a leading advocate for reform under the guidance of its owner/publisher/editor Harlan G. Palmer, also leapt to his defense. The paper argued that, whether or not he was guilty of an indiscretion, the arrest proved the corruption of the LAPD by commercialized vice, the ineptitude of Chief Davis and the ineffectiveness of Mayor Cryer. When the LAPD stepped up raids against gambling houses, speakeasies and bordellos in the weeks after Jacobson's arrest, the paper approved, but it still kept its focus on the vice organizations, revealing that it had learned there were "two rival vice gangs." "One vice gang will furnish one councilman with lists of vice holes of the other and the other gang will furnish another councilman with a list of the joints of its competitors," the paper declared.[44]

The identity of the officers who arrested Jacobson seemed to support claims of a frame-up. For what on its face seemed a small matter, the squad that made the arrest was an impressive set of veteran and high-ranking cops. First, there was Hubert Wallis, vice squad chief. Wallis, a native of England and a former English bobby, had come to Los Angeles in 1907 and risen steadily through the ranks to lead the vice squad in July 1927. Then there was

Captain of Detectives J.F. "Rusty" Williams, another LAPD veteran and former head of the Bunco and Pickpocket squad. A former Michigan schoolteacher, Williams joined the force in 1910 as a detective. His reputation was spotty; in 1920, a bunko artist had asserted that he gave Williams 15% of his profits.

Joining Wallis and Williams was Detective Richard Lucas. Lucas also had a checkered career with the LAPD. In 1919, he was driving a patrol car on east on Third Street when a young motorcyclist shot through the intersection at Figueroa, traveling south. Swerving to avoid the motorcyclist, Lucas crashed into a telephone pole. His partner, Claude H. Wyatt, sustained fatal head injuries. Less than a year later, Lucas was arrested along with another officer, Hubert Kittle, on a charge of liquor possession. The charges did not stick and after a brief suspension, he was restored to duty. He continued as an LAPD officer until January 1924, when he became chief of detectives with the district attorney's office. He lasted one week. On February 1, DA Asa Keyes announced that he had removed Lucas from the position after four investigators reporting to him and two deputy district attorneys threatened to resign. He returned to the LAPD as head of the dry squad, charged with enforcing prohibition laws. Within a few months, he had exchanged gunshots with bootlegger Tony Cornero but he had also been accused of planting a bottle of liquor to frame a Federal prohibition agent and wrecking the home of a man suspected of possessing liquor.

Tagging along was *Los Angeles Times* reporter Albert F. Nathan. Nathan, born in Oklahoma in 1892, was the son of a converted Jew who had ordained as a Methodist minister but eventually found his way to the oil business and moved his family east. In 1910, the family was living in the oil town of Warren, Pennsylvania, where Nathan worked until 1912. He then traveled to Los Angeles via the Panama Canal, arriving in 1912 at the age of nineteen. He found a job at the Oil Well Supply Company. In January 1913, he was run down by a touring car while crossing the street at Main and Alameda outside the company's headquarters. Despite fears that he might be paralyzed, he recovered and joined the *Los Angeles Times*. After breaking a story about a buildup of Japanese warships in Turtle Bay, Baja California, he became one of the newspaper's leading investigative journalists. His specialty was crime, narcotics addicts, the rumrunners of the twenties, and organized graft. He also was known as a fixer for the *Times*, a man who could represent the *Time's* publisher at City Hall or in police department precincts.

The final member of the seemingly impromptu but elite squad was newly appointed Auto Squad Detective Harry Raymond.

Wallis testified that the affair began early Friday evening, as he sat alone in his office in Vice Squad headquarters. A telephone call came in from a person who complained of "wild parties" taking place at a home on Beagle Street. The caller said that a ten-year-old girl was involved and claimed that he had already reported the problem to the Lincoln Heights police station, but nothing had been done about it. Wallis asked the man to identify himself, but he refused, stating only that he was an attorney. After Wallis explained that he had nobody on duty to send to the address on Beagle, the caller threatened to take his complaint further up the police hierarchy.

Wallis claimed he was mulling over the call when Richard "Dick" Lucas stopped by his office with Captain Rusty Williams. When Wallis told them about the call, they offered to go with him to the address after they took care of another matter. A few minutes later, Harry Raymond stopped by Wallis' office and learned of the phone call. Then Al Nathan showed up for a visit that Wallis had arranged earlier that day. He was in Wallis' office about five minutes when Williams and Lucas returned from their errand and said they were ready to go.

The small squad set out for Beagle Street in two automobiles around 8:30 p.m., Wallis, Raymond, and Lucas in the leading car, Williams and Nathan following in a second car. It was a cool evening for early August, the temperature in the low seventies, with a half-full moon. The cops parked their vehicles near a gas station and made their way up the hill on foot. When they reached 4372 Beagle, the three officers from the lead car, including Raymond, sneaked up to a front window. The window shade was partially open, leaving a gap of about six inches from the bottom. According to Wallis, Jacobson and Grimes were visible near the window. Jacobson's arm was around Grimes and he was caressing and kissing her. After a few minutes, Grimes crossed the room to a Pianola and began to play. Jacobson listened for a minute, then crossed and sat on the bench beside her and resumed caressing her. After playing another tune on the Pianola, Jacobson and Grimes moved to another room beyond the police officers' vision.

Wallis said that Raymond and Lucas crept around to the other side of the small house, where a short stairway led to a porch and a second door. They listened for about ten minutes and then noticed a light go out inside. Raymond and Lucas climbed down from the porch, crossed to the front of the house and entered it through an unlocked door opening into the kitchen. In the bedroom, they found Jacobson and Grimes. He was sitting on the bed in his shirt, collar and tie. His pants were on a chair near the bed, along with a woman's dress. Grimes was naked.

According to the officers, the Councilman declared, "Well, boys, you have got me," and then added, "I feel I have been led into a trap." He apologized for his situation, claiming that he only intended to discuss assessments with Grimes and that he and Grimes "had just lost their heads." At one point, he asked for Richard Lucas' gun so he could shoot himself. "I realize that I am all through," he remarked.[45]

At Jacobson's request, the officers took him to the home of Police Commissioner Nathaniel Rodney Webster. Webster was not at home, but Jacobson was eager to talk to him, so the group waited. They waited a long time, long enough that, according to Wallis, Jacobson was ready to give up and let them take him to jail, when Webster's automobile pulled into his driveway.

Although Webster refused to allow the cops and Jacobson into his home, stating he would not discuss police matters there, he agreed to go with them to the Chamber of Commerce Building. With Raymond, Nathan, and Williams following in Williams' car, Lucas drove downtown with Wallis in the front passenger seat. Behind them, Webster talked with the councilman in the back seat. Webster asked Jacobson why he was there.

"Well, I am a man just the same as any other man," Jacobson replied. "I can stand this all right, but they set a trap for me and I walked right into it. I am guilty of what they got me charged with, but they set a trap for me and I walked right into it."

"What do you mean," Webster demanded, "Do you mean these two police officers here set a trap for you?"

"No," replied Jacobson, "These boys have been nice to me, very nice to me. I don't think they had anything to do with it, but I do know who did it."

Webster asked Jacobson who had set the trap, but Jacobson refused to say, telling the commissioner that he would tell him when the right time came.[46]

By the time his trial for resorting began a month later, Jacobson and his attorney, William Anderson, regarded both Webster and DA Keyes as part of the frame-up. Anderson charged Webster had told Jacobson, "This is what you get for writing a letter," an apparent reference to a letter Jacobson had written to the police commission charging that the police were not enforcing anti-vice laws, when he talked with Jacobson that night. In addition, Anderson claimed Keyes had rejected a written statement Jacobson had offered as "no good"—not a strong enough admission of culpability to silence him in the future. Webster and Keyes denied that they had done or said anything to imply that they would let Jacobson go without charges if he agreed to lay off his anti-vice crusade.

By the time of the trial, Jacobson and his supporters also believed that the officers who arrested him were part of the conspiracy. Harry Raymond came in for particular scrutiny. According to one witness, Raymond had accompanied Grimes in the Beagle Street neighborhood a week before Jacobson's arrest. The same witness claimed that several hours before the raid, she observed Grimes, Raymond and Frank Cox, Grimes' brother-in-law, then a member of the LAPD Vice Squad, at the Beagle Street house. Another witness, a young high school boy named Donald Crawford, testified that he watched Raymond and the other cops break in the door of Grimes house immediately after the Pianola music stopped—contradicting Wallis's claim that the cops waited ten minutes after the pair left the front room for the bedroom before busting in. Crawford also described Raymond and another officer, presumably Lucas, stumbling around after the break in, apparently intoxicated.

The judge presiding in the case allowed Jacobson's defense to argue that the councilman had been trapped, specifying that the jury should consider whether "some official or someone in authority in the police department 'induced, persuaded and encouraged' Councilman Jacobson to 'resort' to Mrs. Grime's cottage" and whether Jacobson went to the Grimes house without intending an illegal act. The latter consideration proved crucial. Most jurors believed Jacobson's daughter, who testified that her father visited Grimes to discuss her assessment concerns. The jury deadlocked seven to five for acquittal. A few weeks later, the city prosecutor announced the prosecution would not retry Jacobson, as it was the policy of his office to try misdemeanor cases only once.[47]

There the Jacobson matter stood for the time being. Jacobson returned to his position as city councilman while Chief Davis shifted about the sworn police officers involved in the dubious arrest "for the good of the department." Vice Squad Captain Wallis was reassigned as an investigator for the police commission and then moved again to the Central Division detective squad. A few days later, Davis reassigned him once more, this time to the Hollywood Division. Frank Cox was moved out of Vice to the Newton Division shortly after the trial; a few weeks later, he was sent to the Venice Division.[48]

Richard "Dick" Lucas continued in his positions on the LAPD with no noticeable loss in status. Despite his spotted record, Lucas, like Raymond, was regarded as a key detective within the LAPD. His stature became clear late in 1927, when he and Raymond were chosen to bring back the most notorious Los Angeles murderer of the 1920s, the "Fox."

Charles Crawford
1912 [The Family
Photo Collection
of Linda Burns]

*Kent Kane Parrot [History
of the Bench and Bar in
California, JC Bates 1912]*

Carl Jacobson [Los Angeles Times Photographic
Archive, UCLA Library. Copyright Regents of the
University of California, UCLA Library.]

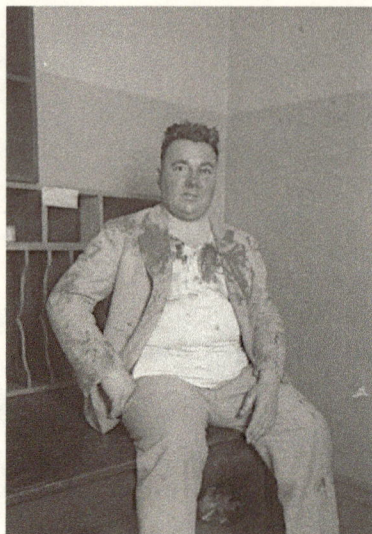

Albert Marco after fight at café [Los Angeles
Times Photographic Archive, UCLA
Library. Copyright Regents of the
University of California, UCLA Library.]

Harry "MileAway" Thomas [Los
Angeles Evening Express, Nov
3, 1927]

Callie Grimes

7: AFTER THE FOX

Shortly after noon on Thursday, December 15, 1927, a young man entered the administrative offices of Mount Vernon Junior High School in the Arlington Heights section of Los Angeles. He was dressed well in a gray herringbone overcoat, dark suit, and hat. The school's Principal, Cora Freeman, was at lunch and the vice-principal was visiting the homerooms of the students, leaving in charge Mary Holt, a senior teacher who also worked as registrar at the school, and a small woman with thick glasses, assistant registrar Naomi Britten.

The young man introduced himself to Britten as Mr. Cooper. He explained that he worked with Perry Parker at the First National Trust and Savings Bank. Mr. Parker had been in an accident, he said, and had sent him to get his daughter. As the startled Miss Britten listened, Mrs. Holt came over and heard the alarming news. He spoke "quietly and courteously," Holt recalled.[49] He offered Parker's address and the bank's phone number for the school officials to call to verify his story. They did not do so, but Miss Britten checked her records and announced that there were two Parker girls, Marjorie and Marion. Mr. Parker had asked only for the younger one, Marion, the young man explained. Britten went to fetch the girl, who was in a class just a few feet away.[50]

A few minutes later, Britten brought Marion into the office. Marion was twelve years old, stood four and one-half feet, and weighed around 100 lbs. She carried some refreshments in her hands from a Christmas party in her homeroom. She grew anxious as Mrs. Holt explained that her father had been in an accident, but when the young man reassured her that he would take her to her father, she seemed eager to go with him. He guided her through the school's doors toward a small coupe parked outside the school building, patting her arm reassuringly as he opened the passenger door and ushered her inside. Then he hurried to the driver's door and jumped in the car. In a few seconds, gears clashing, the car sped away.

Perry Parker had not been in an automobile accident. The next day was his forty-eighth birthday and he was taking a few days off. That afternoon he ran some errands. When he came home shortly after 5:00, he found a telegram awaiting him. Addressed to "P.M. Parker," it was sent from the

Pasadena office of Western Union at 2:45 p.m. "Do positively nothing till you receive special delivery," it stated. It was signed "Marian Parker" and "(George Fox)." His other daughter Marjorie, Marion's twin, had come home alone and she told him of the strange man who had taken Marion. He began calling the residences of some of his daughter's friends to find the girl. After talking with administrators at her school, he called the police.[51]

Parker received a second telegram Thursday evening from the Alhambra Western Union office at 6:20 p.m. "Marian secure. Use good judgment. Interference with my plans dangerous." This one was also signed "Marian Parker/George Fox" and the sender listed his address at 2518 Birch Street in Alhambra. A third communication arrived the following morning, a special delivery letter. Printed across the head was the word "ΔEATH."

ΔEATH
P.M. Parker:
Use good judgment. You are the loser. DO THIS. Secure 75 $20-gold certificates—U.S. currency—1500 dollars—at once. KEEP THEM ON YOUR PERSON. Go about your business as usual. Leave out police and detectives. Make no public notice. KEEP THIS AFFAIR PRIVATE. Make no search.
Fulfilling these terms and the transfer of the currency will secure the return of the girl.
Failure to comply with these requests means no one will ever see the girl again except the angels in Heaven.
The affair must end one way or the other within 3 days—72 hours. You will receive further notice.
But the terms remain the same.   FATE
If you want aid against me, ask God, not man.

Δ∈α Τη

P.M. PARKER:
Use good judgment. You are the
loser. Do This. Secure '15-$20 gold
certificates. U.S. Currency - 1500 dollars -
at once. KEEP THEM ON YOUR PERSON.
GO ABOUT YOUR DAILY BUSINESS AS,
USUAL. LEAVE OUT POLICE AND DETECTIVES.
MAKE NO PUBLIC NOTICE. KEEP THIS'
AFFAIR PRIVATE. MAKE NO SEARCH.
fullfilling these terms with the
transfer of the currency will secure the
return of the girl.
FAILURE TO COMPLY WITH THESE
REQUESTS MEANS - NO ONE WILL EVER
SEE THE GIRL AGAIN, EXCEPT THE ANGELS IN HEAVEN.
The affair must end one way or
the other within 3 days. 72 HRS.
YOU WILL RECEIVE FURTHER
NOTICE,
But the terms Remain the Same.

FATE

IF YOU WANT AID AGAINST ME ASK GOD NOT MAN.

Photo of first letter from Hickman as published in various contemporary newspapers

The warning in the kidnappers' letter came too late. Parker had contacted police Thursday evening and a massive manhunt had already begun. District Attorney Asa Keyes ordered his chief of detectives to assign his entire staff of 125 investigators to the case while the LAPD assigned another 60. Other police agencies throughout the county also allocated detectives. They searched mountain cabins in the Sierra Madre range, questioned suspicious characters, and watched telephone booths and train stations. A few focused on the address on the second telegram, which turned out to be a house for rent. A man matching the kidnapper's description had considered renting the home, they learned. In the LAPD's "rogue's gallery," one investigator found the photograph of a man fitting the school administrators' description of the kidnapper. He took it to show the clerks at the Alhambra Western Union Office. It was not him.

By Friday afternoon, local papers were reporting Marion Parker's kidnapping in their afternoon editions. The news had also gone national. Friday evening editions of papers in El Paso, Texas, and Emporia, Kansas, reported the crime. As the nation soon learned, the kidnapper had seen local papers covering the story while driving through Hollywood. He was on the watch for police.

Around 8:00 p.m. that Friday night, the phone rang at the Parker home. The kidnapper was on the line. "Have you the money and are there any police around?" he demanded. "I am some distance away but will phone you in a few minutes and give you instructions." A half hour later, the phone rang again. A voice said, "Come to Tenth and Gramercy Place in your car and come alone. Dim your lights and don't bring any police if you want to see your child alive." Parker got in his automobile and drove to the location. Harry Raymond, possibly the best detective available and certainly one of the shortest, crouched behind the front seat of Parker's vehicle, a sawed-off shotgun in his hand, while other detectives followed in two vehicles. Parker and Raymond remained at Tenth and Gramercy Place until 11:30 p.m. The kidnapper and his victim did not show.

The following morning, another special delivery letter arrived.

ΔEATH

Mr. Parker:

Fox is my name. Very sly you know. Set no traps. I'll watch for them.

All the inside guys, even your neighbor Isadore b., knows when you play with fire there is cause for burns. Not W. J. Burns and his shadowers either—Remember that.

Get this straight: Your daughter's life hangs by a thread and I have a Gillette ready and able to handle the situation.

This is business. Do you want the girl or the 75—$100 gold certificates U.S. currency? You can't have both and there's no other way out. Believe this, and act accordingly. Before the day's over I will find out how you stand

I am doing a solo, so figure on meeting the terms of Mr. Fox or else

FATE.

If you want aid against me ask God and not man.

Death

Mr. Parker:

Fox is my name. Very sly you know.
∴ Set no traps. I'll watch for them.
All the inside dope, even your neighbor
Isadore B., know that when you play with
fire there is cause for burns. Not W.J. Burns
and his shadowers either — Remember that.
Get this straight: Your daughter's
life hangs by a thread and I have a
Gillette ready and able to handle the
situation.
This is business. Do you want
the girl or the 75-$100 gold certificates
U.S. currency? You cant have both and
there's no other way out. Believe this,
and act accordingly. Before the day's
over I'll find out how you stand
I am doing a solo so figure on
meeting the terms of Mr. Fox or else

FATE.

If you want aid against me ask God not man.

Photo of second letter from Hickman as published in various contemporary newspapers

Included with this letter was one from Marion:

Dear Daddy and Mother:
I wish I could come home. I think I'll die if I have to be like this
much longer. Won't someone tell me why all this had to happen to
me. Daddy, please do what the man tells you or he'll kill me [if]
you don't.
Your loving daughter
Marion Parker
P.S. Please Daddy,
I want to come home tonight.

Dear Daddy and Mother:

I wish I could come home.
I think I'll die if I have to
be like this much longer.
Wont someone tell me why
all this had to happen to me.
Daddy please do what the
man tells your or hill kill
me   youdon't.

Your loving daughter
Marion Parker,

P.S. Please Daddy.
I want to come home tonight

Photo of first letter from Marion Parker as published in various contemporary newspapers

Another special delivery letter followed Saturday afternoon. In it, the kidnapper chided Perry Parker for contacting the police and failing to act as a "Christian and honest man." He explained that he aborted the rendezvous the previous night when he spotted two cars following Parker. "Mr. Parker, I am ashamed of you. I am vexed and disgusted with you! With the whole damned vicinity throbbing with my terrible crime—you try to save the day by your simple police tactics," he remonstrated. Then he invoked Parker's helpless daughter:

> You will never know how you disappointed your daughter. She was so eager to know that it would be only a short while and then she would be free from my terrible torture, and then you missed the whole damned affair.
> Your daughter saw you, watched you work and drove away broken hearted because you couldn't have her in spite of my willingness, merely because you, her father, would not deal straight for her life.

You are insane to betray your love for your daughter, to ignore my terms, to tamper with death. You remain reckless, and with death fast on its way.

A second note instructed Parker on how the exchange of money for the girl would take place:

Δeath
FINAL CHANCE TERMS
1. HAVE $1500 = 75 - 20 DOLLAR GOLD CERTIFICATES - U. S. CURRENCY
2. COME ALONE AND HAVE NO OTHER ONE FOLLOWING OR KNOWING THE PLACE OF MEETING.
4. BRING NO WEAPONS OF ANY KIND
3. COME IN THE ESSEX COACH LICENSE NUMBER 594-995
STAY IN THE CAR

------------------ O --------------------
IF I CALL, YOUR GIRL WILL STILL BE LIVING. WHEN YOU GO TO THE PLACE OF MEETING YOU WILL HAVE A CHANCE TO SEE HER. THEN WITHOUT A SECONDS HESITATION YOU MUST HAND OVER THE MONEY. (THE SLIGHTEST PAUSE OR MISBEHAVIOR ON YOUR PART AT THIS MOMENT WILL BE TRAGIC.)

SEEING YOUR DAUGHTER AND TRANSFERRING THE CURRENCY WILL TAKE ONLY A MOMENT. MY CAR WILL THEN MOVE SLOWLY AWAY FROM YOURS FOR ABOUT A BLOCK. YOU WAIT AND WHEN I STOP I WILL LET THE GIRL OUT. THEN COME AND GET HER WHILE I DRIVE AWAY—AND I WONT GO SLOW THIS TIME. DONT ATTEMPT TO FOLLOW WHEN YOU GET THE GIRL.

BE SURE AND WAIT TILL MY CAR PULLS UP AHEAD AND STOPS AND YOU SEE ME PUT THE GIRL OUT BEFORE YOU START UP. DON'T ACT EXCITED OR THINK I WILL RUN AWAY WITH MARIAN.

I WILL DO AS I SAY AND I HOPE TO GOD YOU WILL HAVE SENSE ENOUGH TO DO EXACTLY AS I HAVE SAID.

WELL, IT'S NOT TO WORRY ME IF YOU BLUNDER AGAIN. I HAVE CERTAINLY DONE MY PART TO WARN AND ADVISE YOU.

FATE --- FOX

Δεατη
FINAL CHANCE TERMS

1. HAVE $1500 = 75-20 DOLLAR GOLD CERTIFICATES - U.S. CURRENCY
2. COME ALONE AND HAVE NO OTHER ONE FOLLOWING OR KNOWING THE PLACE OF MEETING.
4. BRING NO WEAPONS OF ANY KIND.
3. COME IN THE ESSEX COACH | STAY IN LICENSE NUMBER- 594-995 | THE CAR

IF I CALL, YOUR GIRL WILL STILL BE LIVING. WHEN YOU GO TO THE PLACE OF MEETING YOU WILL HAVE A CHANCE TO SEE HER. THEN WITHOUT A SECONDS HESITATION YOU MUST HAND OVER THE MONEY. (THE SLIGHTEST PAUSE OR MISBEHAVIOR ON YOUR PART AT THIS MOMENT WILL BE TRAGIC)

SEEING YOUR DAUGHTER AND TRANSFERING THE CURRENCY WILL TAKE ONLY A MOMENT.. MY CAR WILL THEN MOVE SLOWLY AWAY FROM YOURS FOR ABOUT A BLOCK. YOU WAIT AND WHEN I STOP I WILL LET THE GIRL OUT. THEN COME AND (over)

GET HER WHILE I DRIVE AWAY - AND I WONT GO SLOW THIS TIME. DONT ATEMPT TO FOLLOW WHEN YOU GET THE GIRL.

BE SURE AND WAIT TILL MY CAR PULLS UP AHEAD AND STOPS AND YOU SEE ME PUT THE GIRL OUT BEFORE YOU -- START UP. DONT ACT EXCITED. OR THINK I WILL RUN AWAY WITH MARIAN.

I WILL DO AS I SAY.

AND I HOPE TO GOD YOU WILL HAVE SENSE ENOUGH TO DO EXACTLY AS I HAVE SAID.

WELL, ITS NOT TO WORRY ME IF YOU BLUNDER AGAIN. I HAVE CERTAINLY DONE MY PART TO WARN AND ADVISE YOU.

FATE - FOX
Δεατη

Photo of third letter from Hickman as published in various contemporary newspapers

Once again, a note from Marion was also in the envelope. It read:

Dear Daddy & Mother:

Daddy please don't bring any one with you today. I'm sorry for what happened last night we drove wright by the house and I cryed all the time last night. If you don't meet us this morning youll never see me again.
Love to All
Marion Parker
P.S. Please Daddy:
I want to come home this morning
This is your last chance be sure and come by your self or you

won't see me again. Marion

After receiving the notes, Parker demanded that the LAPD back off. The police, who previously opposed paying any ransom and hoped to capture the kidnapper, had bungled the first attempt to secure Marion's return. Now they agreed that the priority should be to rescue the child.

Around 7:35 p.m. that Saturday evening, Parker received his last call from the kidnapper. He was told to drive to Manhattan Place and Fifth Street and to park alongside the curb in the middle of the 400 block, just north of Fifth

Dear Daddy & Mother:

Daddy please don't bring anyone with you today. I'm sorry
for what happened last night
we drove fright by the
house and I cryed all the
time last night. If you
don't meet us this morning
youll never see me again.

Love to all,
Marion Parker

P.S. please Daddy:
I want to come home
this morning. This is your last chance
be sure and come by your
self. or you wont see
me again. Marion

Photo of second letter from Marion as published in various contemporary newspapers

Street. He left for the rendezvous and arrived at the designated block minutes before 8:00. He parked on the right side of the street. One half-hour later, a small roadster approached. As it passed, a man wearing a white handkerchief over his face peered at him. The car continued down the block and turned on a side street. A minute passed, and then the car returned and stopped alongside his automobile. A man climbed out and walked around the front of Parker's vehicle. He brandished a sawed-off shotgun.

"You know what I'm here for, no monkey business," he said. "Hand over the money."

"Can I see the little girl?" Parker asked.

The man pulled the girl up and showed Parker her head.

"She's asleep," the man said.

Parker thought she was drugged. He gave the man the money. "Can I have her?" he asked.

"Yes, you can have her. I'll drive down a little and I'll leave her just down the street."

The kidnapper drove away slowly and stopped at the southeast corner of Fifth and Manhattan. Parker waited until the car sped off and then ran down the street to his daughter.[52]

A few minutes later, the police arrived at the scene. Two men passing by had called them after hearing Parker's cry of anguish. The father was holding the child in his arms, but, as he recalled, "the body was not complete." Her upper arms and legs were missing. Her eyes were stitched open with a thread that circled her forehead to a piece of linen around her neck.

Detective George Contreras of the district attorney's office arrived shortly. He found Parker standing beside his automobile. Contreras asked where the little girl was and Parker told him she was sitting in his car. "Go and look at her," the distraught father said, "God Bless her little heart." Contreras examined the girl and waited with Parker and other detectives for the coroner. Then he picked up the child and laid her in the coroner's wagon. Autopsy Surgeon Dr. A. F. Wagner, who lived next door to the Parkers and knew Marion and her sister well, would begin examining the body later that night.

That Saturday night a manhunt began that would be even greater than the one that followed the murders of Police Officers Brett and Clester. Radio station KFWB broadcast the news of the child's death Saturday night along with a description of her murderer. The following morning, the Sunday newspaper editions headlined the news. The *Los Angeles Times'* banner, "KIDNAPPED CHILD SLAIN BY FIEND," was typical; throughout the nation, newspapers referred to the kidnapper as a "fiend" or "brute" or "maniac." The manhunt swept up over fifty suspects in the first day, all but four of whom the police quickly released. Among those detained were two mentally unsound persons. Gaylord Barnaman had called radio stations claiming to be the Fox. Police arrested him at a downtown hotel after he made the last of his calls. Evidently, he was not too crazy for the peacetime army, since in a few months he shipped off to the Philippines as a recruit. Lillian Padley, an intoxicated young woman, was arrested after she ran down nearby Manhattan Place, where the killer had dumped Marion's body, shouting, "I didn't kill her, they killed her!" Padley was booked for murder but later released.

Assuming the murderer would try to escape Southern California, the police cordoned off the region. Motorcycle officers patrolled the roads north and south of the city, while a special unit kept vigil on the border crossings into Mexico. A National Guard airplane captured one suspect, Lewis D. Wyatt, on an eastern bound bus in Las Vegas. Wyatt had purchased his ticket with two $20 gold certificates, but, as it developed, the $20 gold certificates were not part of the ransom notes. A month later, he filed for part of the reward for the capture of the actual kidnapper/murderer. He got nothing.

The same impulse that drove Barnaman to pose as the killer and call local radio stations also inspired copycat letter writers to issue threats that further inflamed the public. One note, left on a fire alarm box in Hollywood taunted Perry Parker. "For the trouble you have caused, Marjorie Parker will be the next victim. Nothing can stop 'The Fox' and those who try will know the penalty." Somebody else chalked ΔEATH on the pavement in the middle of 6th Street, right outside the hotel room of LAPD Chief of Detectives Herman Cline, leader of the investigation. However, the pranksters who committed these acts could not compete with the depraved self-indulgence of the real Fox, who sent his final special delivery letter to Parker sometime on Saturday, perhaps after Marion was already dead.

> P.M. Parker,
> Please recover your senses. I want your money rather than to kill your child. But so far you give me no other alternative.
> Of course you want your child but you will never get her by notifying the police and causing all this publicity. I feel, however, that you started the search before you received my warning so I am not blaming you for the bad beginning.
> Remember the three-day limit and make up for lost time. Dismiss all the authorities before it is too late. I'll give you one more chance. Get the money the way I told you and be ready to settle.
> I'll give you a chance to come across and you will or Marian dies.
> Be sensible and use good judgement. You can't deal with a master mind like a common crook or kidnaper.
> Fox-FATE
>
> P.S.—If you want aid against me ask God, not man.

Photo of final letter from Hickman as published in various contemporary newspapers

The following day, a Sunday, an elderly man walking along a roadway in Elysian Park north of the city came across a cardboard box. In it were the girl's arms and legs. Two young boys found the girl's torso shortly afterward. All the body parts were wrapped in newspaper. Later, a suitcase filled with bloodstained newspapers was discovered on the same street.

As detectives examined the packages and suitcase for clues, others followed two leads that had already developed. Autopsy surgeon Wagner discovered a towel with the name of a new apartment building, the Bellevue Arms, in the child's remains. The killer apparently stuffed it inside the body to stanch the flow of fluids. Police surrounded the apartment building and searched its rooms, but they found no evidence linking the murder to the building and observed that the linen closet containing the monogrammed towels was on the ground floor, accessible to anybody entering the building.

The Sunday papers carried not only the kidnapper's description but also the serial numbers of the $20 gold certificates Parker had given him. Early Sunday morning, a Chrysler roadster was found in a downtown parking lot bearing license plates with their edges bent backward to obscure the first and last numbers. The visible numbers matched those Parker had noted as the killer drove away Saturday evening. Police soon learned that the plates belonged to a San Diego automobile, from which they had been stolen earlier in the month. Under the Chrysler's front seat they found Missouri plates. The LA cops contacted Kansas City police, who identified the owner of the Chrysler as Dr. H. L. Mantz of Kansas City. Mantz had yielded the car to a gunman on the night of November 7.

The automobile's discovery broke the case wide open. The driver who abandoned it at the parking station at Ninth Street and Grand, a nervous, flighty young man, according to the parking attendant, never returned, but he left something of great value: his fingerprints. The kidnapper and murderer who posed in his letters as a criminal "master mind" had made the most elemental mistake; in fact, he made several, as soon became clear.

Chief of Detectives Cline contacted his counterpart in Kansas City, Lincoln C. Toyne, to inquire about three suspects with links to Kansas City. Toyne checked the suspects, but while he was doing so, he received a call from former Kansas City Chief of Police Charles Edwards. Edwards had received a telegram from a Los Angeles Probation Officer, Warren Prescott, who had thought of another Kansas City resident, William Edward Hickman, as he read reports of the killing. Six months earlier, Hickman had been convicted of forging checks while serving as a messenger at the First National Trust and Savings Bank, where Perry Parker was an officer. In fact, Parker was the bank officer who fired Hickman after the forgery. Granted probation in part after Edwards persuaded Los Angeles authorities to go easy on him, Hickman had returned to Kansas City.

Edwards had lost contact with Hickman after the young man returned from Los Angeles. He contacted Hickman's mother and then called Toyne back. He told him that Hickman was not in Kansas City and acknowledged that he matched the murderer's description. Toyne relayed the information to Cline, who asked LAPD fingerprinting expert Lieutenant H. L. Barlow to compare the fingerprints found on the automobile to those on Hickman's booking card. They appeared to match. Shortly afterward, Clarence S. Morrill of the State Criminal Bureau of Identification in Sacramento confirmed the match. The murderer was William Edward Hickman.

Hickman was a nineteen-year-old former honor student of Kansas City, Missouri's Central High School, which was located a few miles from Argentine, Kansas, where Harry Raymond spent much of his childhood. Twice he finished second in the *Kansas City Star*'s National Constitutional Oratorical Contest. He was on the football team, the debating club and many other clubs; in his senior year, he was elected class Vice President and served on the Student Council. "An excellent scholastic standing and an unequalled record in extra-curricular activities have and a high standard of ideals will fix his memory in the annals of Central," declared the testimonial beneath Hickman's list of accomplishments in the school's yearbook. This awkward, ungrammatical construction was perhaps the work of Hickman himself, who was on the staffs of both the yearbook and school newspaper.

Despite his stellar background, Hickman had committed numerous robberies, as police soon found out. During the three weeks between Thanksgiving and December 15, he held up several pharmacies. His goal was not to get cash, though he would take money when it was available, but chloroform and other sedatives. In one robbery, the druggist victim claimed he observed another man at the wheel of Hickman's getaway car, but all agreed that he entered their stores alone. In another, a young girl's screams at the sight of his gun sent Hickman into a panic; fearing somebody noted the license plates on his car, he drove all the way to San Diego, where he stole a set of plates for his stolen Chrysler before returning to Los Angeles.

After identifying Hickman as the killer, detectives returned to the Bellevue Arms Apartments with his mug shot. The building's manager identified Hickman as Donald Evans, the occupant of room 315. As the detectives entered the room, they realized that they searched it Sunday morning, while Hickman, posing as Evans, sat in bed and encouraged them to "find the fiend" who killed Marion Parker. On Sunday, they found nothing suspicious; this time, they were more thorough. There were bloodstained towels, traces of blood on the walls, string matching that used to tie the packages containing Marion's limbs, and threads like those that sewed open her eyelids. They also found half of a brazil nut in the wastebasket. It matched another half found in the slain girl's pocket.

Police also showed Hickman's mug shot to the administrators at the Mount Vernon Junior High School and the operators at the Western Union Telegraph Office. All recognized him as the kidnapper. Even the address on the Alhambra telegram proved a clue: it was just four houses from where Hickman was living when arrested the previous June.

The news that police had identified Marion Parker's killer stoked the rage that had engulfed the city over the weekend. The police and press previously had encouraged the public to help find Marion Parker. Brigades of schoolchildren joined the search on Saturday. Scores of calls came into local police departments with tips. Spectators on foot and in automobiles flooded the streets where Marion lived and played. Now that a suspect was identified, the mood became uglier. Already, police had shot one young man who tried to evade a police roadblock in the northern part of the city. Hickman's face was splashed over the front pages of newspapers throughout the nation and men who looked like him were in danger from lynch mobs. One young man who resembled Hickman was brought into the Central Police Station while police with drawn revolvers held back a crowd. In another incident, a traffic officer rescued a young robbery suspect who looked like Hickman from an angry mob. Booked at Central Jail, a few hours later he was found hanging in a cell where sixty other prisoners slept. Although the police surgeon declared he was beaten to death, a coroner's jury determined the death a suicide.

The hunt for Hickman became a regional and even national effort. Portland police wired Chief Davis that their officers were at his command. San Francisco's Police Commission passed a resolution pledging "every possible assistance" to Los Angeles authorities in their attempts to apprehend Hickman. Up and down the coast, eastward in Las Vegas, Phoenix and Denver, police were on the lookout for the fugitive. In Los Angeles, all police officers joined the hunt. The redeployment of 1800 officers who normally managed traffic on downtown streets resulted in bottlenecks that added to the tension and fury of the population. Cops from Bakersfield, San Diego, San Bernardino and the smaller cities of Orange County brought the total officers in the manhunt to 8,000.

The news that Parker terminated Hickman at the bank in June set off speculation that revenge was a motive for the kidnapping. However, Parker remembered the boy as oddly calm when accused of forgery. "He evinced no nervousness and showed very little concern over the seriousness of his actions." Because Parker opposed the court's grant of probation to Hickman for his forgeries, he was surprised when Hickman called him after the trial to ask for his job back. Parker himself said he noticed no resentment or desire for revenge in Hickman's demeanor at the time of the arrest–"no thought of his planning to harm me or members of my family in return for his discharge entered my mind." Hickman, who numbered several prominent men among his mentors, including former Police Chief Edwards, in some twisted way may have viewed Parker as one of his champions.[53]

With most police officers in the western states looking for him, it was just a matter of time before Hickman was captured or killed–or found dead from suicide, as some worried. Hickman himself realized that the authorities had enough to convict him of his crimes, but, as he was "an ace," he believed he could get away. So far, he was doing ok. After the police left his apartment at the Bellevue Arms on Sunday, he packed a bag and took it downtown to store in a locker, and then headed to a theater to watch a motion picture. When the movie was over, he cashed one of Parker's $20 gold certificates at a cafeteria. He later claimed that the cashier, a young woman, kidded him about having a new $20 gold certificate and flirted with him. It amused him to think of her reaction when she realized he was Marion Parker's killer. "I bet she got a thrill when she learned it was me," he would muse.

After the movie, he took a streetcar to Hollywood where he noticed an automobile idling outside a store at the corner of Western and Hollywood. A woman got out and the driver, a man, began to look for a place to park. When he slowed, Hickman climbed in the passenger seat and showed him a pistol.

"You see what this is?" he asked.

"Yes, sir," the driver replied.

"You are going to do just as I tell you to do, won't you?"

"Yes," replied the driver.

"You are not a plainclothesman, are you?" asked Hickman.

"No."

"All right, start your motor."

The driver drove up a block and turned on Russell Street. After he drove half a block, Hickman told him to stop. Keeping his gun on him, Hickman came around to the driver's door and motioned for him to move over.

Hickman put the car in gear and turned south on Normandie. As he drove, he asked the owner questions about the automobile's gauges, its last oil change, why the fan belt squealed. He ran a red light and chided himself, then stopped at another red light at Santa Monica Boulevard. When the light changed, he was still in high gear, but the car, a late model Hudson, powered through the intersection and gained speed. Hickman was impressed. A few minutes later, he stopped and told the owner to get out.

"I know just exactly what you are going to do when you get out of this car," he said. "You are going to call the cops."

"Yes," the man agreed, wondering whether Hickman would shoot him. Then Hickman drove away, leaving the owner, Frank Peck, watching his car disappear over a small hill crossing Normandie, half a block north of Melrose.[54]

After taking the automobile, Hickman drove downtown, removed his belongings from the locker, and drove north on the Pacific Highway. He was stopped at roadblocks three times before he reached Santa Barbara. Unfortunately, the LAPD had not transmitted any information about the stolen Hudson. Each time, after some cursory questioning and helpful words of encouragement from the very man they were looking for, the police waved him on.

On Monday, Hickman arrived in San Francisco and booked a room at the Herald Hotel under the name Edward J. King of Seattle, Washington. The following morning, after having the automobile's oil changed, he took a ferry across the bay and drove east. Figuring that the police would be looking for a man driving alone, he picked up a hitchhiker outside Davis and drove north toward the Oregon border. In Redding, the two travelers lunched at a coffee shop where customers were discussing the terrible murder in Los

Angeles and the reward offered for the killer's capture. Hickman chatted with them about the manhunt before leaving. His hitchhiker decided to stay behind.

In the evening of Tuesday, December 20, James Nelson and Irvin Mowrey were walking along the winding highway that ran north from Redding toward the Oregon border when a green Hudson stopped alongside them. They were both seventeen years old and had traveled to the San Francisco Bay in hopes of getting a berth on a ship as merchant seamen. Having failed to find jobs, they were returning to Portland to spend the Christmas holiday with Mowrey's family. Ten miles back, they had passed Lamoine, California, a small dying lumber town midway between Redding and Mount Shasta. Although the road was uphill and the temperature was dropping, they figured they could make it to Dunsmuir, another ten miles ahead, before resting.

The driver of the Hudson, a young man who looked to be in his twenties, leaned across the front seat, rolled down the passenger window and asked where they were going. Dunsmuir and then Portland, they answered. Well, then, get in, the driver replied cheerfully, he was headed to Seattle and could take them all the way.

The boys threw their duffels in the backseat and climbed in, Mowrey taking the front seat. The driver let the car into gear and started up the road. "I hear they are looking near the border for that Los Angeles kidnapper," he commented as the car accelerated. "I wouldn't want to be stopped riding alone because I've got two quarts of scotch in the back of my car and I want to get to Seattle for Christmas. I've been driving all day."[55]

He looked tired. After a while, he asked whether the boys knew how to drive. Nelson did and took the wheel. The car's owner, who said his name was Peck, the name on the operator's license below the dashboard, settled into the back seat to rest.

A couple of hours later, around 11:00 p.m., they approached the Oregon border. Peck directed Nelson to pull off the road into a secluded spot. Peck had previously said he was in a hurry to get to Seattle—why stop? one boy asked.

"The booze in the car," Peck responded. "Better to wait past midnight. Then it won't be so hot and we can get through OK."[56]

They waited over an hour and then drove over the Oregon state line. Peck was still in the back seat, half-asleep. A few miles beyond the border, a pair of cops stood at the side of the road. One raised his hand for Nelson to stop. The other flashed a light on Nelson and Mowrey for a second and then told them to go on.

At Medford, they stopped at a restaurant and sat at the counter. Peck lowered his hat over his eyes as he asked for a plate of bacon and eggs. "You'll have to wait a few minutes until the cook gets here," the waitress said. Peck did not want to wait so he and the two boys ate cereal instead. While he ate, Peck used only his right hand, keeping his left under the lapel of his coat near a bulge in his pocket. When they returned to the car, Mowrey observed Peck remove a revolver from the pocket and place it on his lap under a blanket.

Eventually, one of the boys asked him about the gun. "For protection," he explained curtly.

Peck took the wheel again. He seemed nervous. He kept looking behind as he drove. They stopped for gas three times and each time Peck asked the station attendant about the kidnapping in Los Angeles. Once Nelson suggested he buy a newspaper, but Peck said he was in too much of a hurry. As they neared Portland, Peck remarked, "That Los Angeles case is the greatest crime in California history."

"Don't know much about it," replied Mowrey. Peck seemed to relax at the reply.[57]

Shortly after noon on Wednesday, they reached Portland. As they entered the city, Peck asked the boys about the interstate bridge into Washington. He also asked about roads leading east. Then he dropped them off at the Congress Hotel at Sixth and Main. As they gathered their bags, Peck stepped from the automobile for a second. As he did, his revolver clattered onto the pavement. He picked it up and tossed it on the front seat of the Hudson. Then he got back in and sped off, heading north.

Mowrey and Nelson walked to the apartment home of Mowrey's mother at 662 Glisan. The boys were exhausted from their long journey and went to sleep in the bedroom. Around 7:00 p.m., Mowrey's mother awakened them. They chatted about the trip to San Francisco for a few minutes, and then the conversation turned to the horrible murder in Los Angeles. Mrs. Mowrey had been following it in the Oregon newspapers. She showed them to her son.

"Why, that's the fellow that we rode in with!" Arthur Mowrey exclaimed, looking at a photograph of Hickman on the paper's front page. "I'm almost sure. It looks a lot like him."

Nelson came into the room and looked at the paper. It did look like Mr. Peck, but neither boy could be sure. They had only seen him in the dark, in profile, with his hat slouched down. Then they remembered his interest in the kidnapping case, his reluctance to purchase a newspaper, which would have had Hickman's picture in it, his revolver, and his nervousness.

"That was Hickman!"

The boys went to the Portland police station and told detectives about the long drive in the big green automobile. The police were not convinced, however. They had already received dozens of reports of Hickman sightings. Still, they wired details of the boys' stories to Los Angeles.

The next morning, a telegram came back from Chief of Detectives Cline of the LAPD. It told of the theft of a green Hudson in Hollywood from Frank R. Peck, who had identified Hickman as the car thief to police Tuesday morning.[58]

After dropping off Mowry and Nelson, Hickman drove north to Seattle. On the way, he picked up another hitchhiker, a sailor who had just completed his enlistment. The sailor took the wheel and guided the Hudson through a heavy fog. They chatted—or joked, as Hickman related later—about the infamous kidnapping and murder in Los Angeles. To Hickman's amusement, the sailor offered his idea on what the murderer was like.

After dropping off the sailor, Hickman was unsure where to head next. He originally planned to go to Spokane, board the Northwest Limited and flee into Canada. He thought of checking with the Automobile Club in Seattle about the roads but decided against it. The weather was unsettled and the passes over the mountains east of Seattle were impassible.

He needed warmer clothes, so he entered a dry goods store around 9:00 p.m. and bought a pair of gloves and long underwear, paying for the items with one of the gold certificates Parker gave him. The salesman thought Hickman was nervous but did not realize who he was until after he left. Then he called Seattle police. Meanwhile, Hickman decided to watch a movie. He found a theater and bought a ticket, but the woman in the ticket booth unnerved him when she looked directly at him. After taking his change, he decided to return to his car. On the way, he stopped at a newsstand to buy a newspaper. As he walked toward the car, he realized that the newsboy was trailing him. Hickman thought he might have to shoot him. The boy kept behind him for two blocks, then let him go.

With the passes in the Cascades east of Seattle blocked by the recent snowfall, Hickman had few options for escape. Doubling back, he stopped at a filling station at Kent, between Seattle and Tacoma, where he passed another gold certificate. Around 6:30 a.m. on Thursday, December 21, he filled his gas tank again in the north end of Portland at a station on Sandy Boulevard, pulling up beyond the pumps to keep out of the light. However, the attendant, Fred King, recognized him and roused the station's owner to call the police. When the police arrived an hour later, King picked Hickman out of a "rogues' gallery" of photographs.

Across the northwestern states, police departments and county sheriffs had geared up to pursue "The Fox." After almost four days on the lam, it was clear that his fate would soon be that of all foxes chased to exhaustion by hounds. The question was where he would bolt to next: north to Canada, south back into California, or east.

King told police that Hickman headed east when he left the filling station. Portland law enforcement authorities broadcast orders throughout Oregon and Washington to stop all automobiles driving east and to be on the lookout for a green Hudson.

The sparsely populated eastern counties of Oregon and Washington, like those of eastern California and Arizona, were hazardous grounds for a fleeing criminal. Their narrow highways were patrolled by stern, experienced sheriffs and their equally severe counterparts in the few cities that dotted the map. Hickman's chosen path, US Route 30, followed the southern shore of the Columbia River through the cities of Cascade Locks, Hood River, and The Dalles to Boardman, where it curved southeast toward Pendleton. He figured he would follow Highway 30 to Boise and Salt Lake City. From Salt Lake City, he could head west to Kansas City and home. The newspaper he bought in Seattle had contained a story of his distraught mother, who feared that he would be killed by police or lynched, and a plea from former Police Chief Edwards that he surrender.

Shortly before noon that Thursday, December 21, the news that Hickman was driving east on Route 30 reached the offices of the *East Oregonian*, the local paper of Pendleton, Oregon. Pendleton, a city of roughly 6,500 persons in 1927, stretched along the two banks of the Umatilla River. In the center of a sheep-herding region, it was famous for its rodeo, the Pendleton Round Up.

When he read the dispatch from the Associated Press, Edward Aldrich, *East Oregonian*'s editor, called his old friend Tom Gurdane, Pendleton's chief of police. Gurdane had been chief off and on for over twenty years. He was a lean, gruff man in his mid-fifties who had spent his life combating gamblers, bunko artists, and pimps as well as opium dealers among the city's sizable Chinese population; he also once smacked a few drunk immigrant laborers with a pick-handle to keep them in line.

Gurdane was with Buck Lieuallen, a state trooper, when Aldrich called. The two men strolled over to the newspaper offices to find out more. Parker Branin, the city editor, handed them the wire. Hickman had used one of his $20 gold certificates in Arlington, 80 miles to the west. If he turned to the southeast at Boardman, he would pass by Pendleton in the big green Hudson within a few hours.

Gurdane returned to his office, where he dispatched his ten officers to cover the secondary roads into and around the town. He and Lieuallan then drove toward Echo, a small town of a few hundred people, twenty-two miles northwest of Pendleton. The road to Echo followed the Old Oregon Trail, a macadam road on the northern bank of the Umatilla River. They had driven about twenty miles when Lieuallan said he wanted to stop for a smoke. "All right," Gurdane replied. "We might as well wait here as any place."

Lieuallen pulled the car to the side of the road at one of its many curves. Before he could take out his pipe, a big green car swung into view, three hundred yards in the distance.

"Here comes a Hudson," observed Gurdane.

Lieuallen looked at it closely. "That's not him. It has Washington license plates. His car has California plates."

"To hell with the license," replied Gurdane. "It's a Hudson and its green."

The two men watched the car speed by. The driver, a young man with dark goggles, looked back at them. It was an overcast day. Gurdane figured there was something wrong when a man wore dark goggles on a cloudy day.

Lieuallen swung the car around and started after the green car. Reaching fifty miles an hour on the rough road, they were soon behind the Hudson. Lieuallen switched on his siren. "You drive the car and I'll do the rest," Gurdane told Lieuallen. The Hudson maintained its speed for another mile before it pulled to the side of the road. Gurdane jumped out with his revolver pointed at the driver, while Lieuallen circled around the Hudson.

"Was I speeding?" the driver asked through his open window.

"What's your name?" Gurdane demanded.

"Peck," replied the driver.

"Where you from?" asked Gurdane.

"Seattle. I've been attending college over there and I'm going to visit my mother."

Gurdane opened the driver's side door and ordered the young man out. As the door opened, a pistol fell on the running board. Gurdane noticed a sawed-off shotgun lying along the base of the driver's seat.

"What are you doing with that gun?" Gurdane demanded.

"It's customary to carry a gun when you are traveling," the driver replied.

"You don't need to keep it between your knees," Gurdane responded.

The driver stepped out from the car and asked again if he had been stopped for speeding. Gurdane scoffed and held the driver's hands together above his head while Lieuallen came around and searched him. "Here's one of the bills," the trooper said. He looked inside the car and spotted seven more $20 bills. The two officers glared at the driver.

"Well, I guess it's over," said Hickman.[59]

News of Hickman's capture flashed through the wires to cities across the nation and around the world. In San Francisco, the afternoon newspapers sold out quickly, and joyful people shouted the news to passersby. In Kansas

City, newspaper boys had to contend with mobs of purchasers when they first shouted that the "boy killer"—the local boy gone bad—had been captured. Hickman's mother collapsed upon hearing the news. Nearly fainting also was LAPD Chief of Detectives Cline, who learned of the capture from Associated Press reporters. Outside LAPD headquarters, motorcycle officers who had gathered for new orders in the manhunt celebrated in a noisy revelry of skidding and toppling motorbikes.

In Pendleton, crowds began to gather in front of the city jail. Gurdane was well aware that the joy and relief Fox's capture brought could change to dangerous passions. The western states had a long history of lynching, particularly when the suspects were of Mexican blood. Five years after Hickman's capture, two other kidnapper/murderers would be lynched in San Jose. The Pendleton crowd appeared more curious than threatening, however. Confident that his police force could keep his prisoner secure, Gurdane declined help from the county Sheriff and state officials.

In Los Angeles, District Attorney Asa Keyes was also concerned about mob action—especially from the rough mountaineers of eastern Oregon. He quickly obtained a grand jury indictment and an extradition order, and then dispatched the district attorney's chief of detectives, George Contreras, to fly to Pendleton along with two LAPD detectives. A small airstrip outside Pendleton, normally used for day flights, was lit by gas fires to aid the plane's night landing.

Keyes' quick actions waylaid some mob spirit, but the possibility that Hickman might escape punishment through an insanity defense worked in the opposite direction. Already, psychologists were debating Hickman's mental state in print and lawyers were assessing legal strategies. After spending an hour with Hickman, a local Pendleton physician declared that the young man was insane. It was not the kind of diagnosis that would sit well with a vengeful mob.

At 6:05 that Thursday evening, District Attorney Asa Keyes and LAPD Police Chief Davis climbed aboard a northbound train heading for Portland. Accompanying them were Chief of Detectives Cline, former Police Chief George Home, Detective Richard Lucas, and Detective Harry Raymond. As the group left for the Pendleton jail, they paused for photographers, Harry Raymond half a head shorter than the other men. The inclusion of the latter two officers, so recently besmirched by allegations they had framed Councilman Jacobson, was remarkable, but only one paper, the *Hollywood Citizen News*, objected to their role. Both detectives were known—and even notorious—for their skill in obtaining confessions. Both were tough and determined, the kind of men who would bring back Hickman, alive and confessed, to Los Angeles, where a jury could convict him and a judge sentence him to death by hanging. "The sickly sentimentality which wars on capital punishment for murder and insists upon the coddling of convicts will have a hard time to justify itself in the case of the slayer of Marian Parker, who, if police theories are correct, is William Edward Hickman, a criminal on probation," editorialized the *Los Angeles Times.* "Society should put the Parker case slayer out of life as quickly as the formalities of the law permit." It was a sentiment felt broadly in the state, with the possible exception of those who would prefer to hang Hickman themselves.

As the band of Los Angeles law enforcement figures journeyed north, Hickman talked freely, if not honestly, with authorities and reporters in Pendleton, particularly Parker Branin. He admitted he took part in the Parker kidnapping but claimed that he did not harm Marion; in fact, he asserted that the two got along, and that he "loved her like a sister." The murderer, Hickman declared, was Andrew Cramer. He spun a long, complex story in which he delivered the kidnapped girl to Cramer, who, to Hickman's horror, returned her dismembered in a suitcase. Only the desire for money propelled him onward with the plot, he explained. Cramer's girlfriend, June Dunning, also helped. While police doubted he had partners, a crime as horrible as the kidnapping, murder, and dismemberment of a child begged for the punishment of more than just one culprit. There were a few odd clues of others involved, such as reports that a woman was overheard in Hickman's apartment urging him to flee the city.

Los Angeles detectives identified a career criminal named Frank Andrew Kramer as a possible accomplice in the crime. Kramer did have a girl friend named Rose Dunning, but he also had an ironclad alibi: he had been in jail since summer. His brother, Oliver Andrew Kramer, also fell under suspicion, but he too had spent the last four months in the county lockup. When told of their alibis, Hickman responded, "That's strange. It can't be." Frank Kramer was puzzled why Hickman was "picking" on him, but he acknowledged that he knew Hickman, most likely because both had spent the previous summer in the county jail.

Without an attorney to quiet him, Hickman was garrulous. Reporters crowded into his jail cell in the center of a large room in Pendleton's City Hall. Putting down a religious pamphlet a minister left him, Hickman recounted in a singsong monotone the story he told on Thursday to Gurdane and Lieuallen. He described how he plotted to kidnap a child of one of the National Trust and Savings Bank employees. Although Parker personally discharged him from the bank, Hickman said he was not motivated by a desire for revenge. Nevertheless, when he decided on the target for kidnapping, Parker came to his mind. Parker's daughter had visited her father at the bank when Hickman worked there. So had the baby of the bank's chief teller, but Hickman figured kidnapping her was impractical—she was too young and might be difficult to control.

He also told of his prior criminal activities, at least those in the period following his return to Kansas City the previous summer. After working for a few weeks at a local theater, he stole a car at gunpoint and robbed several pharmacies in the area. Then, in early October, after stealing another automobile, he took a month long bandit's road trip to Chicago, Washington, Philadelphia and New York City, returning through Columbus, Ohio, where he robbed three stores in one evening. By middle November, he was back in Kansas City but not for long. On November 7, he stole Mantz's car and left Kansas City for the final time, driving south to Texas and crossing New Mexico and Arizona to California. Later that month, he took a short trip to San Francisco, where, suddenly inspired to become a musician, he stole a trombone at gunpoint before returning to Los Angeles. After becoming frustrated by his lack of progress on the instrument, he smashed it and dumped it in Elysian Park.

On November 23, he rented room 315 at the recently completed Bellevue Arms in Angelino Heights. In this single room, Hickman planned the crime that completed his transformation from an "unusually kind-hearted boy" to one of the most despised criminals of the decade.[60]

When arrested for forgery six months before, Hickman had discussed a religious career with Dr. James Hamilton Lash of the Hollywood Congregational Church. Lash gave him a Bible to study, but Hickman later tore it up. After his capture, he would dismiss his talk with Lash as "just a piece of acting." Returning to Kansas City with his mother, he re-entered junior college in early September, claiming he intended to study for the ministry. Four days later, he withdrew from classes, obtaining a refund for his tuition.[61]

This connection between ministry and murder paralleled the unsettling juncture of honor student and criminal. How could this boy, whom some of Pendleton's leading citizens declared a "nice looking man" with a "splendid personality," commit such a horrible crime? Answers, or perhaps more questions, were coming slowly from his old friends, former teachers, acquaintances of his family, and psychoanalysts.[62]

His friends and former teachers described how, despite his earlier ambitions, his attendance, grades and enthusiasm for school clubs and activities began to drop off in his senior year. Perhaps it was merely a case of senioritis, but as graduation approached, he seemed unmotivated and uncertain of himself. Unable to afford college tuition, he sought the counsel of former Kansas City Police Chief Charles Edwards, the father of a friend.

Edwards advised him to apply to Park College, which offered a work/study program that enabled the student to graduate over an eight-year term. Hickman expressed interest in entering the ministry, but within days after his high school graduation, he gave up on the idea of attending Park College. During the summer and fall of 1926, he took and quit a half dozen jobs, enrolled and then abandoned classes at a local junior college. His friends noted that the aimlessness that began in his final year in high school grew more pronounced; what they did not know was that Hickman had found a calling in life—crime—and was about to pursue it.

In Hickman's hometown, Hartford in western Arkansas, some had revolting memories. As a boy, Hickman had "a mania for capturing and torturing stray dogs and cats," recalled his former neighbors. A former schoolmate also remembered that Hickman used to wring the necks of her family's chickens and once did the same to her kitten. Stories like these contributed to the growing debate over Hickman's mental state. Clarence Darrow, who had defended Leopold and Loeb a few years before, argued that Hickman was insane and should not be executed, while Dr. John M Fletcher of Vanderbilt University called Hickman a possible "victim of psychasthenia, that is, he is subject to obsessions over which he can exert no control." The crux of Fletcher's argument seemed to reside in his comment that "It is not human" to commit crimes such as the murder and dismemberment of Marion Parker.[63]

As their train made its way north, Raymond and the other law enforcement officers had plenty of time to keep up with the accounts of Hickman's confessions. The train departed San Francisco at 7:40 a.m. Friday morning after a thirteen-hour ride from Los Angeles and reached Sacramento three hours later. Portland was twenty-two hours ahead. After they arrived there at 8:35 a.m., another train would take them to Pendleton.

In Los Angeles, Joe Taylor, chief inspector of detectives and the man in charge in Cline's absence, dismissed Hickman's claims that he was not the killer and predicted that the big city detectives would break his story soon enough when they got to Pendleton. "Hickman is just trying to frame an alibi which shows on its face to be impossible . . . . Modern police methods are scientific and by adroit questioning detectives soon get to the truth of the matter," he remarked.[64]

Around 5:00 Saturday afternoon, the Los Angeles party arrived in Pendleton. It was already dark and many in the silent crowd of roughly 500 persons carried flashlights and lanterns. Local officials and reporters accompanied the officers to City Hall, where they encountered another large but quiet throng outside the building. Their stylish city suits contrasted starkly with the western attire of the assembled Pendleton citizens. As they passed through the broad doors into the building's central hallway, flash lamp guns boomed and smoke filled the room. Gurdane, in western clothes, and Lieuallen, in his khaki uniform, stepped forward to greet them. The two local heroes were charmed by the warm congratulations and expressions of thanks from the California lawmen. After they shook hands, they headed for the jail cells.

Hickman had learned of their impending arrival earlier in the morning. At first, he bragged that he would match wits with the Los Angeles detectives and prosecutor. Hadn't he outfoxed them before, when he spotted them tailing Parker in the first meeting attempt and when he bluffed his way through three roadblocks north of Los Angeles? He pointed to his virtues: he did not drink, he did not gamble, he did not neck with women, and he smoked very little. After a day of boasting of his criminal exploits and denying responsibility for Marion Parker's murder, however, he grew nervous and his appetite fell off. His fellow inmates taunted him with the threat of a lynch mob. Finally, Cline, Keyes, and Davis appeared in front of his cell. Hickman was lying on his stomach on the lower berth of the bunk bed. He forced a weak smile. The officers did not smile back. "You are the man we want," Cline announced grimly.[65]

Hickman did not get up. "Come on, Eddie, sit up like a man and talk," Cline said, but Hickman would have none of it. One Pendleton jailer entered the cell, grasped Hickman by his shoulder and shook him. His body began to jerk. He cried out, "Marion, Marion, Marion," and looked wildly about the room. Then he rushed at the cell door, banged his head against the bars, screamed, "I did not kill her," and fell to the floor. For a few minutes, he lay on his back, knees raised, eyes rolling, gurgling incoherently, then he grew silent and still. Gurdane came forward and opened the cell door. Cline entered the cell, picked up the small prostrate figure from the floor and laid it on the bunk. "I have a message from Marion," he whispered.

"Man, man, where is she? Come, let me see her face," Hickman pleaded.

"Do you want to know what Marion said?" Cline asked. "Sit up and I will tell you."

Hickman jumped off the bunk, kicking his feet and flailing his arms. He lunged toward Chief Davis shouting, "Marion, Marion, where are you? I love you." A Pendleton jailor restrained him. He stared at Davis. "I have seen those eyes before," Hickman shouted.

Hickman came off his bunk and fell to the floor, squirming. The officers backed out of the cell and locked its door. They had seen enough. They left him on the floor and followed Gurdane and Lieuallen to view the weapons and money that Hickman had with him when arrested. Lucas and Raymond watched them come out of the cells. "Let's get a look at this bird," muttered Lucas. He and Raymond walked into the cellblock.

Afterward, a newspaper reporter asked Raymond if he thought Hickman would talk.

"He doesn't have to," Raymond replied. "His goose is cooked."[66]

The cops believed that Hickman's fit was planned. He had even asked one of his jailers how to appear insane. "Do you just have to talk a little off, or do you rave around?" He decided the latter course was necessary.

Hickman had spent some time earlier that day composing a tract addressed to "the youth of America." "This affair has gained nation-wide publicity and the great reward and search by the police of the west coast show opposition of American people to criminal tendencies," it began.

> Kidnaping and savage murder are the worst of America's crimes and everything should be done to prevent anyone from interfering in any way with the liberty and life of American citizenship.
>
> The young men and college students of America should consider the Parker case as a typical crime of the worst that can happen when a young man gradually loses interest in his family, friends, and his own honesty.
>
> The young men of this country can see that I can pass as an ordinary young man, as far as outward appearances go. Crime in its simplest definition is to have money without work and to enjoy the same place in society as other people and still show no honest effort or intention to be a real man.
>
> Young men, when crime has once overcome your will power to be honest and straight you are a menace to society. Take my example to illustrate this. See how I tried to get what every young man wants, but in becoming a criminal to do so I put my own life in a mess and the way out is very dark. I hope I can do some good by giving you this warning. Think it over, see my mistake. Be honest and upright. Respect the law. If you do these things you'll be happier in the end and you will have gained much more from life.[67]

Hickman's tract, which was published in newspapers throughout the nation, seemed an act of atonement and egoism at the same time. If he could not be the world's greatest criminal, he could be the perfect bad example for all the young men of America. And he, the young man who had excelled in debate contests, would be the one to preach the lesson of his own foul acts.

The Los Angeles cops had hoped to leave that evening with their prisoner, but Gurdane refused to release the prisoner until extradition papers arrived from the governor's office in Salem. He and Lieuallen planned to claim the $100,000 reward for Hickman's capture and wanted the turnover of the prisoner to be by the book. The Los Angeles officials spent Christmas Eve as guests of Gurdane and Lieuallen. Undoubtedly, the men talked over things not normally spoken of on Christmas Eve.

The following day, the Los Angeles officials chartered a Southern Pacific prison car, the Thrall, to return Hickman to Los Angeles. The car had no special markings to distinguish it from other cars on the train, a precaution taken to confuse any mob that might gather along the route. Hickman was to ride in a separate compartment from the officers and reporters. Lucas and Raymond were jointly in charge of a small contingent of Los Angeles cops who would guard each entrance to the car. Nobody was to enter or leave the car while it was in a station.

Hickman had spent a rough Christmas Eve. After the Los Angeles officials left him that evening, he remained on the floor. A physician took his pulse and temperature; they were normal. Gurdane then entered the cell with a reporter who asked Hickman what was wrong with him. Hickman raised one hand and pointed it to his throat. Then he lapsed into what appeared to be a trance, his eyes wide open and staring. After a while, one jailer tested his condition by putting a pair of drunken Indians in the cell. The two scuffled about the cell for a while and began what one newspaper reporter called "an impromptu dance of war and revenge." Hickman regained the appearance of consciousness and cringed in his cell, terrified. Eventually, the Indians quieted and Hickman slept. In the morning, he awakened to the clanking of cell doors. Taking a large handkerchief from his pocket—jailers had removed his belt and scarf—he formed a tight noose about his neck that cut into his flesh. He inserted a finger into the handkerchief and twisted it to form a garrote. Gurdane, at first unable to find the key to the cell for a few seconds, rushed into the cell with a Pendleton jailer and cut the handkerchief. They laid Hickman back on his cot, his face dark and tongue protruding. After a few minutes, they revived him with water.[68]

Disgusted, Cline stood over him. "Listen, Hickman," he shouted, "You wanted publicity and now is your chance to get it. Are you going to be a yellow cur or are you going to brace up and come along on this trip like a man?"

Hickman moaned in response. "Take him up," ordered Cline. Lucas and Raymond stepped into the cell and lifted him to his feet. He went limp. Each detective clamped a handcuff on his own wrist and attached the other end to one of Hickman's.

"Come on, you yellow boy, let's go," Raymond commanded. He and Lucas lifted the young criminal and dragged him out of the cell up the steps that led to the front of the building, where a crowd of several hundred waited in silence. The two officers steered Hickman, his head down and covered by a hat, through a throng of photographers and motion picture cameramen. A cameraman asked Raymond to help him get a clean shot. Raymond step aside and swung Hickman toward the camera as LAPD Detective Inspector Dwight Longuevan, who had secured an extradition order from Oregon's Governor, removed Hickman's hat. "His head hung, his legs failed him, his eyes were haggard, his lips hung loose," wrote *Los Angeles Times* reporter Carlton E. Williams. In fact, there was something histrionic in Hickman's performance. He seemed to have assimilated all the melodramatic expressions of the silent films that he avidly watched. The two detectives led him to the Union Pacific bus. As the bus drove three blocks to the Pendleton Railroad Station, the crowd broke into a run beside it: cowboys, Indian girls, young and old men dressed in rough western clothes. At the station, Raymond and Lucas hustled Hickman into a special Pullman car standing on a siding. The Los Angeles officials and reporters also climbed aboard, as did Gurdane and Lieuallen, who were accompanied by a former motion picture theater owner named Matlock they had hired to represent them to vaudeville houses bidding for their time, and a former judge to help them get the reward money. The crowd surged around the car. Hickman was visible through the window of the carriage, his head down on his chest. He did not look at them.[69]

As the Portland Limited pulled from the station and made its way west through Pendleton, residents along the tracks came out for a final glimpse while the detectives prepared for their interrogation. They had no doubts that they would soon break Hickman. His claim that he had kidnapped but not murdered Marion was full of contradictions, and his pretense of insanity implied that he killed the girl. However, Hickman's fit the previous day, his attempted suicide, and his stupor after boarding the train persuaded Detective Cline to postpone the interrogation. It also gave Raymond and Lucas time to work on whatever feelings of guilt Hickman might have about the murder.

Because of the threat of a large, angry crowd at the Portland railroad station, Keyes and Cline elected to detrain with their prisoner at Montavilla, a suburb outside the city. Even at this small station, a group of curious persons had gathered to watch the train pass, as similar groups had done at every railroad stop after the train left Pendleton. They were treated to the sight of Raymond and Lucas hurrying Hickman from the trail to a waiting police van. He was taken to the Portland City Jail in a convoy of motor police, sirens blaring, where the Los Angeles officers waited until 9:30 p.m., Hickman seated on a cot in a small room handcuffed to either Lucas or Raymond and trembling with fear. Around 9:00 p.m., a crowd began to form outside the building. At 9:40, Lucas and Raymond brought him to the police garage and put him in a police vehicle. The car drove to the Portland railroad station, entering through the yard gates. Lucas and Raymond hustled Hickman across the yard to the Pullman car, now attached to the southbound Cascade Limited, bound for Oakland. At 10:00 p.m., it started for California.

The mobs at Portland and even the small group at Montavilla worried the detectives, who tried to keep the prison car's itinerary secret. Still, the crowds did not seem aggressive, perhaps owing, as one reporter speculated, to a sentiment that hanging was too good for the child killer—or perhaps out of respect for Los Angeles and California, which had the better right to hang him if hanging was to be done. However, the threat of a lynch mob was real; reporters overheard threats from persons in the crowds at Oregon railroad stations, and a rock crashed through a window of the car. Things might get worse when the train entered California, where passions were running very high.

That night, Hickman slept in an upper birth of his compartment, shackled hand and foot to Harry Raymond. "I slept all night," he told a reporter the next morning. "I don't think much of these iron things, though." Turning to Raymond, he quipped, "This is the chain that binds." "Yes, it binds—but it don't stretch like hemp," Raymond replied.[70]

Hickman seemed alert that morning. District Attorney Keyes and Detective Cline decided that it was time to confront the youth. They decided that Cline should conduct the interrogation alone, not only because of his experience in dealing with suspects, but because he had gained Hickman's esteem by treating him as an exceptional criminal. Before he began, Cline let Raymond and Lucas work on Hickman's latent guilt. When the train paused in stations, the two detectives directed their prisoner's attention to children. "Look at that little girl," they said. At first, Hickman only glanced, but as the morning wore on and the train stopped at station after station, the detectives repeated the sentence. "Look at that little girl, look at that little girl." Soon, Hickman shuddered whenever he heard the phrase. Soon, he began to talk.[71]

Meanwhile, in Los Angeles the investigation was proceeding. Police forensic officers found Marion's hair in Hickman's Bellevue Arms apartment. They also discovered blood and human flesh in the plumbing. Dispatches from Los Angeles to the train kept Cline informed of the investigation's progress and furnished ammunition for his interrogation.

The grilling began after breakfast that Monday morning as the train descended from the mountains of northern California into the San Joaquin Valley. At all times, either Raymond or Lucas was present along with Cline and Hickman in the small prisoner's compartment. Cline began by suggesting flatly that Hickman's contention that Kramer killed Marion was illogical. It was a perfect opening move that the former high school debater could not help but counter. "Why is it illogical?" he demanded. Cline asked him to list the key points of his Kramer tale on a piece of paper. Then they reviewed Hickman's entire story. Whenever he asserted something that Cline could disprove logically from discoveries investigators in Los Angeles had made, Cline pointed out the problem but allowed the youth to continue. Each time, Hickman revised his story to overcome the difficulty. Eventually none of it made any sense, even to him.[72]

He shifted gears. He would "adopt the Leopold and Loeb program," he told Cline. He would plead guilty and introduce evidence of mitigating circumstances—in other words, of mental disease. According to Cline, Hickman believed "he could get away with the Leopold and Loeb defense, and he said he wanted the judge to be acquainted with all of the facts of the case." Cline replied he was also anxious for the judge to have all the facts and the best way to ensure he did was for Hickman to write them all out. Hickman began to write in long hand, his left wrist still shackled to Harry Raymond.[73]

Hickman's confession comprised nineteen handwritten pages. After identifying himself and the time and location of the confession, he explained his motivation for his crime. For six months, he had plotted "to kidnap a young person and hold it for ransom . . . as a means of securing money for college." As he had revealed to Branin in Pendleton, he planned at first to abduct another child but finally settled on Marion. After recounting how he tricked the administrators at Mount Vernon Junior High School into releasing the girl to him, he chronicled the more than two days during which he held her. While much of his account focused on his negotiations with Perry Parker, including the aborted meeting on Friday evening, he also described Marion's state of mind and their relationship.

Hickman wrote that Marion became suspicious when they reached Glendale northeast of downtown Los Angeles. At that point, he told her she was kidnapped and that he was demanding $1,500 ransom for her. He bound and blindfolded her, but after threatening her with his .38 caliber revolver, removed the restraints after she promised not to move or call out. As they drove to Los Angeles to mail the first of his special delivery letters to Parker, "Marian sat right up in the seat beside me and talked in a friendly manner. It was very nice to hear her and I could see that she believed and trusted me for her safety." After mailing the letter and then driving to Pasadena to send the first telegram, "Marian and I left Pasadena and drove out Foothill Blvd. beyond Azusa. We talked and had a jolly time. Marian said she like to go driving and went so far as to relate to me that she had a dream just a few days before that someone called for her at the school and in reality kidnapped her." They then returned to Alhambra, where he mailed the second telegram.[74]

Before returning to his apartment with Marion, Hickman took her to a theater in South Pasadena where they watched a film. "Marian enjoyed the picture and we both laughed very much during the vaudeville which followed the picture." Back in his apartment, Marion fell asleep on the couch after taking off her shoes. Hickman slept in his own bed. The next morning, Marion awoke around seven. "She was sobbing and didn't say much." Hickman bound her to a chair with a cloth but did not blindfold or gag her. He then proceeded downtown to send another letter. He included a note from her.

After his return from downtown, Hickman took Marion on a long drive south, past San Juan Capistrano. When they returned that evening, news of the kidnapping had already broken in the afternoon papers. Passing through Hollywood, they heard newsboys hawking evening newspapers headlining the story. "My car was stopped by a traffic light," he recounted. "Marian was beside me and newsboys waved their papers close to us. Marian seemed to be amused by this."[75]

Marion was in the car with him that evening, "parked on Pico between Wilton and Grammercy" when Perry Parker drove by to deliver the ransom. Hickman noticed two cars following Parker and concluded that the meeting was a trap. He returned to his apartment with the girl. "We got back in without anyone seeing us. Marian sobbed a little because she couldn't go home that night but she saw everything and was content to wait till next morning."

Both awoke around 7:30 the next morning. Marion once again slept on the couch while Hickman slept in his bed. Hickman had her write another note to her father, deriding him for having brought the police and predicting that he would never see her again if he did not cooperate. "Marian knew that I wrote her father that I would kill her if he didn't pay me but she knew that I didn't mean it and was not worried or excited about it. In fact, I promised Marian that even though her father didn't pay me the money, I would let her go back unharmed."

Hickman wrote his letter and put both his and Marion's in an envelope, then told her he was going downtown to mail it and afterward they would meet her father. He bound her again to the chair, but, this time, he also blindfolded her. "She said to hurry and come back."

> At this moment, my intention to murder completely gripped me. I went to the kitchen and got out the rolling pin meaning to knock her unconscious. I hesitated for a second and changed my mind. Instead I took a dish towel and came back to where she was sitting on the chair, pushed back in a small nook in the dressing room, with her back turned to me. I gently placed the towel about her

neck and explained that it might rest her head but before she had time to doubt or even say anything I pulled the towel about her throat and applied all my strength to the move. She made no audible noise except for the struggle and heaving of her body during the period of strangulation, which continued for about two minutes.

When Marian passed to unconsciousness and her body stopped its violent struggle, I untied the bandages and laid her on the floor. I took off her stockings, her sweater and dress, and placed her in the bathtub. I got a big pocket knife I had in the apt. and started cutting.

Hickman described in gruesome detail his amputation of Marion's arms and legs, which he wrapped in newspaper and stored in a kitchen cabinet, and the severing of her midsection along the waist. When he finished amputating her limbs, he removed some of the child's internal organs and wrapped them in newspaper. He then hung her body above the bathtub to let the blood drain into the tub and afterward washed the tub to ensure that no stains set in. Once the blood drained, he placed a towel—the one that would prove a key clue in the case—in the torso to absorb any remaining fluids. Then after combing back her hair and powdering her face, he put what remained of her body in a suitcase. In a note at the end of his confession, he explained that he also stitched her eyelids open so it would appear she was alive.

Hickman's confession stunned the LA officials. District Attorney Keyes afterward sat alone in the dining compartment, an uneaten meal before him, before leaving the car complaining of indisposition. He decided not to release the details of the crime, believing them too gruesome for public consumption—especially since Hickman was not securely behind bars in Los Angeles. Still, some newspapers printed them.

Hickman alternated between enjoyment and fear of the crowds that met the train at each station stop. At Dunsmuir, California, which was already part of the tale because it was Mowrey and Nelson's destination when he picked them up, a crowd of 2,000 watched his train pull into the station—a remarkable crowd for a town of less than 2,500 residents. Hickman broke out in a wide smile at the sight, but Cline warned him to restrain his delight—else the crowd might become enraged at his pleasure and storm the car. At another stop, Hickman spotted a woman he thought he recognized. "I think I saw that woman in Portland," he exclaimed, "I bet she has followed me all the way down."[76]

The long ride through the San Joaquin Valley to Oakland was without incident until Benecia, where the train boarded the railroad ferry *Solano* to cross the Carquinez Strait to Porta Costa. There, a large, angry crowd had gathered. Hickman was moved to a baggage car to be interviewed and photographed for the newspapers along with his captors. As the flashlights exploded for the cameramen, there was a sudden commotion outside the car and the sound of hostile voices. "He's in there—make them bring him out. Smash down the doors." Raymond and Lucas, still manacled to Hickman, rushed him to the prison car while Southern Pacific railroad officers shouldered the doors shut. As the train rolled slowly onto the ferry, the rioters hammered at the doors. The officers hammered back with their fists, knocking several men onto the tracks.[77]

Less hostile crowds met the train in Porta Costa and Oakland. Once again, Hickman was brought to the baggage car for the benefit of local reporters and photographers. "He sagged in his clothes, like a doll oozing sawdust," wrote one reporter. "His face, dough white, was expressionless beneath the springing black curls."[78]

The prison car was coupled to the Padre Limited behind the powerful locomotive's tender. The train sped on toward Los Angeles in the early morning, passing small crowds in Santa Barbara and Glendale, and arrived in Los Angeles in the middle of the morning. Despite rumors that Hickman would be taken off the train outside the city and brought to the Central Jail via armed car, the train did not stop until it reached Jackson and Alameda Boulevard, just short of the station, where a small fleet of police cars and two dozen cops with sawed-off shotguns waited. Still shackled to Lucas and Raymond, the youthful killer was rushed into a car and the motorcade sped down a series of back streets to the Hall of Justice. When the police vehicles arrived at the building, Lucas and Raymond hustled their prisoner from the car, lifting him off the ground so that only his toes touched earth, an oversized derby pushed far down on his head, covering his eyes and ears. They carried him through a lane of police guards while a mob estimated at 3,000 persons shouted "Lynch him, string him up!" One man broke through the police line and kicked Hickman as he passed, but police swiftly threw the man outside the line. Once inside the building, Lucas and Raymond hurried Hickman to the county jail in the upper floors. Hickman breathed heavily, winded by the run. Lucas looked down at him. "Well, we made it all right," said the big detective, grinning at his prisoner. "Yes," replied Hickman.[79]

With the successful delivery of Hickman, Harry Raymond's participation in the case ended, with a single exception: both he and Lucas were called by the defense to testify, although in the end only Lucas did so. This surprising development resulted from Hickman's plea of not guilty by reason of insanity. Besides eliciting testimony from psychiatrists of Hickman's mental incapacity, his attorneys also introduced evidence of familial mental illness to the court. Lucas and Raymond's testimony was meant to supplement the defense argument by "stressing the horrid details of the killing . . . to convince the jury that Hickman was insane."[80]

It was essentially the same argument that Dr. John M. Fletcher had made in late December—that it was "not human" to commit such a crime. Yet, a human had committed the crime and other humans were called upon to judge that human. It is barely conceivable that the full text of Hickman's confession, read to the jury by Jerome Walsh, a young Kansas City lawyer and state representative whom Hickman's mother hired to represent her son, created empathy in the twelve jurors for the young murderer. Los Angeles officials and local newspapers had suppressed a key sentence in the confession. "As I cut the limbs and body there were heavy issues of blood and jerks of the flesh to indicate that life had not completely left the body." Now that the jurors heard this appalling statement, a controversy that filled the papers in the last days of 1927 between Autopsy Surgeon Wagner and District Attorney Keyes made more sense. Wagner suggested that Marion died from heart failure because of fright.[81]

> [Hickman] may have attempted . . . [to strangle Marion] but her death was not due primarily to strangulation. There were no marks of contusions or constrictions about the neck, the lungs were not congested but on the contrary were quite pale and bloodless.
>
> The whites of the eyes were not injected (or bloodshot) nor was the face bloated. I knew Marion Parker. She was a nervous child and when he applied the towel about her neck, she realized what was about to happen and her heart stopped as a result of fright and exhaustion.[82]

Keyes responded that Wagner's friendship with the girl, his desire to believe she had not suffered, misled him. However, Wagner's findings and Hickman's confession raised the possibility that the girl was alive when he started amputating her limbs.

Hickman's insanity plea would fail, in part because several times he admitted to interrogators he was faking and once wrote to another inmate for advice in carrying out the deception. Despite testimony by psychiatrists and acquaintances to his mental instability, the jury convicted him on February 9, 1928, after deliberating 45 minutes. He was sentenced to death five days later. His time in the courtroom was not over, however. On December 28, after repeated badgering by detectives who suspected he had killed before, Hickman confessed to the murder of a druggist in Los Angeles on Christmas Eve, 1926. In addition, he named an accomplice, one whose name had already surfaced in the investigation after Marion Parker's death: seventeen-year-old Welby Hunt.

Police had interviewed Hunt when Hickman was first identified as a suspect in Marion's death, crediting him at the time with providing "valuable information concerning Hickman's character and mannerisms."[83] A graduate of Northeast High School of Kansas City, Missouri, in 1926, the same year as Hickman, Hunt had been an outstanding student, making the honor roll in his senior year and serving on the student council in his junior year. He met Hickman when both held part-time jobs at the Kansas City Public Library. In the space of three weeks, along with another youth named Frank Bernoudy, they discovered a common ambition: to become criminals. The trio obtained guns and collaborated in a string of robberies of confectionaries, drug stores and restaurants in the fall of 1926. Afterward, Hunt and Hickman left for California, where they lived with Hunt's grandparents, Abner and Martha Driskell, in Alhambra.

On Christmas Eve, Hickman and Hunt robbed a drug store in the Rose Hills section of Los Angeles. It did not go well. After they entered the store and began to herd the customers and proprietor into a back room, a beat cop walked into the store. The cop pulled his service revolver and a gunfight ensued. Both Welby and the cop were hit. The officer, Donald J. Oliver, was wounded slightly. The pharmacy's proprietor, a young man named Ivy Toms, who recently had graduated from the University of Southern California Pharmaceutical School, was also shot. He died the next day. Hickman took Welby back to a hotel room they had rented in downtown Los Angeles and nursed him.

After the death of Toms, Hickman and Hunt drove to San Francisco, where they committed a string of robberies and car thefts. Returning to Los Angeles by coastal steamer in mid-January 1927, they decided to go straight for the time being. Hunt's grandfather helped both to get jobs as pages at the First National Trust and Savings Bank in downtown Los Angeles, where Perry Parker worked. It did not take long before Hickman saw an opportunity and began to forge checks. Hunt, however, was not implicated in the scheme. He remained in Alhambra after Hickman returned to Kansas City with his mother following his forgery conviction. He continued to work at the bank.

The arrest of Hickman and Hunt for the Toms' killing also prompted police to take a second look at the suicide of Hunt's grandfather, Abner Roberts Driskell, who jumped from the Colorado Street Bridge in Pasadena on May 25, 1927 after scribbling a series of suicide notes on bank withdrawal slips. Ultimately, the police concluded that Driskell killed himself. The Toms case, however, was open and shut; the only issue was which youth fired the fatal bullet. Each blamed the other for Toms' death and both were convicted and sentenced to life imprisonment for the murder.

With the conclusion of the Toms murder trial, the two youths left for San Quentin. Manacled together, they posed for a photographer as they boarded the train, Hickman dressed in a college sweater and an open collar shirt, a hat tilted jauntily on his head, while Hunt looked like a young businessman on his way to work. They slept side by side on the train that night, but when they reached San Quentin, they separated. Hickman entered death row. Hunt headed for a cell in the general population.

A few days later, Hickman had a momentary change of heart and admitted that he shot Toms. He declared that he had been angry with Hunt for telling police that he had said he would like to murder somebody, cut up the body, and "strew it along a highway," but now wanted to exonerate his friend. The news that Hickman had taken responsibility for the Toms' murder elated Hunt, who predicted that he would soon be pardoned or at least have his sentence reduced. His attorney had already filed for part of the reward money, as Hunt claimed that he had told another bank officer that Hickman was behind the crime after reading about it in the papers. While the bank officer, W. H. Rappold, shared the reward, Hunt got nothing. To make matters worse, Hickman soon retracted his confession that he killed Toms.

Hickman's execution was postponed as his lawyers appealed his sentence. Finally, the appeal reached the United States Supreme Court, which declined to hear it.

Hickman, who previously claimed that God was with him when he killed Marion, had converted to Catholicism and spent his final weeks composing letters of atonement. He met a final time with Welby Hunt, who pleaded with him to admit that he fired the shot that killed Toms. Hickman refused to admit to Toms' killing and told Hunt he could not lie for him. Two days later, on October 19, 1928, he was hanged in the view of fifty witnesses, including Detective Richard Lucas, who fainted at the sight of Hickman's body as it writhed at the end of the rope. Because Hickman collapsed a moment before the trap was sprung, the distance of his fall was insufficient to break his neck. He died instead after two minutes of strangulation.[84]

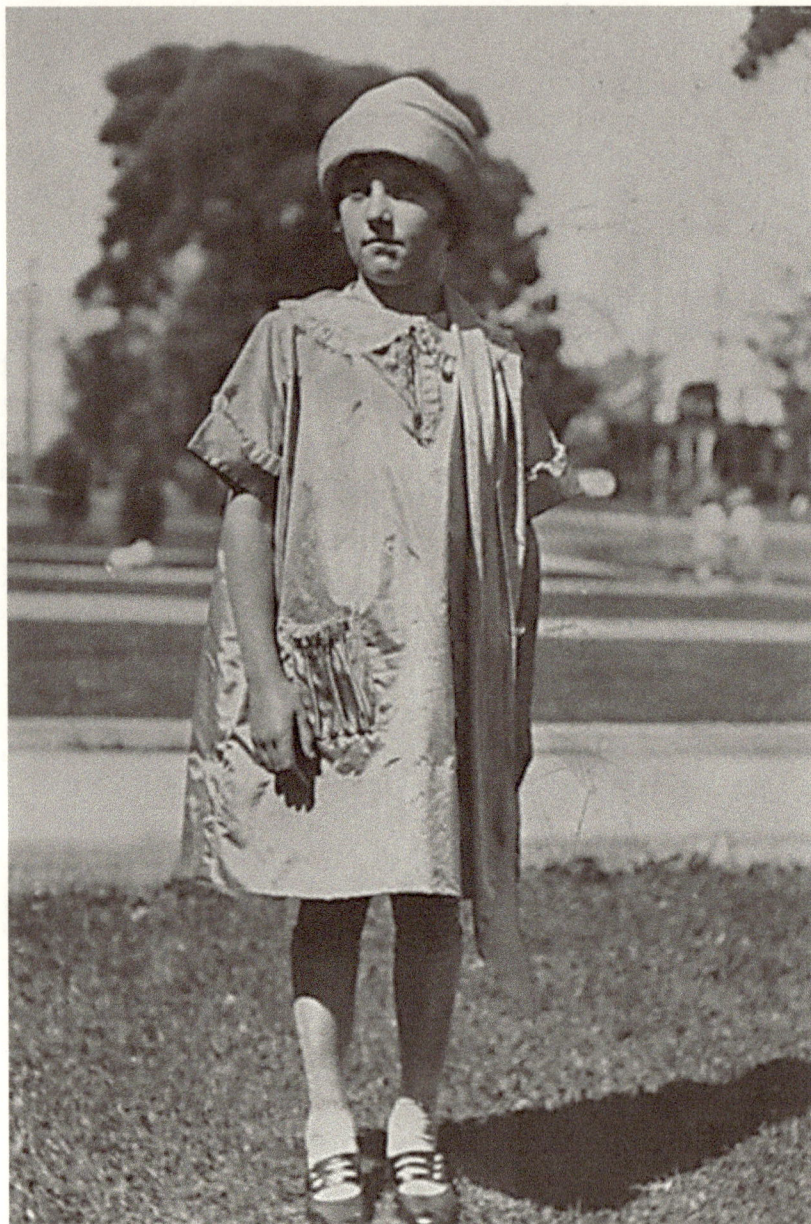

Marion Parker in 1925. [Los Angeles Times Photographic Archive, UCLA Library. Copyright Regents of the University of California, UCLA Library]

Welby Hunt between his attorneys [Los Angeles Times Photographic Archive, UCLA Library. Copyright Regents of the University of California, UCLA Library]

Dick Lucas testifying as defense witness. [Los Angeles Times Photographic Archive, UCLA Library. Copyright Regents of the University of California, UCLA Library]

Hickman handcuffed to Lucas and Raymond at Portland [Oregon Journal Photographs Collection, Oregon Historical Society Research Library.]

Raymond (right) with Police Captain Ray Cato during Hickman trial [Los Angeles Times Photographic Archive, UCLA Library. Copyright Regents of the University of California, UCLA Library]

8: THE JACOBSON BUST REDUX

The ten months following the capture of William Hickman were high points in Harry Raymond's career. Hickman was tried and executed, and everybody involved in his downfall enjoyed the approbation of a grateful city. While the Jacobson case tainted both Dick Lucas and Raymond, their service in the Hickman case helped restore their reputations despite the skepticism of one local newspaper, *The Hollywood Citizen News,* which had condemned the Mayor and the LAPD for using the two officers. In early June, Chief of Detectives Cline put Lucas in charge of a new police unit that the press dubbed the "gangster squad." Joining the squad was Edward D. Brown, a burly detective who had earned his nickname, "Roughhouse," at the expense of many offenders. Shortly before Marion Parker's kidnapping, Brown unceremoniously banished Al Capone from the city after the Chicago gangster checked into a downtown hotel. "Who ever heard of anybody being run out of Los Angeles that had money?" the Chicago crime boss complained as he waited for the train to carry him back east.[1]

Also joining the squad was Detective Harry Raymond.

The new squad's targets were "outside gangsters"—in other words, eastern gangsters who, according to Cline, there were already "too many of them here and too many coming right along." The threat that eastern criminals would bring the lawlessness of Chicago and New York City to LA had long worried Los Angeles civic leaders, who regarded organized crime as part of the corruption of older east coast cities. The city had battled minor criminals from the east since the last decades of the nineteenth century, recognizing that the cheap transportation that transported Midwest farmers eager to buy land also brought thieves and bunko artists. "There are more thieves in Los Angeles than there ever were at one time," LAPD Chief John M. Glass declared in 1894, "They come on in every train."[2] A month later, the *Los Angeles Times* reported that confidence men were tricking San Diego county ranchers into purchasing counterfeit money at a discount. The swindlers, "green-goods men," operating out of New York City, used the mails to distribute circulars to advertise the counterfeit money in the rural communities. When the ranchers reached town, thugs employed by the "green-goods men" stole their good money.[3]

The influx of thieves, pickpockets, con men, and burglars was an annual event as the crooks fled the harsh eastern winters. While the LAPD effectively countered this menace, jailing many eastern criminals and sending others back east, they continued to come each year. In 1920, 80% of the inmates in San Quentin Prison had been born outside the state.

Hostility toward eastern criminals was linked to a belief that Los Angeles, isolated by hundreds of miles of desert on the east and an ocean on the west, was a special place free from the evils of the older eastern cities—crowded tenements filled with foreign-born immigrants, unionism, bossism, criminal enterprises and political corruption. The key proponents of this vision were the publishers of the *Los Angeles Times*, Harrison Gray Otis and his son-in-law and successor, Norman Chandler. After Otis became associated with the paper in the 1880s, the newspaper fought to keep the city and its surrounding region friendly to development and business. On New Year's Day, 1886, as the *Times* surveyed the thriving Southern California region, Otis opined on the men needed in Los Angeles ("Men of brains, brawn and grit") and those who should not come ("Dudes, Loafers, Paupers . . . . Folks who do not wish to obey high-grounded and wholesome laws").[4] As the years passed, the *Times* was a steady advocate of all means necessary to increase the region's prosperity and growth, promoting the digging of an aqueduct from the Owens Valley constructions of dams, and the burgeoning film industry. It also brawled with worker unions both within and without its walls, especially after union activists dynamited its building on October 1, 1910, killing twenty-one newspaper employees.

The newspaper and other local boosters called Los Angeles a "white spot"—a term imported from grey-scale business activity maps published by the National Chamber of Commerce, which depicted areas suffering from poor (solid black) or fair (dark gray) or good (light gray) business conditions. In March 1921, one such map showed Los Angeles as the only area in the nation where business activity was not "at a standstill." After altering the map to show good business conditions in white, the *Los Angeles Times* utilized it in a publicity campaign for the region under the theme "Greater Southern California/Straight Ahead" that was quickly picked up and expanded by business groups throughout the city. A few years later, it re-energized its campaign with a new slogan: "keep the white spot white." Eventually the term expanded to imply not just excellent business conditions, but moral and spiritual values—even the esthetic value of keeping city streets clean.[5]

For law enforcement, keeping Los Angeles a "white spot" meant preventing eastern gangsters and racketeers from competing with local gangsters and racketeers. Police and newspaper reporters knew the identities of these local gangsters, but most citizens had never heard of them and had little understanding of how the local underworld worked. It would take another decade and an event that almost cost Harry Raymond his life before the public began to understand the system and its key players.

Cline's gangster squad went to work quickly, arresting within its first few days a suspect wanted for a San Francisco shooting after a spectacular pursuit through downtown streets. The acclaim the squad received after this arrest was short-lived, however. In July, Lucas and Brown were accused of beating two suspects, throwing them in jail, and falsely charging them with auto theft. The two men, Harry Levin, a 41-year-old Russian immigrant who had been arrested for transporting liquor a few months before, and Theodore Rosner claimed that Lucas and Brown accosted them as they sat in Rosner's car at the corner of Central Avenue and 21st Street. The officers demanded to know if they had liquor in the automobile and then pulled them from the vehicle. Lucas beat Levin mercilessly in the street and continued the beatings at the Central Station, where the pair was booked on suspicion of auto theft. After three days, Lucas and Brown released both men after determining that Rosner owned the automobile. Levin, his face swollen and eye discolored, had a concussion and a fractured nose.

In late July, the squad came under further criticism when it failed to make any arrests in a bootlegger war that had broken out in the North End community near Chavez Ravine. The area was home to many bootleggers, some of whom were easterners, including two former Capone associates. Five men had been murdered in turf disputes, including an elderly resident whose bullet-ridden body was found on an Altadena roadside. The North Civic Center Improvement Association, representing the largely Italian and French neighborhood, condemned the gangster squad's inaction. It ridiculed Raymond, the squad's "outstanding member," and Lucas for not having "thrown one single gunman in jail."[6]

Despite the bad press, Lucas and Raymond, along with Roughhouse Brown, received the choice assignment of guarding presidential candidate Herbert Hoover when he visited Southern California in August.

Raymond's career seemed to be on an upswing, but trouble was right around the corner. In July, Callie Grimes' name surfaced again in the local press. Detectives working a murder case discovered her name and phone number in the victim's address book. The victim, John I. Glab, was found outside his home on Ventura Boulevard. Police suspected that the murderer was his wife, Helen, who would eventually be convicted of the crime, but they currently did not have sufficient evidence to charge her. Grimes' was never a suspect, but she was questioned by detectives, who learned that she met Glab on a street corner and then went "automobile riding" with him a few times in the past few months—after he had married his young wife. Grimes claimed that their relationship was casual.[7]

It is not clear why this brief, second encounter with notoriety motivated Grimes to come clean on her role in the Jacobson scandal. Prompted either by civic duty (to aid in the grand jury's inquiry into bribery cases involving Asa Keyes), remorse (for involving herself in the Jacobson plot), or anger (for not being paid for her frame-up of Jacobson), she declared in an affidavit to the grand jury that Jacobson was framed. Grimes claimed Albert Marco engineered the plot, working with her brother-in-law, Frank Cox, whom she described as Marco's "chief aide," after she related to Cox that Jacobson had tried to seduce her earlier in the week when he visited her home for the first time. At the time of this new allegation, Marco was on his way to San Quentin to serve a two-to-twenty-year sentence for assault with a deadly weapon. In another demonstration of his hot temper, he had shot two men at the Ship Café in Venice after a brawl in the men's room over a verbal sleight.

Grimes alleged that Marco had instructed her to get Jacobson to take off his clothes and given her a bottle of liquor to entice the councilman. He assured her that both the police department and the district attorney's office would look the other way. Marco agreed to pay her $2,500 and an additional $100 for the duration of her life to frame the councilman. However, she had only received $2,140 before the imprisoned Marco told her "there isn't any more" and stopped paying her.[8]

Six days later, Grimes was once again in trouble on a morals charge. This time, she was charged with violating Los Angeles' resorting ordinance. Claiming that they had responded to an anonymous tip that persons in the room at the Continental Hotel at 626 South Hill Street were acting in a "loud and disorderly manner," police busted in to find Grimes and her companion, George A. Keller, with two bottles of liquor. Grimes at first hid her identity, telling police she was Lillian Myers, but Keller told vice squad officers her real name, somehow figuring that it would get the pair off the hook. Grimes continued to insist her name was Myers even after a matron at the Central Jail found a typewritten copy of her affidavit regarding the Jacobson case in her purse. "My name is Lillian Myers," she told reporters, "That's my story and I will stick to it." Badgered by police and reporters to admit who she was, she exclaimed, "What of it? This is just another frame-up!"[9]

In court, Grimes admitted her identity and claimed she had been framed. The LAPD maintained they did not know who she was until told by Keller. Grimes pleaded not guilty to the charges, but less than a month later changed her plea to guilty and received a fine of $10. Keller got twenty days for both resorting and liquor possession.

Grimes' claim that Jacobson had been framed prompted the LAPD to perform an internal investigation. Two police captains, Slaughter and Slater, conducted the investigation, which Deputy Police Chief J. P. Lyons delivered to the police commission on Dec 31, 1928. The report rejected Grimes' allegations. However, the Grand jury had another opinion. On January 16, 1929, it issued a resolution that observed that much witness testimony on the case was contradictory and "neither side is wholly free from culpability." The Jury condemned the police in the Jacobson arrest. In particular, it lashed out at Raymond and Lucas and recommended that the two officers, both of whom had quit the police department that day, should have "no place in the public service of this city or county."[10]

Incensed, Raymond appeared with his attorney at the Hall of Justice on January 30 and threatened to sue each of the 19 Jury members for $100,000 for defamation of character unless they either retracted their resolution or indicted him. The Jury, which was about to disband at the end of its one-year term, responded in mid-February with indictments of Raymond, Lucas, Wallis, Williams, and Frank Cox. Also indicted were Marco, Grimes, and Charles Crawford, though it was widely assumed that Grimes would turn state witness.

For those who understood the politics of Los Angeles' law enforcement and organized crime, Crawford's indictment broadened the case considerably. Newspapers had already reported that he and his associate, Guy McAfee, had submitted affidavits to the grand jury to deny any culpability in the Jacobson matter. With his indictment, the conspiracy to frame Jacobson expanded into the city's political establishment, perhaps even as far as the man who amused himself by sitting in the mayor's chair with his feet on the mayor's desk, Kent Kane Parrot. After all, didn't those few who knew such things know that Crawford was Parrot's man, the director of vice in the political corporation of Cryer's mayoralty?

Charles Henry Crawford was an Ohio native, born in Youngstown on April 22, 1879, the second youngest of 14 children, two of whom died in childbirth. His father, William Wallace Crawford had emigrated from Northern Ireland to Toronto, Canada, where he married Amelia Sprague, an English immigrant, in 1856. In the early years of the Civil War, the couple moved to Youngstown, where William worked as a shoemaker.

In 1896, when the great Klondike gold rush began, seventeen-year-old Charles Crawford traveled to the Northwest along with thousands of miners. He may have tried his luck in gold mining in Saginaw or Dawson, but it is more likely that he remained in Seattle. The northwestern city was the stepping off place for the two main water routes to the Yukon. Men traveling north could buy their equipment in the city and spend their gold there when they returned. Crawford got his start by booking performers for dance halls in the gold rush towns. In 1903, he married Margaret Cordelia Sellers in New York City. By 1910, when she filed for a divorce, he had a small fortune in two Seattle banks, a private yacht, and an establishment by the name of Crawford's Bar on Sixth Avenue. One newspaper described him as a "notorious tenderloiner" when he announced his intention to open a gambling house.[11]

Seattle's vice scene was similar to Los Angeles' a few years before—prostitutes doing business in narrow cribs in a protected area. The arrangement was no secret. The mayor, Hiram Gill, campaigned openly on the platform of segregating vice into a crib district and brought back a former chief of police, Charles Wappenstein, known for his tolerance of vice, to run the operation. However, Wappenstein foresaw more opportunity than did the mayor. Instead of restricting prostitution and gambling to a single, small area, he let it flourish throughout the city and collected a tariff of $10 per month on every prostitute from their pimps. It was a lucrative business for the chief of police. Prostitutes and gamblers flocked into the city to pursue their trade in the safety of civic protection. Even the mayor was surprised by the protected district's success. "Every gambler from Nome to Texas who could get himself a ticket came to Seattle and proceeded to open up [for business]," Gill observed. Described by a contemporary magazine article as "one of the great spectacles of the Pacific Northwest," Tupper and Crawford's establishment, the Northern Club, which they managed along with another notorious tenderloiner, Clarence Gerald, ran around the clock, serving hundreds of customers eager to risk their earnings. Crawford served as the establishment's manager and secretary, while his older brother George was a trustee.[12]

Eventually, the vice scene became too much for the citizens of Seattle, especially the women, who arose from their apathy to support a recall campaign that deposed the mayor. The testimony of Tupper, Gerald, and Crawford led to Wappenstein's indictment for bribery.

After the trial, Crawford moved to Los Angeles, where he purchased the Maple Bar at Fifth and Maple Streets. He had arrived at a propitious time. Ballerino was dead, Savage would be dead in a few years and was no longer a factor in vice operations, and Oswald was on his way to Coos Bay, Oregon. Los Angeles was "Chemically Pure," as Willard Huntington Wright lamented in *Smart Set* magazine. "You will look in vain for the flashing eye, the painted cheek, the silken ankle. No yellow-haired Laisses haunt the dark doorways of the downtown thoroughfares. The city's lights go out at twelve, and so does the drummer's [salesman's] hope."[13] Undoubtedly, such a condition could not be as extreme as Wright portrayed it, nor could it last. There were too many single young men flocking west. Soon after Wright published his article, Cecil B DeMille would ask his boss Jesse Lasky for authority to rent a barn in a place called Hollywood. The Midwestern morals that irritated Wright could never survive the influx of the film industry.

After he bought the Maple Bar, Crawford transformed its upper floor into a bordello and soon opened additional brothels east of Main Street along Fifth, Wall and Maple. Advertised as the place "Where All the Boys Go," the bar became a watering hole for political and criminal figures. Crawford, whom one newspaper described as "one of the best known sportsmen in Southern California," had a talent for organizing. A brief newspaper article in 1915 stated that he represented "organized labor" and planned athletic events and dances for the Labor Temple. By the late 'teens, he had become a leader of the "wets" in the struggle to keep liquor flowing in bars and restaurants in the city and state. Although Los Angeles fell under the Gandier Ordinance, which closed all saloons, prohibited the serving of liquor after 9:00 p.m. in cafés, restaurants, and hotels, and restricted alcohol content in beverages to a maximum of 14 percent, Crawford successfully fought off even more restrictive measures proposed by the local temperance leaders. With national prohibition looming, he predicted optimistically that the café scene would survive with "music, soda-water, and near beer." Months later, however, he was living on his ranch in Antelope Valley and managing a water company.[14]

Crawford's ranch was one of the first assets of his growing Southern California real estate holdings. During the early twenties, he purchased additional properties within the city of Los Angeles, including a 200 by 371 feet bungalow court on Sunset Boulevard in Hollywood. While he may have retained some direct interest in houses of prostitution—according to one madam, he set her up as the manager of the "official brothel" of the Cryer machine on the night that Cryer won the mayor's race in 1921—he moved into what historian Gerald Woods called "an executive job . . . as central broker of police protection." In this capacity, he worked with Kent Kane Parrot, who routinely referred to him issues that touched on commercialized vice in the city. Crawford organized police protection for the vice rackets into a smooth-running machine that withstood a series of police chiefs, newspaper invectives against vice, and even grand jury inquiries.[15]

The preliminary hearings for the trial of the seven indicted men began on February 21. The defendants had hired an array of skilled legal hands. Jerry Giesler, well on his way to fame as Los Angeles' top defense attorney, represented Crawford. Thomas P. White represented Marco. Paul Schenck, brother of Sam, represented Lucas. John C. Cooper and his nephew, Grant

Cooper, a decade away from prominence in the district attorney's office, represented Wallis. Joseph Ryan represented Williams. Joseph Fainer and Cromwell Ormsby represented Cox and Raymond. Leo Daze would represent Callie Grimes once they found her. Ms. Grimes had skipped town.

At first, Grimes' failure to appear in court did not worry the prosecution. Deputy District Attorney George B. Bush observed that, while Grimes was under indictment, she was also a state witness with immunity. Besides, she had informed the district attorney that she was leaving town for a few days on February 10. Others were not so sure. Speculation that she was the victim of foul play to prevent her testimony played out in the newspapers. On February 21, police received an anonymous note that they would find Grimes' body in the ocean off Venice. After over a week, the district attorney's office, frustrated by the continuing inability of the police to locate her, demanded a nationwide search on the scale used to catch Hickman. A warrant was issued for her arrest on March 2. Reporters traced her to San Francisco, where she had stayed with a relative and left her ten-year-old daughter. The relative claimed she had returned to Los Angeles and was ready to testify. The Los Angeles investigators did not believe Grime's relative, however; after they tapped her phone and seized a letter from Grimes with an El Paso postmark, they dispatched a detective to the Texas city. He found her registered under an assumed name in a downtown hotel. Authorities speculated that she planned to flee to Mexico but had halted when a battle between revolutionary forces and the Mexican army broke out in nearby Juarez. Posing as a plumber, a local cop gained access to Grimes' room and arrested her. A few days later, she was on a train to Los Angeles, where, unable to make the formidable bail requirement of $20,000, she was clapped into jail and held in solitary.

Grimes latest escapade soured her relationship with the Los Angeles DA's office. As she evidently left on her own volition, investigators from the DA's office looked for an accomplice in her flight. A detective visited the nearby city of San Bernardino to interview a suspect in Grimes' escape soon after she returned. After she refused to aid the inquiry or help in the trial, District Attorney Buron Fitts ordered her held for trial. He declared that the evidence against the other defendants was enough to secure convictions without her testimony.

The trial got underway slowly as the court struggled to find jurors not already convinced one way or the other about the guilt of the defendants. Jury selection was also complicated by a threatening note found in Grimes' chair after a recess. After Superior Court Judge Walton J. Wood ordered that all persons entering the courtroom be searched for weapons, Defense Attorney Ryan objected, claiming that it might prejudice prospective jurors. When Wood overruled this objection, the defense attorneys moved for a change in venue, arguing that prospective jurors' minds were already made up, particularly by the pro-Jacobson invectives of Robert Shuler, who thundered against the defendants on the radio and at the Trinity Methodist Church. Wood rejected this motion as well.

The prosecution, led by Deputy DA Edward J. Dennison, opened its case by denouncing a "diabolical scheme of the police and underworld with a servant girl" that had been "conceived and designed" by Callie Grimes and her brother-in-law Frank Cox to entrap and photograph Jacobson in a compromising position.[16]

The allusion to other men framed in similar plots was a recurring theme in the trial. A few days later, Jacobson himself testified that another city councilman had been forced into silence. He also claimed that Marco came to his office with a grand jury investigator and offered him $25,000 to desist his anti-vice campaign.

The trial was the inverse of Jacobson's trial a year and one half before. Then Jacobson was the defendant. Now he was the chief witness for the prosecution. The story he told was largely the same. He had innocently agreed to visit Grimes in her home to address her concerns about a street improvement assessment, he followed Grimes into the bedroom to help her assess the value of the home, she offered him whisky, which he refused, and he observed the shadows of two men in the hallway.

> About the time she was showing me the bedroom and as I started to step into it I was given a slap on the neck and fell onto the bed. Next thing I remembered there were four flashlights in the room, like lights coming out of a dim fog. Wallis was standing in the room with my trousers over his arm. I started to get my glasses, which had fallen under a piece of furniture, and someone slapped my hand. I had one shoe on and the other off. It was jerked loose when my trousers were pulled off. Then I heard someone say, "Jerk his collar off."[17]

Jacobson denied the testimony of several defense witnesses, including reporter Al Nathan, Police Commissioner Rodney Webster, former district attorney and now state prisoner Asa Keyes, and even Nute Teeman, a private detective he employed during his own trial and afterward failed to pay. All claimed the councilman had admitted that he "walked into the trap" set by the defendants. Jacobson maintained that he never succumbed to Grimes' enticements and observed that he was "not much of a love-maker," a reflection that may have helped convince some jurors of the innocence of the thin, bespectacled and ascetic-looking councilman.[18]

Callie Grimes' affidavit of the previous autumn would have supported Jacobson's assertions, but Judge Wood declared it hearsay and disallowed it.

The prosecution tried twice to call witnesses with whom Grimes discussed the affidavit before she made it, but the court ruled their testimony inadmissible as well. However, the judge allowed Jacobson's former attorney, William Anderson, to testify that Grimes admitted the frame-up to him eighteen months before.[19]

Although Anderson's testimony seemed to incriminate Marco and Crawford, Judge Wood declared that it could be used only against Grimes herself. He then dismissed the indictments against the two vice leaders. Charlie Crawford, whom reporters and law enforcement personnel familiar with the workings of the local underworld knew as the "Gray Wolf of Spring Street," left the courtroom with a smile on his face. He was out his lawyer's fees—most likely a considerable sum, since he retained Jerry Giesler—and a group of reporters had bamboozled him into shelling over $1,000 in gratitude for their help in convincing Woods to dismiss his case when actually they had done nothing at all. Otherwise, the Gray Wolf had come out of the episode without a scratch. Marco, while pleased at the dismissal, found himself on a train back to San Quentin, where he would serve out his sentence for the melee at the Ship Café.

The case against the remaining defendants—including Grimes—was supported by witnesses who claimed they observed tangential evidence of the frame-up in progress. Harry Raymond was the target of much of this testimony. Two former landlords of an apartment building, John Hyman and Kate Shivers, claimed that Raymond rented an apartment from them at 1027 West 6th Street in Los Angeles after he identified himself as an oilman named J. B. Kelly. Lucas, Wallis and other officers used the apartment for about a month, the Shivers testified, but they abandoned it after Jacobson's arrest. The prosecution contended that the police conspirators originally planned to use this apartment to frame Jacobson but shifted to Grimes' residence when he balked at meeting her there. The defense challenged the Shiver's testimony, however, with that of officers who disputed their description of Raymond as wearing "white flannel trousers, white shoes, a blue coat and a straw hat"—Raymond never wore such an outfit, according to the officers. While two officers acknowledged that the vice squad rented the address, they claimed they used it in the arrests of bootleggers and other vice offenders. In the absence of the real J. B. Kelly, this was the best his defense attorney could manage.

The rebuttal to another charge against Raymond was stronger. A key prosecution goal was to show evidence of preparation for the alleged frame-up. Reports of police activity near Grimes' home in the hours or even days prior to Jacobson's arrest worked toward this end. The prosecution presented neighbors of Grimes who testified they observed police vehicles around her home before the defendants arrived. One witness, Mrs. Fern Carlin, claimed that a few days before the Jacobson arrest, Callie Grimes introduced her to Raymond at the corner of Huntington Drive and Turquoise Street, a few blocks from Grimes' house. Her testimony could have been devastating, but the defense called oilman Raymond R. Kahl, who explained that he was with Grimes the day that Carlin said she met Harry Raymond and that Grimes had introduced him to Carlin by his first name. Carlin's account was further discredited by witnesses who asserted that she spent part of her childhood at a school for the feeble-minded. It did not help when a court official claimed that, when he pointed out Harry Raymond in the courtroom during Jacobson's 1927 trial, she remarked that the balding Harry Raymond had "hair on his head" when Grimes introduced him a few weeks before.[20]

With enough conflicting testimony in the trial to confuse any dozen good men and women, it was perhaps inevitable that the jury would fail to decide. Their task was made more difficult by the instructions of Judge Wood, who, over fervent objections from the defense attorneys, advised them that the resorting ordinance on which Jacobson was originally arrested did not apply to private homes, and that therefore his arrest was improper. Still, the Judge acknowledged, if the police defendants acted in good faith under the misconception that a law had been broken, the jury could acquit them.

On April 21, after fifty-eight hours of deliberation, the jurors told the court that they were split 9 to 3 for conviction of the police officers and 10 to 2 for conviction of Grimes. None believed that they could reach a unanimous decision. Judge Wood dismissed them.

The District Attorney's office retried the case a few weeks later, but this time without Marco and Crawford as defendants, as their cases had been dismissed in the first trial. Again, the jury, split evenly for acquittal and conviction, could not reach a decision. District Attorney Buron Fitts declined to prosecute a third time.[21]

In early July, Chief Davis reinstated three of the accused police officers, Hubert Wallis, Frank Cox, and Rusty Williams. Although one member of the Board of Police Commissioners denounced Davis' actions, the Board accepted the officers' reinstatements a week later.

Dick Lucas and Harry Raymond were out of jobs, however. Lucas was back in the news shortly afterward when police found a cache of rifles, revolvers, and whisky in an apartment he was renting. Neighbors reported that they heard a woman scream in the apartment, which was the scene of many wild parties. The apartment walls were stained with blood. Chief Davis ordered Lucas' immediate arrest, but whether anything came of this incident is a mystery, as Lucas was nowhere to be found, and the papers dropped coverage of it.

A rumor soon surfaced that Raymond was involved in Lucas' disappearance. Supposedly, he was angry over reports that Lucas' wife had asked for a divorce settlement of $150,000, an amount that indicated to him that Lucas had not equally shared funds the two earned through "their associations with the underworld." Years later, Earle Kynette, citing Lucas as his source, claimed Raymond "went up to Dick Lucas' apartment, and, although Dick Lucas was in bed with a heart disease . . . Raymond picked on him and beat him up and that the police found the room the next day full of blood, and a machine gun and several other guns in there." The tale resonated with the September 1929 newspaper reports.[22]

A month later, on Black Tuesday, October 29, 1929, Lucas and Raymond's names both surfaced amid allegations that Davis was protecting illegal vice in the county. Lucas and Raymond, it was asserted, were back on Davis' secret payroll.[23]

Charles Crawford during Jacobson trial   [Los Angeles Times Photographic Archive, UCLA Library. Copyright Regents of the University of California, UCLA Library.]

9: RELIGION AND VICE

After the charges against him in the first Jacobson trial were dismissed, Charley Crawford headed for Europe. It was his second trip to the old continent and it set in motion a chain of events that affected not only Crawford but also many key players in the life of depression-era Los Angeles, not the least of whom was Harry Raymond.

Crawford's decision to visit Europe may have arisen from a craving for culture in a man who had spent his life in the coarse world of organized vice. Crawford, a soft-spoken man, regarded his colleagues in the underworld with distaste. The European vacation may also have reflected his uneasiness with the activities of reform groups in the late twenties. As Crawford and his wife and two children traveled across country toward New York City to embark on their European tour, the two leading candidates to replace Mayor George Cryer pledged to rid the city of "bossism" in its particular local flavor of Kent Kane Parrot. Both candidates also promised change in the LAPD. Councilman William G. Bonelli stated forthrightly that he would remove the current chief, James Davis, while his opponent, John C. Porter, owner of the Auto Salvage and Supply Company and a 1928 Grand Juror, proposed to do the same unless Davis agreed to "work with him."[24] By the time Crawford and family boarded a ship for Europe in New York City, Porter, the favorite of religious reformers, had won the election. Shortly afterward, he asked for the support of Los Angeles' Christian community in a "wholesale cleanup of Los Angeles vice conditions," declaring before a gathering of church leaders, "Los Angeles is the last stand of native-born Protestant Americans."[25] By the end of 1929, he had engineered the elevation of Roy Steckel to LAPD chief of police. Steckel, the former head of the Venice Station, had personally arrested Albert Marco following the latter's drunken rampage in the Ship Café. He was not a friend of the local crime syndicate, as a local FBI agent would report to J. Edgar Hoover a few years later.

Porter's ascension to the mayoralty and Crawford's departure were a victory for religious reformers in Los Angeles, most notably, Pastor Robert Pierce Shuler of the Trinity Methodist Episcopal Church. Born in the backwoods of southwestern Virginia at the base of the Iron Mountains, Shuler had arrived in Los Angeles in October 1920 after spending eight years as a minister in Texas, where he devoted much of his time to fighting liquor interests and segregated vice. He also played a role in the downfall of Governor Jim Ferguson, who was impeached and convicted by the Texas Legislature. Although fervent in his convictions, Shuler had a folksy, self-deprecating sense of humor that played well with Texans and won over many citizens of Los Angeles. He was also a prolific writer, unafraid to reproach his opponents, some of whom responded with lawsuits for libel.

When Shuler departed Texas to seek a better climate for his declining health, he pledged to his fellow Methodists that he would go to Los Angeles, a "great wicked city" as "the same Bob Shuler . . . . I shall dress as I always have dressed, preach as I have always preached, and fight the devil as I have fought him since I was licensed to preach as a seventeen-year-old lad. I expect to be in the middle of every battle for decency in Los Angeles." He had already adapted the moniker "Fighting Bob." Los Angeles soon found out he was not kidding. Before the year was out, he injected himself into a controversy over a jazz jamboree held at the Vernon Country Club in the notorious city of Vernon, a few miles outside Los Angeles' city limits. There some seven hundred young men and women danced and drank whisky until the early morning hours in full sight of non-interfering and often imbibing patrolmen. The *Los Angeles Times* ran a half-page account of Shuler's sermon the following Sunday, "Vernon Country Club versus Decency. Will Los Angeles Stand For It?" complete with photographs of "Fighting Bob" in three pugilistic stances.[26]

Shuler quickly became Los Angeles' most popular and powerful anti-vice crusader. He frequently explored current events in his sermons, making the most of a series of sensational murders in Los Angeles, including Clara Phillips' hammer slaughter of her husband's mistress. Within a few years, he was a serious player in Los Angeles politics and a fierce critic of law enforcement officials, whom he blamed for the county's vice conditions. One of his earliest targets was District Attorney Thomas Woolwine. Shuler called Woolwine, at the time running for governor, the "defender of bootleggers and gambling."[27] He also went after City Prosecutor Erwin W. Widney after Widney refused to take action against a local theater that had shown a movie with a naked woman in it, declaring that the city prosecutor was "more dangerous to law and order than 100 bootleggers."[28] He attacked other political leaders routinely, including Mayor Cryer, Kent Kane Parrot, and various police commissioners. Although he rarely won his political battles, he brought down one police chief, influenced the appointment of another, and contributed to the election of a mayor. However, his fierce fundamentalism, his attacks on rival minister Aimee Semple McPherson, the Knights of

Columbus and Catholicism in general, and his defense of the Ku Klux Klan, limited his influence among more tolerant Southern Californians.

Shuler's ally in the fight against vice was Gustave Briegleb, a Presbyterian Minister who made a name for himself by attacking the film industry. Briegleb advocated drastic censorship of motion pictures, including "a ban on women in abbreviated costumes, no scenes of drinking or smoking by men or women, abolition of all . . . plays and scenes dealing with inharmonious family life, [and] a ban on crime and underworld films." That he did not get his wishes was evident in the industry's prosperity. Briegleb also alleged widespread use of narcotics within the film colony and thundered against official movie censor Will Hays after Hays lifted the blacklist of Roscoe "Fatty" Arbuckle following Arbuckle's acquittal for the murder of Virginia Rappe.

In early December 1923, Shuler and Briegleb brought their tag team act to the Jinnistan Grotto Circus in Prager Park, southeast of the city center. For several years, the local Masons had held circuses in Los Angeles to collect funds for children's charities and a new temple. As soon as it opened on November 30, LAPD Vice Squad Captain Bert Massey visited the event and afterward notified the Grotto's officials that some of their amusement games violated the city's anti-gambling ordinances. As the event sponsors included several councilmen, the mayor, the LA County Sheriff and the Los Angeles City fire chief, Massey's warning served mainly to annoy the event's promoters and amuse reporters. However, it prompted Shuler and Briegleb to contact Police Chief August Vollmer, whom Shuler had helped recruit for chief the previous summer, and demand action. On December 5, the two pastors entered the circus's two-block tent and began sampling the games. Edmund Wilson, writing almost a decade after the event, claimed Shuler won a ham at one game. Whether he took it home and cooked it—and hung the cooked ham above his dining table as his mother used to do when he was a boy in Virginia—is not known, but he and Briegleb circled back to Eighteenth and Hill, where Captain Massey had assembled his vice squad officers. Massey distributed marked silver to the officers, who entered the tents and began playing the games. After a few minutes, ignoring catcalls and jeers, Shuler and Briegleb pointed out the men in charge of the booths to the police, who closed the booths and arrested the men. Finally, the managing director of the circus climbed on a counter in one shuttered booth and began denouncing Shuler and Briegleb until the pair beat a hasty retreat.

The booth operators were booked at Central Station and charged with operating gambling games. Harry Raymond, a grotto member and a Mason for ten years, followed the arrested men to the station and paid their bail of $250 each. The following day, Raymond demanded that the City Prosecutor arrest Shuler and Briegleb for gambling, but the prosecutor replied that the two ministers had acted under police supervision. In the days that followed, recriminations against Shuler and Briegleb, threats of a recall against Mayor Cryer, and an angry tirade against Shuler and Briegleb's "stunt" by a fellow minister roiled the city. True to form, Shuler kept up his invective, delivering a series of venomous sermons a few weeks later, entitled "What do you prefer, Blue Laws or Jew Laws," "When the City Council Looked Like a Jewish Convention," "Putting a new dance law over by stealth," and "Do we want a wide-open, South-of-Europe city?"[29]

Most likely, there was an acrimonious encounter between Raymond and Shuler at the Jinnistan Grotto Circus that December evening. In the coming years, Shuler would link Raymond with some of the worst transgressions of the city's law enforcement, including a charge that Raymond had "a long standing with the underworld."[30]

The *Los Angeles Times* account of the Jinnistan Grotto incident described Shuler and Briegleb as walking "arm in arm." They continued to march together throughout the twenties, although they preached to different choirs. In a chapter of *The American Jitters, A Year of the Slump,* Edmund Wilson asserted that Briegleb's "congregation is made up of a better class of people than Shuler's," and contrasted Briegleb's "much smarter affair than Bob Shuler's rather shabby temple."

> [Briegleb] does not pretend to be a man of the people like Shuler; and though, as program chairman of the Ministerial Union at the time when Shuler was president, they battled side by side against progressivism . . . . [Briegleb] was often criticized by Shuler . . . for his willingness to play the game of the rich.

"Briegleb," Shuler declared to Wilson, "is one of the best fighters for the right who ever buckled on a sword. As I see it, his trouble is that the 'big boys' can feed him stuff."[31]

One 'big boy' feeding Briegleb stuff was Charlie Crawford.

When he departed for Europe in May 1929, Crawford left Guy McAfee in charge of the commercialized vice organization, known as *The Syndicate* or *The Combination.* McAfee, a former LAPD vice office and a shrewd operator of illegal gambling joints, was charged with maintaining order among local vice operators and distributing a levy on their profits to law enforcement personnel.

Like Raymond, McAfee was a Kansas native. Born in Winfield on August 19, 1888, he got his last name from a young scoundrel named Miller McAfee, a Tennessee native who grew up in the small community of Dillon, a railroad stop on the Missouri Pacific Railroad in Dickinson County, where he lived with his uncle Alonzo L Evers, a prominent former Civil War soldier, farmer and judge. Miller McAfee met Guy's mother, eighteen-year-old Jessie Neild, a servant girl, in October 1885, when he was working as a painter in the town of Prairie Dog, Kansas. The marriage lasted only a few months. Miller found his way back to Abilene, where he was convicted of assault and battery in March 1886. In early 1887, he was in Arkansas City, where he intervened in a fight involving a friend, kicking his supine victim in the eye with his boot heel in what the local paper called an "act very cowardly and uncalled for." He received a $10 fine and 30 days in jail. Unable to pay the fine, he would languish in the county jail until March 1887.[32]

These were not Miller's first brushes with the law. In 1877, his seventeenth year, he had moved to Abilene. The city was a few years past its heyday as a rough and tumble cattle town but still not altogether civilized. Miller quickly became notorious for several violent episodes. The first occurred in June 1885. After he was asked to stop using loud and lewd language on an excursion train, Miller struck another man several times and then drew a knife and threatened other passengers. The following afternoon, he argued with an African-American man dining at a restaurant. When the man left the restaurant, Miller followed him and, barking the usual racial epithets, slashed him in the forehead with his knife. Promptly arrested and fined $50 he did not have, he remained in jail.

Despite these episodes, the Abilene newspapers admired him, tracking his progress through his early manhood as he moved from singer to clerk to poster hanger to a brief stint as a St. Louis police officer. Known as "Sugar Spot" or simply "Spot" locally, Miller was a handsome, well-built young man and a favorite with the young women of the area. Jessie Neild was not the first nor the last to succumb to his charms. After serving his sentence in Arkansas City, Miller married another young woman, Mary Conklin, without bothering to divorce Jessie. The couple took the train that evening for San Diego, where in August 1887 he wrote back announcing that he had married a rich San Diego widow, "one of the best ladies in that town" and was making "a mint of money" as an auctioneer. He also explained that the report of his previous marriage to Mary Conklin was "erroneous." What he meant by this is difficult to fathom. His marriage to Conklin, like his previous wedding to Neild, was witnessed by several friends of the bride and groom and documented in the local papers.[33]

Unless some other rascal slipped into the bedroom of the former Jessie Neild, Guy McAfee's birth date of August 19, 1888, suggests that he returned to southern Kansas in December 1887 or early January 1888. By late January 1888, he had returned to California, registering at the Pico House in Los

Angeles on the 23rd and receiving a fine of $30 for disturbing the peace a few days later.

Deserted by her husband, Jessie McAfee raised her son Guy on her own. It is likely that she lived with her father and mother, Samuel and Hannah Neild, who moved to Winfield after a disastrous barn fire destroyed five of their horses and farming implements in 1886. By 1895, she was working in Kansas City, Missouri, as a seamstress while Guy lived in Sioux City, Iowa, with his Aunt Ida and her baker husband. In 1898, the ten-year-old future gambling baron sent a letter to Santa from Sioux City asking that presents be sent to his mother, then living alone in Kansas City.

A few years later, Guy reunited with his mother in Kansas City. He had grown into a tall, thin man, who in later years would be nicknamed "Stringbean." He had a thin, angular face, with a high, sloped forehead and a nose that dived steeply to a wide mouth, all framed by a pair of clownish, protruding ears. They lived together for a few years, but, by 1906, while Jessie remained in Kansas City, Guy appears to have struck out on his own. In 1907, mother and son united again in Seattle, Washington. By then, Guy was a machinist, although when he returned to Kansas that summer to visit his grandmother, he claimed he was a naval engineer. Most likely, he was working in the Puget Sound Naval Shipyard. On May 8, 1907, he married Eva Catherine Nicklason, a young woman from Hood River, Oregon, who recently completed her first year in the Academy at Whitman College in Walla Walla and was now living in Chico, near Bremerton and the shipyard. He was nineteen and she was twenty-five. In October 1908, Eva gave birth to a daughter. By 1910, they were both in Chico, where Guy was making a living as a dairy farmer.

One can imagine what thoughts passed through McAfee's head as he arose early each morning to start his day with the cows. Despite his humble situation, there were signs of aspiration in the young man. Trying to pass himself off as a Navy engineer was one sign. His marriage to a cultured young woman who had studied at a conservatory in Portland was another; how she ended up in Chico, Washington, where she met her future husband, we do not know. One senses that Guy's ambitions must have been too much for his situation, including his marriage. Within a few years, he had left his wife and daughter and moved to Los Angeles.

What is certain is that the future gambler Guy McAfee joined the LAPD in July 1913. Soon afterward, he volunteered for the nascent LAPD flying squad. While he was not chosen for the squad, he found plenty of adventure with the Purity (Vice) squad, playing leading roles in some of the most spectacular vice raids of the 1910s. In 1916, while unarmed, he snatched a package of opium from a quartet of Spanish opium smugglers who drew three revolvers on him. When the fourth smuggler stole back the opium and fled, McAfee ignoring the pistols, chased after and temporarily captured him before being brought to bay by the other three smugglers and their guns.

Much of the battle between the wets and drys, the underworld and the church brethren, the libertarian advocates of an open town and those who wanted to keep the lid tightly on vice, centered on the LAPD and, more precisely, the Purity Squad. McAfee's career reflected the city's collective ambivalence toward gambling, prostitution and liquor. In late 1915, after a series of sensational and well publicized vice arrests, McAfee and his fellow Purity Squad members were dispersed to other police stations. The current police chief, Charles Sebastian, at the time running for mayor, explained that McAfee and the other squad members were "too well recognized by evil doers, including gamblers and prostitutes, for their work to be effective." Squad leader Home, a future chief himself, had another reason: there were "better men for the positions." However, it soon developed that the officers were suspected of protecting some vice establishments while raiding others that had not paid protection money. McAfee and his fellow exiled officers responded by staging an unsanctioned raid in downtown Los Angeles under the noses of the new Purity Squad, netting six gamblers. As the *Examiner* noted, "the alleged gambling house was located in the very center of the city where the present metropolitan squad would have cognizance of it."[34]

In later years, after McAfee had moved to the other side of the law, two legends about his career with the LAPD would be told repeatedly. One was that he had joined the police after watching a cop roll a drunk and concluding the badge was a "license to steal." Another claimed he earned a nickname, "Whistlin' Guy," after fellow Purity Squad members noted that he sometimes made a quick phone call just before they left on a raid. Standing in the full view and hearing of the other squad members, he would dial the number, then casually whistle, "Listen to the Mocking Bird" or some other popular tune while waiting for an answer. His party was never home, nor were there ever anything but empty rooms by the time the squad reached the alleged gambling den or bordello. After a while, other Purity Squad officers suspected that McAfee's whistling phone call routine was a tipoff to the gambler or madam on the other end of the line.

In any case, McAfee's reputation as a police officer began to decline in 1916. First, he was arrested on New Year's Day for illegally hunting on the grounds of the Lomita Gun Club near Sunset Beach. He pleaded guilty to the charges and received a suspended sentence. In September 1916, the district attorney's office investigated allegations that he had accepted a bribe to reduce robbery charges against a medical student. McAfee was cleared in this case, but he was suspended as vice squad leader. In June 1917, he accidentally shot himself in the leg while placing his revolver on a table at this home. A month later, he and three other "purity squad" members were caught playing craps in the assembly room of police headquarters and dismissed from the LAPD. The games had been going on for weeks, according to other cops.

After he was fired, McAfee found work as a fireman with the Southern Pacific Railroad. There he met Wade Buckwald, who remained his close friend over the next twenty-five years, Thomas J. Buckley, Paul Lusk, and George Rivers. The four men enlisted in the US Army the following spring, McAfee as an officer, his friends as privates. McAfee served 18 months, including some time in France with Army engineers, before returning to the US in the summer of 1919. That fall, he was restored to service in the LAPD by Chief of Police Home. On December 20, 1919, working alongside Harry Raymond under the personal direction of Home, he raided two Chinese gambling dens near the old Tenderloin district and another run by Caucasians on West Third Street, crashing through a skylight in one raid to scoop up $1,500 from the tables of the astonished gamblers. Despite this bit of bravado, early in 1920 he was caught up in the same controversy that ended Harry Raymond's second chapter with the LAPD when Assistant City Attorney Jess Stephens declared that the restorations of McAfee and about a dozen other officers dismissed for cause were not legal. While he and the other officers ultimately prevailed in a suit to get their jobs back, McAfee announced soon afterward that he was leaving the force to enter business.

His business turned out to be gambling. Soon he was running gaming dens in downtown Los Angeles under the protection of Crawford and the tutelage of a longtime gambling figure in the city, Milton "Farmer" Page, whom McAfee and Harry Raymond had arrested during a raid in the basement of the Del Monte bar at 223 West Third Street in October 1919. As the twenties progressed, McAfee's star rose in the Los Angeles underworld as Page, who had a propensity for violence, attracted too much attention from law enforcement for Crawford and syndicate leaders.

In McAfee, affable and better educated than most members of the underworld sect, Crawford recognized leadership qualities that would help him control the often-discordant criminal elements of the city.[35] When Crawford left for Europe, McAfee was the natural choice to run vice operations, including managing relations with law enforcement. In Crawford's absence, McAfee reorganized the vice protection racket in the face of the new administration and police chief. By the time Crawford returned, McAfee had control of the racket, which he ran from his mahogany-lined office in the rear of Zeke Caress' bar at 326½ South Spring Street and he was not about to give it back to Crawford. Crawford responded by reinventing himself as a reformer, allying with Gustave Briegleb of St Paul's Presbyterian Church after joining the church and dropping a valuable ring into a collection plate in 1930. Skeptics, including Shuler, questioned the motivation behind the donations from a man who seldom followed a righteous path. Shuler thundered that he would "as soon baptize a skunk as Charley Crawford." Given that Crawford was under indictment for bribery and influence peddling related to a stock market scandal, his conversion seemed hypocritical. Still, after the indictment was dismissed later that year, Crawford donated $30,000 toward the erection of a parish hall in the church. Perhaps a miracle of redemption had occurred.[36]

Crawford's headquarters was a contemporary stucco building at 6665 Sunset Boulevard in Hollywood that was attached to an older wooden frame house in its rear. Real estate firms owned by George C. Copeland and Harry G. Spengler occupied part of the front building. They were separated from the older house by a wooden porch about eight feet wide. Beyond the porch, photographer Roger Fowler had offices in the older house. Crawford's personal office consisted of three rooms in the older structure, while two of his employees, stenographer Lucille Fisher, and his secretary, a young man named Ray Radke, had offices in the front building.

Fisher and Radke were in their own offices at 3:00 p.m. on Wednesday, May 20, 1931, when a handsome young stranger in his thirties sporting a pencil mustache climbed the steps of the porch and walked straight to the door of Crawford's office. Crawford must have been expecting him, Fisher and Radke declared later: he opened the French doors leading to the office, shook hands with the man and ushered him into his office congenially.

Less than an hour later, an ex-newspaper man named Herbert Spencer arrived and asked Fisher to announce him. Spencer, a police reporter and editor with the *Los Angeles Express* for over twenty years, was one of the city's "fixers" who could be called on by persons needing to get out of a jam with the police. He lived well, with an expensive house and expensive cars that made some wonder whether he also took money from the gamblers he counted his friends. He had recently resigned from the *Express* and bought a partial interest in a weekly magazine called *The Critic of Critics* that another veteran LA newspaper reporter, Frederic C. (Mike) Schindler, had started. Crawford was a patron of the magazine, which was attacking other Los Angeles underworld figures, in particular Guy McAfee. According to Schindler, Spencer went to see Crawford about rumors that he, Crawford, owned the magazine. He wanted the rumors quashed.

After Fisher announced Spencer's arrival, the doors to the office closed again. Shortly after four o'clock, Spencer's wife called. Fisher took the call and knocked on the office door. As the door opened, she noted that the three men were seated around Crawford's desk in the rear of the room. Told he was wanted on the phone, Spencer came out and spoke with his wife over the telephone, then returned to the office. A few minutes later, Crawford emerged with the stranger, whom he called Mr. Wilson, a name he used for any guest he did not wish to identify. He asked Radke to show Wilson to the lavatory.

After using the lavatory, the stranger returned to the office. Soon afterward, Fisher heard loud voices and the scraping of a chair. Two shots rang out, one slightly muffled, the other loud and clear. The door of the office opened. Spencer staggered out, his hand on his right chest, blood streaming through his fingers. He stumbled down the wooden steps of the old house, followed a short concrete walkway toward Sunset Boulevard and collapsed in front of the stucco building. Copeland, the real estate agent in the front building, rushed out of his office to help him, then ran back to his office to get water from a cooler. As he did, he thought he heard somebody in Crawford's front office room opening and riffling through desk drawers. A few seconds later the handsome stranger came out of the office, buttoning his coat, and looked about. Seeing Fowler, the photographer, through a window, the stranger asked, "Where did that man go?" He did not wait for an answer, but walked rapidly down the street before breaking into a run.

Inside his office, Charlie Crawford lay on his back, a cigar in one hand, a bullet wound in his stomach. Fisher, Radke, and employees of neighboring businesses rushed to his aid. Somebody called the police. Two patrolmen who happened to be passing on the street in a police car arrived quickly. In a few minutes, Crawford was on his way to the Georgia Street receiving hospital, alive but unwilling to say who shot him, unwilling even to give his own name. That evening, with his brother and Briegleb by his bed, the latter "praying fervently," he died. Just before he did, he told the pastor that "Dave" shot him.

The next day the morning newspapers headlined Crawford and Spencer's murder, printing the police bulletin description of the suspect. "An American, about six feet tall, weighing between 150 and 175 pounds, and between 35 and 40 years of age; hair, brown; a small black mustache; dressed in a neat blue suit and wearing a sailor straw hat, very neat appearance." The police checked Guy McAfee. He did not fit the description, but, as he himself admitted, he was a likely suspect. McAfee had an alibi, however. He gave the police the name of another suspect: Andy Foley, a local gambler making his way up in the local rackets whom Crawford reportedly feared. Not surprisingly, eastern racketeers trying to muscle into Los Angeles were also suspected. Police detective Frank James, responding to a report from LA County Sheriff investigators of warnings heard a month before that Crawford and Spencer were "marked for death" by the underworld, commented, "Crawford and

Spencer were put on the spot. There is no doubt of that. But here's the rub. There are 300 men in town who would have provocation for the job."[37]

Another possible suspect was Harry Raymond. Raymond, some said, hated Crawford because he felt Crawford had set him up in the Jacobson scandal. However, Raymond, five foot six and without facial hair, did not match the witnesses' description. However, it is likely that he also had a hand in identifying Crawford and Spencer's killer. To be sure, somebody had enough insight to put a picture of David Clark, currently a candidate for Municipal Court Judge, in front of Crawford's brother, George, who was in his automobile outside the Sunset Boulevard building when the killer emerged. George Crawford, Radke and Fisher all identified Clark as the third man in the room that afternoon. A bulletin for his arrest went out immediately.

The identification of Clark as a suspect in the killing of Crawford and Spencer set off a news frenzy in Los Angeles. Several months before, he had been a key deputy in Buron Fitts' office and was currently a candidate for Municipal Court Judge. He had prosecuted Albert Marco successfully for the latter's rampage at the Ship's Café. He had targeted gambling boats, liquor interests, and corrupt cops. A more unlikely suspect in the killing of an underworld figure and former reporter was hard to conceive.[38]

Clark surrendered to the DA that evening. He had spent the twenty-four hours after the shooting, driving and walking along the coast as far north as Malibu. He remained tight-lipped about the killings, observing, "Too many men are in the big house because they talked for the newspapers . . . . I'll do my talking in court when the time comes." He continued his campaign for Municipal Court Justice while in jail, his ads calling him "The Man Who Defied the Underworld." Although he lost the election, he received over 67,000 votes.[39]

In the meantime, Joseph Ford, whom Fitts brought out of retirement to serve as special prosecutor in the case, enlisted Harry Raymond to look for evidence to prove Clark's guilt. Raymond discovered that Clark recently attempted to borrow a gun from a Los Angeles policeman. Although the cop refused to lend it, Raymond and his fellow investigators figured Clark might have purchased another weapon elsewhere. They combed pawnshops and gun shops, looking for an invoice linked to Clark. They found one with Clark's name and address at Hoegee's Sporting Goods store on Main Street, dated May 19, the day before the shooting.

The gun was a key element in building a case against Clark, which, although strong, was circumstantial, as prosecutor Ford admitted readily. While there were several persons who identified Clark as the man who followed the dying Spencer out of Crawford's office, none witnessed the actual shooting. In addition, Special Prosecutor Ford could not provide a motive for Clark's actions. He told the jury that he "did not know the motives that actuated Dave Clark, but they were powerful ones. I can only speculate upon it. I am afraid, though, that Dave Clark's head has been turned. I am afraid that life has been too easy for him. I am afraid his handsome face, his remarkable bearing and his wonderful physique have made him selfish. I am afraid he has lost his soul." [40]

Clark's lifestyle had raised eyebrows in the town. As Joseph Ford suggested, he had started out well. An LA native, he had served with the Royal Flying Corps 5th Squadron during World War I after a short stint in the US Navy. After the war, he attended USC's School of Law. Admitted to the California Bar in 1922, he joined the District Attorney's office after four years in private practice. Despite his position and reputation for prosecuting gambling interests, he personally enjoyed the entertainment provided by the underworld, frequenting the top floor gambling parlors of Guy McAfee, sometimes accompanied by the proprietor himself. Indeed, insiders speculated that Clark's fervor in attacking gambling establishments was part of McAfee's strategy to harass competitors and keep control of the city's vice operations. [41]

At his trial, Clark did not deny that he had killed Crawford and Spencer, but instead pleaded self-defense. He told the court that for several months Spencer had advised him to stop attacking vice and the underworld in his campaign. The advice turned into warnings and the warnings into threats. Unnerved, Clark purchased a .38 Colt revolver for protection. He also contacted Crawford for help dealing with the increasingly aggressive Spencer. And he asked Crawford to help get Briegleb's support for his candidacy.

On the day of the shooting, Clark and Crawford met privately before Spencer arrived. Crawford revealed his plan to regain control of LA's vice operations through Briegleb's radio attacks on McAfee. He planned a massive political organization that would control Los Angeles for the near future and boasted that he had four members of the 1931 Grand Jury and DA Buron Fitts in his pocket.

After Spencer arrived, Crawford disclosed his price for aiding Clark. He wanted Clark to help frame Police Chief Roy Steckel. At this demand, Clark said he exploded with indignation.

"Did you want me to frame my good friend Dick Steckel, the chief of police? You dirty low-down skunks! You were indicted for framing Councilman Jacobson some time ago, now you join the church and profess to be a Christian and you throw a big diamond into the plate! You dirty skunk, I am going to leave. I am going out and I am from every platform that I get on, and from every radio I am going to tell the people what happened in this room. You are two rats!"

According to Clark, Crawford tried to pull a gun from his belt at this point. The two men struggled but Clark was able to jam his own gun into Crawford's abdomen and fire. As Crawford collapsed, Clark turned on Spencer, who was advancing on him and shot him as well. Spencer stumbled out the door onto the porch and staggered away.

While police never found Crawford or Spencer's guns, the jury of his second trial for murder (the first having been hung by a single juror voting for conviction) acquitted him.[42]

The murder of Crawford touched off a faux vice crusade by LA law enforcement, resulting in the closure of gambling joints owned by small timers. After the crusade subsided, McAfee's clubs, particularly the Forty-One Club in the penthouse suites of the American Storage Building on Beverly Boulevard, flourished unmolested while the former LAPD vice officer worked with other underworld leaders to consolidate and control operations throughout the city and county.

Gustave Briegleb's role in the final years of Charles Crawford did not serve him well. His onetime friend, Shuler, published a pamphlet entitled *The Strange Death of Charlie Crawford* that, without naming Briegleb, excoriated his role in Crawford's religious conversion. Noting that Crawford also became "quite a religious man" years before when the grand jury began to investigate Seattle's vice conditions, Shuler observed, "His trouble then, however, was finding a preacher who took his sudden change of heart seriously." In Los Angeles, Shuler implied, he found the preacher he needed in Gustave Briegleb, who buried him with tears in his eyes, calling Crawford a "true friend."[43]

Shuler's influence also waned in the coming decade. He lost his radio station license in November 1931. In 1932, he ran as the Prohibition Party candidate for the United States Senate, winning 25% of the vote. Ten years later, he ran for Congress but lost again. He continued to argue for reform, but secular figures, who decried the inevitable corruption and graft that resulted from the criminalization of sin more than the sin itself, soon assumed the leadership of the anti-vice movement.

*Guy McAfee (lower right) with fellow soldiers,
Thomas Buckley, George Rivers, and Paul Lusk.
California, World War I Soldier Photographs.]*

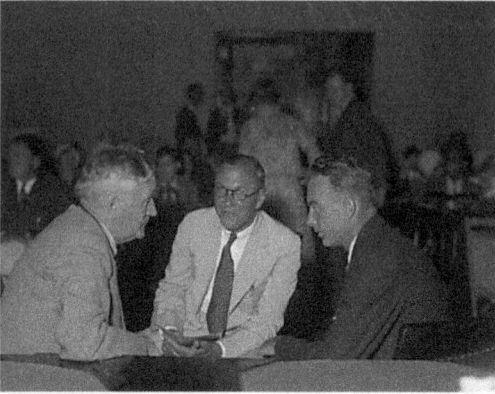

Dave Clark (right) with attorneys during his trial for murder. [Los Angeles Times Photographic Archive, UCLA Library. Copyright Regents of the University of California, UCLA]

Gustave Briegleb [Los Angeles Times Photographic Archive, UCLA Library. Copyright Regents of the University of California, UCLA]

Fighting Bob Shuler Testifying in 1929. [Los Angeles Times Photographic Archive, UCLA Library. Copyright Regents of the University of California, UCLA]

10: RAYMOND UNBOUND

After the second Jacobson trial, Raymond returned to private practice. Over the next few years, he advertised daily in the *Los Angeles Times*. "We never close," proclaimed some of his advertisements. Others referred to "Harry J. Raymond Detectives," the plural suggesting he had a staff supporting him. The newspaper ads offered the range of his services ("...civil and criminal investigations, expert shadowing of anyone, anywhere. Strictly confidential. 23 years' experience.)"[1]

Because most of his work was "strictly confidential," we know little of Raymond's activities of the early and middle 1930s. During his long career as a private investigator, he undoubtedly took on many cases that we will never know about. The private investigator owed his clients discretion and secrecy. In one case, however, we get a glimpse of the working detective. It involved the profligate son of a wealthy San Francisco lumberman named Dandridge Hunt Bibb. From a young age, Dandridge Hunt Bibb Jr. loved a party, particularly when it included wine, women and a little gambling. When he ran out of funds, he just cashed a check for more. After all, his father was a well-known business and political figure in the Bay area and he bore his famous father's name. When he presented a check—usually for services already performed or liquor already drunk—saloonkeepers in the city's Tenderloin figured it must be good.

By 1906, at the age of nineteen, Bibb had already been convicted once of check fraud, but that did not stop him from floating a bad check for $70 to a saloonkeeper named Schiff. When Schiff took the check to the bank, he was told that he had been "bunkoed." Schiff figured the father would soon take care of it. However, Bibb Sr. refused to pay up and even remonstrated with Schiff for having lured his son to a saloon. Schiff could do what he wanted, but, Bibb Sr. explained, his son had shipped out at sea, presumably as a merchant seaman, bound for England.

Schiff took the matter up with the police but, with the boy halfway across the globe, the cops could do nothing. In fact, young Bibb was in Chicago, where he was living the high life at fancy restaurants with chorus girls and had already passed $5,000 worth of bad checks, including one for a $2,000 automobile. Arrested and convicted, he escaped imprisonment after his father's wealthy and influential friends pleaded for leniency. In November, he was arrested again for passing a $50 bad check at a restaurant.

On November 13, 1906, Bibb was sentenced to one-to-fourteen years in the Illinois State Reformatory at Pontiac, Illinois. While the reformatory was established for juveniles between the ages of eight and sixteen, it also admitted a few older inmates who might benefit from educational and manual training opportunities. It is likely that his father's friends persuaded Chicago authorities to send him there instead of state prison. Bibb may have seemed an ideal candidate for reform, especially when one considered his wealthy upbringing, social prominence, and education, including two and one-half years of college. Yet, four years later, he was in trouble again for check forgery.

His newest victims included private individuals and businesses in both Chicago and California. A San Francisco detective tracked him to Jackson, Michigan, where he was living with his young wife and her infant son. This time, the privilege of incarcerating him fell to San Francisco and the state of California. Bibb Jr. explained he had intended to deposit funds to cover the check but was a day too late. Told of his father's refusal to cover the check, he blamed his father's "moody spells" for the parental neglect. In fact, however disgusted he might be with his errant son, the elder Bibb had legal problems of his own. He had fallen into disfavor with his one-time ally, Christopher Buckley, the Democratic Party boss in San Francisco, the same who, for a few years before the turn of the twentieth century, collaborated with Bartolo Ballerino to control Los Angeles's tenderloin district. Buckley had sworn out a complaint alleging that Bibb Sr. sold to another party a parcel of land Buckley had purchased from him already. The charges did not stick, but Bibb Sr. spent a few days in a Washington, D.C. jail cell. Meanwhile, his son was sentenced to five years in San Quentin.

Released from prison on September 1, 1912, after less than two years, Bibb Jr. returned to passing bad checks during a merry month's escapade with a young schoolteacher. He was returned to San Quentin until June 14, 1914. One senses that, by the time he got out of San Quentin the second time, his family had disowned him. His parents had divorced, his sister had married, and his father had quit the lumber industry to exploit patents he held with aviator John Joseph Montgomery, moving to London where he remained until his death in 1927. Once again, Bibb's freedom did not last long. He returned to San Quentin, where he would serve out the remainder of his sentence until January 1915.

For a dozen years after his release from San Quentin, the public record is largely silent on Bibb Jr. The San Francisco Chronicle reported that on Dec 5, 1915, he passed a bad check to a jeweler by claiming it was to purchase a diamond engagement ring for the sister of his landlady. It was a scheme he would use again. In April 1916, he married his second wife, Lenora, in Norfolk, Virginia. The relationship lasted until February 1917. A year later, he was still in Norfolk, serving in the US Army as a second Lieutenant. In the late 'teens through the mid-twenties, he likely spent his time going from city to city, working confidence games or forging checks to make ends meet, and serving minor time when caught. We find him under arrest in Dover, New Hampshire in September 1919 for forgery of a $1,000 check. In 1925, Chicago police sought him for passing $20,000 in bad checks.

What is certain is that, in July 1927, Bibb Jr. entered the home of publishing magnate William Randolph Hearst. He informed Hearst's secretary that he was a friend of Hearst's son and had an appointment with the great man. "Just tell him I'm here," he told the secretary, "He'll understand." While the secretary went to find his employer, Bibb slipped behind his desk and helped himself to six blank checks embossed with the publisher's name. When Hearst appeared, the two men had a short, amiable chat. After he left the Hearst mansion, Bibb forged the publisher's signature on one of the checks he had taken, payable to "George P. Mallary," an alias he used routinely, for $15,000. He opened an account at a New York City bank with the check, withdrawing $6,000 in traveler's checks immediately. It is possible that he mentioned to the teller he was on his way to Los Angeles; when police learned of the crime the following day, they suspected Bibb was headed there.[2]

He was still in New York City, however, where police arrested him on April 3, 1928, along with his wife, Elizabeth. The charges were not limited to check forgery. Bibb and his wife, whom he met in France during the war, were running a profitable auto theft business, shipping cars stolen in the United States to Canada and France and receiving cars stolen in France for sale in the United States. Some 300 automobiles had passed through their hands. Since New York wanted to prosecute him for the Hearst forgery, Bibb stayed in New York while Elizabeth was extradited to Georgia. Fortunately for Bibb (who was no longer Bibb Jr., his father having died in London in 1927), the court had no proof of his prior incarcerations in Pontiac and San Quentin. He received a light sentence of six months to three years. However, the prosecutor, Assistant District Attorney Charles J. Garrison, learned of his prior sentences and set out to substantiate them. In exchange for the dismissal of a charge for possessing a firearm, Bibb admitted his priors and received an additional five years.

After a stretch in Sing Sing, Bibb returned west, settling for a time in Los Angeles, where he courted Nina Ghirardelli, the former wife of Joseph Ghirardelli, heir to the chocolate business fortune.[3] Since the end of her marriage, her fifth, Nina had worked as a private music teacher and the leader of "Nina Ghirardelli's Famous Ladies' Orchestra," which played for local radio shows and patrons of the Blue Bird Cafeteria in the Hayward Hotel in downtown Los Angeles. She was living with her parents, who owned a home valued at $25,000, a significant amount in 1930. Bibb may have seen in her a meal ticket for his advancing years, but it just as possible the whole affair was a long con of with the end goal of passing a bad check, Bibb's specialty. In any case, that is what happened. Posing as J. D. Brooks, one of his usual aliases, Bibb wooed Nina, presumably inventing some background legend to impress a cultured woman who, although no longer young, may well have still possessed some of the radiance of her youth that had already ensnared four husbands, two of whom had been heirs to considerable fortunes. She accepted his marriage proposal sometime in the latter months of 1932. The betrothal required an engagement ring and Bibb was ready with a bad check to purchase one. He suggested Nina introduce him to her jeweler, J. W. Hopkins. The couple picked out a suitable diamond for the occasion and ordered a wedding ring to pick up later, a clever touch that set the jeweler's mind at ease about the worthiness of the $5,800 check that Bibb presented for the engagement ring. On December 23, 1932, the jeweler took Bibb's check and gave him the six-carat diamond ring.

When Nina learned of the phony check, she broke off the engagement. By that time, Bibb had lit off for the east coast.

Raymond began working the case with Detective Lieutenant Frank "Lefty" James in December 1932, after Hopkins complained to the LAPD. In April 1933, Chief of Detectives Joe Taylor received a tip from New York City detectives who were after Bibb for passing a bad check for $3,500. Bibb was on his way to Tucson and intended to cross the border to Mexico. After alerting Tucson police of the fugitive's plans, he dispatched Raymond and James to the Arizona city. The two Los Angeles detectives laid low for a couple of days at the Santa Rita Hotel. At last, Bibb arrived by airplane and checked into the hotel. The Tucson police seized him as he was arranging for a taxi to take him to Nogales, where he planned to board a train for Mexico City. He had a passport under the name R. R. McMullin in his pocket. Sewn in his pant legs were $63,000 in bonds stolen in a $2,000,000 robbery in New York City the previous summer.

Raymond and the other officers sweated Bibb throughout the night. Eventually, he admitted passing a fraudulent check for the diamond ring but maintained he won the bonds in a gambling game. The bonds had been taken on August 10, 1932, from a bank messenger in a violent robbery during which two New York cops were shot. Throughout the nation, police had been on the lookout for them. In fact, police departments kept lists of stolen bonds from various bank robberies, particularly those from the $2,000,000 robbery of the Lincoln [Nebraska] National Bank and Trust Company in 1930. They were easy to negotiate, especially from outside the country. Bibb was not known as a stick-up man, however, and he may have purchased them second-hand at a discount, or perhaps even won them through gambling using the funds he received from selling the engagement ring as a bankroll.

Although the New York authorities wanted Bibb for their investigation of the stolen bonds, Raymond pushed for keeping him in Los Angeles. Hopkins filed a writ of attachment against the bonds to recover his own money while a New York Grand Jury indicted Bibb on bad check charges.

There is no record of what happened to Bibb in the days and months following his arrest in Tucson. The newspapers seemed to have lost interest in him. It is possible that, even with his long criminal record, he received a mild stretch in the county jail. He may also have been returned to New York but ended up walking free after furnishing information about the stolen bonds. In any case, neither his criminal career nor his prison stays were over. In October 1938, he was booked into Folsom Prison as A. D. Brook, a variation on his favorite alias, after passing fraudulent checks in San Francisco County. In 1949, he died at the age 62. A man born into wealth and privilege who instead chose a career of deception and crime, he was buried at the Golden Gate National Cemetery in recognition for his service in World War 1.

In June 1933, six weeks after he clapped Bibb in a downtown LA jail cell, Raymond was appointed chief of the San Diego Police Department by Fred Lockwood, the new City Manager of San Diego. Lockwood was a long serving executive in San Diego's city government who had played critical roles in establishing the Army's Camp Kearny during the First World War and Naval Base San Diego shortly afterward. San Diego's recently elected city council had charged him with finding efficient administrators for city departments. For over a year, a civic group calling itself the Taxpayer's Vigilance Committee had pressured the city administrators to reduce salaries and expenditures; Lockwood himself received a salary of $4,800 per year, a reduction in pay of over 50%. Raymond would receive $3,600 per year.

After being sworn, Raymond declined to lay out his plans for the department, saying only, "the laws will be enforced," and that he opposed salary cuts among the force. "Police officers, who stake their lives and personal safety every day to protect every citizen in the city, should be the last ones to be considered for drastic salary cuts," he declared upon arriving at police headquarters. While this statement met with the approval of San Diego's cops, it may not have sat well with the city council, which was planning drastic cuts for other city employees, including firemen. Like the rest of the nation, San Diego in 1933 was suffering from over three years of financial depression. The city council's demands for wage reductions paralleled the efforts of

Congress and the new Administration in Washington, D. C., which planned to reduce the salaries of federal employees by fifteen percent.[4]

Although ten years of growth in the twenties had nearly doubled its population and raised hopes among its leading citizens that it might fulfill their long frustrated dream of a great southern metropolis, San Diego was still somewhat of a backwater to the burgeoning metropolis 120 miles to the north. Ten years before, its leading citizen, John D. Spreckels, had lamented that San Diego was "not the metropolis and seaport that its geographical and other unique advantages entitle it to be." Why does San Diego always just miss the train, somehow?" Spreckels asked. He then answered his own question: "LACK OF CO-OPERATION." Such an answer might have been expected from a man who had long played a major role in the politics of the city but whose plans and visions were often opposed by other civic leaders. It was not completely fair, however. The citizens of San Diego had united to fund great projects of civic improvement, including the two-year Panama-San Diego Exposition. They had also worked together to bring a railroad to the city, though their early dreams of being the western terminus of a transcontinental line had not been realized.[5]

The real problem with San Diego was its single geographical disadvantage: the mountain ranges to its east, which hindered a direct railroad link from the east and instead channeled tracks northwest along the Salton Sea basin, through the Coachella Valley and over the San Gorgonio Pass into the San Bernardino Valley. San Diego had built a direct link from San Bernardino through Riverside, Perris, Elsinore, Temecula, Fallbrook, and Oceanside but it proved untenable when winter storms turned the Santa Margarita River into a torrent that washed out the tracks. The line that replaced it, running from Riverside to Orange and Santa Ana, then south along the coast to San Juan Capistrano and Oceanside, did not altogether bypass the LA basin. In 1906, Spreckels began planning a railroad between Yuma and San Diego along the border between the United States and Mexico. The route crossed California's Imperial Valley and climbed over 2,000 feet up the Jacumba Mountains before heading south for eleven miles, including three miles of tunnels and wooden trestles, above the steep Carrizo Gorge. The task of building the railroad inspired engineers who plotted the track bed along treacherous terrain to nickname it the "impossible railroad." It was impossible for more than the engineering challenges of the Carrizo Gorge. To bypass the mountain ranges further west, the railroad dropped into Mexico, passing through the cities of Tecate and Tijuana before re-entering the United States through Tijuana. While the detour resolved some of the daunting geographical challenges to the railroad, it exposed it to the chaos of a nation on the verge of decades of political turmoil and banditry. Along with the 1907 recession and First World

War, which dried up funding for the railroad, the dip into Mexico proved an additional impediment to its success. By 1932, the desert heat, earthquakes, landslides, floods and tunnel collapses that beset the fledgling railroad had combined with Mexican revolutionaries and bandits to make the impossible railroad almost impossible to operate.[6]

The more favorable geographical location of Los Angeles enabled it to receive a higher number of Midwestern immigrants than San Diego in the half century after the United States seized California, leading to greater investments in business and industry. San Diego's natural harbor remained underdeveloped until the Navy established a base in the early twenties. Meanwhile, Los Angeles' own man-made harbor, which as late as 1920, the *San Diego Evening Tribune* and the *San Diego Union* dismissed as the "San Pedro lagoon" and continued to ridicule into the twenties, met the region's commercial seaport needs. By 1930, San Diego had one-eighth the population of Los Angeles. Still, its nearly 148,000 residents made it the 53rd largest city in the United States and the fourth largest in California.[7]

The San Diego police force Raymond led was one-tenth the size of Los Angeles', which in 1932 had a staff of 2,379 officers spread across 15 substations and 388 motor vehicles. Still, for a man who had supervised just a handful of subordinates as chief of police of Venice and head of the district attorney's detective staff, it was a large organization, with 227 officers in three substations, twenty-four of whom were motorcycle cops, and seventeen prowl cars equipped with one-way radios. It was also an unhappy force; four factions, each supporting different men for chief, had vied for power over the past few years while unaffiliated cops struggled to keep their jobs. During the last six years, six chiefs had come and gone. One, Percy Benbough, a San Diego businessman, tried to reorganize the force, transferring officers to new assignments. Despite his knowledge of San Diego politics (he later served as mayor), he lasted less than two months.

As in Los Angeles, rumors that a "ruling clique" controlled the police, allowing some gamblers to operate while others could not, were often repeated in city hall. Except for a single exception, during the late 'teens, twenties, and the first years of the 1930s, the department was run by a succession of short time chiefs. Several found themselves hampered by intrusive city councils on the one hand and resistant staff on the other. Raymond's predecessor, Robert Newsom, resigned on June 2, in order to give Lockwood free rein in selecting his subordinates; privately, he expressed his frustration with the politics of the position.

Raymond had been selected because of his "reputation for efficiency in force management" and as a man "with a record of getting things done."[8] Twenty-five years as a detective had taken him throughout the west and as far as Chicago and New York City, gaining him a wide reputation as a skilled and resourceful detective. He had driven the coast route to San Diego many times chasing automobile thieves. In fact, one of his earliest cases as a private investigator brought him to San Diego in pursuit of Dr. Otto William Houck, whose trade was to court elderly women and "borrow" money from them, and then disappear.

Raymond found his new office decked with flowers from local supporters. Hundreds of telegrams also arrived from friends and colleagues throughout the country. Not all San Diegans were happy he was the new chief of police, however. Two councilmen had voted against him, preferring a local man for chief, and several local aspirants for the job were "keenly disappointed" an outside man was selected. More significant was the unhappiness of the *San Diego Sun*, which complained, "all the talk about bringing in August Vollmer or some other internationally known police officer was merely propaganda to prepare us for bringing in Mr. Raymond."[9]

Soon after being sworn into office, Raymond's troubled reputation came to haunt him. On June 10, two local San Diego attorneys, Edger B. Hervey and W. K. Brown, told council members that in 1932 Raymond and another man, whom they did not identify, attempted to persuade San Diego police officers, including Police Chief Harry Scott, to go easy on a pair of con artists recently arrested in the city. One Raymond supporter on the council demanded that the attorney back up their charges with company records, declaring, "It is a well-known fact that there are always disgruntled job seekers and opposing political factions" trying to besmirch a new administration. In fact, rumors tying Raymond to LA underworld figures were swirling around city hall.

The following morning, Saturday, June 10, the council held a special session to hear the charges against Raymond. The new chief was allowed to choose whether the meeting should be open to the public, and he decided it should. First to address the crowded council chamber were Hervey and Brown, who related that in 1932, a man known as Ed Rice came to Brown's office complaining of police harassment. Two cops, identified as San Diego Chief of Detectives Kelly and Detective Jobbins, had arrested Rice and his friends as vagrants and were trying to run the whole group out of town. Brown said he told Rice all he could do was to arrange for a six month suspended sentence contingent on Rice and his friends leaving town. When Rice retorted, "Everyman has his price," Brown told him flatly neither Chief of Police Scott nor the detectives would take a bribe, and he himself wanted nothing to do with the case. At that point, Rice asked Brown to look up Harry Raymond's phone number in a Los Angeles Directory. As Brown listened in, Rice dialed the number. "He called the person on the other end, Harry,"

Brown told the council. "He said the boys were here and that five of them were arrested and that things were getting pretty hot. He said he wanted Harry to come prepared and to get ahold of Joe Fainer."[10]

Raymond came with attorney, Russell E. Parsons, an associate of Fainer. Around the same time, Rice visited the home of Police Chief Scott, the former chief told the council. Scott was not at home, but Rice talked with his wife, alluding in passing to a figure of $8,000. While Scott claimed he did not regard it as a bribery attempt, it was the same amount, in $1,000 bills, that was in Parson's possession when he and Raymond later visited his office to discuss Rice.

> [Raymond] asked me what could be done about Rice. I told him there was nothing doing in spite of claims some of the men made that they had fixed the chief, district attorney, and others. While we were talking the other man reached in his pocket and pulled out some folded currency. He seemed to be counting it. I don't know what he did it for. They told me that all they wanted in the cases was a suspended sentence so the men wouldn't have to leave town.
>
> I said I wanted Rice to surrender himself—he was out on $1,000 bail—so I could talk to him about these statements that he had fixed officers. I knew he hadn't fixed me.

Questioned further about the money, Scott declared, "I saw a $1,000 bill and I heard him count to eight."

Two San Diego detectives involved in the Rice bunko case, Jobbins and Kane, had already expressed concern to Scott that Rice threatened to get them fired, claiming he had "real pull" in the city. Scott told them not to worry. "Put him in jail and throw away the key," he advised them.[11]

Despite the stack of $1,000 bills, Scott did not believe Raymond and Parsons were trying to bribe him. Raymond wanted information on confidence men he was pursuing, Scott recalled. Chief of Detectives Kelly, who joined the meeting in Scott's office, corroborated Scott's impressions. Raymond did not try to get the San Diego police to ease up on Rice, he related. "We talked about bunko cases and Raymond said he was on the trail of bunks, including one Kent B. Marshall, who was supposed to have bunked a retired police lieutenant named Connolly." Kelly added that Rice entered prison on May 12, while Fainer told the council that Raymond furnished information leading to Rice's arrest in Oakland. The same information led New York police to arrest Marshall.

San Diego County District Attorney Thomas Whelan spoke before the council as well. Whelan explained he asked for a delay in Raymond's appointment so he could find out more about him. "I had heard Raymond was a clever detective but felt there should be a delay to investigate." After his request was denied, he drove to Los Angeles to get more information on Raymond, particularly about the Jacobson affair. "The whole mess didn't look so hot and that was why I wanted the council to look into it thoroughly," the district attorney declared.

It is doubtful the council gave the Jacobson matter much consideration, although one councilman observed, "It seems odd that two captains and some others would be tailing down a morals case. After Whelan read from the Jacobson trial testimony, San Diego Mayor John F. Forward told the chamber that he had checked Raymond's reference with the Automobile Club of Southern California. "I never heard a man given a more laudable report," he declared.

When given his chance to respond personally to the allegations, Raymond insisted he visited San Diego during the Rice affair to obtain information about Kent Marshall. He was working for Connolly, the former LA cop whom Marshall had defrauded out of $22,500, he explained. Rice called him between eight and ten times from San Diego to give him information on Marshall but never asked him to "fix things up" in San Diego. The councilmen were curious why Rice cooperated with Raymond. What did he want in return? "To squash the beef" Connolly had against Rice, Raymond said—to settle the dispute between the two for a return of half Connolly's losses. To the councilmen's surprise, he stated he kept good relationships with confidence men in order to keep an eye on them. They did not resent it when he arrested them, he explained, as long as the charge against them was fair.

After hearing from Raymond, the council voted unanimously to exonerate him. They accepted his statement he acted under the orders of a superior officer in the arrest of Jacobson. Hervey and Brown, who started the investigation with their report of Rice's phone call, followed up a few days later with an open letter to Raymond expressing their satisfaction with his exoneration and pledging support for him in the future. Overall, Raymond had a clean bill of health from those who previously doubted him. However, he was not in the clear.

The City Charter League, an organization founded in 1932 to "assist in carrying into effect the intent and full purpose of the new charter" persuaded District Attorney Whelan to convoke the grand jury to investigate the manner in which Raymond became chief. The league had already taken on the city government in several cases where, in its opinion, city officials were not keeping to the letter and spirit of the charter passed by voters in April 1931. It now argued that the charter mandated that the selection of chief of police was the responsibility of the city manager alone and that councilmen were prohibited from influencing him in his task. In fact, it was a misdemeanor for councilmen to try to influence the city manager in appointing the chief.

The *San Diego Sun* had already charged that Raymond had been selected by city councilmen prior to Lockwood's formal appointment, claiming that, "the council had made up its mind about who should be chief of police before it had made up its mind as to who should be city manager and the appointment was only a gesture of compliance."

For four days, the grand jury heard testimony from the mayor, the city manager, the previous city manager, and all the councilmen. All denied having influenced or attempted to influence City Manager Lockwood's decision to appoint Raymond as chief of police. However, in view of a report in the *San Diego Union* in April that Councilman Dan Rossi had visited Raymond in Los Angeles (and obtained a copy of a book Raymond had written entitled *How I Convicted Five Murderers of Los Angeles Police Officers*), it is difficult to believe Rossi, at least, was entirely innocent. According to the *San Diego Union*, three other councilmen had also actively supported Raymond's appointment.

Raymond does not seem to have been bothered by the investigations. On taking office, he focused on curbing traffic violations in the city, declaring its high fatality rate was a "blot on the reputation of the city." He also launched an anti-vice campaign, declaring, "I don't know if there is any vice in the city or not" but, if there were, he expected the vice squad to clean it up. The squad raided some brothels and gambling joints. Within a few days, whatever vice the city offered before was gone. In fact, since 1912, when San Diego shut down the notorious Stingaree District along the waterfront, to where many prostitutes fled when Los Angeles closed its crib district, there had been little prostitution or gambling in San Diego. The Mexican border town of Tijuana just a few miles south fulfilled San Diego's illicit entertainment needs, which grew as the Navy settled in after World War 1.[12]

An immediate problem was the threat of some 2,500 left-wing radicals preparing to descend on San Diego. Raymond declared there would be no repetition of the Memorial Day riots that occurred just days before he became chief—in fact, he would not allow demonstrations of radical unionists at all. Undoubtedly, this was a position that gained him favor with the conservative citizens of San Diego. The city had not suffered a serious radical union disturbance since 1912, when members of the International Workers of the World flocked from throughout the nation to protest an ordinance banning public speaking in a six-block area in downtown San Diego. Local police and armed residents had responded with violence against the protesters.

Attacking vice, traffic fatalities, and radicals was a good strategy for a new chief in 1933. It needed to be supplemented by a focus on reducing violent crime, but that would come later. Raymond now concentrated on the San Diego Police Department's internal organization. After the city council agreed to allow him to fill four open positions on the force while denying his request to hire any additional officers, he quickly reorganized the department, shifting approximately 100 officers to new duties. He also returned Lieutenant George Sears, who had been "shipped" to the La Jolla substation two years before, to the central Vice Squad. Additional changes came quickly. The reorganization angered many within the clique-ridden department, but it indicated the new chief's determination and vision.

His supervisory duties notwithstanding, Raymond found time to take personal action in several cases. On June 28, he slipped back into Los Angeles to arrest Charles Gilsten, an east coast rumrunner and member of a gang that specialized in the theft of securities. Gilsten was on his way by plane from New York to Los Angeles with stock certificates worth $20,000 that had been stolen from a bank messenger in New York City on May 25. Like his friend Dandridge Bibb, Gilsten claimed he won the certificates in a crap game. Raymond brought him back to San Diego but had to release him after the San Diego district attorney declined to file charges, noting that neither he nor Raymond had jurisdiction in Los Angeles County where the arrest was made. Raymond kept the bonds, however, turning them over to the insurance company.

The Gilsten affair did not sit well with all San Diegans, however. The *San Diego Sun* caustically observed that Raymond was a "clever detective" but he had no business in doing the work of Los Angeles law enforcement.[13]

More problems for Raymond quickly followed. In the middle of his second month as police chief, around 8:30 in the morning on Tuesday, July 18, Dalbert Aposhian, the seven-year-old son of a clothing cleaner and Baptist Minister, left his father's store at 1351 Fifth Avenue with his friend, nine-year-old Jackie Confar, to go to the Kress Store a few blocks south. According to Jackie, after visiting the store, the two boys parted, Dalbert heading for the San Diego Zoo while Confar went to his mother's fur store. When Dalbert did not return to his father's store that evening, his parents contacted police, who began searching the city for him.

In the following days, police searched throughout the area for the missing boy. Attendants at the zoo were familiar with the boy, but they had not seen him on the day he went missing. However, several sightings were soon reported. He was seen playing near his father's store in the late afternoon of the day he disappeared. A taxicab driver claimed Dalbert approached him early Wednesday morning—the day after he disappeared—at the corner of Second Avenue and Broadway and asked to sleep in his taxicab. The boy claimed he was from Pasadena and was visiting his aunt in San Diego. As the cabbie left to pick up a fare, he noticed the boy walking north on Second Avenue. On hearing the taxicab driver's report, his mother speculated the boy had become confused. He lived in San Diego but had an aunt in Pasadena, not vice versa.

After suspending a planned drive against illegal slot machines in the city, Raymond mobilized the police force to search for the boy, who they believed had run away from home and was afraid to return for some unknown reason. Three hundred Boy Scouts searched Balboa Park. More sightings of young Dalbert were reported in the next few days. Then, on Monday, July 24, six days after he disappeared, sailors on a Navy vessel found his body, fully clothed in the garments in which he disappeared Tuesday morning, floating about 100 feet off North Island in San Diego Bay.

It was a horrific sight. The boy's eyes were gouged out, his ears and tongue were cut off, and the right wrist was almost severed. Dr. D. F. Toomey, the county autopsy surgeon, estimated that he had been dead four or five days. When the surgeons opened the child's head, they found evidence of a severe hemorrhage. The skull was not fractured, but the discolored throat bore signs of strangulation.

Chief Raymond and Captain Kelly conferred with the autopsy surgeon and the coroner. All agreed the child had been tortured and murdered before the body was thrown into the sea. The mutilations had occurred before death.

After the meeting, Raymond admitted he had no suspects. When asked how he would investigate the crime, Raymond declared, "We are going to do police work." Police work involved searching Balboa Park and deserted boats, shacks and other possible hiding places along the waterfront for the murder site. It also meant rounding up the city's degenerates and any vagrants unlucky enough to be around when police detectives or patrolmen came looking.[14]

Outrage over the murder spread nationwide. In San Diego, women's organizations demanded action by county and city law enforcement and governmental agencies against "known degenerates, feeble-minded, congenital perverted and all irresponsible criminals." When the police were unable to find a suspect quickly, the *San Diego Union* expressed its exasperation. "No definite clues! No indications of an immediate arrest." District Attorney Whelan blamed the Aposhian atrocity on the "laxity of judges and probation officers in dealing with degenerates."

"It may be that we are not making the headway in this case which some persons think we should make," Raymond responded, "but I am confident that we will find the slayer of the Aposhian boy. I admit that Monday night we were up against a blank wall. But now the outlook is brighter for capturing the perpetrator of this crime, certainly one of the most dastardly in the history of California."[15]

Raymond's attitude did not sit well with the *San Diego Sun*. Even before the Aposhian death, the paper had played up claims the city was in the midst of a "crime wave" and editorialized that the once competent police force had grown flabby under his leadership. Now it editorialized on the front page that authorities, particularly the new chief of police, had to "Stop San Diego's Crime Wave."

> Some time ago we imported a chief of police who has a reputation as a detective. He may not be to blame but it is obvious the underworld felt welcome here since his arrival. The department has been in a ferment since he came. His appointment was admittedly political . . . .[16]

The *Sun*'s editorials and crime coverage reflected a national-wide dread and rage. It seemed criminals were ascendant everywhere, and the authorities were unable to stop them. Shortly after Raymond took over as police chief, gunmen killed four law enforcement personnel, including an unarmed FBI agent in an attempt to free a prisoner at the Union Station in Kansas City. Criminal bands—led by the likes of Bonnie and Clyde, John Dillinger, Baby Face Nelson, and Alvin Karpis—were terrorizing the Midwest, earning infamy that would be retold in scores of pulp magazines, Hollywood films, and books over the coming decades. Throughout the summer of 1933, newspapers in San Diego and elsewhere recounted kidnappings and the threats of kidnapping daily. A chief who seemed complacent about the threat of crime—as Raymond did when, after a series of burglaries and robberies over the July 4th weekend, he observed that San Diego crime outbreaks were cyclical and caused by "outside criminals [who] go down to Tijuana, do a little gambling, and turn a little job on the way home to make up for what they've lost"—was asking for trouble.[17]

Kidnapping for profit was not the only form of the crime, of course. Kidnapping of children by sexual predators was a menace that involved all social and economic classes. Young Dalbert's murder evoked this latter threat, prompting newspapers to compare his death to William Hickman's slaying of Marion Parker. The newspapers also focused on six recent unsolved slayings in San Diego County, some with sadistic elements.

The first murder involved ten-year-old Virginia Brooks, who disappeared while on her way to school in 1931. After weeks of searching and false reports of sightings of the girl in Arizona, Los Angeles, Portland, and San Francisco, a sheepherder's dog found the girls' mutilated remains in a burlap sack near the Camp Kearny military base.

Brooks' murderer was never identified, nor was the killer of Louise Teuber, an eighteen-year-old woman who fled her parent's home after a fight with her father. Picnickers found her body at the base of Black Mountain in northern San Diego County a month after the discovery of Brooks' mangled body. Naked except for shoes and stockings, she was hanging by the neck from an oak tree in a half-sitting position, her feet touching the ground, a rope stretching over a tree limb and fastened to a bush twenty feet from the tree.[1] The murderer of prostitute Dolly Bibbens, beaten and strangled in her San Diego apartment a few days before Teuber's body was found, also was never identified.[1] While a man was tried for the death of Hazel Bradshaw, whose body was stashed in some bushes in a Balboa Park Boy Scout Camp after she was stabbed seventeen times in May 1931, he was acquitted.

More recently, in Raymond's first month as chief, a thirty-seven-year-old contractor named Claude Trader disappeared after climbing into a car with a man who asked him to estimate a painting job in Escondido. Trader's body was found among some wild grape vines on San Pasqual Road. He had been shot in the temple. A San Diego City policeman, Gerhard Cordes, soon emerged as the key suspect. Eventually acquitted, Cordes would slash a woman's throat a year later and murder a second in Texas in 1952.

While the police continued searching the waterfront for clues in the Aposhian death, the *Sun* engaged the former San Diego County Psychiatrist, T. Coe Little, to produce a psychological profile of the killer.

> The sadist was a young man, not over 30 years of age. Eliminate from consideration all middle-aged, elderly or old men. The evidence on the child victim's body plainly points to a young, full-blooded man, physically strong.
>
> Sadistic torture was continued through a period of 48 hours. The number of mutilations reveals this. Such extended orgy of blood lust could only be the set of a young man. Incredible as it seems, the child victim could have been kept alive during that long period of torture.
>
> The mutilation did not occur outdoors. Eliminate all futile search of open air places, the waterfront or parks. Such protracted torture as revealed by the child victim's body could not have been continued in an open place without detection. Nor would such a place fit the perverted requirements of the sadist.
>
> Seek some secluded house where such an extended orgy could have been perpetrated undetected.
>
> An old man would have satisfied his abnormal tendencies by one or two slashes. A middle-aged man could not have continued the torture of perversion for more than a short period. Look for a young man, who vented his sadistic fury in the privacy of a house until his victim died, and then transported the body by car to the bay, where it was thrown into the water.[18]

In the days following the discovery of the corpse, police detained several men, but none was bound over for trial. Los Angeles County Sheriff Eugene Biscailuz dispatched Virgil P. Gray, one of his tops investigators, to help San Diego Sheriff Ed F. Cooper investigate the county's unsolved murders, but Gray was not authorized to enter the Aposhian investigation.[19]

On August 2, another Los Angeles cop, Detective Chief Joe Taylor, announced he had the Aposhian killer in custody. Raymond and Captain Kelly rushed to Los Angeles to take custody of the man, a nineteen-year-old named Phillip Edwards. Edwards claimed he befriended the boy on Tuesday, July 18 and then took him via streetcar to a secluded area in East San Diego, where he hit him on the head with a large rock. Later that evening, he stole a car and transported the body to the waterfront, where he cut off his ears and performed other mutilations with a butcher knife, disposing the body parts in a jar he threw in the ocean.

Sailors from the Navy base searched the water outside the San Diego Rowing Club, where Edwards said he sank the bottle after he weighted it down with an iron bar in a gunnysack. However, several of Edwards' friends came forward to declare they were with him throughout the day on which Dalbert disappeared. Around 11:00 a.m., when Edwards claimed he was with the Aposhian boy, he had rented a rowboat from the club and rowed out to a naval vessel in the harbor searching for a sailor friend. Other inconsistencies in his narration soon led Raymond to doubt his confession, though Kelly and Captain S. J. McCaleb of the LAPD believed it. Edwards modified his statement to adapt to the unsought alibis of his friends but finally gave up the game and admitted it was a hoax. "I did it to effect a reconciliation with my estranged wife," he declared, but police were finished believing anything he said. After he drafted a telegram to a national magazine offering his life story for $2,000, he belittled the police for having fallen for his hoax and alleged Los Angeles police had "forced . . . his confession." His family and the district attorney agreed the best place for him was a mental institution.[20]

Raymond now had no suspect in the Aposhian death. He had even bigger problems, however. Los Angeles Coroner A. F. Wagner had journeyed from Los Angeles on the behest of San Diego County Sheriff Cooper and LA Sheriff Detective Virgil Gray to participate in a second autopsy on Dalbert's body, which had been exhumed for the purpose. Wagner joined with several other doctors to suggest that the apparent mutilations of the corpse were the work of fish and sea crabs.

Other San Diego authorities rejected Sheriff Cooper and Wagner's contentions. Deputy District Attorney John T. Holt, assigned to the case by District Attorney Whelan, reacted with contempt. "[T]he Sheriff offers a new contribution to science," he remarked, "He has discovered a fish that can commit such an attack upon a human as only another human can commit; a fish that is particularly 'choosy' in selecting morsels on which to feast; a fish that could choke the child, drain every drop of blood from his body, and then replace the clothing without the sign of a blood stain or clot, and without even tearing the clothing to get to parts of the body that could not be reached without literally tearing the clothing away." Investigators from the DAs office also recalled that other bodies recovered from sea had not exhibited similar disfigurement. Dr. Percy S. Barnhart of the Scripps Oceanography in La Jolla also disputed whether any marine life would eat a human body.[21]

Chief Raymond's response was even stronger. Cooper's theory was "too ridiculous to be considered" and an "insult to the intelligence of the people of this county." Raymond released a written statement declaring the entire staff of the San Diego Police Department, aided by law enforcement agencies and veteran groups throughout the state would continue to "work hard and never stop until the atrocious murder and all other murders heretofore committed in our community will be solved." Raymond continued,

> There is no place in San Diego for degenerates, murderers, racketeers and criminals. Unjust criticism at this time by certain politically minded individuals and publications only lend aid and comfort to these enemies of society. I ask that all service clubs, women's organizations and citizens continue their co-operation with the police department to the end that the elimination of all degenerates, criminals and racketeers will become a reality instead of a hope.[22]

Casting the investigation as a crusade against the city's "degenerates" placed Raymond in the camp of the women's club leaders who demanded a roundup of local sexual deviants. While the council voted not to hear the demands of the women's organization until the police had time to pursue the Aposhian killer, one councilman suggested the city petition the California legislature to sterilize all convicted degenerates. A letter-writer supported his idea, praising similar action in Germany by its new chancellor, Adolf Hitler.

How much this was a strategic move on Raymond's part is hard to tell. In late July, *The San Diego Union*, responding to the Aposhian death, editorialized against "known degenerates who roam at large under no surveillance." The paper complained the police department was a "political fief" that needed to obtain "the best professional police administrator available, pay him a salary commensurate with his job, keep his hands off details and insist plainly and openly upon results." The current police department operates "as a collections agency, 'bearing down' here, easing up there, suiting itself to the plans of some unofficial boss and shifting its men and jobs about as that boss, or bosses, may dictate," the newspaper complained.[23] Clearly, it did not think the city had found the needed man when it hired Harry Raymond.

On August 8, Raymond blasted the Sheriff again, complaining that instead of focusing on unsolved murders in the county, deputies were wasting their time arresting "petty criminals and alleged prostitutes." He asked the Sheriff to cooperate in finding the killer responsible for the "fiendish slaying of Dalbert Aposhian." George Aposhian, doctors and morticians also ridiculed the Sheriff's theory. "I say the boy was murdered unless we have trained fish in our bay that can undress a person, perform an operation upon him, and then redress him," declared J. D. Smith, the mortician who directed the mortuary where the original autopsy was conducted. "The boy's clothes were in perfect order. Every button was buttoned. I think the theory of drowning was out of the question because there was no water found in the lungs. The lacerations on the tongue was too far back in the mouth to have been done by fish."[24]

Following the second autopsy of Dalbert's body, Wagner returned to Los Angeles with a portion of the boy's neck to perform a "pathological examination" for evidence of strangling. He issued a detailed report analysis five days later. After first observing that a finding of death by homicide would be unavoidable were there evidence of mutilation by a sharp knife or spermatozoa in the boy's large intestine, Wagner tested each of these claims in sequence. In the end, his conclusion was clear. "The only logical conclusion to be reached," Wagner declared, "Is that the child was drowned and subsequently mutilated by marine animal life."[25]

Sheriff Cooper issued a statement accompanying Wagner's report that pulled few punches. He charged that Raymond, Coroner Gunn, and Autopsy Surgeon Toomey "made statements to the press ridiculing [me] without first having made a thorough examination of all the facts I had secured in my investigation." Charging that Toomey's statements about the cause of Aposhian's death were "made on assumption and not on facts," he listed seven points where the Autopsy Surgeon mischaracterized or mishandled evidence. As for Raymond, Cooper asked, "Why did not the chief of police ascertain the true facts before questioning my efforts in solving the case? Why did not Chief Raymond accept my co-operation when the strength of my office was tendered him? How can he explain to the public of San Diego why Jackie Confar was not questioned for several days after Dalbert's disappearance? Why did he not take advantage of the statement made by Jackie Confar that 'Dalbert is in the bay.' Why, if Chief Raymond knew that the Edwards boy was lying, as he stated, did he let the entire police department waste three whole days running down Edwards' fake and ridiculous statements?"[26]

In addition, Sheriff Cooper had noted discrepancies in the account of Dalbert's friend, Jackie Confar. Cooper pressed Confar, who admitted that Dalbert had not left him to go to the zoo but insead joined him in a trip to the waterfront Tuesday morning. He recounted their adventures along the bay that morning: meeting other boys, playing on a junk pile of discarded wheels, crank cases, wires and other engine parts, climbing on top of a train engine, watching boats unloading lumber. A few boys who were fishing gave them some bait and an improvised hook, he recalled. Jackie and Dalbert dropped their fishing line in the water beneath the pier and waited for a fish to bite. A few times, they descended through an opening in the planks to check if they had caught anything. Finally, they decided to try the other side of the pier. They dropped down through the opening and began crossing under the pier on some boards laid on the substructure, the older boy in front and Dalbert following with a rope tied to a gunnysack. After Jackie took a few steps along the pathway, however, he lost confidence in the sturdiness of the thin boards. He told Dalbert to lead them back to the surface. Dalbert turned around, shifting the rope from one hand to the other, took a couple steps, and fell.

Jackie heard him splash in the bay. He crept up to where Dalbert had fallen and looked down. "He was hitting at the water just like you do when a lot of wasps get after you," Jackie told the investigator. "He was just hitting at the water, first one and then the other. He was moving his mouth around—think he had it full of water."[27]

Jackie watched his friend trying to swim for a few seconds. He said nothing. Then he climbed up to the top of the pier. A few older boys were there. Jackie did not speak to them. He returned to the store of his father and mother. When they asked where he had been, he replied that he had been at the Kress department store. He did not tell them about Dalbert.

When the Sheriff's investigator asked him why he had not tried to help Dalbert or gone for help, he told them he was scared. Dalbert's father had warned him never to take Dalbert to the waterfront.

Harry Raymond had lost skin in the dispute with the sheriff. In the coming weeks, his detectives struggled to regain traction. Even the district attorney, caught between the two main law enforcement bodies of his county, was unsure whether to continue the investigation. Reluctant at first to grant a "John Doe" warrant for the murderer, he agreed to do so after talking again with the physicians who attended both autopsies. On August 17, Coroner Gunn closed the case in his office, filing it officially as a murder, a legal act that would help keep it open until police found the murderer.

Meanwhile, Raymond returned to other duties. He shuffled personnel between jobs and locations, actions that no doubt annoyed many of those impacted, including residents of South Beach. Along with Mission Beach and Pacific Beach, the community had been plagued for over a year by a burglar the local newspapers dubbed the "bedroom bandit." A group of citizens, led by a deputy district attorney named John Holt complained Raymond had transferred experienced officers out of the community and replaced them with men unfamiliar with the area. They demanded not only the return of the former officers but also ten additional cops until the bandit was captured. Raymond declared the police were doing all they could do to capture the man, who died a few months later when a private citizen whom he awakened shot him.

However, the new chief was acquiring new supporters as well as new detractors. The South Beach citizens' complaint was offset when another group of citizens, the California Defense League, representing Mission Bay and Pacific Beach, issued a proclamation praising Raymond for the efficient patrolling of the area and asked him to help reduce telephone toll fees for their district so more citizens could afford phones to call police when necessary.

Inevitably, with strained resources, some groups would feel underserved; it was more remarkable there were citizens and communities satisfied with the police protection they received. However, criticism of his performance was mounting day by day, until the *Sun* demanded his resignation in an editorial on August 22. Raymond responded to the editorial that day. "Somebody must have a distorted sense of humor if they are circulating the rumor that I intend to resign," he declared. "I will be in office long after some of my critics are gone."[28]

A week later, Raymond took some friends to the Hofbrau at the corner of State and C in downtown San Diego. The restaurant had opened a month before, serving newly legal beer and offering dancing to Eddie Wheeler and his Fox Theater Orchestra. According to the *Sun*, which, unlike other San Diego newspapers, took care to detail the event, Raymond entered the establishment with his three friends shortly after midnight. The place was busy and he and his party had to wait for service. The delay annoyed Raymond. He was further annoyed when the bartender, assuming a dollar bill Raymond held over his shoulder was in payment for the drinks, took it from his hand. Raymond scolded the bartender, threatening to show him "what will happen to this place," and stormed out of the restaurant. A few minutes later, several police officers arrived with Vice Squad leader Lieutenant George Sears and demanded all dancing stop in compliance with a city ordinance requiring all dance halls to close at midnight. When the Hofbrau's owner protested that the police were singling out his establishment, Sears contacted Raymond, who radioed all patrols to close all open beer establishments in their area. Several late night establishments were shut by the order while Sears' men waited outside the Hofbrau with a paddy wagon, into which they directed inebriated customers leaving the café.

After the incident, the *Sun* renewed its calls for Raymond's resignation. Raymond responded to the criticism, which was coming not just from the *Sun* but other San Diego papers and prominent citizens as well, by claiming he was merely enforcing a law the city council passed in July. He stated he had taken action against the Hofbrau and other beer halls after numerous complaints and his own direct observation. His self-justification, however, did not win over his critics, including City Manager Lockwood. On September 2, Lockwood fired Raymond, stating,

> He hasn't executive ability. He cannot reorganize, and much reorganization is necessary in the police department. He is temperamentally unfit for the job. He simply isn't the man for the job.[29]

Lockwood appointed former Police Chief Jack T. Peterson to succeed Raymond. Peterson, whom Raymond had transferred "to the sticks," began returning others similarly exiled back to the central station.

While some observers believed Raymond's firing was the result of conflicts between various police and political factions within San Diego, it is clear his zeal also played a larger role. Readers who have spent long years toiling in organizations will recognize the pattern: an ambitious, "visionary" manager is brought in from the outside and proceeds to rough everything up, reassigning personnel, establishing new goals, enforcing new requirements, disciplining and threatening long serving staff. Meanwhile, the rank and file grows sullen and resentful. Eventually, the new manager makes a mistake and the oppressed pounce. Finally, without acknowledging their own mistakes, his superiors cashier him, declaring he is not fit for the job. The employees are left to wonder why management thought he was right for the job in the first place.

Raymond had served as police chief in Venice fifteen years before and led the Los Angeles District Attorney's detective squad briefly in the mid-twenties, but these jobs involved supervision of only a handful of subordinates. He had never demonstrated serious executive ability, never had to manage men who supervised other men or budgets. He did not have the "reputation for efficiency in force management" the San Diego City Manager claimed he possessed when he hired him; he was a skilled detective, a tough cop, a fearless man, that was all. His fiercest critic, the *San Diego Sun*, perceived his limitations from the start, and even took to mocking him as an "imported . . . crime detector."[30] The paper, which, like other San Diego organs, wanted a "reorganization" of the San Diego Police, complained loudly that Raymond's energetic, if perhaps misguided, reassignment of personnel was nothing more than a "shake-up" that ignored civil service rules. To some extent, his successors achieved the "reorganization" the papers demanded by simply undoing the transfers Raymond had engineered, thus reorganizing the force back to its former organization.

As the *Sun* acknowledged after Raymond's dismissal, it had opposed his appointment from the start. Despite pledging to give him a chance, it pounced on him almost immediately. From the perspective of eighty-five years, the idea he alone was responsible for the "San Diego crime wave" of the summer of 1933, much of which involved robberies and psychopathic murders, seems absurd; the paper began to blame him less than one month after he took office. His dismissal, however, was inevitable. He demonstrated that, while a brilliant detective, he was not temperamentally fit for managing a large staff. He let his temper get the better of him repeatedly, refused to indulge reporters, and was curt, short, and narrow-minded in his definition of what the job of police chief entailed in even a moderately sized city. It required not just "police work" but PR work as well.

Why did they pick him in the first place? One paper, the weekly *San Diego Herald,* had an answer. Throughout the three months of Raymond's tenure, the *Herald* decried Raymond's focus on controlling petty vice in the city, complaining the whole purpose of his anti-vice campaign was to establish a "closed" town that would enable corrupt politicians to extract payoffs from vice figures. Alternatively, and somewhat contradictorily, the paper viewed the anti-vice campaign as the machination of Baron Long, a Los Angeles business and gambling figure and a partner in the Agua Caliente racetrack. Long and several San Diego councilmen wanted to close the city so sailors and citizens looking for gambling or sex would head for Tijuana, just across the open border. Either way one cut it, in the *Herald's* view, Raymond had been a tool of vice leaders.

The Aposhian case remained open with the San Diego Police for seventy more years. Although the San Diego police continued to hunt Dalbert Aposhian's killer, their pursuit became less newsworthy and more futile as time passed. Press attention shifted to the bit players caught up in the dragnet over the purported torture slaying. Phillip Edwards earned himself time in the county road camps for his false confession; when he got out a year later, he was sent to a mental ward after passing bad checks at several downtown San Diego merchants. Another temporary suspect in the case, E. Bassett Curtis, who two young boys claimed had shown them indecent pictures and attempted to molest them, received four months in jail. In 2005, San Diego cold case detectives and medical examiners determined the original examination by Toomey did not recognize the signs of feeding by fish and crustaceans. The San Diego Police Department formally closed the case.

The Man Who Never Was: A Newspaper Artists Conception of the Murderer of Dalbert Aposhian [San Diego Sun, Jul 27, 1933]

Consensus of opinion by various psychiatrists gives the following description of the fiend murderer:

Young man, 30 years or less.
Physically strong.
Smooth faced, no outstanding facial peculiarities.
Well-dressed.
A car owner or driver.
Owner or tenant of a house, not a homeless vagrant.
Sly, secretive, a lone wolf.

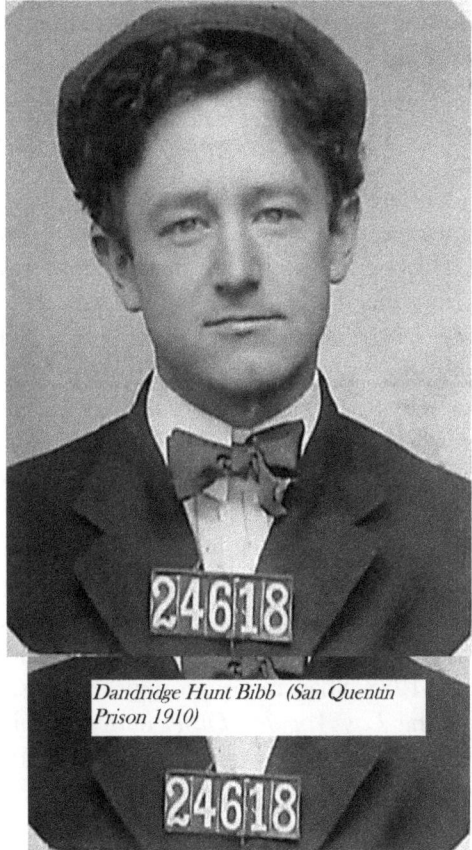

Dandridge Hunt Bibb (San Quentin Prison 1910)

11: LA ON THE SPOT

Harry Raymond returned to Los Angeles in early September 1933. He had not been away completely. As the *San Diego Sun* noted, in San Diego he had lived in a hotel room and returned to LA frequently. Whether his wife, Beulah, accompanied him, is not clear but it is not likely. He probably had not shuttered his detective business, either. The building that housed it at 238 West First Street in downtown Los Angeles was damaged in the March 1933 Long Beach earthquake, but Raymond's frequent absences from San Diego suggest that he supervised some   staff—perhaps subordinate operatives, including a former sports reporter named William Smith, throughout the summer.

Major changes had taken place in the City of Angels since he became San Diego's chief of police. There was a new mayor and a new but familiar police chief.

The new mayor was Frank Shaw, a property investor and businessman in the southern section of the city. Shaw was a Canadian by birth, and whether he had been legally naturalized as an American citizen became a matter of debate in the 1933 mayoralty election. His family had moved to Hays, Kansas, in the 1880s when he was a young boy and, after a few years homesteading in Colorado, had wound up in Joplin, Missouri. After working as a grocery salesman in Joplin, Shaw had moved with his wife, Cora, to Los Angeles around 1908. He continued to work as a salesman in the grocery business until 1925, when he was elected to the Los Angeles city council as a representative of the city's eighth district. In 1927, he was endorsed by the Central Labor Council, which was trying to unionize city employees, and the Cryer/Parrot administration. He won re-election easily. The *Los Angeles Times*, although a fervid opponent of the Cryer/Parrot administration and organized labor of any stripe, had also endorsed him.

In 1928, Shaw ran for county supervisor, again with Parrot's support. This time, the *Los Angeles Times* endorsed his opponent, incumbent J. H. Bean, labeling Shaw "the wheel-horse of the Parrot-Cryer machine." Four years later, however, the paper supported Shaw for a second term, calling him a man of "integrity, capability, and industry" and praising his accomplishments in controlling the county's budget and reducing taxes, always key goals of the paper's publisher, Harry Chandler. The following year, however, when Shaw ran for LA mayor, the *Times* backed incumbent Mayor John C. Porter, claiming that Shaw was again in the clutches of Parrot, who was attempting a comeback after being shut out of city politics during the four years of Porter's mayoralty. Despite the *Times'* opposition, which targeted Shaw's dubious citizenship, Shaw won the election with the endorsements of former Mayor Cryer, who lost to him in the primary, and Gustave Briegleb.[1]

After taking office, Shaw reconstituted the police commission, replacing all existing commissioners with his own selections, one of whom, Harry Earl Munson, played a minor yet crucial role in the events of the coming years. While Shaw left the decision to retain Roy Steckel or appoint a new LAPD chief to the police commission, his wishes were clear to observers. A few days later, James E. Davis was restored to the job of chief of police, while Steckel was demoted to a deputy chief position. Although he pledged to ensure that the nation would soon know Los Angeles as "the one locality where organized crime does not and cannot flourish," Davis' restoration to the chief's office represented a resurgence of the Parrot/Crawford/McAfee syndicate.

Like most Caucasian Angelenos, Davis was not a native. He was born in Whitewright, Texas, in 1889 into a poor, fundamentalist family. A patrolman between 1912 and 1920, he rose in the LAPD ranks to head the vice squad in the mid-1920s. Selected as chief in 1926, he built a reputation for tough, unfiltered threats against criminals. He declared that the LAPD "would hold court on gunmen in the Los Angeles streets" and threatened to reprimand officers who showed mercy to criminals. "If the courts won't eliminate them, I will," he threatened.[2]

Davis quickly reconstituted the gangster squad. Soon after Raymond returned from San Diego, the new chief announced that he was considering appointing him to the squad, having already brought Dick Lucas back to the LAPD to head it.

> It is my intention to obtain the services of all persons who have a real knowledge of gangsters and their activities so that we may root them out from Los Angeles and its environs and keep them out. Dick Lucas has, in my estimation, the greatest knowledge of gangsters of any person outside the police department.[3]

Raymond, Davis continued, had "a vast knowledge of the same class of criminals [as Lucas] from a different angle," would also be "of great help to us in this campaign against organized crime."

The return of Lucas displeased many police critics, who considered him a brute. Unfazed, Davis replied, "You can't stop gangsters by slapping them with a powder puff."[4] The comment revealed the "class of criminals" he wanted to target: not the sophisticated, politically savvy racketeers, such as Charlie Crawford or Guy McAfee, but the small, violent packs of hoodlums who at the time were terrifying the nation, the bank robbers, kidnappers, highwaymen, auto thieves, and stick-up men. The only exceptions to this rule were racketeers from the east coast, who were never welcome no matter how genteel they pretended to be. In April of the following year, former Chicago "beer baron" "Spike" O'Donnell was convicted of vagrancy and escorted to the train station by Lucas and other cops on the gangster squad. "O'Donnell . . . doesn't want any part of Los Angeles and I do not believe that Los Angeles wants any part of him," declared District Attorney Buron Fitts, adding, "the whole problem of law enforcement is to keep the city clear of easterners who desire to 'horn in.'" Fitts' declaration was an unambiguous admission of the deeper goal of law enforcement in Los Angeles in the period. Keep the easterners out of the county, so that the local rackets—particularly gambling and prostitution, the "victimless" crimes—could operate undisturbed.[5]

During the early years of Cryer's mayoralty, the local crime syndicate had worked well despite the occasional nuisance of figures like Jacobson, but in the last years of the twenties, it began to lose its grip. Cryer and Parrot had argued and split, the mayor retiring and Parrot failing to engineer a viable replacement for him. The new mayor, John C. Porter, stood with religious reformers such as Shuler and Briegleb. Buron Fitts was now the district attorney and an unknown quantity. Marco, the city's top pimp, was in San Quentin.

The eclipse of Charlie Crawford by Guy McAfee was perhaps the worst blow to the syndicate. McAfee was a skilled organizer, but his control over Los Angeles County vice was not firm. Gangsters unaffiliated with the syndicate—whether eastern or homegrown—kept trying to "horn in." The smooth payoff system that Crawford had operated fell into disarray. Lower level vice operators found themselves besieged by competing bagmen, each demanding bribes to keep law enforcement from shutting their operations.

The threat eastern gangsters posed for the local underworld was highlighted in December 1930 when a gang of ex-cons led by former Illinois bootlegger Ralph Sheldon kidnapped bookie Zeke Caress, owner of the old Jim Jeffries Bar at 326 ½ South Spring Street, and his wife. Sheldon wanted $100,000, but Caress negotiated the couple's freedom for checks totaling $50,000. Caress arranged for one of his gambler friends, Les Bruneman, to go with several members of the gang to an offshore gambling ship to cash the checks. While waiting at the dock for a taxi boat, they were confronted by two Long Beach police officers. A gunfight erupted and one cop was wounded critically. Police captured Sheldon immediately. The rest of his gang were eventually rounded up and sent to prison. Caress and his wife were uninjured, but the message for Southern California gamblers, both offshore and onshore, was clear. They were on the spot.

While the LAPD had a key role in maintaining the home field advantage for local vice leaders, the district attorney also played a major part. From 1928, when he took over after the downfall of Asa Keyes, Buron Fitts occupied the DA's office.

Fitts was a young man who had risen rapidly in California politics. Born on March 22, 1895, in the tiny northern Texas town of Belcherville, his family moved to Los Angeles in 1905 by way of Chickasha, Oklahoma. Young Buron, as ambitious and hardworking as a Horatio Alger hero, spent his spare time outside school cutting grass and delivering newspapers. By the time he attended Manual Arts High School, he held a Saturday job as a meat cutter in the Arlington Market and a Sunday job for a Westlake (now McArthur Park) pharmacy. By 1913, he was working in his father's real estate business.

Fitts' appetite for a legal career was whetted by the trials growing out of the bombing of the *Los Angeles Times* building in 1910. He secured part-time jobs carrying records for court stenographers and eventually made his way into the law office of Earl Rogers. In 1916, he completed night classes at USC's School of Law and was admitted to the bar, starting a partnership with two of Roger's junior partners, Frank Dominguez and Harry Dehm.

At this point, his career took a detour. It was 1917 and the United States had entered World War I. Fitts, who somehow had found time to join the National Guard during his high school days, was ordered to Fort Rosecrans, South Dakota. Later, at Camp Lewis in Washington, he was commissioned a second lieutenant detailed to Company I, 364th Infantry, 91st Division. After further training at Gondrecourt, France, he served on the front as a scout. In late September 1918, weeks before the armistice, he was wounded in the leg. The injury left him lame for the rest of his life.

After a year of convalescence in France and at San Francisco's Letterman Hospital, during which he met and married his first wife, Fitts returned Los Angeles. There, he established a law firm with Joseph Ford and Henry Bodkin. He also joined the American Legion, winning an executive position with its Los Angeles branch and quickly rising to become California State Commander. With anti-radical hysteria sweeping the nation, the Legion spearheaded the local repression, including attacks on the International Workers of the World, which was trying to organize the dockworkers at San Pedro. The Legion's brutal suppression of the Wobblies and other radicals earned Fitts and the legionnaires the praise of Mayor "Pinkey" Snyder, who also commended the police for "looking the other way" while the legionnaires busted heads. The following year, Fitts energetic leadership gained him a position on the Legion's National Executive Committee.

Fitts' harassment of the IWW led to a special appointment with the district attorney's office in 1920. Working under the supervision of Asa Keyes, Fitts prosecuted the Wobblies under California's Criminal Syndicalism law. His zeal earned him a permanent position as a deputy DA. Three years later, he was promoted to chief deputy.

Fitts continued his activities on behalf of veterans groups during the early twenties, working for legislation that authorized county boards of supervisors to levy taxes for patriotic halls and lobbying in Washington and Sacramento. In Los Angeles, he obtained financing for the Patriotic Hall, an eight story building on Figueroa Street that soon became notorious, along with the Hall of Justice, for overruns that doubled its cost from $509,234 to $1,250,000.

His strength with veterans aroused the interest of Governor Friend Richardson, whose pocket vetoes of several veteran-sponsored bills had lost him support among ex-servicemen. Richardson persuaded Fitts to run with him for the 1926 Republican nomination for Lieutenant Governor against the counter ticket of C.C. Young and Frank Merriam. Although they rejected Richardson's bid for re-nomination, Republican voters chose Fitts over Merriam. Young and Fitts went on to win in the general election.

After serving less than two years as Lieutenant Governor, Fitts ran for the seat of Los Angeles County District Attorney after Asa Keyes announced his retirement. He declared his candidacy while a patient at the veteran's hospital, where he was undergoing treatments to save his injured leg. This dramatic announcement underscored that his campaign would rely once again on the support of his fellow veterans. This old mainstay was joined by a wide spectrum of diverse groups, including Harry Chandler and the *Los Angeles Times*. With no serious opposition, Fitts won easily.

Shortly before Fitts took over as DA, the 1928 Grand Jury, which included both future mayor John C. Porter and future councilman John Anson Ford, returned indictments against Asa Keyes. It fell to Fitts to prosecute his former mentor. The successful prosecution of Keyes and his cronies may have boosted Fitts standing among the voters but it cost him the sympathy of others, especially among the press, who objected to the enthusiasm with which he prosecuted his old mentor. In their view, Fitts should not have bitten so hard the hand of the man who had fed his career in the district attorney's office.

Fitts served as district attorney throughout the thirties, winning re-election in 1932 and 1936. While civic reformers and anti-vice crusaders initially looked favorably on him, they soon questioned his honesty. They charged he was too cozy with the motion picture studio heads, smoothing out legal difficulties for the stars and producers. In 1934, for instance, he and former police chief and current LAPD Captain Roy Steckel released Abe Gore, a theatrical magnate, after he served only three days of a thirty-day sentence for reckless driving. This favorable treatment went beyond what some considered justifiable avoidance of "unnecessary scandalmongering" to what one writer called "the extreme of collusion with attorneys to protect the stars, producers, and their underlings when they got into difficulties." Rumors also circulated that Fitts was covering up evidence in the 1924 murder of William Desmond Taylor despite the fact he occasionally reopened the case with grandiose predictions of an impending solution. A few years later, similar allegations formed around the apparent suicide of Paul Bern, Jean Harlow's husband.[6]

Other charges against Fitts involved his handling of vice activities in the county, particularly gambling. Even while he huffed and puffed over offshore gambling boats, casinos operated openly on the mainland. One close observer was unequivocal in his interpretation of Fitts' policies. Charging that Fitts' "principal source of income is from the sale of gambling concessions," he dismissed the DA's "ceaseless warfare against outside racketeers attempting to organize in our city "as a subterfuge to distract the public. Not only did Fitts protect local gamblers, he used the public's fear of "Eastern gangsters" to protect the locals from outsiders "muscling in on the local trade." When Fitts did go after the locals, some believed he did so half-heartedly, his convictions coming after public and press attention became too great for him to let the accused slip free.[7]

Still, many Angelenos were convinced this trim, energetic, and somewhat accident-prone man, with his neatly combed medium brown hair, narrow intelligent face, penetrating eyes, oversized nose and game leg, which he tossed in front of him like a log, kept the city a haven from the crime-ridden ethnic slums of the east, a "white spot." Others were troubled by his failure to win convictions in several cases involving organized crime, politics and big money. And they were annoyed by the way Fitts' leg always seemed to act up whenever he came under heat for some act of corruption or another, sending him to the hospital and generating sympathetic stories in the newspapers.

One case, dubbed the "Love Mart Case" by the Los Angeles press, haunted Fitts for several years. It began when a procuress named Olive Day left her suitcase with a sixteen-year-old prostitute whose services she recently sold to J. P. Mills, a multi-millionaire with ties to Agua Caliente gambling interests. Mills regularly paid Day to bring him young virgins. Inside the suitcase, the young girl's brother found a diary detailing the last five years of Day's sordid life, including her transactions with Mills and other wealthy Angelenos. The brother took the diary to the district attorney's office. Within a few weeks, Day and her lover/accomplice, William Jobelmann, were arrested for pandering, while three of their clients were indicted for statutory rape. Of these, the most famous was Alexander Pantages, a Los Angeles theater magnate already under trial for raping a young actress, Eunice Pringle.

Fitts moved to dismiss other charges against defendant Mills in order to use him as a witness against Day and Joblemann. After one judge denied his motion, the case was tried in the courtroom of Judge Wilbur C. Curtis. Fitts told Curtis that his witness, the sixteen-year-old prostitute, had married and, eager to put her past behind her, now refused to testify. He also reiterated that he wanted to use Mills as a witness against Day and Joblemann. When Curtis disagreed and ordered him to proceed, Fitts rested the case without calling any witnesses. Reluctantly, Curtis discharged all three defendants. Mills went free, but police rearrested Jobelmann and Day. The latter was eventually convicted.

Shortly afterward, Lucien Wheeler, a private investigator employed by Mills, and Fitts' sister, Mrs. Berthal Gregory, engaged in a series of transactions involving orange grove acreage owned by Fitts' parents. The net result was a clear and seemingly unwarranted profit for the Fitts family. Rumors of the deal began to circulate in political circles, where it was interpreted as a bribe in exchange for Fitts' petition for a dismissal of the charges against Mills. After Fitts challenged the grand jury to investigate the charges, the state Attorney General named a special prosecutor with little experience in graft investigations to head the inquiry. Appearing before the jury, Fitts spoke freely and at length of the transactions. His candid testimony, which one veteran observer attributed to his confidence in the friendliness of the jury and the special prosecutor's inexperience, convinced the jury members that no crime had been committed. But not everybody in the city was persuaded.

In September 1932, a group of prominent citizens formed a secret organization called The Minuteers (known popularly as the Minute Men), intending to collect evidence of corruption in local government. The Minuteers' focus on fighting "graft, bribery, and governmental corruption" demonstrated the secular nature of their campaign. For the most part, the organization's senior members were attorneys and businessmen, not church leaders and churchwomen as were previous anti-vice crusaders in the city. Unlike Shuler and Briegleb, they were more concerned with how illegal vice fostered governmental corruption. Prostitution, alcohol and gambling were secondary concerns to them, important only in that illegal, commercialized vice made graft inevitable.[8]

As private citizens, the Minuteers had no power to issue subpoenas or compel testimony, but they could furnish information to law enforcement. The DA's office was closed to them however. Fitts attacked the group for besmirching Los Angeles, declaring that,

From the standpoint of organized gang groups, Los Angeles is today the white spot of the United States, and it seems to me that every business man and every citizen interested in the good name and good repute of this community should emphatically resent the attempted assassination of the good name of this community by a small clique of disgruntled politicians who seek power by perfecting a Nazi type of organization.[9]

As Fitts' antipathy to them foreclosed any cooperation from his office, the Minuteers' best hope for honest and thorough investigations lay in the Grand Jury. Despite legal requirements that a member of the DA's staff be present at their deliberations, it was possible for the grand jury to slip the reins of the DA and his deputies and probe matters on its own. As grand jury investigations endangered the smooth operation of vice enterprises, the Parrot/Crawford/McAfee syndicate had long made control of juror selection a key goal, as made evident by Dave Clark's testimony that Charlie Crawford had bragged that he had in his pocket four members of the upcoming 1931 jury.

In 1933, the Minuteers supported the candidacy of Judge Raymond Cheseboro for City Attorney against Edwin Werner, who, along with his wife, Helen, was rumored to have instituted a patronage system for county tax assessor jobs. Also supporting Cheseboro was Edward F. Otto, a real estate broker struggling to make ends meet who had taken a job soliciting funds for the Cheseboro campaign. Otto's technique was to call potential donors and claim to be the judge himself. If they did not fork over a donation, he became offensive, according to Cheseboro, who fired him after learning of his abusive phone calls. Afterward, Otto approached a downtown barber with a proposition. If the barber could put him in touch with a member of the grand jury, he would furnish information about corruption in Los Angeles and pay the barber $1,000 for his help. The barber refused to take any money, but he passed on the information to his barbershop partner, Wayne Jewell, who just happened to be the son of grand juror Oriel A. Jewell. Otto and Wayne Jewell met and agreed that Otto would pay Jewell $400 "for expenses" to convince his father to start an investigation into Werner. By the time of the meeting, however, the elder Jewell had learned of Otto's activities and reported them to Fitts. Fitts put his investigators on the case and soon had enough evidence to get an indictment against Otto from the same grand jury Otto tried to influence. He also procured indictments against two Minuteers working for the Cheseboro campaign, Raymond Haight and attorney Thatcher Kemp. After a sensational trial in the summer of 1933, during which the defense exposed Fitts' shady relationship with "Queen Helen" Werner, who admitted to helping finance his 1932 campaign with contributions from tax court appraisers whose appointments her husband controlled, the presiding judge dismissed the charges against Haight for insufficient evidence. Several weeks later, Otto and Kemp were also acquitted.

Although he did not convict the Minuteers, Fitts' blunt tactics was a warning to the reformers, who now knew how hard and fast he could hit. His furious countercharge convinced them he was their principal opponent. The *Los Angeles Times*, which editorialized against the Minute Men's "reckless statements" and implied the timing of the Minuteers' foray to Sacramento was political, was also high on their list.

After Fitts' indictment of their leaders, the Minuteers focused on the DA himself. The twisted paper trail of purchases and sales of his father's orange grove acreage in 1931 following the Mills dismissal still haunted Fitts. Although the 1931 grand jury had refused to indict him, with the 1934 Grand Jury he faced a row of reformers who suspected him of trying to control their reformist agenda instead of compliant, machine-picked henchmen. His intimidating style came to work against him now. One writer described him as "long . . . accustomed to dominating Grand Jury proceedings," who "frequently chided and hotly catechized jurors who sought to go deeply into investigations which Fitts decided should be taboo."[10] The reformers on the grand jury mistrusted his insistence that a deputy DA be present whenever the jury or its special committees met. They also suspected he deliberately filled the jury's time with unimportant investigations. Eager to get on with their agenda, they excluded his deputies from their sessions only to discover some jurors were Fitts loyalists who kept him apprised of their activities.

The conflict escalated in late May 1934 after the County Board of Supervisors denied the jury's request to redirect funds earmarked for audits to their vice investigation. The rebuff was widely perceived as a victory for underworld figures threatened by the impending investigations. For months, gambling bosses had nervously watched the pre-battle maneuvering in the grand jury room, halting operations whenever the reformers seemed to be getting their way. The casino operators put together a common fund for countering any investigations and hired private detectives to shadow reformers and grand jurors. When the supervisors denied the jurors funds for open-ended investigations, the gamblers foresaw victory, one crowing, "We have the grand jury stopped. They'll never get a dime!"[11]

For Fitts, however, the denial of funds by the supervisors proved a dangerous turn of events. Although the jurors did not have funds to investigate graft generally, money was available from the state for investigations of county supervisors and district attorneys. The grand jury's graft investigation, before somewhat diffuse, now focused on Fitts. Not that the funding limitation was the sole motivation for this change of strategy. Rumors of the jurors' antipathy to Fitts bruited about Hall of Justice corridors for several months. There was little doubt that Superior Court Judge Fletcher Bowron, who selected the jurors, viewed the district attorney with suspicion.

By late spring of 1934, the split between the grand jury and the district attorney was in the open. Bowron charged Fitts was out to "embarrass the Grand Jury." The jury's foreman, Dr. John Buckley, accused the DA of attempting to "bulldoze and embarrass and intimidate the grand jury." Bowron and other reform leaders belittled Fitts' renewed war against gambling, which focused on penny ante card games, betting between tennis players and golfers, and raids against offshore gambling boats while it ignored the gambling casinos downtown and on the west side.[12]

Before the hostile 1934 Grand Jury, Fitts could not repeat the easy testimony he gave before the friendly 1931 Jury. Speaking guardedly, he endured a week of cross-examination. Although he dodged a bribery indictment without perjuring himself before the current jury, his frank 1931 testimony came back to haunt him. The jurors, noting discrepancies between it and his more recent testimony, issued an indictment accusing Fitts and his sister, Berthal Gregory, of perjury.

Fitts struck back with characteristic vigor, charging the indictment was politically motivated. Represented by Jerry Giesler, Joseph Scott, and Jack Gilchrist, three of the city's foremost lawyers, he continued his attacks in the courtroom, attempting to have the indictments set aside as prompted by "bias and prejudice."[13] His attorneys convinced the California Supreme Court to throw out a second indictment that grew out of his failure to pursue fraud charges against his sister and her husband in a misguided mortgage venture. Fitts' staff and supporters also kept the pressure up on the DA's accusers. An investigator for the jury, reporter Charles "Brick" Garrigues, recounted how Tom Cavett and another detective from the DA's office beat him when he arrived with documents for the Superior Court justices. Later, according to Garrigues, Cavett tried to push him down the stairway of the Hall of Justice. Fortunately, Cavett checked himself when a nearby elevator opened to emit a potential witness. Another Fitts loyalist, Los Angeles Times reporter Al Nathan, the same who played a part in the Jacobson arrest, threatened newspaperman James H. Richardson, a onetime ally of Fitts who had since turned on the DA.

Delaying tactics kept the case from coming to trial until January 1936. In the meantime, Fitts continued as district attorney. Fearful of a continuance of the crime-busting investigations and remembering the 1928 "runaway" Jury, which indicted not only DA Asa Keyes but also Albert Marco, local political bosses and underworld leaders schemed in late 1934 to ensure the 1935 Grand Jury was compliant to vice interests. Their strategy was to reverse Bowron's success in selecting the previous jury panel and to pack the new jury with "anchors" to slow the more zealous, reform-minded jurors. With "anchors" in place, the district attorney's office could keep the jury's collective nose out of the underworlds' business by concentrating on the grand jury's traditional duties: indicting labor organizers, petty criminals, and vice purveyors unaffiliated with the city's power elite.

The strategy worked. The 1935 Grand Jury lauded Fitts in its annual report and condemned its predecessor. "It is an easy matter for a grand jury to criticize public officials, to besmirch their character and reputation and through politically and selfishly inspired motives to bring government into disrepute." On the same day the annual report was published, Fitts was acquitted after his attorneys argued that the 1934 Grand Jury issued the perjury indictment because it failed to find any evidence of real corruption in the orange grove transactions.[14]

District Attorney Buron Fitts emphasizing a point. [Los Angeles Times Photographic Archive, UCLA Library. Copyright Regents of the University of California, UCLA Library]

12: THE CORNER POCKET

How long Raymond remained on the gangster squad after returning from San Diego is not clear, but a report in the *Los Angeles Times* indicated that he was still associated with the LAPD as 1933 ended. A few months earlier, he had considered creating a "detectives correspondence school" in National City, south of San Diego and moving his detective agency there, but nothing seems to have come from this idea except that National City residents were treated to an exhibition of photographs from his career. Four months later, the *Los Angeles Times* reported that he helped apprehend a bunko artist engaged in a variant of the Spanish Prisoner swindle. The man, who claimed to be the former physician of the late Czar Nicholas of Russia, had lured several LA citizens into financing a lawsuit to recover $43 million frozen in a San Francisco bank. Previously, he spent time in prison for having practiced medicine without a license. The story identified Raymond as a *private* detective.

In September 1934, Raymond was reported in Las Vegas, where he helped the local police shadow and arrest a suspect in the rape/murder of Celia Cota, who was strangled and suffocated in the back yard of her San Diego home a month earlier. San Diego police released the man after they questioned him, however.

After returning from Las Vegas, Raymond became chief of the Automobile Club of Southern California's Auto Theft Bureau. He held the position until January 1936, when he crashed his automobile into a telephone pole on North Main and Wilhardt Avenue in the Dogtown district of Los Angeles. Before lapsing into unconsciousness, Raymond said a stolen car he was chasing forced him off the road. At the Georgia Street Receiving Hospital, doctors discovered he had a fractured skull and a compound fracture of the right leg. There was some doubt whether he would survive. He regained consciousness the next day, however. The paper printed a large photograph of him lying prone on a hospital bed, bandages wrapping his forehead. Discharged to his home at 955 Orme Avenue in Boyle Heights in mid-February, by the end of the month he was able to move from a reclining position to a wheelchair.

While Raymond recuperated, the Los Angeles vice syndicate continued to evolve. A new force had entered Los Angeles' organized crime scene with Frank Shaw's election in 1933: Frank's younger brother, Joe, a former lieutenant in the US Navy and now the mayor's personal secretary. Forty-three years old, Joe had come up through the ranks, serving as an executive officer on several ships, and working with the service's intelligence bureau. He was a tough, stern man, disregardful of courtesy, accustomed to giving brusque orders and seeing them obeyed, impatient of red tape and bureaucracy. After his brother's election, he took the lead in negotiations with the Navy to develop a fleet air base at Allen Field on Terminal Island. He also took charge of promotions and appointments in the police and fire departments. It was not long before Joe was known by the allusive sobriquet, "the corner pocket," which referred both to the location of his office in City Hall and his key position within his brother's administration. If you wanted anything done, whether it was a favor, a contract, or permission to open an illegal gambling joint, you went to see the "corner pocket."[15]

As the mid-thirties progressed, the Shaws grew dissatisfied with the trickle of loot from organized vice payoffs that flowed to the mayor via the Parrot/McAfee syndicate and plotted to direct the enormous take straight to the mayor's office. Joe Shaw reached into the LAPD for allies, acquiring the services of the LAPD's Special Intelligence Unit, led by Earle E. Kynette. Kynette reported directly to him, bypassing Police Chief Davis.

Forty-one years old, Kynette began working in the Special Intelligence Unit in 1934 as a detective lieutenant. He had a diverse past. Born in Iowa in 1893, he had fathered an out-of-wedlock daughter in 1911. In 1917, he met Phillipa Gunter while both were performing at a vaudeville house in Chicago. The couple, who married in Santa Ana in May 1918, took up rooms in Los Angeles at the Southern Pacific Station building near the corner of Fifth and Central Avenue, an area known for bordellos and prostitutes. Like many young actors, they may have come for the city's burgeoning film industry. The marriage did not fare well at first. In October 1918, Phillipa sued for an annulment, claiming she was underage when they married. She had been 17, not 22 as was recorded on the marriage certificate. Her father, a prominent Montgomery, Alabama, attorney, had not approved of the marriage and did not wish her husband to get his hands on his extensive Texas land holdings. The marriage endured for a few more years, however. Kynette enrolled in the Pharmacy College of the University of Southern California, graduating in 1922. He was an active student, a correspondent on the school newspaper, a yearbook staffer, and a member of the student body government. He and his wife also became the Southern Pacific Station Hotel's managers.

Earle and Phillipa had two daughters. The first, Jeanne, was born in August 1921, but died before her first birthday. In 1923, Phillippa gave birth to Adele Lois. The marriage did not last much longer. After graduating from USC in 1922, Kynette and his wife continued to manage the furnished rooms at the Southern Pacific Station building, but by the following year, Kynette, with or without his wife, was offering rooms at 1610 S. Figueroa. In 1924, he moved to Pomona to take a job as a pharmacist for the Central Drug Company in that city.

By 1925, Kynette and Phillipa had divorced. Kynette soon remarried, once again to a teenager, Eunice, aged 17. They may have met at Jocelyn's Beauty Shop in the Brack Shops building in downtown Los Angeles, where Earle was working as an "artist"/hair bobber. Why he had left his Pomona job is not clear—perhaps to obtain his Master of Arts Degree from USC in Chemistry. In any case, Kynette's second marriage lasted about as long as his first. By 1927, his current young wife filed for divorce, complaining that Kynette forced her to entertain his former wife, Phillippa. While the divorce was called off, the former Mrs. Kynette and her daughter, Adele, who would become a prominent physician at the University of Pennsylvania, remained in Los Angeles to the consternation of the current Mrs. Kynette until 1928, when, having earned her high school diploma at night school, Phillippa decamped with her daughter to Texas.

Kynette joined the LAPD in 1925, finishing second in his class at the Police Training Academy, where he excelled in both physical and mental tasks. Some sources report that Albert Marco and the Los Angeles crime syndicate of Charles Crawford helped him get a job with the police. According to this tale, Kynette was a pimp for a couple of the girls in Marco's bordellos. Kynette impressed Marco with his "ambition, intelligence and boldness." While there is no documentary evidence that Kynette was an underworld mole when he entered the LAPD, it is curious that he was in the Ship Café in 1928 when Marco shot two men and earned himself a stretch in San Quentin. In fact, Kynette became a defense witness for Marco, claiming that he observed another man fleeing the café after the gunplay.[16]

Kynette's connection to Marco may have been a factor in the autumn of 1927, when Purity Squad leader Sydney Sweetnam arrested him for extorting money from prostitutes. (Sweetnam himself had faced similar charges twice before in his long career as a vice and purity squad member.) The next day, Police Chief Davis released Kynette from jail and sent him back to his job as a patrolman. Later, when the Police Board found Kynette guilty of accepting a bribe and dismissed him from the police force, Davis convinced the police commission to reinstate him with full back pay.

Despite his missteps, Kynette advanced rapidly in the LAPD. He was a Sergeant in 1927 when he arrested a member of Tony Cornero's bootlegging gang, James S. Fox, for illegal possession of a firearm. Fox had killed two men in a gunfight in front of the St. Regis Hotel on west Sixth Street the year before but convinced a jury he had acted in self-defense. By the following year, Kynette had made Detective Lieutenant. Along with Harry Raymond, he was one of Davis' confidential investigators. Davis' critics claimed that Kynette and Harry Raymond held their jobs through underworld influence.

After Steckel took over as police chief from Davis in late 1929, Kynette's connection to Davis may have been a hindrance to his career. In December 1929, as Davis' hold on the position of chief became tenuous, Deputy Chief Steckel returned Kynette to patrolman. By 1931, he had worked his way back to acting detective lieutenant only to be bounced back to a uniformed officer later in the year. It was a bad time for him. His wife, Eunice, again filed for divorce. This time the alienator of her husband's affections was a sick dog on which Earl allegedly spent too much time and money. The divorce was granted. Soon afterward Kynette married eighteen-year-old Eleanor Charbonneau from Glendora, Mississippi. His new wife would give birth to his third daughter, Eleanor Ann, in late 1936.[17]

With Davis' return to the chief's office in 1933, Kynette's star began to rise quickly. Davis promoted him to acting detective lieutenant and in October of that year transferred him to a new "anti-hoodlum" unit, reporting directly to him along with two other officers, McKinley Robison and Stanley Stone. The three detectives set about solving the September 1932 robbery of actress Mae West outside her apartment in Hollywood. After trailing a suspect for several months, they arrested him in December. They sweated him for thirty-six hours until he confessed and named a friend of West as his accomplice.

By spring of 1934, the "anti-hoodlum" squad had been informally rechristened the "intelligence bureau." Kynette took over leadership in April with the departure of Stone to the Vice Squad. In November 1935, he was promoted to full detective lieutenant and assigned to the Metropolitan Division. About this time, the unit was renamed the "Special Intelligence Unit" [SIU] and established its headquarters in a dingy storeroom at 311 East First Street. Whether the "intelligence bureau" reported to Captain Warren Justin of the Metropolitan Division, to Chief Davis, to Joe Shaw, or to all three would be a matter of dispute in the years to come. However, its mission became clear as its investigations accumulated. To begin with, it performed normal police work, conducting investigations of criminal activity. For example, in March 1934, Kynette arrested the promoters of a "Musical Review" charity event planned for the Shrine Auditorium for violating city ordinances that required promoters to donate a significant proportion of the funds collected to the charity they advertised. Two defendants were convicted and both received a year's imprisonment. In 1936, the intelligence squad shadowed Robert S. James, a West Eighth Street barber whose wife had drowned in a fishpond outside their La Crescenta home the summer before. Kynette's men rented a bungalow next door to James' new home on LaSalle Street and snuck inside while he was out to install listening devices. For days, they eavesdropped on him and his niece, who worked as a manicurist at his barbershop. Finally, they heard sounds of lovemaking and burst through the windows to confront the couple. James was arrested for incest and was convicted on morals charges. Although condemned to prison for from 3 to 150 years, he did not have to serve out the sentence. An accomplice confessed to helping him try to kill his wife by sticking her foot in a box of rattlesnakes and, when that did not work, drowning her in a bathtub. James was hanged in 1942 for his wife's murder.

Fighting crime was not the intelligence squad's only job, however. Kynette, under direction that came from Joe Shaw and Chief Davis, also focused on "subversive elements"—which included detractors of the police department, the mayor, and even the underworld. The case of John Langan, a Hollywood dialog director with a background in mineralogy who sued the LAPD in Federal court in early 1936, showed how far Kynette and the SIU was willing to go to protect the Shaw administration. Returning from Arizona, Langan had been detained at Blythe on the California border by the Los Angeles "bum blockade," a force of 136 LAPD officers that Chief Davis had dispatched to prevent Dust Bowl migrants from entering California. With support from the American Civil Liberties Union and two prominent attorneys, John C. Packard and James Carter, Langan charged that the blockade violated the 14th Amendment and asked for $5,000 in damages.

Langan may well have underestimated the determination of Los Angeles officials to prevent impoverished migrants from overwhelming local resources. Despite widespread condemnation from other states (except for Florida, which also experienced a surge of migrants during the winter months), the blockade continued, while Kynette and the SIU set about to smear Langan and his lawyers as dangerous radicals. Posing as reporters from *Time Magazine*, they interviewed and photographed Langan and his attorneys. Afterward, no story ran in *Time,* but pamphlets began appearing in Los Angeles containing photos of Langan with the two attorneys, whom the accompanying article identified as known communists. Langan's associate in the Arizona mining venture was threatened with prosecution for violating pollution ordinances at his LA County plant if he continued to collaborate with Langan. Langan's wife, a British subject, received anonymous phone calls warning she would be deported unless her husband dropped the suit. Uniformed LA Police officers tailed Langan's attorneys. Kynette's men tapped their phones.

In early March, Langan visited the mining site in Arizona, where he learned that two men claiming to be federal agents had told Langan's business associates that he was a communist and warned that anybody who worked with him would lose his job. While camping alone in the desert outside the small town of Cleator, Langan decided that his lawsuit was putting too many others at risk. He wired his attorneys to discontinue it immediately. Instead, Carter took a train to Phoenix and drove to Langan's camp. The two men discussed the suit and their fears over the threats and harassment they had both experienced. Langan regained his courage and directed Carter to continue the lawsuit.

Before the trial began, Kynette visited Langan's Los Angeles home one evening. The two men left together. Just before midnight, Langan's wife called attorney Carter to report that her husband had not returned home. Langan was not in court the next day, either. His attorneys received a message from him asking again to have the case dismissed. Although Carter and Packard presented the letter to the judge and acknowledged Langan had signed it, they told the judge that they suspected the message was coerced, and that Langan was being held against his will. Appalled, the judge ordered the case to continue and demanded that Langan appear in court before he would grant a dismissal. A few hours later, a disheveled Langan appeared. To many in the courtroom, he appeared hung over. He seemed a "dejected, beaten, frightened man." He repeated his request for a dismissal. This time the court agreed.[18]

That evening, Langan released a statement explaining that "more studied thought and deliberation" had convinced him that the police border blockade was good for the state. He denied that anyone had coerced him to drop the case and praised the police department. A few days later, he wrote a letter to Chief Davis praising Earle Kynette for his help in understanding the issue. Some regarded it as sarcastic.

Chief Davis rewarded Kynette's efforts in the Langan matter in May 1936, promoting him to captain "for efficient and meritorious service in the Langan case." While many suspected that Kynette had strong-armed Langan into abandoning his lawsuit against the LAPD, the two men became friends, bonding, perhaps, through their mutual interest in theater. Three years later, however, the friendship ended when Langan's wife, an actress whose professional name was Joan Manners, subpoenaed Kynette as a witness in her divorce suit against Langan.[19]

About the same time that he was pressuring Langan to drop his lawsuit against the LAPD, Kynette and the SIU took on two investigations that resonated in the coming years. The first involved Lyndon "Red" Foster, a hot-tempered civic gadfly and perennial candidate for office who published a monthly political scandal sheet called *The Equalizer*. Foster was a fierce critic of Los Angeles' governmental and political leaders, including Mayor Shaw and his brother, Joe. He also battled other civic activists, who differed, however slightly, with his views. In 1929, he got into a fistfight on the City Hall steps with another civic gadfly/investigator, Joe Buchta, who a few years later would regale the FBI with tales of the Los Angeles underworld. A year later, he was arrested for disturbing the peace outside the Los Angeles City Council chamber. He fought a supporter of Minuteer Raymond Haight outside the convention hall of the Progressive Party soon afterward. Ten years after his set-to with Buchta, Foster gave another gadfly a black eye outside City Hall. His next reported bout was in a Long Beach courtroom, where he traded punches with a local attorney.

Foster also had unkind words about the LAPD and, in particular, the SIU and Kynette. In mid-December 1935, somebody took enough offense at his criticisms to lift a wooden plank bearing a bomb to the second-story window of his apartment at 359 South Cochran Avenue. The bomb blew apart the window and its frame and hurled bricks into the room, splintering the furniture. A curtain rod speared the doors of his Murphy bed. Asleep below the closet, Foster was unhurt.

Foster had plenty of enemies, but few of them had the skillset to build a bomb. Not one to hold his tongue, he speculated on who might have tried to kill him. "The underworld didn't do this. It's not organized. People don't do these things unless they have protection. The Police Department didn't do it. It came right from the mayor's office."[20]

The most recent edition of Foster's *Equalizer* had attacked "religious racketeering." The term covered a broad range of schemes designed to profit from the spiritual yearnings of its victims. What Foster meant by it has been lost to us along with the issue of the *Equalizer* in which his exposé appeared, but in 1936 religious leaders in Southern California were incensed by the activities of Charles E. Kelso, founder of the Spiritual Psychic Science Church. Kelso offered to ordain ministers in his church for $10; for $15, one could purchase a Doctor of Divinity degree and for a mere $30 one would be elevated to the high office of Bishop. It was a good deal for some would-be ministers, including at least one mallard duck, ordained as Reverend Drake Googoo. The establishment church figures, bound together in an organization named the Los Angeles Ministerial Assembly, prayed to the state and federal governments for relief from such cut-rate ordination.

The term "religious racketeer" also applied to religious figures who used their pulpit to extort money from gambling bosses. While reformers often faced accusations that their real goal was simply to hound vice figures until they were paid off, those that had established themselves as ministers of faith had a leg up on the game.

For a time, one of the Shaws fiercest critics was evangelist Rheba Crawford. Born in Wisconsin in 1898 to a Salvation Army Adjutant General and his wife, Rheba followed her parents' footsteps into the ministry. By her late teens, she was a Salvation Army leader in Atlanta, Georgia, well known as a writer and organizer as well as a "tambourine girl" who used her instrument as a collection plate. In 1918, the Army sent her to New York City to take charge of collecting donations and saving souls in the Broadway theater district. Overcoming cynicism and ignoring leers, she developed a rapport with the Broadway crowds that included several prominent directors and actors, including George M. Cohan. Newspaper reporter and fiction writer Damon Runyon based the heroine of one of his short stories on her that was eventually developed into a hit musical, *Guys and Dolls*. "She is tall, and thin, and has a first-class shape, and her hair is a light brown, going on blond, and her eyes arc like I do not know what, except that they are one-hundred-percent eyes in every respect," Runyon wrote of her fictionalized character. In 1927, Cecille De Mille produced a movie based on her New York ministry, "The Angel of Broadway," with Leatrice Joy playing the lead character.

Crawford espoused a tolerant form of Christianity that suited her worldly audience. "I don't pretend to know everything about God. And I think it would be impertinent for me to give people a blueprint of heaven. I try to build up a spirit of mutual helpfulness and tolerance in this life. I can't understand hard and fast Christianity."[21] The Broadway crowds loved her, and she loved them as well, declaring, "I conquered Broadway because I have the soul of Broadway myself and its mind and heart as well. I love Broadway and understand it. It is the greatest street in the world and has the biggest heart." She spurned multiple offers to join the cast inside the theaters and even to take screen tests for the motion pictures.[22]

Newspapers throughout the country related the charming phenomenon of the theater district's popular missionary girl, christening her the "Vamp of the Salvation Army" and "The Angel of Broadway." The crowds that gathered to listen to her preach on the steps of Cohan's Gaiety Theater at 46th and Broadway soon became so large that they blocked traffic. One frustrated police officer decided to take action. On Oct 16, 1921, Officer Emerson Taylor pushed his way through the 2,000 persons gathered around her and demanded that she desist. When Crawford told him she had a permit to hold the open meetings, he replied that the permit did not allow her to block traffic.

When she refused to stop, he placed her under arrest. As he escorted her to police headquarters, members of her audience began to follow menacingly. Taylor whistled for backup and two officers arrived. By the time Crawford and her trio of captors reached the West 47th Street Police Station, the crowd had grown even larger and noisier, men and women jeering and catcalling the police while young boys climbed the police station steps and perched on its windows. At one point, cops had to beat back several men who had charged the station doors. Inside, the alarmed police called for support. Off-duty cops soon arrived and threw up a cordon at Eighth and Ninth Avenues.

An associate of George M. Cohan paid Crawford's $500 bail. The case was soon dismissed on the urging of theater owner Edward F. Albee and columnist Walter Winchell, who years later recalled that Crawford "was an inspiring speaker and had the best looking legs this side of the Mississippi."[23]

After taking a short break on her doctor's orders because of nervous exhaustion, Crawford held a meeting at the Winter Garden Theater, and then traveled to San Francisco to be with her parents. While there, she preached at the Congregational Church as a guest speaker.

Back in New York City in early January, Crawford found that the Salvation Army's leadership had wearied of her celebrity. She resigned her post and began a career as an evangelist, commencing with a massive meeting at the Selwyn Theater. Four thousand persons attended, but many more were unable to squeeze into the theater. During the next twelve months, she preached along the southern seaboard, from Virginia to Florida. By this time, if not sooner, she had cultivated a mid-Atlantic accent, trilling her Rs dramatically.

During the remainder of the decade, Crawford preached intermittently. She had originally planned to evangelize for five years, but, in March 1924, she married St. Petersburg, Florida publisher and advertising agent Harold Sommers, a crippled war veteran she met at one of her services. For two years, she retired partially to married life but found the St. Petersburg social scene tedious. Her own experiences with Broadway chorus girls and the down-and-out of New York City were not material for polite conversation. After she convinced Sommers that she needed to return to the pulpit, she moved to California, where she became the pastor of the Fruitvale Congregational Church in Oakland. In August 1928, she announced that she and her husband had separated. Eighteen months later, a week after the dissolution of her marriage to Sommers, Crawford married Ray Splivalo, a wealthy San Francisco businessman and sportsman, and announced that she had given up preaching from the pulpit because the public objected to "divorced women being so indiscrete as to fall in love and remarry." However, she pledged to continue to preach via radio to all "the shut-ins and stay-at-homes from her new home in the Hollywood Hills."[24]

The radio broadcasts, which featured African-American spiritual singers, lasted a month. By July, Crawford had embarked on a new career. She claimed that, while she vacationed in Mexico with her new husband, Mexicans asked her about gubernatorial candidate Mayor James Rolph of San Francisco. When she returned to California, she went to work for Rolph's election. She began a speaking tour in the San Joaquin Valley but found herself in hot water with the American Legion when she broke a rule prohibiting political campaigning at posts by praising Rolph. Unfazed, she continued her speaking tour, including radio talks, throughout the summer, using street corners as her preferred venue. After Rolph's election, Crawford vied for the state cabinet post of director of the Department of Social Welfare, a position sought by two other Rolph campaign aides. Crawford got the job, but several current board members quit their unsalaried positions in protest over her selection.[25]

After serving over three years, Crawford returned to the pulpit as an assistant to evangelist Aimee Semple McPherson in December 1934. McPherson had returned from her European tour in September and was contemplating a mission to the Orient. In early January, Crawford accompanied her on a triumphant march in honor of McPherson's twenty-fifth anniversary as a religious leader. The parade wound through the downtown streets culminating on the Los Angeles City Hall steps, where Mayor Frank Shaw waited to greet McPherson. Later that month, McPherson set out for Japan, leaving Crawford in charge of the temple.

Crawford's choice of subjects for her Sunday sermons at the Angelus Temple, while embellished with her "tremendous, dramatic, illustrated" style, soon moved from the spiritual to the political. After a joint sermon with McPherson entitled "Am I My Brother's Keeper," she launched into spiritual reflections with provocative, gimmicky titles such as "Welcome, Tax Collector" and "Chiselers"—the latter beginning "We are all chiselers" but quickly evolving into an entreaty that all "carve a course guided by inspiration from God." Within a month, she moved to politics, using her pulpit to deliver "The Truth About the Relief Program," in which she decried the federal and state programs as suffering from "confusion, lack of decision and the failure of responsible officers to personally survey difficult situations." Two days later, she accused the Los Angeles County Board of Supervisors of condoning mismanagement and negligence.[26]

In June, Aimee Semple McPherson returned to the Angelus Temple podium with sermons even more theatrical than those she presented before. Crawford was dispatched "to the field," specifically, Texas, for a month's

223

evangelical tour, McPherson explaining, "Now that I'm back in the Temple, there is no use for her to stay here, too." It was the first public sign of trouble between the two women.[27]

Back in Los Angeles in early August, Crawford resumed her diatribes against local vice conditions and indifferent local politicians. In April, she had joined with several civic leaders to congratulate Police Chief Davis "for his untiring efforts on behalf of the citizens of Los Angeles and the efficient work of his department . . . [including] the excellent record made by the chief in curbing crime in Los Angeles." But now she began to focus on the failure of the mayor and the police to combat illegal gambling in the city. In mid-August, she sent a letter to the Los Angeles City Council charging that Albert Marco, who was deported following his stay in San Quentin, was directing vice operations in Southern California from Mexico, including "twenty-three houses of ill fame, nine openly operated gambling houses, seven slot machine establishments and six bookmaking places." The city councilmen responded variously to her allegations, maintaining that the matters had already been turned over to Chief Davis, that it was not the council's but the grand jury's duty to investigate payoff allegations, that those who complain about gambling houses play cards in their own homes, and that every few years a new City Council embarks on a vice crusade only to find that jurisdiction for such matters falls within the mayor's office and police department. The *Los Angeles Times'* "City Hall Gossip" column commented wryly, "the pastoress . . . writes the Councilmen and others letters about atrocious conditions in the town, and then, for fear they don't read their mail, talks about it on the radio."[28]

The unresponsive city government did not deter Crawford, who continued her crusade, reading the addresses of gambling houses and bordellos on her radio broadcasts and threatening a recall movement against Mayor Shaw and Police Chief Davis. To counter her claim that Los Angeles was "overridden by criminals, gangsters and racketeers," Shaw cited police department statistics showing a drop in violent crimes over the past two years. For his part, Davis responded that he needed more money to combat vice but noted that most vice locations Crawford publicized were closed or private clubs.[29]

Going after the Los Angeles vice syndicate was dangerous, as former councilman Jacobson could have told her. In April, Crawford reported that she was threatened with a "morals frame-up" after she criticized Los Angeles' relief effort. In late August, while leading the singing of a hymn, a drunken 28-year-old pipefitter and former British Navy sailor tried to punch her on the Angelus Temple podium. The man had no connection to anybody or anything other than alcohol but Crawford claimed illegal gambling interests had put him up to the assault. While mistaken about this, she was not wrong a week later when, responding to the board of police commissioners' decision to increase the LAPD's secret service fund, Crawford suggested sarcastically that the department should "take the two undercover officers who have been shadowing me and put them on the vice squad."[30]

In fact, Earle Kynette's Special Intelligence Unit was tailing her. Joe Shaw had directed Kynette to combat political enemies of his brother, whose authoritarian leanings were clear when he commented that Crawford's threat of a recall was typical of persons who want to "dictate to men in public office." The SIU was also monitoring the activities and conversations of her husband and his associates. Governor Frank Merriam had appointed Raymond Splivalo as auditor of the California State Railroad Commission earlier that year. Now Splivalo was working with a group of local functionaries and scoundrels in a shakedown of Los Angeles gamblers. The SIU placed a bug in the office of one conspirator, Clinton Baxter, a former Los Angeles Board of Health Commissioner and currently the treasurer of the California Republicans, Inc. Although the California Republicans were not officially connected to the Republican Party, either nationally or statewide, it boasted some important Republican figures as members, including former LA Mayor Frederick Woodman and Superior Court Judge Goodwin Knight. According to one of the conspirators, private investigator Wilbur Le Gette, the organization's secret purpose was to shake down the city's gambling interests. SIU operatives listened in as Baxter and Orville Forrester, a local narcotics addict, former bootlegger, hijacker, extortionist, and burglary fence who had been arrested three times for attempted murder, boasted of how they would soon take over illegal gambling in the city, run out the Shaws and send Earle Kynette to the "sticks." Repeatedly Baxter picked up the phone to confer with Ray Splivalo while Kynette's men listened.[31]

Other members of the group included Le Gette's wife Helen, former Sacramento lobbyist Nate Elliot, and Eliot's wife Florence, who was Helen Le Gette's sister and Rheba Crawford's former secretary. Andy Foley, a well-known gambling figure and an early suspect in the murders of Charlie Crawford and Herbert Spencer, rounded out the group. In late summer of 1935, while Rheba Crawford was attacking illegal gambling dens in Los Angeles, Splivalo and other members of the group purchased one of several former "Q" boats a British syndicate had brought to the West Coast to establish a coasting service between the various ports of northern Mexico and California. Originally a "speedy and heavily armed affair that slopped along disguised as a tramp freighter in war-time sea lanes that submarines made dangerous" in order to lure unsuspecting subs to come within range of its concealed five-inch guns, the vessel in question had already survived a series of failed enterprises. Rechristened with each change in service, it became the *Star of Hollywood* in early 1933 after its owners abandoned plans to use it for cruising the South Pacific and instead anchored it off Ocean Park as a gambling ship. It also failed in this new task. Los Angeles District Attorney Fitts filed criminal charges against its promoters, arguing that they deceived investors who expected a cruising, not gambling ship. After the *Star of Hollywood* was moved to a new anchorage off San Pedro, police banned water taxis from taking patrons to the ship. Before it could cease operations, hijackers with machine guns attacked it on a speedboat. By some uncharacteristic good fortune, it was rescued from this assault when a Coast Guard patrol boat arrived in time to scare the speedboat away. Later that year, the owners tried to restart gambling operations in Santa Monica Bay, but Santa Monica and LA County officials thwarted it from operating by prohibiting water taxis from ferrying patrons to the ship.[32]

Nate Elliot was the ringleader in the latest episode of the *Star of Hollywood*'s career. Elliot told the Le Gettes, Splivalo and others that he had obtained written legal opinions from former Los Angeles City Prosecutor Lloyd Nix and other maritime authorities that, despite the events of the previous year, the *Star* could operate legally in the bay as long as it stayed outside the three-mile international limit. It was a lie, but he got away with it and obtained $35,000 from the group to purchase the ship and prepare it for use. However, when the time came to anchor the boat in the Santa Monica Bay and open the tables, Elliot admitted that the district attorney "might pinch" the operators and any patrons aboard. The boat was then towed to Santa Barbara, much to the consternation of Santa Barbara officials. After weeks of legal dueling between Elliot and Santa Barbara, the boat caught fire. Two crewmembers were badly injured. Eliot had it towed back to San Pedro at the end of September. It passed out of his hands to continue its meandering path as a fishing barge, offshore restaurant, and phoenix gambling boat—rechristened the *Monte Carlo* in the early 1940s.[33]

Rheba Crawford did not learn of the *Star of Hollywood* venture until Splivalo told her about it in the fall 1935, weeks after the boat caught fire. Splivalo, a "sportsman" in his youth, a term which connoted both a love of athletics (in his case, tennis and polo) but also a fondness for horse racing and betting, agreed to finance a gambling boat scheme—"provided," he said, "It's legal." His stipulation to Elliot that he "wouldn't go" for any prostitution on the boat indicated the distinction that he and others in the investment group made relative to vice enterprises in Los Angeles. Rheba Crawford may have exercised a similar discrimination or she may have simply been a dupe in the schemes of her husband and his friends. However, Aimee Semple McPherson testified under oath that before leaving on a trip to Honolulu in the fall of 1935, Rheba told her she expected a payment of $130,000 from Los Angeles gamblers. When the shocked McPherson asked her if she were joking, Crawford said, "They paid off in other cities so why not here?" By the time of her testimony, however, the relationship between the two evangelists had soured; Rheba had launched a million dollar defamation of character suit against McPherson for referring to her as a "Jezebel" and "mistress of a high state official." During the trial, McPherson's attorney called Orville Forrester to the stand. Forrester testified that Crawford told him she ended her anti-vice crusade because "she had a chance to become friends with the [city] administration—a chance to make a deal." Her decision to side with the Shaws left him vulnerable to Kynette and his men, Forrester declared. They had followed him and once, after forcing his automobile to the side of the road, threw acid on his tires.[34]

One chronicler of Los Angeles in the mid and late thirties claimed that Forrester used Crawford's radio broadcasts to extort payoffs from the vice interests, supplying her with the addresses of only those gambling houses and bordellos that refused to pay him. According to the same account, Kynette revealed Forrester's scheme to Crawford in early 1936 and furnished her with recordings from the dictographs he had placed in Baxter's office and Le Gette's home to prove the point. The disclosure may have contributed to an intestinal illness that struck her days later. After a brief stay at a Glendale sanitarium, Crawford returned to her sermons at the Angelus Temple and her weekly radio broadcasts. Instead of lambasting the Shaw administration, she now was one of the mayor's supporters.

One way or the other, Kynette had "cooled" Crawford's reformist spirit. She was no longer a threat to either the Shaw administration, the vice syndicate that ran the city, the system of payoffs that kept the LAPD's upper brass happy and the gamblers in business or the individuals and enterprises that profited from the corrupt status quo. However, her sudden conversion from reformer to supporter of the Shaw administration had been noticed by other critics of LA's vice underworld.

Aimee Semple McPherson, Mayor Frank Shaw, and Rheba Crawford share a podium in 1934. [Los Angeles Times Photographic Archive, UCLA Library. Copyright Regents of the University of California, UCLA Library]

Rheba Crawford, the Angel of Broadway [Original photograph by Sergzis Alberts; Author's personal collection]

Joe Shaw [Los Angeles Times Photographic Archive, UCLA Library. Copyright Regents of the University of California, UCLA Library]

13: THE ACORN

After Rheba Crawford's sudden shift from critic to supporter of the Shaw administration, the usual church figures, such as Briegleb and Shuler, and a small cadre of political pamphleteers like Foster, were once again the main voices of the anti-vice movement. In addition, secular reformers continued to press for changes to the county's law enforcement personnel. In the spring of 1936, the Minuteers, who were a significant factor in the 1933 victory of Ray Chesebro over tainted Los Angeles City Attorney Erwin Werner, endorsed *Hollywood Citizen-News* publisher Harlan Palmer for district attorney against Buron Fitts. While Fitts had beaten his perjury indictment early in 1936, he was vulnerable to a different verdict from the voters. For years, Palmer had railed against public corruption through his newspaper. Despite a lack of prosecutorial experience, he appeared to be an uncompromising and dangerous opponent of organized vice. He accepted a draft by his supporters on the condition that he would not have to campaign, but even without much personal effort, he ran a close race to Fitts, who garnered endorsements from *The Los Angeles Times* and professional organizations within the law community. Palmer's performance in the election gave reformers hope, especially when they observed that he beat Fitts in the areas outside Los Angeles city limits.

Still, Fitts' re-election and the popularity of the Shaw administration bode well for the continuing profitability of Los Angeles' organized vice syndicate. Although there was a fair amount of jostling in local organized crime circles, with eager outsiders, including ambitious easterners such as Bugsy Siegel, trying to muscle in, the locals still held the cards. Kent Kane Parrot, the former political boss during Cryer's mayoralty, was now the syndicate leader, having assumed the liaison position between the political/police spheres and those in vice after Charlie Crawford's death in 1931. As an attorney, he could represent gambling and other vice interests without exposing himself to charges of influence peddling. He could also act legally as a fixer, demanding large retainers from clients, which, after taking his cut, he passed on to government officials to expedite permits or quash legal actions.

As he had during his earlier career in the Cryer administration, Parrot kept largely out of public view. The press was fascinated by his studied inaccessibility and aura of power. A. Brigham Rose, attorney for the reform interests, once remarked that one "cannot receive an audience with him except through other members of the [criminal] syndicate." Years before, a reporter described Parrot "[shooting] a thrill into the courtroom" when he testified in the libel suit of former Mayor Cryer against Robert Shuler.

> There was a certain easy confidence about this 'boss' as he sank into the witness chair that held the jury and spectators in tense expectation. The Parrot right hand went casually up to the judge's desk and the Parrot left arm over the back of his chair. The Parrot smile, a disarming weapon, a boyish good-natured grin in sharp contrast to the normally stubborn jaw and combative eyes, was directed at the jury. Several women jurors resolutely refused to meet it.[1]

Part of Parrot's allure was his sophistication, unusual among those who ran LA's criminal enterprises in the 1930s. Even Grant Cooper, who defended Rusty Williams at the Jacobson conspiracy trial and worked as a Deputy DA under Buron Fitts, remembered him as a "gentleman." This gentleman, whom future Supreme Court Chief Justice Earl Warren recalled years later as a man of "somewhat ominous reputation," had a rough edge one ignored at his own peril, however. As Arthur Brigham Rose remarked, "Parrot's decisions are final, and his judgments are terrible; they have no restraint. It is reliably reported that he is deemed accountable for more than one one-way ride hereabouts."[2]

As much as Parrot avoided publicity, from time to time he found his name in the newspapers, usually under unfavorable circumstances. Repeatedly during the thirties, he was called before local and state investigators without ever suffering an indictment or a charge of any kind. He appeared before the 1934 Los Angeles County Grand Jury, which was investigating gambling within the county. Parrot, telling reporters he had "no idea" why he was summoned, testified for twenty minutes. Nothing came from the grand jury's investigation, which ended as its term lapsed. The 1935 Grand Jury had little interest in pursuing vice conditions, but it considered summoning him when it investigated the death of actress Thelma Todd. Parrot and Todd were frequent companions at Southern California nightclubs.

In 1935, Parrot also testified before California legislative committees looking into corruption in the award of liquor licenses through the Board of Equalization. Twenty-five complainants charged that the liquor control office in Los Angeles, led by former LAPD Captain Bert Massey, referred license requests to local politicians for approval. The Board's former local office manager, Marie Toretsky, who had resigned because of conflicts with Massey, identified Parrot as one of the local politicians involved. Two other staff members claimed that Parrot frequently telephoned Massey to instruct him about issuing liquor licenses. When he called, he concealed his identity, using the alias of Mr. Quinn, they alleged. Once again, Parrot denied everything. "I never telephoned to the State Board of Equalization in my entire life," he declared, "and I doubt if I would know Massey if I saw him. I know him only casually."[34]

In December 1935, Parrot and his future wife, Lucille Cary Armstrong, the former wife of automobile pioneer Earl V. Armstrong, flew from Ensenada in the company of Guy McAfee. When the plane arrived at Lindbergh Field, an Immigration Service agent filled out a flight manifest, listing the addresses of three passengers as 7351 Biltmore Hotel, Los Angeles. The address was a transcription error. Since the dissolution of his marriage to Virginia Burrows Pierce in 1929, Parrot had lived at the Biltmore Hotel in downtown Los Angeles, an opulent mixture of renaissance, baroque, and beaux arts architectural themes that is still a leading hotel in the city. In the twenties and thirties, it was the favorite venue of the rich and powerful, a meeting place not only for business and political conventions but also for the underworld. "The fact that the politicians and leaders of the gambling and vice interests often operate out of the hotel has given rise to the use, by those who consider themselves in 'on the know,' of the euphemistic phrase, 'The Boys at the Biltmore,'" observed June Hallberg, a young graduate student at UCLA in 1937. Parrot occupied a suite of rooms, numbered 7313 and 7315, on the southeastern corner of the Biltmore Hotel's seventh floor. Their commanding view of Pershing Square and downtown Los Angeles was appropriate for the key position he now occupied within the city's vice establishment. Many contemporary observers failed to notice the central role he continued to play in the life of the city, dismissing him as a has-been. Parrot must have appreciated their disregard. As always, he had no need for publicity. It is not surprising that, while McAfee's name was entered without artifice on the Immigration form at Lindbergh Field, Parrot resorted to his ready alias, J. B. Quinn. Armstrong was listed as Mrs. Quinn. She would become the third Mrs. Parrot a month later.

As head of the syndicate, Parrot managed the complicated relationships between gamblers, politicians and the police, often holding meetings in his suite. One such meeting took place in early 1934, when he hosted a gathering of syndicate leaders to deal with the dispute between Police Commissioner Harry Earl Munson and a real estate agent named Ralph Gray. Both Munson and Gray were old friends of Harry Raymond. Munson was a farmer's son from Sheridan, New York, a small town along the banks of Lake Erie some thirty miles southwest of Buffalo. In 1909, he had married a Sheridan farmer's daughter, sold plumbing fixtures for a year, and then moved with his wife to Los Angeles, a place about as far away from the frigid winters of Sheridan as he could get. After a few years working as a building contractor with offices on Spring Street in downtown Los Angeles, he took a job as a salesman with the California Provision Company, a wholesaler of meat and groceries. Three years later, he purchased a restaurant on West Pico. In the mid-twenties, he and his wife moved to San Diego, where he launched a real estate career, specializing in small farms and agricultural acreage in Chula Vista, and achieved some prominence in local affairs, serving on chamber of commerce committees and San Diego city commissions. However, when the economy skidded in 1929, real property values plummeted and the market for farm acreage dried up. Munson left San Diego and for a time lived in Tulsa, Oklahoma. By 1933, he was back in LA, trying to make a living by selling distilled water.

Where Raymond first met him is not clear. Both arrived in Los Angeles about the same time and there were abundant opportunities for their paths to cross. Both were Masons, and Munson's restaurant on West Pico was close to Raymond's headquarters at the Southern California Automobile Club. In any case, the two friends ran into each other in early February 1933. Eager to help an old friend, Raymond suggested that Munson join the campaign of County Supervisor Frank Shaw, who had just announced that he was running for mayor of Los Angeles. Munson took the advice and before long, his home became a district headquarter for the campaign.

Ralph Gray was another real estate broker on the skids. Gray came to Los Angeles as a teenager with his family, headed by his father, an attorney. He was a chauffeur for about a dozen years, driving taxicabs and hearses, before jumping into the surging real estate market of the twenties. Like Munson, in 1932 he was looking for alternative ways to make money. Raymond sent him to Munson, who agreed to take him on as a campaign worker at the daily rate of $15, plus $5 for the use of his car. Gray accompanied Munson on visits to prominent contributors to the Shaw campaign, including some who made their money from gambling. He was with him in Guy McAfee's office when the gambling kingpin handed Munson $10,000 for the campaign.

Gray had also gone with Munson to the offices of Robert J. Gans, the wealthiest and most socially prominent member of the Los Angeles vice syndicate. Gans owned the Gans Company, which his older brothers Jonas and Moses established in 1898 as J. J. Gans and Brothers, a wholesaler of cigars and other tobacco products. He had come to LA at age nineteen in 1905 and worked his way up as a clerk and later a salesman to become a full partner in the firm in 1914.

In the late 1910s, the J. J. Gans Company began to manufacture and distribute coin-operated vending machines. At the time, they were called *slot machines*, a term lacking the later connotation of gambling devices. Since the 1880s, manufacturers had come up with ingenious uses for such devices. They dispensed prayer and hymnbooks, one-day insurance policies, postage stamps, opera glasses, pharmaceutical pills, veterinary prescriptions, hot coffee, chewing gum, candy, and even prescription eyeglasses. By the early 1890s, the machines were the consumer novelty of the time, ubiquitous in both large cities and small towns in the United States and Europe. "There is hardly anything that you cannot do nowadays by dropping a nickel in the slot," observed the *Washington Star* in 1891. They also stimulated the ingenuity of petty criminals, some of whom never pilfered from a living being but were happy to cheat a slot machine by inserting worthless slugs or nickels attached to strings that could be pulled back once the product was delivered.

Entrepreneurs soon grasped that games of chance could be replicated on the machines. One of the earliest applications was a horse racing game, where bystanders could bet on mechanical racehorses mounted by tiny metal jockeys that ran around a track under a glass dome. Replicas of card games, in which the player bet against the machine itself, enriching the slot machine owner or lessee, soon followed. As the gambling machines proliferated legal authorities began to suppress them.

Much gambling action took place in cigar stores, a natural gathering place for men looking for entertainment. Cigar vending machines had been popular since the 1880s, when they were used to circumvent blue laws that prevented shopkeepers from selling cigars on Sunday. It is likely that the J. J. Gans Company entered the vending machine business by selling or leasing these machines and gravitated to distributing and manufacturing gambling devices. Their business activity can be traced in the reports of periodic crackdowns by local law enforcement agencies. In 1917, a salesman from the firm was fined $200 by an Orange County court for placing gaming machines in poolrooms and cigar stores throughout the county. The following year, a series of raids in Santa Monica and Venice, the latter led by Chief of Police Harry Raymond, drove the betting machines from the seaside communities.

The Gans brothers were not deterred by the raids, however, nor by similar police actions in the decades that followed. The profits from their machines enabled them to counter police and prosecutors with skilled lawyers and sympathetic politicians. After his brother Jonas died in 1926, Robert became one of the city's most important campaign donors, backing candidates that would go easy on his slot machine business. He also grew rich, purchasing a nine-room home on South Van Ness and later an even more palatial property on Las Palmas in Hancock Park, Los Angeles' premier neighborhood.

While Gray had not observed Robert Gans' campaign donation to Harry Munson, he had seen McAfee's $10,000 contribution and suspected that Gans made a similar one. Campaign funds flowed so freely through Munson's hands that it made little sense when, after the election, he told Gray that he was unable to pay him for his work. Gray had worked 163 days during the campaign, earning over $3,000. Munson paid him only $270. The amount Munson still owed was a significant debt in 1933, almost 5/6 of the annual salary that Harry Raymond would be promised the same year to serve as San Diego's chief of police. Whether Munson possessed the funds to pay Gray would be a matter of dispute between the two men for the next four years and result in catastrophe for Harry Raymond and many prominent figures in the city of angels.

Raymond was serving as San Diego's police chief when he learned that Munson had stiffed Gray. On one of his trips back to LA, he visited Munson, who was then a police commissioner courtesy of newly elected Mayor Shaw. While Los Angeles police commissioners were paid less than $50 per month, those willing to serve the interests of the LA underworld syndicate could do well, a fact that Harry Raymond knew. Still, Munson insisted that he could not pay Gray. He was broke, he claimed.

Raymond did not believe him. He decided to poke around in Munson's life. He discovered that Munson was involved with a Mrs. Meyers, who formerly ran a Tulsa, Oklahoma, bordello, where Munson had met her a few years before. They had reunited in Los Angeles soon after Munson returned to the city. Raymond went to have a go at her, but by the time he did, she was on her way back to Oklahoma. A rogue cop named Eddie Keim, soon to be under investigation for shaking down LA bookies, had paid her bills, and Munson had seen her to the train. Raymond did not have the woman, but he had enough to squeeze Munson. Moving a woman back and forth across the country to serve as one's mistress could be regarded as a violation of the Mann Act, which made the transportation of persons across state lines to serve as prostitutes a federal crime.

Raymond sent Munson a telegram demanding that he resign as a police commissioner "for the good of Los Angeles." After receiving it, Munson sought help from Gans. Gans, whom one reporter dubbed "our own local Prince of Monaco," summoned Raymond to his office. What was the point of the telegram? Gans asked. Raymond explained that Munson owed Gray money and he was determined that he would make him pay it.[5]

Gans decided not to get involved in the matter, and Munson held firm to his protestation of poverty. Raymond, by now out of his San Diego job, figured the Tulsa woman was key to breaking Munson. He and Gray drove east to Tulsa on the recently designated Route 66, where they found and interviewed Meyers. What she told them was enough to convince them they had something to force Munson to pay up. Raymond dispatched another telegram to Munson with the same message as before. Resign. Coming from Oklahoma, it had teeth.

Raymond and Gray hurried back to Los Angeles, where, in mid-February 1934, they drove to a spot a few blocks from the Biltmore Hotel and parked. Leaving both Gray and his revolver in the automobile, Raymond entered the Biltmore's lavish entrance and rode the elevator to Parrot's office on the seventh floor. Waiting for him were the kingpins of the Los Angeles vice syndicate: Kent Parrot, Bob Gans, and Guy McAfee. Also present was Harry Munson.

The conference of such an august group of scofflaws reflected the importance they placed on Harry Munson's position as police commissioner, if not on Munson himself. The commissioners not only set the payroll levels for the LAPD, they also influenced the department's policies and sometimes intervened in administrative matters. For the past year, first as a collector for contributions to the Shaw campaign and now as a valuable ally on the Police Board, Munson had done their bidding. It soon became clear, however, that their loyalty had limits. Raymond had the goods on Munson. A detailed accusation that he had violated the Mann Act by helping a prostitute move to Los Angeles and then return to Tulsa would sink him even if it could never be proven in court. Parrot, McAfee, and Gans must have seen the problem clearly. As Munson tried to defend himself, it became even more certain. However loyal to them Munson may have been, they knew that Mayor Shaw could find somebody else for the Board of Police Commissioners to protect their interests.

As for Harry Raymond, they all knew him. If, as some would allege, Raymond threatened to expose their campaign donations, it did not work. The three syndicate leaders declined to do anything more than usher Munson out of his job. Later, they may have reflected that it would have been better just to pay off Gray and perhaps Raymond as well. That day, they agreed only that Munson had to go.

He did not go far, however. After resigning from the Board of Police Commissioners on February 21, 1934, he continued to work as a bagman for the LA syndicate, funneling cash from gamblers to the Shaw administration and the LAPD hierarchy. He kept rooms at the Hayward Hotel in downtown Los Angeles, one of the premium hotels of LA and the site of many political and business meetings. In April, Gray forced him to admit in Superior Court to a $2,900 debt. Still, he did not pay up.

Ralph Gray [Courtesy of Lisa Gray]

...y Munson (second ...n right) with 1931 ...e Commissioners ...s Angeles Times ...ographic Archive, ...CLA Library. ...yright Regents of ...e University of ...lifornia, UCLA Library]

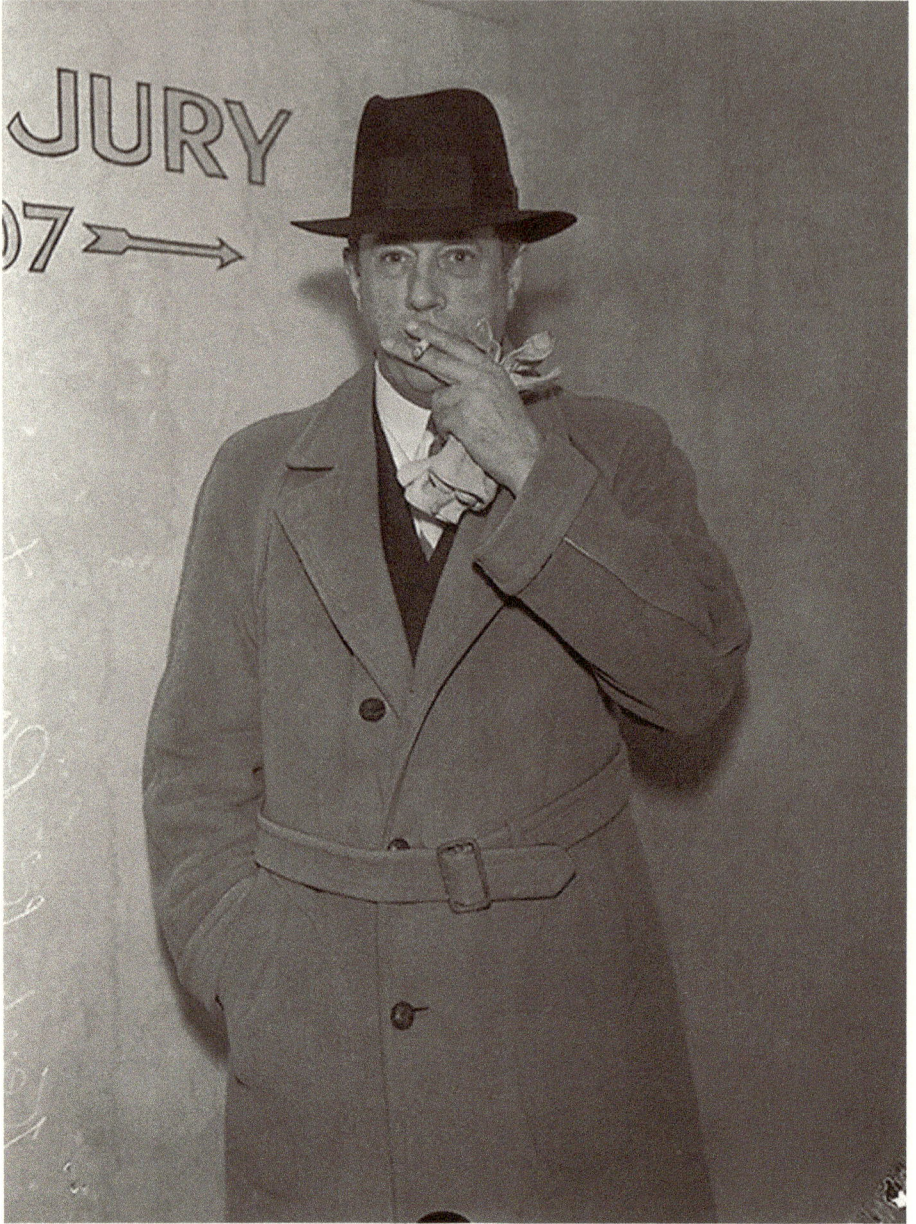

Kent Kane Parrot in 1935 [Los Angeles Times Photographic Archive, UCLA Library. Copyright Regents of the University of California, UCLA Library]

14: BATTLE IN THE GRAND JURY

There is little trace of Harry Raymond in the two years following his January 1936 automobile accident. How long he convalesced is not certain, but his injuries, including a compound fracture of one of his legs, were serious enough to keep a normal man in a wheelchair or on crutches for at least five months. By October, he was able to travel to Dallas for a convention of the International Association for Identification, which honored him with a lifetime membership. Although no longer employed by the Auto Club, Raymond made money. He had sufficient income to rent a two-bedroom bungalow in the Boyle Heights section of Los Angeles for himself and Beulah. In the fall of 1938, he bought a new Chrysler Royal. Most likely, he had returned to work as a private detective and was taking on jobs with the LAPD. A newspaper in Yuma, where he and LAPD Lieutenant W. R. Porter stopped for the night in March 1937 on the way home from the funeral of former Phoenix police chief George O. Brisbois, reported that he was associated with the Automobile Club of Southern California. At some point during the two years after his automobile accident, he began to share his knowledge of LA's organized crime with the city's reformers, who continued to battle with the political and police powers that enabled gambling and other forms of vice to flourish.

In April 1937, LA County Supervisor John Anson Ford ran against incumbent Mayor Frank Shaw. Ford had the support of reformers but not Briegleb and Rheba Crawford. However, when he assailed vice and corruption within City Hall, he earned strong rejoinders from the *Los Angeles Times*, a key Shaw supporter, which panned him for his failure to name the civic officials and high-ranking police officers he claimed were corrupt. Damaged also by allegations that he was a radical supported by communists, Ford failed to win endorsements from any major Los Angeles newspaper and lost the election to Shaw, who collected fifty-four percent of the vote. While only a quarter of registered voters cast ballots, the results indicated that the citizens of Los Angeles were largely satisfied with the Shaw administration. "The Shaw campaign has been based on the record of the city government in the four years he has been Mayor," the *Times* declared. "The city government works evenly and smoothly. The police department, although sadly depleted in personnel and finances, has reduced the rate of crime and has prevented the disorder characteristic of other major American cities. Withal, the police department has not interfered unnecessarily with the citizens."[1]

While the endorsements of the *Los Angeles Times* and other Los Angeles newspapers were important to Shaw's reelection campaign, monetary support from LA's underworld syndicate was critical. According to the *Hollywood Citizen-News,* after spending $2 million to re-elect Fitts in 1936, the underworld contributed $1.5 million to Shaw's reelection campaign.

With Shaw's re-election and that of Fitts the previous year, Parrot, McAfee, Gans, and other members of LA's underworld syndicate could look tranquilly on the prospects for continued profits in 1937. The syndicate leaders must have calculated that the major threat to their power came not from law enforcement, the press, or reformers but from the ambitions of the mayor, his brother, and a host of outsiders, both eastern and local. Joe Shaw had allied himself with a group of Italian mobsters who had long pecked away at the crumbs the syndicate let drop in the city, including Johnny Roselli, a close associate of Columbia Pictures head Harry Cohn, and Jack Dragna, a mafioso who had been around LA for years without much success. Roselli and Dragna had teamed up before, launching several ill-fated adventures, including a short-lived dog track in Hollywood. Shaw had also brought into his camp former vice squad officer Rusty Williams and veteran racketeer Andy Foley. Meanwhile, former bootlegger Tony Cornero, relatively inactive since serving a two-year prison sentence at McNeil Federal Penitentiary for violating prohibition laws, was about to float a gambling ship off the Santa Monica coast with his brother Frank. For ten years, Cornero had been fighting the Internal Revenue Service's claim that he owed $307,000 in back taxes. Despite a decade of hijackings, robberies, fires, union disputes, and suicides that plagued the gambling ships—not to mention DA Buron Fitts' vigorous legal assaults on the vessels—Cornero saw his financial salvation on what he considered the high seas.

Other racketeers found opportunities in the smaller cities and unincorporated areas of the county. Benjamin "Bugsy" Siegel, a New York associate of imprisoned Charles "Lucky" Luciano, began investing in gambling operations in Hermosa and Redondo Beach as early as 1936. Dave Clark, the killer of Charles Crawford and Herbert Spencer, owned part of a Hawthorne tango parlor and represented other tango parlor operators as they clashed with local police and the county sheriff.[2]

In late July 1937, the attempted assassination of another county gambling figure set the city and county on edge. George Lester "Les" Bruneman, owner of a Redondo Beach gambling joint named "The Surf" and several bookmaking establishments, was strolling along the boardwalk on the Redondo Beach pier with a young woman when he passed two smartly dressed young men, who were later described as "Latins" or Italians, leaning over the pier railing. Suddenly the two men whirled and fired three shots at the couple. One penetrated Bruneman's lung. One of the men yelled, "I got him" before both disappeared in the crowd. Police later found a .45 caliber automatic pistol in a nearby parking lot and another in the sands of a vacant lot.[3]

Bruneman was a well-known figure in Los Angeles gambling operations. A San Francisco native, he had joined the merchant marine as an ordinary seaman in 1918 at age twenty. He was good with his fists, in and out of the ring, so good that he was booked for attempted murder after fracturing another man's skull in a Los Angeles fistfight in 1925. When he arrived in LA is not clear, but by 1923, he was running a bootleg joint named the Cabaria Café on North Main Street with Jesse Orsatti. He also became a gunman in Farmer Page's battles with Tony Cornero.

In 1930, Bruneman played a key role in the kidnapping of Zeke Caress by members of the Ralph Sheldon gang, which ended in a gun battle with Long Beach police that left a patrolman paralyzed for life. Although Caress told police that Bruneman had accompanied the gunmen at his request to obtain ransom money from an offshore gambling ship, Bruneman was tried along with Sheldon and two members of his gang for shooting the patrolman. The jury declined to convict any of the defendants, convinced somehow that it mattered that the police fired first. Six months later, however, police obtained a confession from James Gatewood, another gang member, which implicated Bruneman as part of the kidnapping plot.

Bruneman decided not to wait around for another trial. While Sheldon and his compatriots, including Orsatti, were tried, convicted and sent to prison for kidnapping, Bruneman hid in Canada. Two years later, in February 1934, he surrendered to LAPD detectives in Hollywood. Tried and convicted on the strength of Gatewood's testimony, he won a retrial on a legal technicality. In the meantime, Gatewood had taken a job as a seaman and left the state. Without his testimony, the prosecution had no case. Bruneman was set free to return to his former career. He began to muscle his way into gambling establishments throughout the county, bumping heads with Italian mobsters Jack Dragna and Johnny Roselli.

Los Angeles County law enforcement reacted to Bruneman's shooting with its usual short-lived vigor. While Bruneman lay struggling to survive in a Torrance hospital bed, his heavily armed friends guarding the door of his room, DA Buron Fitts announced the beginning of what the *Los Angeles Times* described as a "gambling purge." Fitts warned that the attack on Bruneman "may develop into a war between various factions of gangsters and gamblers." Characteristically, the DA warned of "an influx recently to Los Angeles of out-of-town underworld characters bent on intrenching themselves in this community." The following day, the *Times* redefined the "purge" as a "War . . . on Gang Rule." LA County Sheriff Eugene Biscailuz echoed Fitts' warning about "eastern criminals" invading the county. LAPD Chief James Davis pledged his support, but qualified that, "There are no gangsters in [the city of] Los Angeles." His view was seconded by Mayor Shaw, who observed that racketeers had "congregated outside the city limits, in neighboring communities and unincorporated county territory."[4]

Davis and Shaw's assessment about the presence of gangsters and racketeers within the city may not have been accurate, but it turned out to be prescient. Most gambling hall operators and bookies quickly fled or went into hiding in the face of grand jury subpoenas. The anti-vice campaign mainly netted low-level offenders and their patrons.

On July 19, two days before the attack on Bruneman, restaurateur Clifford Clinton attended a mass meeting at the First German American Methodist Church along with religious and secular reform leaders, including Bob Shuler and Dr. Allan M. Wilkinson, a Hollywood physician and church leader. Thirty-six years old, Clinton had been born into a missionary family. He had spent some of his childhood in China, where he was moved profoundly by the hunger and starvation he witnessed among the Chinese people. In the early twenties, he followed his father into the cafeteria business in San Francisco, promising his staff that they would get 95% of the profits.

In 1931, he moved to Los Angeles, opening a Polynesian-themed cafeteria on South Olive Street, followed a year later by a second location on South Hill he called the "Penny Cafeteria," where a penny bought a meal of stew, coleslaw, and Jell-O with a cup of coffee. The cafeterias were popular but not profitable. On opening the first, Clinton declared it the "cafeteria of the golden rule." While meals had a set price as in other restaurants, Clinton's patrons were allowed to pay what they wished, which could be nothing at all. In the hard times of the depression, ten thousand meals were served free-of-charge during one 90-day period. Somehow, Clinton made ends meet, and in 1934, he opened a third cafeteria with a redwood forest theme on South Broadway. He also became president of the Restaurant Alliance, an organization founded to meet the requirements of the National Recovery Act, an experience that gave him his first taste of civic engagement.[5]

Clinton had the square, determined face of a modern day technocrat. It was also the face of a Baptist preacher. He was a religious man but also practical. His father taught him to organize for efficiency and cut waste, and his cafeterias proved that he had learned his lesson. In 1934, Los Angeles

County Supervisor John Anson Ford appointed him to lead an investigation of conditions at the new Los Angeles County General Hospital. Clinton's committee identified reforms that saved the hospital $120,000 annually. Unfortunately, the reforms also interfered with the petty graft enjoyed by the Shaw administration's allies. After the committee's report became public, newspapers sympathetic to Mayor Shaw attacked both it and Clinton. Stink bombs exploded in his cafeteria and professional "floppers" tripped in his restaurants or fell down stairs, then followed up with damage suits against the restaurants. Other patrons filed suits alleging food poisoning. While none of the suits were ever settled or made it to trial, their message—and that of the stink bombs, harassing health department inspections and unaccountable increases in property tax assessments—was clear. Clinton had made some powerful enemies.

In 1936, Supervisor John Anson Ford convinced Superior Court Justice Fletcher Bowron to nominate Clinton for the 1937 Los Angeles County Grand Jury. Bowron submitted Clinton's name, which was drawn along with twenty-nine others from a raffle wheel containing 130 names. Clinton was then appointed to the jury by Justice William Aggeler, who stressed that the jurors should "diligently inquire into public offenders against the people" and "act diligently, faithfully, and courageously" if they believed that public officials were "guilty of corrupt or willful misconduct in office." Ignoring advice from the chairman of the previous grand jury to "be content to be a mill and grind out what [the District Attorney] . . . bring[s] you," Clinton proposed that the current jury investigate the open flouting of vice and gambling laws in the county. Opposed by Foreman John Bauer, a wealthy owner of a paint-manufacturing firm with city government contracts, the motion failed, but Clinton persisted. After Dr. Wilkinson presented evidence of Los Angeles' organized crime operations to the grand jury, Clinton and several other jurors began their own investigation.[6]

After the meeting at the First German American Methodist Church, Clinton and other attendees agreed to support Rev. Wendell L. Miller's request to Mayor Shaw to deputize a small group that could make arrests of gamblers and operators of bordellos. Shaw struggled to respond to Miller's request. At first, he reacted furiously, claiming, "politically ambitious persons who use unsubstantiated vice allegations as their step-ladder to notoriety" had organized the July meeting. But he also endorsed the vice investigation of the United Church Women of Los Angeles that the meeting spawned, declaring, "[W]hen they make their report Los Angeles will get the truth." After thrashing about for a few days, he agreed to Clinton's request for a meeting with a self-appointed group called the Citizens Independent Vice Investigative Committee (CIVIC) in the mayor's office. Clinton recalled that after he "made a clear statement, as previously approved [by the committee], laying out our aims and intentions, and stating we wanted the mayor's authority to act," Shaw reacted angrily, accusing the reformers of being "snoopers, busy-bodies, and self-seekers" who had opposed his re-election. However, he ultimately granted them the authority they had requested, despite Police Chief Davis' accusation that the real goal of the committee was to begin a recall election the following year.[7]

Shaw's official recognition of CIVIC lasted just over a week. Davis' argument that CIVIC was a political danger to the mayor convinced him to revoke his support. In a blistering letter to Clinton, who was now the committee chairman, Shaw condemned the group as "temperamentally incapable of distinguishing sincere investigation from irresponsible snooping . . . calculated to destroy confidence in the duly elected representatives of the people." He charged that CIVIC had violated its pledge to shun political activities and was failing to restrain its members from "irresponsible utterances." Shaw claimed that CIVIC members were meeting secretly with "discredited and repudiated political demagogues" to find "ways and means of circumventing the will of the people." CIVIC, the mayor charged, was attempting to set itself up as a "citizen's grand jury" contrary to the "American form of government." Clinton's participation in CIVIC, the mayor alleged, was inconsistent with his duties as a grand jury member.[8]

In the coming months, the Shaw administration and its supporters in the press and grand jury rooms continued to attack Clinton. His restaurants, guided by the principle of the Golden Rule, were besieged by what he described as "a long stream of . . . unkempt folk who sat in our lobbies, congregated around our entrances and in our dining rooms, seating themselves with our better dressed guests, causing annoyance." The "unkempt folk" were directed to the restaurants by Shaw administration employees. After receiving their free meals, some claimed they had been poisoned. City officials began challenging the restaurant's compliance with health ordinances.[9]

In September, Clinton filed a $1 million lawsuit against his detractors through A. Brigham Rose, an anti-vice attorney recommended by Harry Raymond. Rose was a flamboyant lawyer whose courtroom antics annoyed judges and had already earned him three citations for contempt of court. While Clinton's lawsuit against his detractors went nowhere, the partnership of Clinton and Rose would prove effective over the next twelve months.[10]

Other members of CIVIC came under attack by the Shaws and their allies. In September, a scandal broke out involving Allan M. Wilkinson, another prominent CIVIC member. In 1936, Wilkinson helped manage a dramatic religious spectacle at the Los Angeles Coliseum based on Lord Edward

Bulwer-Lytton's novel, *The Last Days of Pompeii*. Sponsored by the Los Angeles Federated Church Brotherhood to benefit a new mountain camp for underprivileged boys, the event was to run for 10 nights. It was billed as "one of the largest and most impressive spectacles that has ever been given in Los Angeles" with a cast of 750 actors and an artificial Mount Vesuvius as high as the Coliseum's upper seats. "[T]he show will feature chariot races, bacchanalian frolics, martyrdom of Christians and the color and life of the old Roman city," one newspaper reported. Elephants and lions were to take part in the display, along with tableau actors covered in bronze. Each night, the drama concluded as a replica of Mt. Vesuvius erupted in a massive fireworks show.[11]

Charles H. Duffield, the leading pyrotechnics expert in the United States, came from Chicago to produce the show. Duffield had put on the spectacle and others like it for forty years, making a good profit for himself and the institutions that hired him. With a popular motion picture of the same name playing in the theaters, "The Last Days of Pompeii" must have seemed a sure moneymaker for the Church Brotherhood and Duffield, who was to receive $27,500 for his efforts. Unfortunately, two weeks before the grand opening a three-way squabble broke out over the Church Brotherhoods' rental of the Coliseum between the Coliseum Commission, the County Board of Supervisors, and the Los Angeles City Council. The Coliseum Commission agreed to charge the Church Brotherhood $1,000 per night for the use of the Coliseum, but the Board of Supervisors overruled it and let the stadium for no charge, asking only that the Church Brotherhood pay for cleanup. When the contract reached the City Council, several councilmen condemned the arrangement, pointing out that other charities were charged $2,000 per night. As the Church Brotherhood was stalling to get a reduction in the cleanup fees and had not signed the contract, the City Council took over the lease negotiations itself. After a week, the Council and the Brotherhood agreed to a rental fee of $5,000 for all ten days plus an additional $5,000 to cover the cleanup costs.

While the terms of the final lease seemed favorable to the Church Brotherhood, it soon became clear that the organization had badly mismanaged the financials. After four days, despite decent attendance, including some well-known Hollywood film actors, the event was in serious financial difficulty, owing $3,500 to the Coliseum Commission and $22,500 to Duffield. In desperation, Wilkinson reached out for additional donors. Two unlikely benefactors came forward: gambling kingpin Guy McAfee and slot machine tycoon Bob Gans. McAfee offered a $4,400 loan and Gans gave $400. In late August 1937, during a grand jury investigation into rumors that certain anti-vice reformers demanded payoffs from vice leaders, Wilkinson explained that McAfee offered the loans to prove that "even a gambler has a heart." He testified that, a few days after receiving the loan he had visited McAfee in his office with Glen Phillips, pastor of the First Methodist Church of Hollywood, and the three men had knelt together as Phillips prayed that McAfee might be led from his life as a gambler. Afterward, McAfee told them he was impressed by the prayer and pledged to give up gambling, but only slowly, as quitting suddenly might shock his nervous system.[12]

Wilkinson stated that he thought taking the loan from the arch-gambler of Los Angeles was justified as long as "it was in the service of the Lord." However, his account brought ridicule and discredit on his work as a reformer. He had been played by McAfee, a point the *Los Angeles Times* made in an editorial when it observed that "the revelation that Guy McAfee was the angel of the Church Brotherhood . . . is less interesting than the story, if it could be had, of just how McAfee came to make the gift and who suggested it to him."[13]

A few days later, Duffield, disconsolate over the failure of the show and the financial loss he was facing, wrote a note to his wife stating, "It took the Church Brotherhood to break me" and shot himself in the head with a pearl-handled revolver. While he survived the suicide attempt, the bullet demolished one of his eyes and left the other useless.[14]

By accepting donations from McAfee and Gans, Wilkinson lost credibility as a reformer. At Shuler's insistence, he resigned from CIVIC, but the other members of the organization, led by Clinton, declined his resignation. A few weeks later, however, the County Board of Supervisors removed him from the County Welfare Commission. It was a rapid and steep fall for the veteran churchman. It also damaged the credibility of CIVIC and Clifford Clinton. Accusations of hypocrisy were dangerous to reformers. Even worse were accusations that their real interest in attacking gamblers was to elicit payoffs or take over vice operations. The indictment and eventual guilty plea of another CIVIC leader, Robert Coyne, for attempting to extort two Huntington Beach gamblers and trying to bribe Santa Monica officials to allow him to set up a bookmaking joint, did not help matters.[15] Nevertheless, Clinton and CIVIC pressed on. Clinton and his supporters conducted at least a dozen raids on Los Angeles bordellos, including some on Central Avenue, a key commercial area in the African American community, using grand jury badges to convince the operators of their legal authority. In September, Clinton obtained permission from the grand jury to present his own criminal inquiry and issue subpoenas on his own. The following week, he brought Wilbur Le Gette before the somewhat mystified jurors. He also announced that he had subpoenaed Rheba Crawford, who, from her bed in the Queen of Angels Hospital, reacted with indignation, declaring that she didn't know "what it was all about" but suspected that she was about to be made the "goat in a political plot."[16]

Over the next few weeks, Clinton pursued his investigation in the face of mounting opposition from Foreman John Bauer and a majority of his nineteen fellow jurors. The jury room discussions were heated. Fearing witness intimidation or corruption, Clinton refused to disclose the goals of his investigation. All his fellow jurors knew—and all the newspapers reported—was that prominent officials, underworld characters, and Rheba Crawford were implicated. Annoyed by Clinton's tactics, most other jurors dismissed the testimony as hearsay and suspected that it was designed to discredit city officials. Finally, Bauer refused to allow further testimony, declaring, "We are not going to be led around by the nose by one man." In response, Clinton and Brigham Rose filed a writ of mandamus in Superior Court to force the jurors to hear the evidence. The petition accused the other jurors of blocking the investigation and criticized the district attorney's office for failing to support it. Fitts responded that he had offered Clinton full support for his investigation but only "in compliance with the laws governing such investigations" and not "in a scheme to further the political ambitions of Mr. Clinton." Clinton then attempted to have the Superior Court remove six jurors because of conflicts of interest. Superior Court Judge Emmett Wilson rejected this attempt and Rose's writ of mandamus, ruling that only Superior Court Justice Charles W. Fricke, officially in charge of the grand jury, could approve Clinton's petition. Fricke had already advised Clinton that it was necessary for him to disclose the goals of his investigation and the names of his prospective witnesses before he would support him.[17]

Clinton's investigation was finished for the time being, but events were in the saddle.

After the first attack on his life in Redondo Beach Les Bruneman spent several months recuperating at the Torrance and Queen of Angels hospitals. Afterward, he hid out in a ranch north of Phoenix, his home for a few years in the late 1920s, planning to relocate to Dallas as soon as he recovered his health. He knew people in Dallas and could start anew there. By October, however, he was back in Los Angeles with sponsors who wanted a new gambling establishment in the basement of the Montmartre Café in Hollywood and another in Palm Springs, a favorite vacation spot of wealthy film producers and actors. On the evening of Sunday, October 25, 1937, he was in the Café Montmartre in Hollywood with Alice Ingram, an attractive young blonde who had nursed him at the Queen of Angels Hospital. They had spent the day together, eating breakfast at a ranch in Montebello, and then enjoying an afternoon tryst at Bruneman's apartment in Los Angeles. After dinner and some highballs, they left the Montmartre to meet Alice's sister and her boyfriend at the Roost Café, a small beer parlor housed in a rustic single-story wooden frame building at the corner of West Temple Street and Benton Way, not far from Alice's apartment on Coronado Terrace. Overhung by a tall eucalyptus tree, it looked like a country roadhouse. Two stone steps led up to a wide wooden porch and narrow front door, beyond which a small parlor of a half dozen tables, two booths, and a short bar with tall stools were squeezed into a twenty by sixteen room.

It was shortly after midnight when Bruneman and Ingram arrived at the Roost. Alice's sister Mary and her boyfriend, Robert Palden, were waiting for them at a table in the center of the room just inside the door. Four or five other patrons were scattered around other tables and at the bar. Alice introduced Bruneman to the café owner, Roy Huddle. Bruneman ordered a round of drinks for everybody in the establishment.

After about thirty minutes, long enough for Bruneman to order two more rounds for the house, Alice's sister and her boyfriend began to quarrel and moved to another table to talk things over. Around a quarter to one, Bruneman gave a few quarters to Elaine Huddle, Roy's wife, to put in the jukebox. She was dropping them into the coin slot when she noticed two men coming up the porch toward the front door. Assuming they were customers, she walked over to greet them, but they burst into the room before she reached the door. They were both in their early thirties, of medium height, with dark complexions. They were both dressed immaculately in expensive brown suits and hats with complementing ties. They both had revolvers in each of their hands.

Bruneman looked up just as a bullet smashed through his glasses into his left eye. He fell back onto the floor as the gunmen continued to shoot, his two revolvers useless on his belt and in his hip pocket. Alice leapt to her feet. Two stray bullets hit her leg and shin and she dropped to the floor.

As the two gunmen backed through the front door, a café worker, Frank Greuzard, a young man with more courage than sense, rushed after them. Elaine screamed at him. "For God's sake, don't go out there!" but it was too late. One gunman warned Greuzard to get back, but the youth, perhaps hoping to get a glimpse of their automobile's license plate, rushed through the door onto the porch. He took two bullets in his abdomen and heart.[18]

Inside, Bruneman was stretched out on his back, bleeding from twelve bullets. Three struck his head, and the rest peppered his stomach, chest, abdomen and legs. Mary Ingram was screaming hysterically and her sister Alice, oblivious to the fact that she had been shot herself, shouted at her to shut up. The other patrons began to rise from behind the chairs where they had ducked when the gunplay began. The restaurant's bartender, peering out a side window toward Benton Way, saw the two gunmen dash into a small sedan in which three men waited. As the car drove off into the fog, he could see that it had no rear license plate.

In the days after the slaying of Bruneman and Greuzard, LA city officials issued their usual proclamations. Mayor Shaw declared, "gangsterism will not be permitted to get a foothold in Los Angeles." "The law enforcement agencies of Los Angeles city and county have established a fine record in keeping the metropolitan area free from racketeers and gangsters," he declared. The LAPD, led by Homicide Captain Bert Wallis, speculated that the gunmen had come from the east—likely St. Louis or Chicago—to finish the job that local hoods botched months before in Redondo Beach. Sheriff Biscailuz pledged his support in combating the renewed threat of eastern gangsters. However, District Attorney Buron Fitts declined to start a separate investigation, leaving matters up to the city and county police agencies. The *Los Angeles Times* opined that the shootings were "a call to police action, swift, sure and decisive . . . . Headlines call it a 'gamblers war,' but it is plainly the ugly head of gangland racketeering itself in this community."[19][20]

On the day of Bruneman's funeral in San Francisco, a second act of violence shocked Los Angeles. In the early morning of Friday, October 29, a bomb filled with chloride of potash exploded outside the kitchen wall of Clifford Clinton's palatial home on Los Feliz Boulevard as a green sedan sped away. Clinton was not at home, but he arrived within a few minutes as the smoke continued to pour from a large hole in the wall. His family, asleep in the upstairs bedroom when the bomb detonated, was unhurt. Two hours later, Clinton received a phone call. "Well, what do you think of that little puff-puff we gave you?" a voice asked. "We just wanted you to know how it feels to have the floor boards come up in your face. Next time we'll lift the whole house."

"There is no question but this is a reprisal for my efforts in attempting to get rid of gambling and vice in Los Angeles County," Clinton later declared. "I have received several threats in the past weeks."[21]

Clinton's comments touched off another dispute in the grand jury room. Led by Foreman Bauer, the majority demanded that Clinton "conform with the law and declare such evidence as he asserts is in his possession, of the commission of a public offense, in order that this jury may conform with the law and proceed with an investigation thereof." Clinton responded by stating that he had proved that the "grand jury is contaminated by insidious influences and that the criminal complaints committee has no place of standing in the law." He vowed to protect his sources until a judicial review answered his charges that some grand jury members were compromised by sinister influences.[22]

The battle between the Clinton-led minority and the grand jury majority continued throughout November and December. It was a war of attrition, with Bauer charging Clinton and his supporters on the jury with contempt for refusing to testify about their evidence of vice and corruption while Clinton, through Rose, charged that Bauer committed contempt when he failed to recuse himself in a case where he was an interested party. At one point, Clinton was forced to reveal whom he believed were the leaders of LA's gambling and vice industry, but he did so by using the letters of the alphabet to designate the underworld figures instead of their names.

The term of the 1937 Grand Jury ended on December 31. Bauer put forth the jury's obligatory report, blasting Clinton and his cohorts in and outside the Grand Jury.[23]

Clinton and the minority faction responded with a lengthy report addressed to the Superior Court of Los Angeles County. It outlined the operations of "a powerful, greedy, cruel, ruthless underworld political machine supplied with an abundance of funds from the growing profits from illicit operations, including protected gambling." It also named twenty-eight individuals and families operating vice establishments within the county, including Guy McAfee and Bob Gans but omitting Kent Kane Parrot. And, it declared that the "law enforcement agencies of the County, the District Attorney, the Sheriff and the chief of police of Los Angeles, work in complete harmony and never interfere with the activities of the important figures in the underworld."[24]

While Superior Court Judge Fricke refused the minority report, ruling, "[t]here is no provision under law by which a minority report may be filed," the document was the most thorough description of the Los Angeles syndicate and its control of law enforcement, prosecutorial, and political agencies since the vice scandal of 1909. Still, the argument of the 1937 Grand Jury report was powerful. Clinton and his allies inside and outside the jury room did not provide clear evidence of criminal acts that could be prosecuted in a court of law. The syndicate was too powerful, too well organized, too deeply embedded in Los Angeles civic affairs, and too well represented legally for anything but the most determined and well-supported prosecutor or politician to oppose it.

It is easy to imagine that in some alternative world, faced with an indifferent public and its representatives, Clinton would have given up his fight against the dark powers he had opposed for twelve months and retired from the field to run his restaurants. Still, change was coming. With Joe Shaw's help, easterners *were* moving in, bringing the dispassionate, professional violence that LA's populace had long feared. The Bruneman slaying was not the first gangster assassination in Los Angeles history—two east coast hoodlums were gunned down a few years before in a downtown restaurant in reprisal for deeds done in New York City—but it was the first since prohibition that appeared to result from territorial rivalries between gangsters. The descriptions of the suspects as "Latins" or Italians and speculation they were from out of town fed fears of an impending gangster war reminiscent of those of New York City and Chicago. Middle class Southern Californians who had been indifferent to the regions' vice were becoming alarmed.

A. Brigham Rose (left) and Clifford Clinton [Los Angeles Times Photographic Archive, Charles E Young Research Library, University of California at Los Angeles]

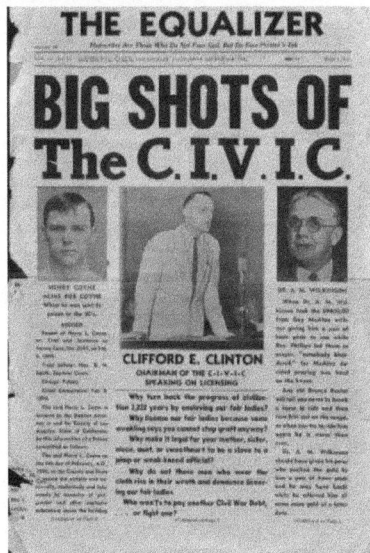

Red Foster's Equalizer attacks CIVIC leaders [Wendell Miller Collection, Special Collections & Archives, University Library, California State University Northridge]

George "Les" Bruneman in
1934 [Los Angeles Times
Photographic Archive,
UCLA Library. Copyright
Regents of the University
of California, UCLA
Library]

Roost Cafe, site of the Bruneman murder. [The J. Paul Getty Museum, Los
Angeles. George Watson, 1937, Gelatin silver print, 7 × 21.4 cm.]

15: EXPLOSION

While local newspapers headlined the dramatic infighting between grand jurors, the dispute between Munson and Gray continued through 1937. After Munson filed in federal court for bankruptcy protection, Gray hired reform lawyer Brigham Rose to oppose Munson's petition. On June 17, Raymond accompanied Ralph Gray to a preliminary hearing on Munson's bankruptcy petition. When they arrived, Raymond observed Earle Kynette in the courtroom's foyer talking with Munson. He knew Kynette well. They had worked together on the murder trial of Frank Rocco and Dominic Leo for the gangland murder of Carmine Buono in 1929.

The two detectives greeted each other and talked shop for a few minutes. Kynette wanted Raymond's help in finding Geraldine Williams, the former wife of Orville Forrester, who had figured in the Buono case. The conversation was friendly until Raymond asked him why he was "fooling around" with Munson. Munson, Kynette responded, was a friend of his and Joe Shaw. He added he had heard there would be an accusation made against a prominent political figure. He wanted to know who and what was involved. "If you want to know what's going on, you get a front seat and sit down in there and listen and you'll find out," Raymond retorted.

From that point, according to Gray, watching from across the hall, things got ugly. Kynette chided Raymond for drinking too much, alluding to a recent incident at the 411 Club in downtown Los Angeles, a popular night club with the Hollywood set, where a drunken Raymond got into a scuffle that resulted in a woman breaking her ankle. Raymond accused Kynette of getting his information from Buron Fitts.

After the hearing, the two men met again outside on the sidewalk outside the Hall of Records. Raymond recalled, "[Kynette] said in substance this: 'This is an election year and you know what this money is for.'"

Raymond was still puzzled about Kynette's interest in the case. "Which office do you work from, anyway?" he asked.

"I work from the chief's office but I get my orders from Joe Shaw, and this has got to stop," Kynette responded. "You can't put the heat on the administration."

Incensed, Raymond told him he would make sure that Gray got the money that was due him. Alluding to Munson's claim that he was bankrupt, he told Kynette, "A man can't ride around in a 1937 De Soto sedan and have $150 suits and have a suite of rooms at the Hayward Hotel and have his meals brought upstairs and a private barber shave him unless he has got some money," he told Kynette.

"I'm going to see that nothing happens to Munson," Kynette retorted. "I head the intelligence squad, you know."

"What are you going to do with me?" Raymond demanded.

"You'll find out later," Kynette said.

"Well, you've bamboozled people long enough as far as I'm concerned," Raymond said. He turned to walk away.

"Don't get too tough," Kynette warned. "Don't forget what happened to that little boy—Red Foster."

Raymond knew he was referring to the bombing of Foster's apartment. "I know what happened to Red Foster," he responded, "But from what you say, I guess you know more about it than I do."

The Munson bankruptcy hearing was continued to September 1, at which time Gray would testify that Munson received a campaign donation between $10,000 and $12,000 in cash for Shaw's election from Guy McAfee, the money bulging from both of his pockets as he left the gambling baron's office.[25]

According to Kynette, the Special Intelligence Unit's surveillance of Harry Raymond began in July 1937, after Jack Southard, an investigator in District Attorney Buron Fitts' office, asked him to place a Dictaphone in Raymond's home. Southard suspected Raymond was involved in several criminal activities, including an assassination attempt on Fitts himself. In March 1937, Fitts and his wife had hosted a dinner party for a few friends, including Jerry Giesler and his wife, at his palatial home on East Royal Oaks in Duarte. After the dinner, Fitts went to visit his father, who lived a quarter mile away on Foothill Boulevard (now Royal Oaks Drive). While his guests retired to the living room, Fitts drove down his long driveway, which ran between groves of orange trees. At the entrance to the driveway, he glimpsed a dark sedan with its lights out parked behind some bushes. Three men were in it. As he passed the automobile, it burst out onto the road behind him and pulled alongside. Sensing danger, Fitts slammed on the brakes and the car roared past. As it did, two shots rang out. One bullet penetrated his left forearm. Another crashed through his front windshield and lodged in a sun visor. While his arm was broken by the bullet, the bleeding stopped soon after Fitts reached his parents' house a few minutes later. He was taken to the Good Samaritan

Hospital on Wilshire. The county launched an extensive investigation into the assault.

Although Fitts suspected union agitators, angered by his indictment of strikers at the Douglas Aircraft Company, were behind the attack, rumors reached him that Harry Raymond was in the area at the time of the shooting. According to Southard, Raymond was "mixed up in several things," including a scheme to force Los Angeles beer parlors to purchase their liquor from San Diego breweries. Believing Raymond was tailing him and Deputy DA Eugene Williams, Fitts assigned an operative to shadow Raymond. In the fall, when Clinton challenged the integrity of members of the grand jury, Fitts suspected that Raymond, Le Gette, and James Alexander, an African American private eye who specialized in the African-American neighborhood along Central Avenue, were part of a conspiracy to produce "false affidavits" designed to discredit grand jurors.[26]

On September 21, Earle Kynette directed one of his subordinates, Lieutenant Daniel M. Draper, to rent an apartment in Boyle Heights under a fictitious name, John M. Craven. The apartment took up half of a forty feet long and twenty-three feet wide single story building in the rear of a narrow courtyard of barrack-like residences on the 2700 block of 7th Street. Its front door opened on a small living and dining room, from which doors led to a bedroom and kitchen. What interested Draper and his boss were the dwelling's ready access to phone lines and its back door that opened onto a gravel alley running sixty-five feet to Orme Avenue. A window looked out the porch toward the front driveway and porch of Harry Raymond's residence at 955 Orme.

A few days later, Draper and two other SIU members moved into the apartment. Kynette ordered Draper to install a Dictaphone to record conversations in the Raymond home. That night, neighbors watched as the police officers ran telephone wires from the apartment's bedroom to the roof of another courtyard building and up a telephone pole on the northwest corner of Orme and 7th Street. A final wire would connect to a telephone box at Raymond's home.

The SIU's surveillance of Raymond lasted four months, from mid-September 1937 to mid-January 1938. The stakeout of his home began around September 25. For the first month, two officers were assigned to the apartment, Leo F. McDonald and Delbert T. Phegley, who watched Raymond's residence from 9:00 a.m. to 11:30 p.m. In October, Fred A. Browne and Roy J. Allen joined them. The quartet worked in two shifts of two men each, the shifts changing at 3:30 a.m. and 3:30 p.m., covering all twenty-four hours.

Kynette instructed his detectives not to keep any written records but to report the license plates of all visitors to the Raymond home. In particular, he was interested in any cars bearing Nevada plates. According to Kynette, the DA's office suspected Raymond of having criminal ties to the nascent gambling mecca. While in Las Vegas—again, according to Kynette, who claimed to have a "man" in the desert city—Raymond stayed with Art Schreiber, a Las Vegas underworld figure who in the late 1920s was part of a protection racket for bootleggers headquartered at the Arizona Club. Kynette also suspected Raymond of transporting stolen goods and narcotics to Las Vegas. He speculated that Raymond had something to do with the attacks on Les Bruneman as well, which some surmised Nevada gunmen had perpetrated. However, he had no evidence to back his suspicions and his staff did not observe any vehicles with Nevada tags at Raymond's residence.

Watching Raymond's home must have been a tedious assignment. Raymond had few visitors—Wilbur Le Gette and Ralph Gray were the only ones the four cops reported. They did not hear anything of consequence. Perhaps wary of the Dictaphone skills of the police and DA's office, Raymond used the small front porch of his bungalow-style house to talk business.

While four detectives remained at the spy house, other operatives from the SIU trailed Raymond after he left home each morning. He was a late riser, often not awakening until 9:00 or 10:00. He had not completely recovered from his automobile accident a year before and still walked with a cane. Every other day, he visited his doctor's office, and twice a week he had his leg massaged at the YMCA. Three operatives were detailed to watch him: Ralph G. Selby, James Le Berthon, and later Richard Emery. They alternated the assignments, which included monitoring the Civic Center Building where Brigham Rose had his office. Besides following Raymond to medical appointments and afternoon massages, they tracked him as he stopped at liquor stores or caroused bars. He was drinking heavily and at least once returned home in an angry mood. Detectives in the spy house watched as he "chased" his wife from the house."

Raymond also regularly visited Police Chief Davis at police headquarters. Several times, he rode with the chief to a dentist's office in Hollywood where Davis was receiving treatment. Neither man spoke about the SIU although both knew Kynette's operatives were watching Raymond. In fact, both the chief of police and DA Fitts received reports on the Kynette's investigation of Raymond throughout the last months of 1937. However, the reports never disclosed that the SIU had rented an apartment near Raymond's house. Kynette was keeping the spy house secret from all his superiors, including his direct supervisor, Warren Justin, Metropolitan Division Captain.

In mid-November, Raymond drove downtown shortly after midnight with Ralph Gray. After parking along Broadway between First and Second Street, he entered the Civic Center Building to meet with Rose while Gray strolled down Broadway toward First Street with a friend. "As I was about to return to Raymond's car," Gray recalled, "I saw Captain Kynette come out of a café and walk toward the machine. I backed across the street and watched. Kynette tried all the doors. He appeared to be working on one door when he spotted me watching. He moved away from the car quickly and stepped into the shadow of a doorway. There he waited until I walked on down the street and hid behind a telephone pole. Then he hurried from his place of hiding and disappeared up the street."[28]

After this incident, Raymond asked the parking attendant at the lot he normally used on Broadway, between Second and Third Streets, to keep an eye on his new 1938 Chrysler Royal.

Although Kynette had allocated six out of his nineteen men to watch him, Raymond was not the only person the SIU was monitoring. Allen and Browne, who joined the spy house group in late October, were assigned to follow Wilbur Le Gette, Rheba Crawford's former associate. After Crawford's conversion to a Shaw supporter, Kynette directed the two operatives to stalk James Alexander and put others outside Rose's office building.

The targeting of other suspects by the SIU did not diminish the shadowing of Raymond. In fact, Kynette's detectives became more aggressive. Toward the end of 1937, Roy King, a parking lot attendant, spotted Officer Allen examining Raymond's car in the lot at 234 South Broadway. A couple of weeks later, Raymond had an encounter with Kynette and his squad. He and Gray were meeting with Rose in his office in the evening of Monday, January 10. Gray and Rose left to eat while Raymond read the paper. After a few minutes, Raymond went downstairs to look for them. He first checked the Log Cabin Coffee Tavern across the street from the Civic Center Building on Broadway. Not finding them there, he strolled toward the Lotus Café at 136 South Broadway. They were not there either, so he turned to check the Log Cabin again when he heard somebody say, "There goes the son of a bitch, now." He looked back to see Kynette with a group of men. For a moment, Raymond considered confronting them, but he was still walking with a cane and there were four or five of them, more than he thought he could handle with a bad leg. He continued to the restaurant, where he found Gray.[29]

Later that week, on Thursday, January 13, Raymond and Gray met again in Rose's office. They were planning for what they expected to be a climactic hearing before the bankruptcy referee in the Munson case later in the month. Raymond would testify about Munson's connections to the Shaws and the gambling money behind Frank Shaw's two successful campaigns for mayor and Buron Fitts' recent campaign for District Attorney. The day before, Rose had won a two-week continuance in the hearing. Although the bankruptcy referee denied his request to have Gans and McAfee testify at the hearing, he allowed Rose to subpoena their records. Rose asserted that McAfee was dodging subpoenas because he worried that he would be forced to admit that he had contributed a large sum to the campaign to re-elect Buron Fitts two years before. After the hearing, a United States Marshall had rushed to a Main Street café where McAfee was supposedly lunching with Gans, but neither man was there by the time he arrived.

As the three men discussed strategy in Rose's office, two of Kynette's detectives, Richard Emery and Ralph Selby, were outside the Civic Center Building surveying persons entering and exiting the building. Emery had parked his car on Broadway in front of the auto park and taken up a position across the street. Selby was in his car near the lot's south entrance. Shortly after 9:00 p.m., Raymond left the building, crossed Broadway and entered the parking lot. After a minute, his new Chrysler Royal pulled onto Broadway and turned left on Second Street. Selby followed him down Second, passing through the Second Street tunnel.

Raymond sensed that he was being followed. He turned quickly down a dark street and switched off his lights. Selby anticipated the move and held back. When Raymond took a definite turn toward the east, heading home, Selby let him go. He drove back to police headquarters. He was there around 11:30 p.m. when Kynette stopped by. Selby gave him a verbal report on that night's stakeout, then the two left headquarters for home. They lived near each other in the hills north of the city. Selby followed Kynette along Echo Park Avenue until he reached Effie, then he turned toward his home on Lake Shore. Kynette continued to his own home on Cerro Gordo.

About the same time, Harry Raymond was going to bed. After Selby stopped tailing him, Raymond drove home unobserved. Nobody watched him when he arrived home, either. Although Officers Allen and Browne had relieved McDonald and Phegley at the spy house at 3:30 that afternoon, they spent most of the evening keeping an eye on the parking lot at 234 South Broadway. Parking attendant Roy King watched them cruise slowly past the lot several times, Allen driving and Browne in the passenger seat scanning the lot for Raymond's Chrysler Royal. Around midnight, they pulled into the lot. King asked them if they wanted to park. They told him they were looking for "two girls and a man in a Ford." Then they headed back to the spy house.[30]

While Raymond knew he was being watched and suspected that his telephone was tapped, he was unaware that 125 feet from his front door Kynette's spy squad had set up shop. On the morning of Friday, January 14, however, the spy house across from Raymond's home was empty. Phegley and McDonald had not shown up for their usual shift from 3:30 a.m. until 3:30 p.m. Allen and Browne were both downtown at SIU headquarters, waiting for Kynette.

It was a mild morning, the temperature in the low 60s. Rain was in the forecast, the first of many storms to come that year. Around 9:50 a.m., Raymond came out the front door with his wife. He had been up since 8:00 and she had arisen earlier. Harry, who usually dressed in a white shirt and bow tie, had put on some old clothes to take his new car to have its brakes adjusted. Although dressed casually, he was carrying his gun. Beulah was going with him. She and a neighbor, Lotta Edwards, who lived across the street, were going grocery shopping. The two women regularly went to the market together. Since Lotta's husband, Rolla, became ill late in 1937, Harry had assumed the responsibility for chauffeuring the women.

Beulah crossed the street to Lotta's home at 954 Orme and Harry walked across the front lawn to the garage. While she talked with Lotta and Rolla, Harry removed the padlock and opened the garage doors. Then he opened the car door and climbed into the driver's seat. Sitting back deeply into the seat to stretch out his injured leg, he twisted the ignition key and pressed down the clutch and accelerator pedals. Then he pushed the ignition button, sending a surge of electricity from the car's battery to a makeshift bomb attached to the automobile's starter motor.

Later, Raymond remembered only falling back onto the seat after the explosion lifted him to the car ceiling. He tried to climb out of the car, but he could not use his right foot or left hand. He was bleeding profusely from a cut to the main artery in his left wrist and dozens of other places. While Rolla Edwards and several neighbors pulled him from the automobile onto the front lawn, Beulah rushed into the house to phone an ambulance.

His injuries were extensive. He had multiple lacerations on his right leg and his left foot, and his right forearm and right ankle were broken. He was conscious, however, and remained so as surgeons at the Georgia Street Receiving Hospital, led by Dr. Charles Francis Sebastian, son of former Mayor John Sebastian, removed between thirty-five and forty pieces of wood and metal from his body during the next four hours. The operation was the first of eighteen that Raymond endured over the coming weeks. Almost 350 objects would be removed from his body.

Lying on the ground awaiting the ambulance, Raymond had been contemptuous of the bomber. "This is a rotten way to try to get a man. They didn't know but what my wife or some other person would be the first to enter the car this morning."

The bomb would be quickly identified as a six-inch pipe filled with black powder packed tight with oakum. Later experts, including John Parsons, a young rocket scientist who a few years later would help found the institution that eventually became the Jet Propulsion Laboratory, claimed that smokeless powder was the key ingredient. It was a powerful device. The explosion was heard a mile away and shattered windows throughout the neighborhood. The garage walls were demolished; only the four corner posts remained. Underneath the automobile, the bomb gouged a large hole in the garage's concrete floor. The car itself was wrecked. The bomb had smashed the engine block and most of its auxiliary components. Bits of the dashboard and floorboards were lodged in Raymond's legs.

Raymond claimed that it was the third time somebody had tried to kill him in recent months. However, his friend Joe Taylor, chief of detectives for the LAPD, did not think the bomb was intended to kill him. Observing that it appeared to have been placed next to the engine block and not underneath the floorboards, Taylor speculated it was meant only to scare him, but the bomber had underestimated its explosive power. However, explosive expert Parsons later argued it was placed under the floorboards.[31]

While the doctors worked on removing shrapnel from his legs, Raymond, under a local anesthetic, talked with reporters and officials in the hospital. Among the first to arrive was Clifford Clinton. After whispering with Raymond, he charged that the bombing "was a deliberate attempt by the organized underworld to put him out of the picture. I believe this bombing can be blamed on Raymond's connection with the bankruptcy case of Harry E. Munson, former police commissioner, and his knowledge of the connections of Guy McAfee and Bob Gans, gambling czars." As Clinton spoke, District Attorney Buron Fitts, identified one month earlier as a beneficiary of Munson's campaign collection efforts, listened. Fitts had rushed to the hospital to pledge his support to finding the perpetrators of what he called an "outrage," adding, "We're going to get the men who perpetrated this dastardly attempt on Raymond's life. I intend to spare no resource of this office to run these men to the ground." Raymond refused to talk with him. Outside Raymond's room, Fitts claimed that Raymond asked him to investigate the bombing, but Rose was clear that Raymond did not want Fitts involved in the investigation. "Raymond will talk of this case to no one but me and his close friends on the police force," he told reporters.[32]

There was little question in Raymond's mind who put the bomb in his car. "If I could get off this bed, I could put my hands on the men responsible for the bombing in 10 minutes," he told Rose. "I know who pulled this job." He also claimed he knew much more and what he knew would soon rock the entire city. "I'll blow the tower off the City Hall," he predicted. Raymond said he had entrusted reports documenting the Los Angeles underworld's connection with prominent Los Angeles officials with friends in San Diego, Seattle, and New York. At his request, Rose contacted the men, who made plans for immediate trips to Los Angeles. "Within 24 hours we shall have in our possession the evidence which will wipe [the vicious gangsters and killers] out of existence," Rose exulted. "What these killers sought to do to Harry Raymond was the most stupid thing they could have attempted. They chose the one man—singled out the one man in all this city—who could be the means of showing up the whole rotten system which has for so long taken a dirty and heavy toll here."

"We've got the rats at last, and it was a long, tough fight," Rose continued. "Now, maybe the attorney general will listen when we ask him to appoint a special prosecutor to come in here and mop up." Rose had already asked for state intervention from the California Attorney General, who directed one of his special agents to discuss the case with Fitts.[33]

Raymond seemed determined to take matters in his own hands as soon as he was able, telling reporters "I think I know who did this, I'll take care of the investigation in my own way," but he had already confided with two men he trusted from the Homicide Squad, Warren Hudson and Aldo Corsini. "These boys are all right, and I'm willing to trust them to go the limit in this thing," he told reporters. The two detectives had arrived at Raymond's home a few minutes after the bombing. After inspecting the garage and automobile, they questioned Raymond as they rode with him in the ambulance to the Georgia Street Receiving Hospital. At the hospital, they were joined by Homicide Chief Bert Wallis. Raymond told the trio of Homicide detectives that he suspected that Earle Kynette and the Special Intelligence Unit were behind the bombing.[34]

Earle Kynette arrived at the SIU offices at 11:00 that morning. His second in command, Sergeant William L. Murphine, had called him earlier at home to report the bombing. When he arrived, he found Murphine, Allen and Browne in the office. There was nobody at the spy house. Around 12:30, he drove to Raymond's house and watched while Police Chemist Ray Pinker searched the automobile and debris in the demolished garage for bomb fragments. Afterward he followed the tow truck dragging the damaged vehicle to a salvage yard. While he was there, Beulah Raymond and Harry

Raymond's younger brother James came by with Ralph Gray. They had come to retrieve Harry's personal items from the Royal's rear seat, including a scrapbook. Kynette handed it to them.

Returning to his office, Kynette took a call from Assistant Chief of Police George Allen, who asked him to call Homicide Captain Wallis. Wallis informed him he was a suspect in the Raymond bombing and that his detectives, Corsini and Hudson, wanted to search his house. Kynette agreed and contacted his lawyer.

After leaving a message for his attorney, Kynette picked up Roy Allen and Fred Browne and returned to Raymond's home. The crowd from the neighborhood had dispersed, leaving a single cop, H. L. Bain, to guard the scene. Kynette drove past the house once, then came back a few minutes later and parked. He asked Bain, who was sitting in a patrol car, whether the police had canvassed Raymond's neighbors. Bain replied that he did not know and that he had been ordered only to guard Raymond's property. Kynette chatted with him for a few minutes about Raymond, alluding to some of Raymond's misadventures as a police chief in Venice and San Diego and allegations that Raymond was trying to force beer dealers in Los Angeles to use San Diego-brewed beer. He did not mention what he was still hiding from everybody else outside his squad, including his superiors in the LAPD: 125 feet away his men had been watching Raymond's home since September.

While they waited for Kynette, Detectives Corsini and Hudson investigated another suspect in the Raymond bombing, LAPD Sergeant Tom James. Rose had pointed them toward James, who until recently was a member of Kynette's squad. James was a colorful figure in Los Angeles, a flamboyant, outspoken man whose unrestrained opinions frequently got him in trouble. Born in Morgantown, Kentucky in 1895, he joined the US Navy at seventeen and became a merchant seaman four years later. By 1926, he had left the seas for the LAPD. His penchant for sowing dissension among the ranks led Police Chief Davis to exile him to the "sticks" repeatedly, first to the Sawtelle Division on the far west side, then to the largely undeveloped San Fernando Valley. In those remote, empty precincts, he found plenty of room for self-expression of the kind that displeased his superiors. Davis figured it was better to keep him close-at-hand, and assigned him to direct traffic at the busy intersection of Seventh and Broadway. Eight hours of "dodging flivvers," as a *Los Angeles Times* columnist put it, should have taken the fight out of him, but James' disgruntlement with the Cryer administration and Davis spurred him on. He joined the mayoralty campaign of John Porter. In 1929, the newly elected mayor rewarded his services by elevating him to the position of special investigator in the mayor's office. By early 1930, he held the rank of Acting Captain and was the head investigator for the Board of Police Commissioners.[35]

James' rise under Porter was rapid, and so was his fall, owing to his talent for making enemies. In May, he resigned his investigator's position to return to duty as a patrolman, citing "political events of the last year." In the following months he was transferred from one assignment to another, from 77th Division to Hollywood Division to Chinatown Division and finally back to "the sticks"— the San Fernando Valley.

It soon became clear why his career had nosedived: he had broken with Porter. In December, he was subpoenaed by a grand jury investigating the Porter campaign's expenditures. The jury ordered him to produce records of his investigations during his tenure with the police commission. His apostasy from the Porter administration and its supporters and his big mouth (while working as a crossing guard in Van Nuys, he told an undercover investigator for the LAPD that Mayor Porter, Police Chief Steckel and Reverend Bob Shuler were "in on the big payoff in Hollywood) prompted Steckel to dismiss him from the police force in May 1931.[36]

For four years, James fought futilely for reinstatement to the LAPD through police boards of inquiry and the court system. In the meantime, he kept up his attacks on Porter and Steckel through articles in the *Critic of Critics* and a 68-page pamphlet entitled *Chief Steckel Unmasked.* His friendship with Herbert Spencer, editor of the *Critic of Critics,* involved him tangentially as a witness in the Crawford/Spencer murder. He became active in the Prohibitionist Party, attending the National Convention in Indianapolis as a delegate in 1932 and running as a candidate for the Electoral College the same year. He festooned his Chevrolet with banners and placards attacking Porter and Steckel, covering the automobile so completely that *Los Angeles Times* columnists speculated wryly about its actual color. While he normally parked it at Second and Broadway, he moved it about depending on his mood and whatever political fight he had decided to wage. One afternoon, he parked the car in a red zone in front of City Hall and leaned on the horn until two uniformed cops hustled him inside the building. He then tried to help them find an ordinance in the books that would allow them to charge him. The cops released him.

The 1933 mayoralty campaign between Shaw and Porter afforded James an opportunity to get back at his nemesis. Despite his support for Shaw, Shaw's police commissioners blocked his reappointment, possibly with the urging of Police Chief Davis. A year later, however, the influence of another ex-sailor, the mayor's brother, likely led to his reinstatement at the rank of sergeant. He had learned the wisdom of loyalty to the signer of his paychecks and soon had a job with Kynette's squad, charged with keeping an eye on

Clinton, Wilkinson, Coyne, and other members of CIVIC, whom he despised as hypocrites.

Rose believed James had been on the other end of a series of harassing phone calls he received in previous months. "Harry [Raymond] has been an old friend of mine for years," he told the detectives. "Lately since I have been fussing around with this Munson matter, he did drop in my office almost daily. From time to time, I would receive these calls over the phone. 'Is your big undercover man Raymond around? Can he reach the phone? Well, have him shove it up his ass.' This has been going on for some time."

Rose told the detectives he believed Kynette was behind the bombing and that James was one of his "chief stooges." He encouraged the detectives to check James' rooms at the Astor Hotel at Second and Hill. "My hunch is he has lots of stuff in his room," Rose said. "I would check up on this guy's activities last evening." Assistant Chief Allen summoned James to his office, where detectives Corsini, Hudson and Pinker waited. The three detectives accompanied James to his room at the Hotel Astor, where they searched for material that might have been used to make a bomb. The Astor's rooms were not large. It did not take the detectives long to find nothing.[37]

The three detectives returned to City Hall, where Homicide Chief Wallis informed them that Kynette had just left his office. Joined by Homicide Captain Dalton H. Patton, they intercepted the spy squad leader in the basement garage. Pinker told him he was a suspect in the Raymond bombing and that they needed to search his home. Kynette was not happy with the news, but he agreed to take them to his house. However, first he needed to stop off at SIU headquarters to get a package of clothes he had purchased for his infant daughter. He drove with Corsini to the SIU office.

While Corsini waited in the car, Kynette entered the office. Phlegely and McDonald were doing their normal 3:30 shift at the spy house on Kynette's orders, but several other squad members were also there. Kynette told them that the detectives were going to search his house. After ten minutes, Corsini, tired of waiting, came into the office and the two men departed.

They drove to the corner of Echo Park and Sunset Boulevard, where they met with Patton, Pinker and Hudson. As the two cars drove toward his house, Kynette complained that it was ridiculous and unfair to search his home. Corsini assured him it was just routine and suggested they pick up something to drink. Kynette pulled over at a liquor store to buy some whisky and beer while Corsini waited. The detectives in the second car waited behind them.

Around 6:00, they arrived at Kynette's home at 1501 Cerro Gordo Street, a small house of about 1200 square feet that he had built the year before on a vacant hillside corner lot. Kynette mixed some drinks in the kitchen. Afterward the five men relaxed in the living room, talking about their children.

Eventually the conversation turned to the Raymond case. Kynette recounted his activity the previous night. After a meeting of Army Reserve Officers between 8:00 and 10:00 p.m., he had carried out a confidential mission for Davis. Kynette explained he worked for Chief Davis, reported only to Davis and that Davis was out of town. Patton ordered him to file an LAPD Form 72 to account for his movements the previous day and to send it to Wallis.

After explaining to Kynette that they were looking for bomb-making material, Pinker and Hudson began to search Kynette's house, the other detectives following along to watch. After searching the small house for a few minutes, the five men returned to the living room. Kynette mixed another round of drinks. He told them he spent the morning trying to fix his Frigidaire refrigerator and was planning to tackle a problem with the fireplace vent next. When they finished their drinks, Kynette led them to a room in the basement. There Pinker found a short piece of pipe that seemed similar to that he found at the bombing site. He told Kynette he thought he should take the pipe for examination. "Don't make an ass out of yourself," Kynette growled. Pinker put it in his pocket.[38]

The group then entered the detached garage at the rear of the property. It was a square building, 18 x 18 feet, opening onto a narrow street angling away from Cerro Gordo. Kynette opened the back door and switched on a light. A bench ran along the south and east walls. Pinker trained a flashlight on the bench and spotted a small coil of paired white and black wire and another spool of bell wire. He continued searching the garage, flashing his light on the darkened sections while the other men looked about idly. Then he returned to the black and white wire.

Kynette watched him carefully. "It's just bell wire," he said and turned to switch off the light. While Kynette's back was turned, Pinker slipped the spool of white and black wire in his pocket.[39]

The following day, a Saturday, Raymond's health took a turn for the worse. Dr. Sebastian told reporters that the next forty-eight hours would decide whether he would survive. He lapsed into a coma several times during the day. DA Fitts and Joe Taylor tried to question him but had little success. He did not want to talk to Fitts at all. "Get out of here," Raymond barked at him, his voice failing. "I don't want your help." Finally, Sebastian asked Fitts and Taylor to suspend questioning until his condition improved.[40]

He was better on Sunday, well enough that he had Rose telegram his friends in San Diego, Seattle, and New York to defer their journeys to Los Angeles with copies of his trove of incriminating documents. While he rested, the LAPD detectives continued their investigation. Pinker examined bomb fragments under a microscope while other detectives concentrated on questioning underworld figures. Many had left the city.

The syndicate leaders were not the only ones absent that weekend. Mayor Frank Shaw had departed on the Santa Fe Chief for Washington the day before the bombing to lobby Congress to provide financial support for intracoastal steamship lines. Police Chief Davis was also out of town, attending an international marksmanship contest as leader of the Los Angeles Pistol Club in Mexico City. Mayor Shaw's brother, Joe Shaw, was also in the Mexican capital. Late in the evening of January 15, Kynette tried to call him at his hotel. When Shaw did not answer, Kynette tried to locate Chief Davis. After calling several restaurants in the Mexican capital, he finally reached Davis at his hotel. The two men talked for seventeen minutes about the bombing and possible suspects in the crime. They agreed there were many persons who wished Raymond dead. Davis ordered Kynette to find out who had acted on the wish. Kynette did not mention that he was himself a suspect in the bombing.

After making little headway over the weekend in questioning Los Angeles underworld figures, Detectives Hudson, Corsini and Pinker questioned Raymond's neighbors on Monday. They soon learned that a group of mysterious men, whom the neighbors referred to as "G-Men," had rented an apartment near Raymond's house in September of the previous year. One neighbor, noting that the men parked their cars blocks away from the apartment and suspecting that the "G-Men" were actually crooks, recorded the license plates of their vehicles. Hudson checked them and discovered they belonged to Special Intelligence Unit members. It was the first time that anybody outside the SIU learned that Kynette's men had rented the apartment.[41]

The discovery of the spy house was kept from the press and public for two days while the Homicide Squad detectives searched the apartment. Inside, they found evidence of the electronic surveillance of Raymond's home: a hole drilled in the bedroom floor through which telephone wire stretched to a neighboring bungalow and from there to a telephone pole on the street corner, where it connected with a wire terminating in the junction box of Raymond's home. They also found a large floor radio that was modified to function as a speaker, enabling the SIU members to listen to conversations without wearing earphones. There was little sign of domestic use in the apartment. The refrigerator was empty, the bed appeared unused, and the bathtub was dusty. Only empty beer cans and overflowing ashtrays suggested habitation.

While Corsini and Hudson were searching the spy house, Chief of Detectives Joe Taylor interviewed Raymond at the Georgia Street Receiving Hospital. His condition had improved considerably over the weekend and he was able to furnish Taylor with additional information about the bombing. As Taylor and Homicide Chief Wallis began to build a case against Kynette, Assistant Chief Allen telephoned Chief Davis, who was still in Mexico City, to alert him to the developments. Afterward, Davis made plans to return by plane to Los Angeles.

One neighbor whom the police detectives interviewed on Monday was George Sakalis, a produce vendor who lived across the street from Raymond. The night before the bombing, Sakalis was awakened shortly after midnight by the voices of men. He looked out the window and saw three men, two tall and one short, in the alley outside his bedroom. Sakalis lost his temper and warned the men that if they did not go away, he would get his shotgun and shoot them. He didn't own a shotgun, but the men left so he didn't need one. Two hours later, when he left for the central market, he noticed that the lights were on in the apartment adjoining the alley, where the G-Men stayed. He could hear men talking inside it.

At 5:30 Wednesday morning, less than a week after the bombing, Sakalis left the downtown produce market with his truck filled with fruits and vegetables. He stopped by his house briefly and then headed for his first stop, Hoover High School in Glendale. As he drove, he noticed a black sedan behind him. On 36th Avenue, the sedan sped up and cut in front of him. Sakalis veered left to avoid it. As he did, he glanced over at the sedan. He thought he recognized the two men as members of the group that had rented the apartment across the alley from his home.

Sakalis continued on his way, the black sedan following. On San Fernando Road, the sedan again tried to cut him off, but once again, Sakalis evaded it. Around 7:00 a.m., he reached the high school, where he delivered his produce and drank a cup of coffee as he told the cafeteria workers about the black sedan.

The next stop on his route was on Caleb Street in the Verdugo Mountains north of Glendale. Sakalis followed Hillcrest to the entrance of the Camp Clarence Edwards, a Boy Scout retreat, at the foot of Sherer Canyon. As he slowed to downshift before a steep grade, the black sedan swung beside him and forced him to the side of the road. He stopped his truck and threw it into reverse, but before he could back up the passenger from the car, a big fellow in his forties, opened the door and pulled him from the truck by his hair.

"How's your friend, Raymond?" he demanded. Then he smacked Sakalis on the head.

"I don't know nothing about it," Sakalis responded, "I never read the newspapers."

"You act dumb," the big fellow said. He slugged Sakalis in the stomach. "You keep your mouth shut about Raymond."

Bewildered, Sakalis looked at the man in the car. He had on a reddish brown suit with a belted back.

Sakalis reached in his left pocket and pulled out four one-dollar bills. "Boys, I am a poor man," he said. "I am working 18 hours a day. I am making a living for my babies."

The big fellow took the four bills. In Sakalis' hand was also a business card with Detective Corsini's name on it. The big fellow looked at it. "So, you know him personally, too?" he asked. He punched Sakalis in the stomach again. Sakalis doubled over. The big fellow hit him twice more in the stomach. Then he hit him in the chest. Finally, he grabbed Sakalis and flung him into the driver's seat of his truck. "You keep your mouth shut," he said.[42]

The big fellow climbed back into the black sedan. It made a U-turn and proceeded down Hillcrest. Sakalis sat in his truck for a few minutes, dizzy and nauseous. He felt he was about to vomit but didn't. Then he shifted into gear and drove toward his next delivery.

Afterward, he called his neighbor, Rolla Edwards, and told him what had happened. Then he returned home and lay on his bed. Around 7:00 p.m., a cop knocked on his door. The police were rounding up witnesses in the neighborhood to identify the men who had occupied the spy house. A report of Sakalis' assault had reached Chief of Detectives Joe Taylor, who dispatched the officer to pick him up. Sakalis tried to hide in the bathroom, but the cop was insistent. At last, Sakalis joined Beulah Raymond and some residents of the bungalow apartments on 7th Street for a ride downtown in the police cars.

The DA had filled a room with the members of the SIU squad along with other cops and investigators to serve as decoys. Homicide Squad detectives guarded the SIU Squad. All were present except Roy Allen, who had left town that afternoon. Kynette was there, as was Fred Browne, who arrived late after being ordered to attend by Homicide Chief Bert Wallis.

The men were sitting around, some playing cards. Fitts told them to stand up. He asked the residents to pick out the men they saw coming and going from 2711 E 7th Street. A few of them did so, selecting both SIU squad and decoys. Fitts turned to Sakalis. Did he recognize either of the men who beat him up that morning? Sakalis, nervous and trembling, looked around. The big fellow was not there, but he spotted the driver of the car in his reddish brown suit with the belted back. Sakalis looked at him. Fitts asked again if he recognized anybody.

Sakalis said he didn't.

Afterward, Fitts took Sakalis to his office, where he showed him a photograph of a man. Sakalis examined it carefully. It was the big fellow. Roy

Allen, one of the senior cops said. Sakalis looked at the photo. It looks like him, he said. Maybe.

The following morning, Sakalis telephoned his attorney, Frank Seaver. He told Seaver that he recognized not only Allen but also Kynette, the man in the reddish brown suit with the belted back. Seaver advised him to keep to his business, to sell his vegetables and take care of his children. The Raymond affair was all politics, he told him. Better stay out of it.

After Raymond's neighbors left that evening, Fitts called in Kynette, Draper and three other SIU squad members to his office, where Deputy DA Eugene Mathews questioned them. All refused to answer any questions, citing the Fifth Amendment's protection against self-incrimination, that right "and all other rights." All claimed that they could only reveal secret police information to their direct superior. Other questions taxed their memories.[43]

Following the interrogation, Fitts had Kynette and Draper arrested for illegal wire-tapping. They were booked and released on $2,000 bail.

The arrests marked a growing rift between the district attorney's office and the Los Angeles Police Department. Fitts told reporters, "The case has simmered down to the point where no one not a member of the police department is being considered as a suspect." The LAPD top brass objected to Fitts' comment heatedly. Assistant Police Chief Allen, the LAPD's senior officer in Chief Davis' absence, declared there was not enough evidence to charge the officers. On January 24, ten days after the bombing, Police Chief Davis, home at last, also sought to exonerate Kynette and members of his squad. "After a thorough and complete investigation of all angles of the case," Davis declared, "I am satisfied beyond a doubt that no member of the Police Department had anything to do with the bombing of Harry Raymond. Kynette's surveillance of Raymond was a routine matter prompted by knowledge of the latter's acts in connection with groups which are antagonistic to the city government," Davis explained. "That is part of the intelligence unit's work—to investigate such groups just as it is part of government intelligence units to investigate groups inimical to the government of the nation." Whether Davis' exculpation of Kynette and his men convinced anybody in the city is doubtful, but it confirmed the views of critics who believed Davis and the Shaws used the SIU as a political cudgel against any person or group that threatened their power.[44]

Fitts reacted to Davis' statement with a mollifying letter, but asked that Davis at least suspend Kynette from active duty. Davis refused. Kynette and Draper would remain on active duty until Fitts presented sufficient evidence to warrant suspending them. Fitts then directed his efforts toward presenting his case to the 1938 Grand Jury. He withdrew the wire-tapping complaint against Kynette and Draper, instead charged Kynette and two unnamed cops with attempted murder. He also announced that one SIU cop had made a statement "tantamount to a confession" and had furnished damning evidence against Kynette. The seriousness of the charge forced Davis to suspend the captain from duty. On Jan 27, Kynette surrendered in Municipal Court and posted bond.[45]

Fitts' arrest of Kynette and Draper surprised some observers who expected the district attorney to close ranks with the LAPD and mayor's office. Still, Attorney Rose was unimpressed. "We're just waiting for these fellows to get finished with their political razzle-dazzle and then Harry and I will step in and solve this case without any hokus pokus," he declared.[46]

Fitts was moving fast, however. On September 24, he held a second "show-up" of SIU squad members in the Homicide Squad offices to obtain positive identification from two key witnesses in the case. The first was Beulah Raymond. She claimed that a few weeks before the bombing she observed a man looking over the Raymond's garage.

"He had a flashlight," she recalled. "It was a kind of amber shade, and he was going up and down the corner of the garage."[47]

The garage was only fifteen feet from her bedroom window. Beulah saw the man's face clearly in the moonlight and by the light cast upward from his flashlight. He was looking intently at the southeastern corner of the garage. "He wore a reddish brown suit, one of those sport suits with a belted back, and a gray hat without about a two-inch band, and it was pointed in the corner," she declared. Harry was not at home. She called the police, but by the time they arrived a few minutes later, the man was gone. When Harry returned, he dismissed the incident. "He laughed at me about it, because he said he didn't know why a man would have a spot light on a moonlit night."[48]

In the "show-up," Beulah Raymond identified Earle Kynette as the man she observed that night.

The second key witness was George Sakalis. This time, Roy Allen was present. Allen had not attended the first "show-up" at the DA's office on January 19. Instead, he left town in the afternoon for a cabin near Big Bear Lake. Fitts claimed that he departed despite a telephone call from Captain Wallis to ask him to report to the police station. Allen disputed the allegation, claiming he left to use vacation time he had accrued and did not know that he was wanted by detectives. His departure touched off a manhunt and much consternation for his twin brother, Lloyd, who was also a policeman; after Roy's photograph was splashed across the pages of local newspapers, Lloyd was twice detained on streetcars by zealous citizens.

Sakalis arrived at the "show-up" in the Homicide Bureau with his brother-in-law. He was nervous and talked rapidly in a thick Greek accent. Homicide

Captain Wallis tried to calm him, but Sakalis broke into tears as he looked over the eighteen men of Kynette's squad. He identified several of them as men he had seen around the neighborhood but said that Allen was not the man who beat him up on January 19.

In a radio broadcast on January 30, Fitts condemned intimidation against Sakalis and other witnesses. "I am just as convinced that Capt. Kynette—with the probable assistance of others—planted the bomb that blew up Harry Raymond as that my name is Buron Fitts," the DA declared. He claimed that he had overwhelming evidence collected by his investigators "against almost unbelievable odds—with retaliation and intimidation constantly threatened." A few days later, he announced that he would broaden the investigation. "I have ordered my staff to enlarge the scope of their inquiry into all of the ramifications of the reported local graft and corruption system." Although this seemed a direct attack on the Los Angeles crime syndicate and corruption within the Shaw administration, Fitts was careful to separate himself from Clinton and the reformers, religious and secular. "From time to time as apparently reliable information is gathered either by my men or brought in from other sources the information will be placed before the grand jury for such action as that body sees fit. However, we are not going to confuse the grand jury by placing before it any wild rumors or half facts which may originate from unreliable or misinformed persons."[49]

Sakalis was not the only person threatened after the bombing. Joseph Fainer, Raymond's personal attorney who had been appointed a special prosecutor in the case, placed his wife and four-year-old son on the ocean liner Matsonia headed for Honolulu after the family received several phone calls threatening "another Lindbergh case."[50] Other persons associated with Raymond also received threats, most notably Ralph Gray, who was called to the telephone in the Georgia Street Receiving Hospital lobby on the night of the bombing. The voice on the phone had asked, "How is Mr. Raymond this evening?"

Gray replied, "Mr. Raymond is resting better, thank you. Who is this?"

In a slow, deliberate tone, the voice replied, "That is too bad. The next time we will do a better job. You are next, Mr. Gray."

"Why am I selected for this honor?" Gray asked.

"If you stick your nose into other people's business, that is too bad. We will get you, Mr. Gray, and we will do a better job than we did on Mr. Raymond, maybe tomorrow, and maybe next week or maybe next month. We will get around to you. We are warning you that we will get to you."[51]

Indignation over the bombing and the threats against witnesses mounted as the days and weeks passed. After he denounced Mayor Shaw and Police Chief Davis for their "cool indifference to public opinion" and "assaults upon

American civil liberties," Clinton joined representatives from various civic, church and labor organizations to form the Federation for Civic Betterment and demand that Governor Frank Merriam appoint a special prosecutor to look into LA County's vice and political corruption. The new organization did not seek to replace Fitts, however. Fitts' vigorous investigation of Kynette and the SIU persuaded the city and county reformers that this time he would do his job. Manchester Boddy, *Los Angeles Daily News* editor, applauded Fitts three days after the bombing for his condemnation of the "dastardly" and intolerable violence against Raymond, though he pointed out that for a long time Fitts had tolerated such acts. For whatever reason, Fitts had decided to make a break with the LAPD and Shaw administration and to ride the wave of public indignation touched off by the Raymond bombing rather than be swamped by it. Mayor Frank Shaw tried to ride the same wave, but was unsuccessful. After expressing confidence in the police and dismissing evidence of police involvement in the bombing, he altered course and appointed a citizen's commission to investigate the crime. The strategy failed. First, several city council members rebuffed the idea. Then four of the persons selected for the committee declined to serve. By February 1, all seven appointees had notified the mayor that they could not serve on his committee.[52]

Fitts received his most important endorsement on February 7, when Raymond publicly expressed confidence in him. "I have the utmost confidence in Buron Fitts, Gene Williams and Joseph L. Fainer," he declared in a written statement from his hospital bed. "I know they are doing everything humanly possible in the investigation for presentation to the grand jury of evidence with relation to my being bombed. I have been an investigator for many years, and if there was the slightest doubt in my mind about their seriousness and sincerity in this matter, I would not hesitate to tell the public about it."[53]

Intersection where Buron Fitts was shot. [Los Angeles Times Photographic Archive, UCLA Library. Copyright Regents of the University of California, UCLA Library]

Fitts examining his damaged automobile. [Los Angeles Times Photographic Archive, UCLA Library. Copyright Regents of the University of California, UCLA Library]

(L-R) Clifford Clinton, Beulah Raymond, "Tipper," and L. E. Berger in Raymond living room. [Library Special Collections, Charles E. Young Research Library, UCLA]

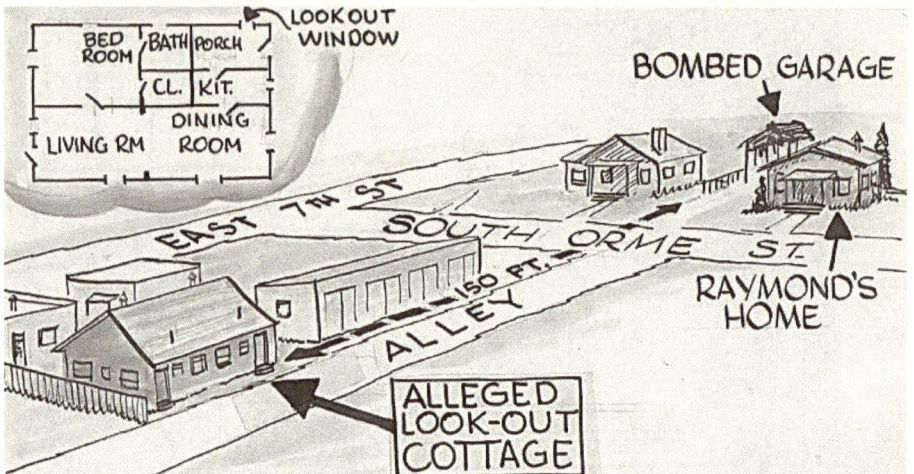

LOOKOUT WINDOW

BED ROOM | BATH | PORCH | CL. | KIT. | DINING ROOM | LIVING RM

BOMBED GARAGE

EAST 7TH ST.

SOUTH ORME ST.

150 FT.

ALLEY

RAYMOND'S HOME

ALLEGED LOOK-OUT COTTAGE

Contemporary Diagram of SIU spy house and Raymond's home. [Los Angeles Times Photographic Archive, UCLA Library. Copyright Regents of the University of California, UCLA Library]

Clifford Clinton examining Raymond's damaged automobile [Library Special Collections, Charles E. Young Research Library]

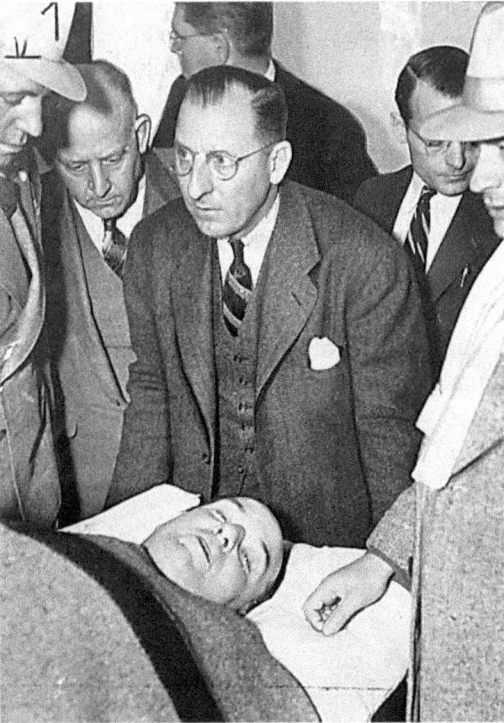

Buron Fitts leans over injured Harry Raymond. Clifford Clinton is behind Fitts. [Library Special Collections, Charles E. Young Research Library, UCLA]

16: THE TRIAL AND RECALL

While Fitts focused on the trial of Kynette, Browne, and Allen, the case's wider implications were reviewed in the press and on the radio. On January 31, the *Los Angeles Examiner* published an investigative report accusing the Shaw administration of underworld ties and identifying former police commissioner Harry Munson as an underworld courier. Ten days later, *Examiner* editor Manchester Boddy predicted that Fitts' investigation might prove to be the "real thing." Boddy compared Los Angeles' repetitive vice controversies to a toy carousel where the "vice, corruption, payoff, [and] cleanup business" go "round and round" only to halt when public interest wanes, leaving all the metal figures in the same places they began. Fitts was changing that. "*Potentially*, Fitts' action is more important than any event . . . in law enforcement circles since the bombing of Harry Raymond . . . . [He] has plunged boldly and openly into the real hot spot of what promises to be a fight to the finish to rid Los Angeles of invisible government." Boddy's enthusiasm for the investigation reflected the dawning realization among reformers that big changes might be on the way.[54]

In mid-February, Fitts brought his case against Kynette to the newly impaneled 1938 LA County Grand Jury. He had declared that he would first present evidence linking Kynette and the SIU to the bombing of Lyndon Foster, but before the jury, he focused only on the Raymond bombing. Once again, all SIU members involved refused to testify, asserting their Fifth Amendment right against self-incrimination and claiming their information was privileged. Frustrated by the police officers' stonewalling, the grand jury ordered the seizure of the squads' records. The records revealed that Kynette and his men not only watched Raymond but also many prominent citizens and reformers, including *Hollywood Evening-News* publisher Harlan G. Palmer, John Anson Ford, Buron Fitts, Lyndon Foster, and San Francisco private detective Ed Atherton. They also recorded Clifford Clinton's radio broadcasts and produced investigative reports on him and other reformers. It was further evidence that the SIU viewed critics of the Shaw administration and police as subversives.

Fitts brought Sakalis, Beulah Raymond and Ralph Gray before the grand jury. In the preceding weeks, the terrified produce vendor had gained the courage to tell the district attorney and police investigators what he had been telling his friends, his customers, and even his priest: Roy Allen was the man who had beaten him while Earle Kynette watched in the car. On February 19, testifying before the grand jury, Sakalis named both Kynette and Allen as the men who followed and assaulted him. Word that he would finger Kynette and Allen had already escaped from Fitts' office. In mid-February, a short, bespectacled man approached Sakalis at the Central Market and offered him $3,000 to "keep his mouth shut." When Sakalis refused the bribe, the man told him he would be sorry.[55]

Beulah Raymond testified that Kynette was the man she saw examining the side of her garage door, while Gray described the threatening phone call he received at the Georgia Street Receiving Hospital and claimed he recognized Kynette's voice. Fitts also called expert witnesses who testified that wire taken from Kynette's garage matched wire fragments found near Raymond's demolished automobile. The witness's testimony convinced the grand jury to indict Kynette, Allen and Fred Browne. Following the indictments, Fitts ordered county Sheriff deputies to guard Beulah Raymond and George Sakalis. Two deputies watched over the peddler, riding with him to the market in the morning and on his route during the day.

The trial of Kynette, Allen, and Browne began on April 12. The three had been held without bond since their indictments on Feb 18. During that time, Kynette had grown a thin mustache, changed the way he parted his thinning hair, and donned glasses. The changes may have been intended to confuse Beulah Raymond and Sakalis, as the prosecution contended. If so, they backfired. They made the detective look more sinister and were not enough to fool either eyewitness. Neither hesitated to identify him.

The trial lasted until June 16. The prosecution's evidence divided broadly into scientific evidence and eyewitness testimony linking Kynette, Allen, and Browne to the bombing. The defense responded with an array of counter-experts and challenges to the credibility of the prosecution's eyewitnesses. Among the prosecution experts were Jack Parsons and William Harper of Cal Tech. Harper provided damning testimony that the wire found by Pinker in Kynette's garage and that found around Raymond's garage was from the same manufacturer and spool. Not surprisingly, the defense paraded several of its own experts to question his findings, including explosive experts from the movie industry. The conflicting testimony of chemists with advanced degrees likely confused the jurors but that of the eyewitnesses, including Sakalis, Beulah Raymond, and Ralph Gray, was enough to convict Kynette. It was hard for the defense to dispute that there was little opportunity for anybody except the SIU cops to plant the bomb, given that they had Raymond under 24-hour surveillance.

The testimony that most hurt the three defendants came from the victim himself. Harry Raymond had undergone multiple operations since the bombing. On January 23, hospital attendants moved him by ambulance from the Georgia Street Receiving Hospital to the California Hospital on South Hope Street while the injured detective held a revolver under the covers of his gurney.

On April 29, Raymond was guided into the courtroom in a wheelchair by his nurse. With a suit coat over his hospital robe, Raymond detailed his increasingly hostile encounters with Kynette over the past year, his involvement in the Munson case, and his movements on the night before and the morning of the bombing. As he described the moments immediately before he entered his automobile and started the engine, the thought that his wife might have been a few feet behind him when the explosion occurred brought tears to his eyes. Attorney Fainer had to ask the court for a brief recess to allow him to recover his composure.

The defense attorneys declined to cross-examine Raymond, claiming there was no advantage in cross-examining a sick man. As he was wheeled from the courtroom, Raymond responded scornfully. "All these attorneys poured poison on to me in their opening statements to the jury, but when I got on the witness stand they didn't have a word to say. You can draw your own conclusions."[56]

After the prosecution rested its case, however, the defense tried to pour more poison on Raymond. Some of it was rebuffed by the prosecution, which blocked testimony from several witnesses purported to support Kynette's contention that Raymond was involved in an unseemly incident at the 411 Club, a nightclub in downtown Los Angeles. Some of the poison got through, however, delivered by Kynette. He strived to persuade the jury that Raymond was "a very dangerous" man who needed to be watched for the public's protection. He recounted much that was known publicly and privately about Raymond, whom he labeled as a "man of two coats," and charged that Raymond was fostering a rumor that Buron Fitts' assassination attempt resulted from a spat with a woman. His attack on the bombing victim may or may not have had an impact, but in taking the witness stand, he exposed himself to the prosecution's cross-examination. His snide intimations that the evidence against him, particularly that contained in the SIU documents, were planted led to a series of angry interchanges between him, the prosecution attorneys, and the defense team.[57]

At one point, prosecutor Williams demanded whether Kynette believed that his duty as SIU head was to investigate all persons who criticized the city administration. Kynette did not answer, but Police Chief Davis had already responded to the same question shortly after the bombing when he declared that the SIU investigated persons and groups "antagonistic to the city government." On the witness stand, resplendent in his black uniform, Davis described the unit's duties as investigating "criminal political elements in the city, elements attempting to harass the police department, thereby destroying morale. . . . Many criminals are working with political elements to embarrass the police department, hampering its work and thereby furthering their own ends," he declared. The prosecution attorneys made sure the jury knew that the SIU's charter also included protecting the mayor. Fainer declared that the SIU's "primary purpose" was to harass and roust opponents of the city administration. When Davis left for the lunch recess, a large crowd outside the courtroom heckled and booed him. The police chief stopped and shook his fist at them.[58]

The jury found both Kynette and Allen guilty of the malicious use of explosives. Kynette was also convicted of attempted murder and assault to commit murder. One juror told reporters, "Kynette's own testimony did more to convict him than the State's prosecution. Police Chief Davis' testimony also was detrimental to the defense." From his hospital bed, Harry Raymond praised the convictions although he was unhappy with the acquittal of the third defendant, Fred Browne. "There's only one thing to do now, that's get out and clean up the rest of the goon squad—and that we are going to do," he promised.[59]

While Raymond's focus was on the trial, Clifford Clinton and his allies were busy achieving a larger goal: the removal of Mayor Shaw and the election of a reform administration that would drive illegal gambling and corruption from the city. Raymond's bombing may have had nothing to do with CIVIC's campaign, but Clinton made use of it and the frequently reported claim that he employed Raymond to investigate civic corruption. As Clinton's grandson later declared, "CIVIC wanted to make the most of the Raymond bombing." Although Raymond testified that he had never been in Clinton's employ, the persistence of the claim suggests that informally, at least, and perhaps through their common attorney, A. Brigham Rose, Raymond furnished Clinton with some material for his anti-vice campaign.[60]

Shortly after the bombing, Clinton moved his campaign to the radio, broadcasting first on KEHE and later on KFI. The Raymond bombing, the trial of Kynette, Allen, and Browne, became major themes during the coming months as Clinton and his son led the recall effort against Mayor Frank Shaw. During the trial, Clinton recounted each day's testimony, tying the attack on Raymond to the political campaign to remove Shaw.

Shaw at first pretended to ignore the campaign. "This office is snowed under right now answering an average of 1000 inquiries a day from people in the East who wish to know how their relatives here fared in the flood," he declared as the effort to collect signatures for his recall began. A week before, a series of rainstorms had drenched Los Angeles, Riverside and Orange counties, killing more than 100 persons and destroying over 5,000 homes and businesses. As the months passed and the recall campaign gained momentum, Shaw's supporters fought back, sometimes with subterfuge, such as sending fake petition gatherers into the streets to collect voter signatures that they later discarded. Shaw fell back on an old theme in Los Angeles politics, declaring that, "Back of this recall are a handful of racketeers who have preyed upon the public in this city for years and who have, during my time in office as Mayor, been irked to find an honest and sincere effort to decrease crime and vice—a campaign which has finally reached a point where Los Angeles is recognized by Federal authorities as a law enforcement white spot in the nation."[61]

Despite the Shaws' counter-efforts, the reformers obtained enough signatures to qualify for a recall election. The Federation for Civic Betterment considered three candidates to replace Shaw should they win the first item on the ballot, which was to remove him from office. Only one, Assemblyman Sam Yorty, was eager for the job, but even his supporters agreed that his pro-union positions and firebrand style made him too far to the left to win. At last, after recently defeated mayoralty candidate John Anson Ford declined to run again, Judge Fletcher Bowron reluctantly accepted the nomination. While some progressives balked at his candidacy, regarding him as too conservative, others took a pragmatic approach, one progressive leader even declaring it represented a combination of "the leftist elements and labor with the rightest middle class church people." Despite support from the *Los Angeles Times*, who argued that Shaw was being unfairly blamed for Kynette's roguish behavior, Shaw was recalled by an almost 2 to 1 majority and Bowron elected.[62]

As he took office, Bowron characterized himself as even-handed, middle-of-the-road, and unconcerned with organized vice unless it corrupted city government and the police department. He pledged to "go slow" with the reform of the city departments, including those that bore on the police. However, in the next months, he quickly replaced most city commissioners, including the entire police board. In November, Police Chief Davis retired, claiming he was doing so to protect his pension, which a firing might threaten. In early March 1939, Bowron's newly appointed police commission forced twenty-three high-ranking LAPD officers to retire. Among those cashiered were Harry Raymond's longtime associates and friends, Joe Taylor and Hubert Wallis. Also retired was Assistant Chief George Allen, who had supported Kynette in the first days after the bombing, and deputy chiefs Roy Steckel and Stanford J. McCaleb.[63]

Officially, the terminations were explained as steps to improve efficiency and reduce the ratio of executive officers to patrolmen. However, as the *Los Angeles Times* noted, the "official reason that the department is overstaffed at the top, is not convincing" and that the argument that the officers practiced "outmoded and inefficient" methods made little sense when one considered their replacements used the same methods. The dismissals, the paper opined, were a response to charges that "Los Angeles is again 'wide open' in the matter of vice." The officers were longtime upper-level managers in the LAPD when the crime syndicate of Parrot, Crawford, McAfee, Gans and scores of lesser lights could run their vice operations unhindered in the city. Some may not have had a direct role in keeping the syndicate in business, but none worked hard to put it out. Reform was impossible as long as they were in power.[64]

Seated from left: Fred Browne, Roy Allen, Earle Kynette. [Los Angeles Times Photographic Archive, UCLA Library. Copyright Regents of the University of California, UCLA Library.]

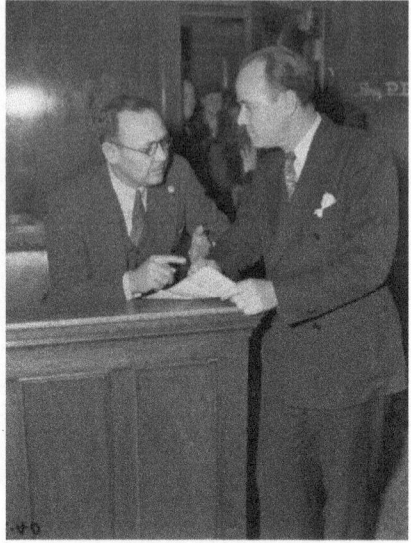

Kynette with glasses and mustache with Robert Noble. [Los Angeles Times Photographic Archive, UCLA Library. Copyright Regents of the University of California, UCLA Library.]

Police Chief James Davis testifying at trial. [Los Angeles Times Photographic Archive, UCLA Library. Copyright Regents of the University of California, UCLA Library.]

Harry and Beulah Raymond outside their home after Harry's release from hospital

17: DYING FALLS

In the days and weeks following the dismissal of the twenty-three LAPD executive police officers, the Los Angeles crime syndicate of Parrot, McAfee, and Gans began to collapse. Bowron had pledged action against the syndicate shortly after his election. "We have our McAfee and our Kent Parrot," the mayor-elect observed. "They continue to campaign and determine the policy of the administration. As far as I am concerned, I'm going to break the power these men have. It has been the most sinister influence we've had for years." In June, the *Los Angeles Times* noticed a change in the gambling scene. The players had headed offshore. "On the gambling boats, and there are quite a number anchored along the Coast, can be seen many of the former crap dealers, wheelmen and card dealers who a year ago could be found up and down Spring Street." One who had taken to the high seas was Farmer Page. Others found lucrative outlets elsewhere. "Guy McAfee, long a man of mystery in local gambling and political circles, has moved at least a large part of his operations to Las Vegas and may be in the market to dispose of his holdings in this city," the *Times* noted. "[Los Angeles] is too big a city now for one man to run," McAfee declared. "I don't want any more of its headaches. I hope Mayor Bowron keeps it closed. That'll be good for Las Vegas."[65]

The desert city had long relied on Southern California to sustain its economy. Until 1905, only a few dozen ranchers, farmers and miners lived in the area, but its strategic location between Salt Lake City and Southern California and an abundant water supply from artesian wells made it an ideal stopover for travelers. Around the turn of the 20th century, Senator William A. Clark of Montana, a wealthy copper miner who had branched into newspapers and trolley lines in Butte and San Pedro before bribing his way into the US Senate, began plans for a railroad to connect Salt Lake City to Los Angeles and San Pedro. Clark purchased 2,000 acres of land in the Las Vegas valley that he subdivided and sold to fund a water stop and depot for his railroad. With the railroad's completion, Las Vegas grew to just under 1,000 persons by 1910. Incorporated in 1911, it was a stable city of small cottages and streets lined with umbrella trees and elms. Most of its citizens worked either in the railroad yard or as miners. A second railroad line connected the mining towns of eastern Nevada to the Salt Lake City/San Pedro tracks.

While for its first decades, mining and the railroad were the backbone of the small city's economy, some of its prominent citizens and entrepreneurs sought sources of revenue not subject to the fluctuating values of gold and silver. Gambling had been legal in Nevada since the early days of its statehood. One of its earliest hotels contained a gambling casino. While the state outlawed gambling in 1909, Las Vegas continued to allow it in "Block Sixteen," an area set aside legally for the sale of liquor. Throughout the 1910s, city leaders debated legalizing or at least decriminalizing forms of gambling. As the silver mines served by the railroad played out and railroad jobs associated with the Tonopah line disappeared, the search for more sustainable industry became urgent.

Divorce was one solution. It had long been a moneymaker in Nevada, especially for the state's northern cities, where the terms the "Reno Marriage" and "Reno Divorce" were already current when Las Vegas incorporated. Las Vegas' location along the railroad line to Los Angeles made it a natural destination for those wanting a quick beginning or ending to a marriage, but it did not have the infrastructure to compete with Reno, which boasted a continuing social scene, a "divorce colony," with jobs and entertainment to fill up the requisite waiting period. Gambling, however, required less of a time-commitment than did divorce. In fact, you didn't even have to be a Nevada "resident" to lose your money at a saloon.[66]

The debate over gambling in Las Vegas took a sharp turn in the twenties when plans for a dam in Boulder Canyon became public. Some foresaw that water from the new dam would boost the area's agriculture. Others recognized that the dam would bring hundreds if not thousands of well-paid workers eager for rest and recreation to the city. It would also attract tourists, in particular those driving up from Los Angeles on the improving highways. A series of advertisements by Thomas Carroll, a Las Vegas real estate developer, crystallized the vision by calling on state leaders "TO MAKE NEVADA THE PLAYGROUND OF THE UNITED STATES" by legalizing open gambling.[67]

In 1931, as construction of the Boulder Dam began, Nevada legalized casino-style gambling. Las Vegas grew despite the ongoing national economic depression, with hotels and casinos cropping up on Fremont Street and along Highway 91, which McAfee later nicknamed "The Strip."

In July 1935, after the Mexican government banned gambling, the Las Vegas Chamber of Commerce invited hotelier Baron Long and other Agua Caliente casino owners to move their enterprises to Las Vegas. While the Agua Caliente gambling executives declined the invitation, after the Raymond bombing, Bowron's election, and the termination of syndicate-friendly cops in the LAPD, McAfee and other Los Angeles underworld figures were ready to move to the desert.

The troubles of LA gamblers came at an opportune time for Las Vegas. After the completion of the Boulder Dam, gambling receipts from construction workers fell off, and the city was in a recession. Las Vegas businessmen recognized that the path to continued growth still rested with the metropolis to its southwest. For Los Angeles' bold and well heeled, Las Vegas was only a two-hour flight aboard Western Air Express. It could also be reached by Union Pacific trains, including the brown and yellow streamliner the "City of Los Angeles" or by an automobile ride up US 66 and 91, a fast and improving route.

McAfee had obtained a license to operate games in the city in 1930, but only games without a bank, which made it difficult for the house to make a profit. His financial condition was not good when he left Los Angeles in 1938. The IRS was after him for unpaid income taxes, and there were rumors that he was almost broke. However, he had enough funds to purchase the Pair-O-Dice casino on Highway 91 a few miles outside of downtown. It was an unpretentious gambling hall, with a couple black jack tables, a single faro bank, one roulette wheel, and a craps table, but McAfee grasped its potential. He upgraded it to attract the clientele he had served in Los Angeles and reopened it as the 91 Club. In the next two decades, he became one of Las Vegas' premier casino operators and investors, developing the Frontier Club and the Golden Nugget. In August 1951, he purchased the Last Frontier Club and Silver Slipper Casino in what was at the time the largest hotel deal in Las Vegas history.

Other LA gambling figures followed him to Las Vegas. After struggling unsuccessfully to legitimize his offshore gambling boats during the mid-forties, Tony Cornero was shot at the front door of his Beverly Hills home after he made plans to open a casino in Mexico. Afterward, he saw the wisdom in moving to Las Vegas instead and joined with his old bootlegging rival Farmer Page and McAfee to build the Stardust Hotel in 1954. Another LA gambling figure, Tutor Scherer, also collaborated with McAfee in casino projects.

The Las Vegas enterprises of McAfee and other LA gamblers were the primary legacy of Los Angeles's underworld syndicate. LA had already wrested its water from regions hundreds of miles beyond its limits and built a harbor with stone filched from Catalina Island. Now it located in the fledgling desert community its solution to the clash between the moral severity of its Midwestern migrants and the hedonism of its youth and film industry. Las Vegas, created to fill the needs of Southern California, first with a railroad connection to Salt Lake City and eastern cities beyond, and later to satisfy LA's appetite for electric power, became LA's playground, where Angelenos could do what they could not do at home.

While McAfee headed for Las Vegas, Kent Kane Parrot decided that it was time to retire. He had settled his tax problems with the IRS, perhaps with the help of producer and fellow gambler Joseph Schenck, whose tax evasion schemes would land him in federal prison a few years later. By the time of Raymond's bombing, Parrot already had one foot out of Los Angeles and into Santa Barbara, where, since the early twenties, he had spent the summers with one wife or another, playing golf and hobnobbing with the idle rich. He had purchased undeveloped land in Hope Ranch in 1926, but the property would pass from his hands as part of a divorce settlement with his second wife before he could carry out his plan to erect a large estate there. By 1938, he had left Los Angeles political and business life for a beachfront home next to the Miramar Hotel in Montecito. In the coming years, his name came up in the Los Angeles papers only occasionally, and usually in unfavorable contexts. In 1941, he testified before the grand jury investigating tax evasion charges against two amusement machine operators who had taken tax deductions for bribes they paid to public officials. True to form, Parrot told reporters, "I know absolutely nothing about this matter" while denying press reports that he represented the organization involved in the bribes, the California Amusement Machine Operator's Association. A year later, a state Assembly Committee reported rumors that agents of former Governor Culbert Olson's re-election campaign attempted to shake down the operators of sardine fishing packing companies in Monterey for permits. While most operators refused to pay for the permits, Parrot and his partner, whose brother was a member of the State Fish and Game Commission, purchased one for $10,000. Parrot said that he wanted to get in the sardine business because "It is a racket where one dollar will get you five without doing anything." Naturally, Parrot denied any wrongdoing, although he admitted he owned a large share of the Lone Wolf Packing Company in Moss Landing.[68]

After the sardine flap, the social activities of Parrot's ex-wives, one of whom was now a famous author and the other a close friend of Greta Garbo, and his son, who was beginning a military and diplomatic career, took up more newspaper print than did the former political boss of Los Angeles. While his wife continued to be a prominent socialite, Parrot lived as a recluse for the last years of his life.

Bob Gans, the third member of the syndicate troika, remained in the public eye for years to come, not as a sinister political and gambling figure but as a leader in the Jewish community. After selling his slot machine business to Samuel "Curly" Robinson, another amusement machine figure, he served as President of Mt. Sinai Hospital from 1942 to 1951. He also led an organization dedicated to funding Jewish settlements in the state of Israel.

All three syndicate leaders died within a few years of each other, Parrot in March 1956 from cancer, Robert Gans of a heart attack three years later, and Guy McAfee after a stomach operation the same year. Death soon cut a large swath in the ranks of other men and women who played parts in the vice drama of pre-war Los Angeles. Both Tutor Scherer and Cornero died of heart attacks in the mid-fifties, the latter succumbing while playing craps at the Desert Inn. Farmer Page survived multiple heart attacks until the final one got him in 1960 at his home on 6th Street in Los Angeles. Dave Clark, who gunned down Charlie Crawford and Herbert Spencer in 1931, lived long enough to murder again. In 1953, he killed the wife of his best friend. He died in Chino State Prison the following year.

Deposed Mayor Frank Shaw passed away in 1958. He had attempted a political comeback in 1941, running against incumbent Fletcher Bowron and finishing fifth behind his predecessor as mayor, John C Porter, who was making his second attempt at a comeback. Shaw spent some of the years after his recall filing and fighting lawsuits emanating from the Raymond bombing. In August 1938, Raymond had sued him, his brother Joe, Police Chief Davis, Earle Kynette, Roy Allen, and Fred Browne and other SIU members as well as twent John Does representing vice interests in Los Angeles. A year later, however, Raymond dismissed the lawsuit. Shaw claimed in 1940 that he never paid Raymond a penny.

In October 1939, Shaw launched a defamation suit against Warner Brothers, claiming that the studio's film, *The Man Who Dared*, was based on the Raymond bombing and that it implicated him in a murder plot. The lawsuit was settled out of court, Shaw receiving $7,500. The terms of another lawsuit Shaw brought in 1943 against McFadden Publications, which had published a series of articles in *Liberty Magazine* entitled "The Lid Off Los Angeles" by Frank Allhoff and Dwight McKinney, were not disclosed. Nor were the settlement terms of a lawsuit he filed against McFadden for an article penned by Nelda Clinton, Clifford Clinton's wife, entitled, "My Husband's Death Struggle with the Vice Czars of Los Angeles." In return, Clifford Clinton abandoned a libel suit against Shaw. All claimed they did so to concentrate their energies on the war effort. Finally, in 1955, Shaw sued William Bonelli, whose book *Billion Dollar Blackjack* connected him to Raymond's bombing.

Frank Shaw's brother, Joe, died in 1965. He had been convicted of selling civil service jobs in 1939. Two years later, an appeals court reversed his conviction, ruling that civil service commission employees who altered examination scores as part of the scheme were accomplices in the crime and therefore could not testify against him. Without the testimony of these functionaries, there was no case. For years afterward, Joe fought charges that he acted corruptly during his brother's mayoralty. He had some success. An associate of Clifford Clinton admitted in court that he fabricated a story claiming that Joe and his chauffeur, Peter Del Gado, smuggled a half million dollars into Mexico under the floorboards of an automobile. The tale had reached Clifford Clinton, who was eager for negative information about the Shaws. Clinton had passed it to the writers of the *Liberty Magazine* article.

In 1949, Joe ran for mayor against his nemesis, Fletcher Bowron, and lost badly. A few weeks later, his reputation was further tarnished when he was called before the grand jury to testify in a vice investigation. He took on Bowron once more the following year by attempting to organize a recall of the recently re-elected mayor. Bowron fired back angrily, claiming that Shaw was part of "an unholy combination" that aimed to bring back the days of his brother's regime. While the unholy combination gathered enough signatures to force the recall election, the effort failed.[69]

Despite convicting Kynette and Allen for the bombing, Buron Fitts came under attack from Clinton and the reformers when he ran again for district attorney in 1940. Bowron opposed him as well. So did Joe Shaw, who was smarting from his prosecution for graft and the vitriol Fitts' deputies heaped on him and his brother during the Kynette prosecution. Fitts was favored to win re-election after having led in the late August primary by 34% against 25% for his chief opponent, John Dockweiler. In the November final election, however, Dockweiler gained almost all the votes that went to other candidates in the primary, winning with 60% of the vote. It was a crushing rejection for the longtime and always embattled prosecutor, but Fitts was not the man to crawl away beaten. He started his own private practice and later associated with an established law firm. He also continued to address community organizations, using the super-patriotic themes he had repeated during twenty years in public life. With a war in Europe and the threat of war imminent in the United States, it was a fine time to warn of menacing domestic forces and fifth columns.

In June 1942, amid rumors that he would again seek an elected office, Fitts joined the Army Air Corp with the rank of major. He was wounded in northern Africa a year later when a fragment from a high explosive shell hit him in the face. He also served in the Pacific campaign, piloting B-17s and reaching the rank of Lieutenant Colonel before being discharged by a medical board in 1947. After his return to civilian life, he resumed his law practice, contemplated running for office several times, spoke at public gatherings on themes of patriotism and internal vigilance, and, his health failing and bothered by LA's smog, retired in his seventies to Three Rivers in Tulare County, California. In 1973, he was found dead in the driveway of his home. Despondent over poor health, he had shot himself in the head.

In 1942, the grand jury indicted Clifford Clinton along with Mayor Fletcher Bowron, Deputy DA Grant Cooper, Police Chief Clemence Horrall and four police officers, including chemist Ray Pinker, for illegally wiretapping suspects in a vice investigation. Clinton was serving in the US Army when the indictments were announced. As the Army had discovered Clinton's food service skills and was using the restaurateur to redesign its mess procedures at Fort Benning, the charges were dismissed. After serving eighteen months, he returned to Los Angeles and his restaurant business. He stayed active in city politics, but his influence, which had led some of his detractors to allege he was becoming a new city boss, waned substantially. In 1945, he ran unsuccessfully for mayor against his old ally Bowron. Eight years later, he ran for a seat on the Board of Education but lost badly. Much of his efforts after the war focused on his restaurants and philanthropic projects, such as the Meals for Millions Foundation, which he created in 1946 to distribute multi-purpose food packages to the world's hungry. He died in 1969 after suffering a heart attack at his home.

Rheba Crawford died in 1966. She had bitterly denied Clinton's allegations that she was involved in a shakedown racket. In 1940, after LAPD investigators examined her bank records for 1936-7, she scolded the Los Angeles Police Commission for permitting a "goon squad" to violate her privacy rights. The commission issued a statement clearing her of any offenses and the matter died. Ill during most of the war years, she resumed her calling as an evangelist in 1945, touring the south for several years before remarrying in 1948. Most of her last eighteen years were spent with her third husband, Imperial Valley rancher Arthur Lawrence Lambertz, occasionally preaching and serving briefly as a coordinator for senior affairs in Los Angeles County.

Raymond's friend Ralph Gray made a run at City Council in 1940 with Clifford Clinton's support but lost. He died in November 1966. His nemesis, Harry Munson, had died almost twenty years earlier of a heart attack. At the time of Munson's death, the *Los Angeles Times* published a short obituary for him on the first page of its "City News" section. The article did not mention Munson's dispute with Gray and the role it played in the Los Angeles civic upheaval of 1938. A world war had intervened, and already the city was moving on.

Two other figures in the Raymond bombing died soon after the bombing trial. Fred A. Browne, who was found not guilty, died of a heart attack in February 1939. Roy Allen died in May 1942 from heart disease in the San Quentin Prison hospital with Earle Kynette, a hospital orderly, by his side. Allen had continued to protest his innocence until his death.

Earle Kynette never admitted guilt in the Raymond bombing, either. After failing to win a second trial, he entered San Quentin in September 1940 after two years in Los Angeles County jail. Over the next seven years, his attorneys continuously appealed his conviction, filed writs of habeas corpus, and beseeched authorities for parole or a pardon. Harry Raymond fought their efforts at every turn with impassioned letters to the governor. In November 1945, Kynette was scheduled for release on December 1, his sentence having been reduced by credits for good behavior and work in prison harvest camps in the Sacramento Delta. The camps, established during the war to ease labor shortages, were notorious for enabling misbehavior among inmates. One official complained that prisoners "came and went as they pleased, enjoyed their liquor and women without interference, and in general lived like anything but convicts."[70]

Raymond fought Kynette's release fervently. "As the victim of the most dastardly crime in the police annals of the nation," he wrote to Governor Earl Warren, "I protest with all vehemence I can muster against the freeing of Earle E. Kynette as a mockery on justice and a travesty on law." He gained access to Kynette's prison records, where he found that the state accidentally credited Kynette twice for the same 48 days of war contract work. On November 30, the Director of the Department of Corrections announced that Kynette's parole would be delayed until early February because of the mistake. The delay gave Raymond more time. He claimed he had been warned that after Kynette's parole his own life would be in jeopardy. On February 8, the day that Kynette was scheduled to walk through the gates of San Quentin, the California Adult Authority announced that his parole had been revoked "because the length of incarceration was not commensurate with the gravity of the offense."[71]

Kynette had to wait two more years for his release. The parole board noted that he had been a model prisoner, serving as a Red Cross instructor during the war. "Nine years, nine tough years for something I didn't do," the former LAPD captain grumbled as he left San Quentin and headed to work at a Hayward, California ranch. He no longer had a family to rejoin. His wife, Eleanor, after moving to Pittsburg to be near her older sister, had divorced him in November 1945 alleging that he did not share his prison camp pay of $3/day with her. She soon remarried.[72]

Once again, Raymond responded angrily to the news of Kynette's release, declaring, "The parole is a mockery and travesty of justice." According to Kynette, in the following twenty-four months Raymond "hounded" him continuously and interfered with his attempts to find work. He also claimed that Raymond offered to leave him alone in exchange for $5,000.[73]

In December 1950, a pair of Oakland patrolmen observed Kynette staggering down a street. As they approached, he tossed aside a green prescription bottle filled with pills and capsules. The cops took him to jail, but he was so intoxicated that they were unable to fingerprint him. After checking out a false address in Pittsburg that he had given them, they located his rooms in Oakland, where he was working as a pharmacist. There they found two hypodermic needles and two dozen bottles of pills.

Raymond swung into action on the news of Kynette's arrest, writing to Governor Earl Warren to demand that his parole be revoked. Oakland police held him as they awaited chemical analysis of the pills found in his hotel room and those he had thrown away on the street. Kynette claimed they contained nitroglycerin for his heart ailment. He tried to get the drunk charge dismissed, complaining that it would jeopardize his pharmacy license, but the court rebuffed him, and he pled guilty. In mid-January 1951, he was sent back to San Quentin, where he remained until May 1952.

After his second release in 1952, Kynette regained his pharmacist license. During the next ten years, he lived in the San Francisco Bay area, continuing his downward path. In 1954, while visiting Dagmar, his youngest daughter born out of wedlock in 1911, he got into a minor traffic accident in Los Angeles. After a patrolman interviewed him, Kynette abruptly left the scene while the patrolman was busy calling into his headquarters. LA police issued a warrant for his arrest for drunk driving. As the patrolman had not performed a sobriety test before Kynette left, he could only base the warrant on the smell of alcohol on Kynette's breath. In the end, the charges were dropped after a key witness failed to appear.

The Los Angeles drunk driving charge was a prelude to a tragic event. In July 1955, Kynette, then working in a drugstore in the town of Twain Harte, was traveling in an automobile owned by Hayward, California resident Clarence Bitting near Sonora on California State Route 108 when a car approaching in the opposite direction swung into its lane. Bitting's automobile swerved and climbed up the side of an embankment before toppling over onto its roof. Bitting and Frances Wahlstrom, sister of his former wife, Eleanor, were both killed, and Kynette was badly injured. After he told police officers at the scene that he was driving the car, he was charged with felony drunk driving. However, at his trial, he claimed he had not been behind the steering wheel. "I wasn't even driving the car," he told the Judge. "I can prove it. If I had been driving, I would have chest injuries." As there was no proof that he was the driver or that his actions had caused the accident, the charges were dismissed.[74]

While he retained his pharmacy license until October 31, 1967, where Kynette worked in the latter fifties is not clear. By 1960, he was living in Oakland. In September of that year, he married Annie Matilda Guild. He was now in his 67th year. She was 61. The marriage lasted four years, but the couple likely separated long before they divorced on November 20, 1964. They were probably living apart when, on July 3, 1963, he went on a drinking binge in Oakland bars with a younger man named Ira Dunn. Afterward, the two staggered to Dunn's skid row apartment, where they drank some more. Dunn then tried to rob him. When Kynette resisted, Dunn stabbed him in the arm and abdomen. Kynette was taken to Oakland's Highland Hospital; Dunn went to jail.

Kynette died in June 1970 just short of his 77th birthday. There was no mention of his death in the newspapers. His era and misdeeds were over.

It is certain that after Kynette's final release from prison, Harry Raymond continued to monitor his post-prison travails. It is likely that he thought of some action he could take—perhaps another letter to the parole board or even the pharmacy licensing commission. However, Kynette had not been found guilty of drunk driving in either case and he was beyond the reach of the parole board, his parole having been final in 1952. Legally, he was beyond Raymond's grasp.

During the last decades of his life, Raymond must have continued to earn a living as a private detective. However, the only record of his detective work after 1939 is a New York columnist's brief comment that he was investigating the murders of Walter and Beulah Overell. The couple had died aboard their boat in Newport Beach harbor when dynamite sticks stashed in one of the vessel's bunks exploded. Because the heir and prime suspect, the couple's daughter, was acquitted along with her fiancé, several insurance companies were on the hook for $122,000. Whether Raymond was under contract or freelancing is not clear.

Raymond's alliance with Clinton and Bowron withered during the years after the Kynette trial. In 1939, he ran for the Los Angeles City Council for the Boyle Heights district in a field of seven, three of whom were former councilmen of the district. He adopted a populist theme in announcing his candidacy, declaring that he would continue to defy the underworld. "I am a poor man, and my campaign will be a poor man's campaign, supported by the common people." Both Mayor Bowron and Clifford Clinton backed other candidates in the race. Raymond finished fourth behind the three former councilmen. After his loss, except for an occasional biting letter, he stayed out of politics.[75]

Bowron's discharge of twenty-three senior LAPD officers in 1939 had infuriated Raymond. Years later, after Bowron failed to win re-election to a fifth term, Raymond wrote him a harsh letter exulting his loss.

> Just to remind you that you were not elected to the Office of Mayor in September 1938 recall election of Frank Shaw. Shaw was recalled by the voters; and as you were the only one on the ticket you automatically became the Mayor; the voters had no other choice.
>
> You were just the incident and accident on that alleged reform ticket, and any other person who would have been on that ticket would have been Mayor of Los Angeles.
>
> Fletch, you rode into the Office of Mayor in September 1938 on my broken bones, and our many friends. After becoming Mayor in 1938, you stooped to the same tactics that you have used in the recent election, but this time you failed and failed miserably.
>
> . . . you purged 23 of our finest and most efficient Ranking Officers of our Police Department, each with more than 20 years experience as such; all with outstanding reputations as Law enforcement officers, not only in the City of Los Angeles but throughout the United States and Foreign Countries.[76]

Harry lived with his wife Beulah at 955 South Orme until 1942, when the aging couple moved a quarter mile away to 2800 ½ Oregon Street. There they lived until 1950, when they moved to 316 S Rampart Blvd. Harry made frequent trips to National City, where he once considered relocating his detective business, to visit with his friend, publisher William Clay Silver, and his wife, Anna. He also continued to carouse bars, particularly those around a somewhat seedy stretch of Main near the corners of 12th and Pico. After his younger brother enlisted in the army, Harry came by from time to time to check on his sister-in-law and nephew. His sister-in-law did not like Harry, but she politely let him take Jim, a boy of eleven, on afternoon excursions. Harry took the boy with him from bar to bar in downtown Los Angeles, where the young boy watched as Harry's old friends greeted him. He remembers Harry picking him up proudly, placing him on the bar and exclaiming, "This is my nephew! Anybody want to fight?"[77]

On July 11, 1956, two San Diego police officers observed Harry staggering on the sidewalk at the corner of 4th Avenue and Nutmeg. Neither officer had been with the San Diego Police Department during Raymond's short stint as chief. Unrecognized, Raymond was booked on a charge of public intoxication. Although there is plenty of evidence that Harry sometimes drank heavily, it is possible that he had suffered a stroke, a malady sometimes misdiagnosed as intoxication. Sometime in July, he became bedridden in his home at 316 South Rampart Blvd by heart problems. He survived nine months, succumbing on Monday, April 1, 1957. Masonic services were held at the Rosedale Cemetery Chapel on April 4. In addition to his wife Beulah and his younger brother, James, 200 persons attended the services. Among them were figures from law enforcement of the past decades, including Frank "Lefty" James, head of the LAPD's gangster squad in the 1920s, former Police Captain Robert Kallmeyer, former LA County Undersheriff Arthur Jewel, and one of Raymond's fellow detectives with the Southern California Automobile Club in the early 1920s, Jim Reynolds. Also present were current leaders of the LAPD and Sheriff's office: Sheriff Eugene Biscailuz, LAPD Captain Jack Donahoe, and Chief of Detectives Thad Brown, who would become chief nine years later.

After Harry's death, Beulah lived in their apartment at 316 South Rampart Blvd. for a short time, surviving on social security benefits and the couples' savings. For a time, James Raymond, Harry's younger brother, paid part of her rent but eventually found himself unable to continue supporting her. He drove to her apartment to tell her he could no longer afford to help her, knocked on the door and heard steps approaching. "Beulah," he began, and then explained why he had come. She did not open the door and she did not speak. After a few moments, he heard her steps withdrawing inside the apartment. It was his last contact with her.

In the early sixties, Beulah moved a block away to 276 ½ South Rampart, where she died on August 23, 1976. She was buried in Angelus Rosedale Cemetery in Los Angeles, not far but not especially near the crypt of her husband. In the years after her husband's death, the turbulence of the eras he lived through and played a small but important part was replaced by a different and even greater turmoil. The moral reform leaders of the twenties and thirties became a thin, weak voice drowned out by advocates of free sexuality and self-indulgence. Legal gambling was thriving in Las Vegas and soon would spread across the nation, shielded by Supreme Court restrictions on the state's authority over Amerindian reservations. Los Angeles' law enforcement, which had fought to keep eastern criminal groups from challenging the homegrown syndicate, soon were faced with a homegrown explosion of gang violence and crime financed by the sale of narcotics. When compared to the chaos of the decades that followed Raymond's death, those of his time now seem almost quaint.

Guy McAfee breaks ground on the 91 Club, Las Vegas, 1939 [Los Angeles Daily News Negatives, UCLA Library, Copyright Regents of the University of California, UCLA Library]

BIBLIOGRAPHY

Allison, Ross. *Spooked in Seattle : A Haunted Handbook.* Cincinnati, Oh, Clerisy Press, 2011.

Ainlay, Thomas Jr. and Gabaldan, Judy Dixon. *Las Vegas: The Fabulous First Century,* Arcadia Publishing, Charleston, SC, 2003.

Joseph Clement Bates. *History of the Bench and Bar of California.* San Francisco, Bench And Bar Publishing Company, 1912.

Blackmar, Frank W. *Kansas; a Cyclopedia of State History, Embracing Events, Institutions, Industries, Counties, Cities, Towns, Prominent Persons, Etc. . . . with a Supplementary Volume Devoted to Selected Personal History and Reminiscence.* Chicago, Standard Publishing Company, 1912.

Bonelli, William G *Billion Dollar BlackJack.* Civic Research Press. 1954. Print.

Briggs, Arthur E. *Southern California Renaissance Man.* UCLA Oral History. Print.

Burke, Colin B. *America's Information Wars,* Roman and Littlefield, Lanham, Maryland, 2018.

Burdette, Robert J., ed. *American Biography and Genealogy, California Edition, Volume 2,* pp 799-810, The Lewis Publishing Company, Chicago/New York, 1912.

Buntin, John. *L.A. Noir : The Struggle for the Soul of America's Most Seductive City.* New York, Three Rivers Press, 2009.

Callis, Tracy and Johnson, Chuck. *Boxing in the Los Angeles Area, 1880-2005,* Trafford Publishing, Victoria B. C. 2009.

Carr, Horace. *Los Angeles, City of Dreams,* D Appleton-Century, New York, 1935.

Castanien, Pliny, *To Protect and Serve: A History of the San Diego Police Department and its Chiefs,* 1889-1989, San Diego Historical Society, San Diego, 1993, 58.

Chamberlain, Ernest R. "FITTS: Protector of Womanhood", manuscript draft in Clinton Collection, University of California at Los Angeles Special Collections.

Robert Glass Cleland. *California in Our Time, 1900-1940. [With Plates and a Map.].* Alfred A. Knopf: New York, 1947.

Clinton III, Edmond J, and Mark A Vieira. *Clifton's and Clifford Clinton : A Cafeteria and a Crusader.* Santa Monica California, Angel City Press, 2015.

Cohn, Alfred A. *"Take the Witness!"* New York, New York Home Library, 1943.

"A Rationale of the Law of Kidnapping." *Columbia Law Review* 53, no. 4 (1953): 540-58.

Crawford, Richard. "The Brief and Hectic Career of Chief Harry Raymond." http://www.sandiegoyesterday.com

Davis, Carlyle Channing. *Olden Times in Colorado,* Philips Publishing Company, Los Angeles, 1916.

Daniels, Bebe and Ben Lyon. *Life with the Lyons: the Autobiography of Bebe Daniels and Ben Lyon.* London. Odhams Press Ltd., 1953.

Deener, Andrew. *Venice: A Contested Bohemia in Los Angeles,* University of Chicago Press, Chicago, IL, 2012.

Dewey, Thomas. *Twenty Against the Underworld.* Doubleday and Company, Garden City, 1974.

Domanick, Joe. *To Protect and To Serve: The Century of War in the City of Dreams.* Pocket Books, Simon and Schuster, New York, 1994.

Gale, Neil, "The History of Chicago's "Red-Light" Vice Districts", *The Digital Research Library of Illinois History Journal.*

Finney, Guy. *Angel City in Turmoil.* Amer Press. Los Angeles, 1940.

The Great Los Angeles Bubble. Forbes, 1929.

Fox, Stephen. *Blood and Power, Organized Crime in Twentieth-Century America.* William Morrow and Company, New York, 1989.

Fulford-Jones, Will. *Time Out Los Angeles,* Time Out Guides, London, 1997.

Garrigues, Charles H. *You're Paying for It! A Guide to Graft.* Funk & Wagnall's, New York, 1936.

Gebhard, David and Winter, Robert. *An Architectural Guidebook to Los Angeles,* Gibbs Smith, Salt Lake City, 2003.

Gottlieb, Robert & Wolf, Irene. *Thinking Big: The Story of the Los Angeles Times, Its Publishers and Their Influence on Southern California.* G. P. Putnam & Sons, New York, 1977.

Guinn, James Miller, *A History of California and an Extended History of Los Angeles and Environs Also Containing Biographies of Well-known Citizens of the Past and Present ·* Volume 1. United States: Historic Record Company, 1915.

Haight, Raymond. "Indicted! How a City Political Gang Got Its Man." *Scribner's Magazine,* March 1934.

Hallberg, June. *Fitts/Palmer Campaign for District Attorney.* M.A. Thesis, UCLA, 1939.

Jennings, Dean. *We Only Kill Each Other,* Prentice Hall, 1967.

Kurashige, Scott. "Between 'White Spot' and 'World City': Racial Integration and the Roots of Multiculturalism," in Deverell, William and Hise, Gregg. *A Companion to Los Angeles,* John Wiley and Sons, Chichester, 2014.

Kooistra, AnnMarie. *Angels for Sale: The History of Prostitution in Los Angeles 1880-1940,* University of Southern California, PhD Dissertation, 2003.

Lacey, Robert. *Little Man, Meyer Lansky and the Gangster Life.* Little, Brown and Company, New York, 1991.

Larson, Arnold B. *Newspaper Reporting in the Twenties: Reflections,* University of California, Los Angeles, Oral History Program, 1970.

Lawler, Oscar. *Los Angeles Attorney,* UCLA Oral History, 1962, Interviewed by Doyce Nuns.

Leach, Josiah Granville, *History of the Bringhurst family with notes on the Clarkson, De Peyster, and Boude families.* Philadelphia J.B. Lippincott, 1901.

Livingston, Alberta. "The Strangest Third Degree," *True Detective Mysteries,* McFadden, Jan 1930

Longstreet, Stephen. *All Star Cast, An Anecdotal History of Los Angeles.* 1977.

Lowell, Douglas L., "The California Southern Railroad and the Growth of San Diego", *Journal of San Diego History,* San Diego Historical Society Quarterly, Fall, 1985, Volume 31, Number 4.

Martin, John. "Patriotism and Profit: San Diego's Camp Kearny *Journal of San Diego History,* San Diego Historical Society, San Diego, CA, Volume 58, Fall 2012, no. 4.

May, Allan. "Cleveland's Sly/Fanner Murders," *Crime Magazine,* www.crimemagazine.com.

McKinney, Dwight & Allhoff, Fred. "The Lid off Los Angeles," *Liberty Magazine* November 11, 1939.

McPhail, Elizabeth C. "Shady Ladies in the 'Stingaree District' When The Red Lights Went out in San Diego", *Journal of San Diego History,* San Diego Historical Society Quarterly, San Diego Historical Society, Volume 2, Number 2, Winter, 1973; *SDU,* Jan 23, 1921.

H. W. McQuat 1951, "History of the Los Angeles Harbor" In: *First Conference on Coastal Engineering.* Long Beach, CA, 1950.

McWilliams, Carey. *Southern California: An Island on the Land.* Gibbs Smith, 1973.

298

Moehring, Eugene and Green Michael S. *Las Vegas: A Centennial History,* University of Nevada Press, Reno, 2005.

Moody Eric N. "Nevada's Legalization of Casino Gambling in 1931/Purely a Business Proposition", Nevada Historical Society Quarterly, Summer, 1994.

Moore, Charles. *The City Observed: Los Angeles,* Vintage Books, New York, 1984.

Muir, Florabel. *Headline Happy,* Holt Publishing. New York, 1950.

Nasatir, Abraham P. "Chileans in California during the Gold Rush Period and the Establishment of the Chilean Consulate." *California Historical Quarterly* 53, no. 1 (1974): doi: 10.2307/25157486.

Netz, Joseph. "The Great Los Angeles Railroad Boom of 1887", *Annual Publication of the Historical Society of Southern California,* Vol. 10, No. 1 / 2, (1915/16).

Newton, Michael. *Stolen Away: The True Story Of California's Most Shocking Kidnap-Murder.* Simon and Schuster, New York, 2000.

Nichols, Chris. "Charting the 127-Year History of Clifton's, Downtown's Most Glorious Resurrected Building," *LAmag.com,* Aug 19, 2015.

O'Hara, Mary. *Flicka's Friend,* G. Putnam's Sons, New York, 1982.

Olender, Terrys T., *For the Prosecution, Miss Deputy D.A.,* Chilton Co., Philadelphia 1961.

Outland, Charles. *Man-Made Disaster: the story of St. Francis Dam.* Arthur H. Clark Company, Glendale, California, 1963.

Polley, Martin ed., *The History of Sport in Britain 1880-1914,* Routledge, London, 2004.

Pourade, Richard F. *The Rising Tide,* Union-Tribune Publishing, 1967.

Rayner, Richard, A Bright and Guilty Place: Murder, Corruption, and L.A.'s Scandalous Coming of Age. Doubleday, 2009.

Rasmussen, Cecilia. "Ramparts Site Was a Noir Landmark," *Los Angeles Times.* Sept. 9, 1999.

Rodman Willoughby, *History of the Bench and Bar of Southern California.* William J. Porter, Los Angeles, 1909.

Runyon Damon, "The Idyll of Miss Sara Brown," *Collier's Magazine,* Jan 28, 1933, 41.

Sann, Paul. *The Lawless Decade,* New York, Fawcett World Library, New York, 1971.

Schwartzberg, Beverly. "Lots of Them Did That": Desertion, Bigamy, and Marital Fluidity in Late-Nineteenth-Century America, *Journal of Social History,* Volume 37, Issue 3, Spring 2004.

Shanks, Rosalie. "The IWW Free Speech Movement: San Diego, 1912, *Journal of San Diego History,* San Diego Historical Society Quarterly, San Diego Historical Society, Volume 19, Number 1, Spring 1974.

Shmelter, Richard J. *USC Trojans Football Encyclopedia,* McFarland & Company, Inc., Jefferson, North Carolina, 2014.

Shuler, Robert. "The Jacobson Outrage." *Bob Shuler 's Magazine,* September, 1927.

The Strange Death of Charlie Crawford. Los Angeles, 1931.

Shuler, Robert, Jr., *"Fighting Bob Shuler of Los Angeles,"* Dog Ear Publishing, Indianapolis, Indiana, 2011.

Siegel, Fred. *The Future Once Happened Here,* The Free Press, Simon and Schuster, Inc., New York, 199.

Sitton, Tom. "The 'Boss' Without a Machine: Kent K. Parrot and Los Angeles Politics in the 1920s." *Southern California Quarterly.* Vol. 67. No. 4. Winter 1985.

Los Angeles Transformed, University of New Mexico Press, Albuquerque, New Mexico, 2005.

Sitton, Tom, and Deverell, William, ed. *Metropolis in the Making: Los Angeles in the 1920s.* University of California Press, 2001.

St. Cloud, Vern. "Bombing the Lid Off Los Angeles," *Official Detective Stories.* May-November 1938.

St. Johns, Adela Rogers *Final Verdict,* Doubleday & Company, Garden City, New York, 1962.

Starr, Kevin. *Material Dreams.* Oxford University Press. New York, 1990.

Stoker, Charles. *Thicker'n Thieves.* Sidereal Company, Santa Monica, California, 1951.

Story, Harold, H. *Memoirs of Harold H. Story,* UCLA Oral History, UCLA, 1967. Interviewed by Elizabeth I. Dixon.

Sutherland, Vincent. "Raymond Bombing Sequel to Chandler-Shaw Deal." *People's World,* Feb. 2, 1938.

Tygiel, Jules. *The Great Los Angeles Swindle,* University of California Press, Los Angeles, 1994.

Jonathan Turley, "Laying Hands on Religious Racketeers: Applying Civil RICO to Fraudulent Religious Solicitation," 29 Wm. & Mary L. Rev. 441 (1988).

United States Senate, Special Committee to Investigate Organized Crime in Interstate Commerce, United States Senate, HEARINGS, Nevada-California, November, December 1950, March 1951. United States Government Printing Office, Washington, D.C., 1951.

Vaus, Jim. *Why I Quit Syndicated Crime.* Van Kemper Press, 1951.

Walton, John. *The Legendary Detective: The Private Eye in Fact and Fiction.* University of Chicago Press, 2015.

Weinstock, Matt. *My LA.* Current Books, New York, 1947.

White, Leslie. *Me Detective.* Harcourt, Brace and Company. New York, 1936.

Wilkerson, Tichi & Borie, Marcia. *The Hollywood Reporter.* 1984.

Wild, Mark. *Street Meeting: Multiethnic Neighborhoods In Early Twentieth Century Los Angeles,* University of California Press, Berkeley and Los Angeles, Ca, 2005.

Willard, Charles Dwight. *The Los Angeles Herald's History of Los Angeles City,* Kingsley, Barnes and Neuhar Co., Los Angeles, 1901.

Wilson, David. *Not Just Evil: Murder, Hollywood and California's First Insanity Plea.* Diversion Books, New York, New York, 2016.

Wilson, Edmund. "The Queen of the Angels", *The American Jitters, A Year of the Slump,* New York, C. Scribner's Sons, 1932.

Winston, Janet S., MD, Yeh, I-Tien, MD, Evers, Kathryn, MD, Friedman, Adele K. MD. "Calcium Oxalate Is Associated With Benign Breast Tissue: Can We Avoid Biopsy?" *American Journal of Clinical Pathology,* Volume 100, Issue 5, 1 November 1993.

Wolf, Marvin J. and Mader, Katherine. *Fallen Angels,* 1986 and 2012.

Wolsey, Serge G. *Call House Madam.* Martin Tudordale, Inc., New York, 1941.

Woods, Gerald. *The Progressives and the Police: Urban Reform and the Professionalization of the Los Angeles Police.* UMI Dissertation Information Service, Ann Arbor, 1973.

Wright, Willard Huntington "Los Angeles: The Chemically Pure", *The Smart Set Magazine,* Mar 1913; John Adams Thayer Corporation, New York, London, and Paris.

Yankel, J. Heim. "Who Shot Our Buron' . . . And Why?" *Clifford Clinton's Civic Digest,* December 1939.

A Complete Set of Surveys and Plats of Wyandotte County and Kansas City, Kansas, G.M. Hopkins, Philadelphia PA, 1887.

Atlas of Kansas City, Kansas etc., Rascher Insurance Map Publishing Company, Chicago, Illinois, 1893.

Atlas of Kansas City, Kansas etc., Rascher Insurance Map Publishing Company, Chicago, Illinois, 1893.

People vs. Earl E. Kynette, Roy J. Allen Fred A. Browne. Digest of Testimony. Joseph Shaw Papers, Special Collections, UCLA Research Library.

301

The People of the State of California vs. Earl E. Kynette Roy J. Allen Fred A Browne John Doe and Richard Roe. Joseph Shaw Papers, Special Collections, UCLA Research Library.

The People of the State of California vs. William Edward Hickman. California State Archives. (People v. Hickman (1928) 204 Cal. 470, 476).

Touring Topics, Vol XIV, No 1, January 1922 Automobile Club, Los Angeles, CA 1922.

General Catalogue of the Officers and Students of The Philips Exeter Academy 1783-1903, The News-Letter Press, Exeter, New Hampshire, 1903.

The Paen, Vol 18, Exeter, New Hampshire, 1902.

The Standard, A Weekly Insurance Newspaper, Boston, MA, Jun 10, 1904.

University of Southern California, *Yearbook 1909-1910*, Vol. 4, No. 1, March 1909; Vol. 5, No. 1, March 1910.

Stare Decisis University of Southern California School of Law, 1909, 76.

Rodeo, University of Southern California, 1907-1910.

The Druggist Circular, Vol LXVI, #4, Apr 1922, 147, New York, New York.

INDEX

ENDNOTES

Key to major sources:

BACK   Bakersfield Californian
CT   Chicago Tribune
HCN   Hollywood Citizen-News
IDN   Los Angeles Illustrated Daily News
LAT   Los Angeles Times
LAE   Los Angeles Examiner
LAEE   Los Angeles Evening Express
LAH&E   Los Angeles Herald and Express
LAR   Los Angeles Record
OAKT   Oakland Tribune
OSE   Ogden Standard-Examiner
SAR   Santa Ana Register
SCEE   Santa Cruz Evening News
SBCS   San Bernardino County Sun
SDET   San Diego Evening Tribune
SDS   San Diego Sun
SDU   San Diego Union
SFC   San Francisco Chronicle
SFCALL   San Francisco Call
SFE   San Francisco Examiner
SMT   Santa Maria Times (Santa Maria, California)

THE YOUNG DETECTIVE
[1] *LAH,* Jan 28, 1921, B8.

[2] Rosella's widowed mother joined her daughter and Albert in Nickerson after Harry's birth. She saw opportunity in the little city. Before long, she had purchased several properties, including four houses formerly owned by jeweler D. C. Gilbert, one of the city's most prosperous and energetic citizens, who got the properties back when he and

Rosella's mother married in October of the same year.

³ *Hutchinson Herald* (Hutchinson, Kansas), Feb 1, 1879; Feb 13, 1879; Aug 28, 1880; Sept 2, 1880; Apr 30, 1881; Nov 2, 1883. *LT,* Sept 2, 1880.

⁴ The killer was Logan Montgomery. *Emporia News,* Nov 24, 1881, p. 4.

⁵ Kansas Prohibitory Law, As Amended by the Murray Bill. Also, the New Pharmacy Law, G. W. Crane and Company, Topeka, Kansas, 1887.

⁶ *Emporia Gazette,* May 9, 1896, 1; May 11, 1896, 1; Jul 30, 1898, 1; Aug 1, 1898, 4. *Emporia Daily Republican,* Aug 1, 1898, 4; Aug 5, 1898, 4. *Emporia Democrat,* Aug 5, 1898, 5. *Topeka State Journal* (Topeka, Kansas), Aug 11, 1898, 5. *Argentine Siftings,* Jan 16, 1886, 1.

⁷ Harry's absence from public documents during the period 1900-03 is intriguing because of later rumors, promulgated by his enemies, that he spent some time in a Cheyenne prison. The author contacted Carl Hallberg of the Wyoming State Archives. Mr. Hallberg was unable to find any record of a Harry Raymond in the Laramie County District Court index, Laramie County District Court criminal appearance docket, Penitentiary inmate register, Laramie County sheriff's jail register, Cheyenne city marshal jail register, or the Wyoming newspapers online.

⁸ *Idaho Statesman,* Apr 20, 1893, 8; Apr 23, 1893, 5. *Salt Lake City Herald,* Apr 23, 1893, 2; Apr 25, 1893, 3.

⁹ *Idaho Statesman,* Apr 20, 1893, 8; Apr 23, 1893, 5. *Salt Lake City Herald,* Apr 23, 1893, 2; Apr 25, 1893, 3.

¹⁰ *LAT,* Jan 14, 1906; Oct 28, 1906.

¹¹ *Willard,* 339-340.

¹² *Clare Sentinel,* Mar 31, 1904; Oct 28, 1904; Jun 7, 1907; Dec 3, 1909; Apr 1, 1910.

¹³ *LAT,* Jan 29, 1910, ii, 16.

¹⁴ *LAT,* Feb 13, 1910, 9.

¹⁵ *LAT,* Sep 22, 1902, 3.

¹⁶ *LAT,* Jan 28, 1910, ii, 14.

¹⁷ *LAT,* Feb 02, 1910, ii, 6.

¹⁸ *LAT,* Feb 26, 1910, 5.

LA THROUGH THE PEEPHOLE

² *New York Sun,* July 11, 1913, 6.

³ *LAT,* Mar 19, 1910, 15, 22.

⁴ Guinn, James Miller, *A History of California and an Extended History of Los Angeles and Environs Also Containing Biographies of Well-known Citizens of the Past and Present · Volume 1.* United States: Historic Record Company, 1915, 268.

⁵ Sanbury Insurance Map, Los Angeles, 1888. *LAT,* Mar 23, 1896, 9; Nov 11, 1935, ii, 1.

⁶ *US Federal Census/*Los Angeles, Jun 1880. *LAH,* Jan 26, 1890; Nov 25, 1895; Jan 10, 1900.

⁷ *LAT,* Nov. 15, 1902.

[8] Cohn and Chisholm, *Take the Witness*, 9-10 quoted in AnnMarie Kooistra, *Angels for Sale: The History of Prostitution in Los Angeles 1880-1940,* University of Southern California, PhD Dissertation, 2003 27.

[9] *LAT,* Nov 15, 1902. *Kooistra,* 45.

[10] *LAH,* Apr 27, 1889. *LAT,* Feb 25, 1896, 8.

[11] *LAT,* May 11, 1895.

[12] *LAT,* Feb 17, 1903.

[13] *LAT,* Nov 29, 1903; Dec 1, 1903; Dec 12-16, 1903; Jan 13, 16, 1904; Feb 1, 1904; May 6, 1904; Nov 30, 1904; Mar 18, 1907; Mar 26, 1907. *LAH,* Dec 18, 1903.

[14] *LAH,* Jan 30, 1895.

[15] *LAT,* Aug 06, 1904, 13.

[16] California Voter Registration 1886/San Francisco County Districts 33-36. *LAT,* Jul 20, 1892; Jul 22, 1892.

[17] *LAT,* Feb 6, 1889, 2. *LAH,* Sep 23, 1894; Oct 24, 1894.

[18] *LAT,* Dec 28, 1894; Dec 29, 1894; Mar 19, 1895; Apr 23, 1895; Aug 31, 1895. *LAH,* Mar 19, 1895; Apr 23, 1895; Jun 18, 1895; Dec 5, 1896.

[19] *LAT,* Oct 1, 1897; Aug 8, 1898. *LAH,* Oct 4, 1898; Aug 4, 1898.

[20] *LAT,* Aug 9, 1898; Aug 11, 1898.

[21] *LAT,* Aug 9, 1898; Aug 11, 1898.

[22] United States Federal Census, 1870, Fredonia, Ozaukee County, Wisconsin. *Los Angeles City Directory,* 1895-1912. *LAT,* Oct 2, 1901; Jan, 19, 1902; Nov 12, 1902; Sept 13, 1903; *Los Angeles City Directory,* 1895, 1897, 1899, 1900, 1901.

[23] *LAR,* Mar 18, 1904, 1.

[24] *LAT,* Feb 6, 1904; Feb 10, 1904; Feb 17, 1904; Mar 27, 1904; May 3, 1904.

[25] *LAT,* May 16, 1906, 13.

[26] *LAT,* May 06, 1906, 13.

[27] *LAT,* Oct 26, 1905.

[28] *LAT,* Mar 18, 1907.

[29] *LAH,* Dec 31, 1906; Jan 17, 1909.

[30] *Los Angeles City Directory, 1907,* 124. *LAH,* Jan 27, 1909; Mar 26, 1909; Jun 29, 1907; Jul 1, 1907; Jul 2, 1907; Mar 6, 1907. *LAT,* Jul 3, 1903; Jan 21, 1906.

[31] *LAH,* Jan 12, 1905. *American Biography and Genealogy, California Edition, Volume 2,* pp 799-810, The Lewis Publishing Company, Chicago/New York, 1912. *LAT,* Jul 29, 1907; Jul 30, 1907.

[32] *LAH,* Apr 14, 1909.

[33] Ballerino's will left his nothing to his wife, $5 to each of his children, $13,000 to various friends and $5,000 to a convent. The rest of his estate went to the nurse who tried to snatch the will from him a few years before. The family, less wife Maria, who also died in 1909, contested the will. So did the woman who earlier sued him for breach of promise. The final settlement, reached in 1921, was a compromise between the nurse and family members

[34] After the Montefalcone burned and sank off Long Beach, Oswald and his brother George bought an interest in a dog-racing track in Compton called the Southern California Kennel Club. It turned out to be a bad idea. Although the track had operated since the

early twenties, Los Angeles County District Attorney Buron Fitts harassed it into bankruptcy in late 1933. When Oswald and his brother refused to cooperate with a court-appointed receiver, they were arrested and convicted for contempt of court. However, the US Circuit of Appeals reversed the decision. It was the culmination to his life of crime without punishment; he died in April 1941.

[35] *LAT,* Dec 10, 1907; Jan 5, 1908, ii, 11.

[36] The anti-liquor crusade in Los Angeles reflected the same phenomenon that had furnished plentiful would-be suckers for Greene and his gang: the migration of Midwesterners to the warm climate and fertile soils of Southern California. In an essay in *Smart Set Magazine,* March 1913, Willard Huntington Wright noted this phenomenon.

...the inhabitants of Los Angeles are culled largely from the smaller cities of the Middle West, leading citizens from Wichita, honorary pallbearers from Emmetsburg, Good Templars from Sedalia, honest spinsters from Grundy Center- all commonplace people, many of them with small competencies made from the sale of farm lands or from the lifelong savings of small mercantile businesses. These good folks brought with them a complete stock of rural beliefs, pieties, superstitions and habits-the Middle West bed hours, the Middle West love of corned beef, church bells, Munsey's Magazine, union suits and missionary societies. They brought also a complacent and intransigent aversion to late dinners, malt liquor, grand opera and hussies. They are a sober and phlegmatic people with a passion for marching in parades and wearing badges. They are victims of the sonorous platitude; at concerts, they applaud the high notes and they vote for their pastor's choice of candidate. [Willard Huntington Wright, "Los Angeles: The Chemically Pure", *The Smart Set Magazine,* Mar 1913; John Adams Thayer Corporation, New York, London, and Paris.]

[37] *LAH,* Oct 4, 1912.

[38] *LAH,* Oct 5, 1912; Oct 18, 1912.

[39] *SBCS,* Dec 12, 1913, 1; Dec 13, 1913, 1; Dec 16, 1913, 4; Dec 18, 1913, 1. *Long Beach Press,* Dec 13, 1913, 10.

[40] California State Archives, Sacramento, California, Secretary of State California State Archives Folsom Prison Registers. *Daily Eastern Oregon,* Mar 10, 1915, 3. *Democrat and Chronicle* (Rochester, New York), Apr 4, 1912, 16. *Brooklyn Daily Eagle,* Mar 24, 1912, 5. *The New North-West* (Deer Lodge, Montana) Dec 31, 1892, 5; Jan 21, 1893, 3; Jan 13, 1894, 1. *Anaconda Standard,* Jul 16, 1896, 6; May 22, 1898, 14; Mar 30, 1899, 4; Dec 28, 1902, 9; Jun 17, 1903, 4. *Phillipsburg Mail,* Oct 9, 1896, 1; Nov 27, 1896, 4; Dec 31, 1896, 1; Jan 22, 1897, 4; Apr 30, 1897, 2; Dec 13, 1901, 8. *Butte Daily Post,* Feb 6, 1903, 6; Nov 12, 1903, 3; Nov 21, 1904, 8. *Butte Miner,* Aug 22, 1903, 1. *Stockton Evening Mail,* Feb 26, 1908, 8. Letter from Charles E. Sligh to Governor J. R. Toole, undated, Montana State Prisons, Prisoner Records, Box 71/19, Montana Historical Society Research Center, Archives, Helena, Montana.

https://www.spanamwar.com/32ndMichigan.htm

VENICE CHIEF

[1] *LAT,* Oct 26, 1916, 3.

² *LAT,* Nov 29, 1916, 17.

³ *Santa Monica Evening Outlook,* Oct 24, 1916, 6.

⁴ *Hancock Democrat,* Nov 2, 1916, 8.

⁵ Another newspaper report linked Irene Barrett to a suspicious death in Colorado over a dozen years before. An Iowa man in the company of a woman Myrtle Wright had died at the resort town of Pegaso Springs in 1901. An autopsy revealed arsenic in his stomach. Myrtle Wright and her male companion were arrested, but the evidence was not strong enough for trial. A few years later, she was involved in another mysterious death in Pueblo. A Colorado physician named A. R. Clock, who had attended the dying man, identified Myrtle Wright as Irene Barrett. However, after reviewing his claims, both the DA and the defense attorneys rejected Clock's assertions, citing evidence that Irene Wright/Barrett was living with her then husband, Charles Wright, in New York at the time of the alleged murder.

⁶ *LAT,* Nov 29, 1916, 17.

⁷ *LAH,* Mar 6, 1917; Dec 20, 1916; Nov 22, 1917; Feb 2, 1917; Jul 12, 1917. The internecine battles of the Venice Trustees were covered in the *LAH, LAEE,* and *LAT* in the decade of 1910-19.

⁸ *LAH,* Aug 6, 1918. *LAT,* Aug 20, 1918, Part ii, 8; Aug 31, Part ii, 2.

⁹ *LAH,* Nov 22, 1917; Jan 5, 1918; Jul 26, 1918; May 3, 1918; May 4, 1918; Jul 31, 1918; Aug 14, 1918; Sep 10, 1918. United States Petition for Naturalization, Box 10, # 944. *LAT,* Aug 23, 1918, ii, 5.

¹⁰ *LAH,* Aug 12, 1918. *LAT,* Aug 21, 1918.

¹¹ *LAH,* Sep 12, 1918; Sep 13, 1918, 1. *LAT,* Sep 13, 1918, ii, 1; Sep 14, 1918.

¹² *LAH,* Aug 23, 1918; Oct 15, 1918; Oct 14, 1918; Oct 22, 1918; Apr 28, 1919.

¹³ *SBCS* Aug 31, 1918. *OAKT,* Oct 26, 1918.

¹⁴ *LAH,* Apr 28-9, 1919.

AUTO CLUB DETECTIVE

¹ *LAH,* Sep 27, 1919; Jan 29, 1920; Oct 2, 1919; Nov 14, 1919, 1, 6; Jul 10, 1920; Feb 3, 1920, 1, 17; Sep 10, 1919. *LAT,* Jan 14, 1920, ii, 3; Feb 25, 1920. *Woods,* 63-66. *LAEE,* Jan 14, 1920, 3; Feb 2, 1920, 1. *LAR,* Jan 28, 1920, 1; Feb 2, 1920, 2; Feb 3, 1920, 1; Feb 4, 1920, 2; Feb 5, 1920, 1; Feb 7, 1920, 1; May 27, 1920, 1; Jul 10, 1920, 1.

² *LAT,* Feb 16, 1916; Aug 26, 1917; Apr 2, 1919.

³ Raymond's driving skills were likely honed during a cross-country trip he made with Beulah and friends in 1917. *Leavenworth Times,* Aug 2, 1917, 6. *LAT,* Aug 14, 1922, ii, 1; Nov 15, 1922, ii, 11; Jul 8, 1923, ii, 3; Sep 21, 1924.

⁴ *LAT,* Jun 23, 1921.

⁵ *LAT,* Jun 1, 1922.

⁶ *OSE,* Jan 1, 1922, 7

⁷ *LAT,* Dec 24, 1919, 6; Jan 4, 1920, vi, 1; Dec 27, 1921, ii, 1, 7. *Lima News* (Lima, Ohio), Oct 18, 1919, 8. *Detroit Free Press,* Jun 1, 1919, v, 1. *Bakersfield Morning Echo,* Nov 1, 1919, 2. *Mojave Miner and Our Mineral Wealth* (Kingman, Arizona), Dec 28, 1921, 1.

⁸ *LAEE,* Dec 23, 1921, 5.

[9] *LAE,* Mar 7, 1914, 19; Apr 23, 1914, 11; Apr 29, 1914, 12. *LAT,* Oct 5, 1914, ii, 6; Oct 21, 1914, ii, 8; Nov 4, 1914, vii, 4; Jan 3, 1915, ii, 15; Jul 14, 1915, 11; Apr 20, 1917, 6; Jan 9, 1918, ii, 6; May 15, 1918, ii, 2; May 17, 1918, ii, 1; May 4, 1919, vi, 8; Dec 17, 1920, ii, 6; Nov 27, 1921, 176; May 17, 1924, 5; Jul 31, 1927, ii, 6; Feb 26, 1928, 148. *Riverside Daily Press,* Jul 24, 1914, 4; Aug 8, 1914, 6. *SDU,* Mar 8, 1914, 2; Mar 10, 1914, 7; Mar 12, 1914, 11; Sep 22, 1929, 24; Oct 20, 1921, 14. *SBCS,* Oct 31, 1914, 7. *Commercial West,* Vol 41, Jan 7-24, 1922, 29. *Coast Banker,* Apr 1922, 446. *SAR,* Sep 22, 1917, 9. *Long Beach Daily Telegram,* Oct 21, 1914, 9. *Pomona Progress,* Nov 3, 1914, 10.
https://www.ivpressonline.com/storiesfromthepast/stories-from-the-past--sept-niland-drea-only/article_e9c11606-ba02-11e8-95eb-833d545383e6.html.

[10] *Williams News,* Dec 30, 1921, 1.

[11] *LAT,* Aug 14, 1922; Apr 18, 1923, ii, 11; Jun 28, 1923, ii, 10; Apr 22, 1924; Aug 13, 1924; Sep 13, 1924; Sep 21, 1924; Feb 6, 1924; Mar 19, 1924.

[12] *LAT,* Feb 23, 1924; Mar 29, 1924; Apr 13, 1924; May 3, 1924; May 11, 1924; May 24, 1924; May 25, 2924; Jun 26, 1924. *LAR,* Feb 6, 1924, 7; Mar 19, 1924, 1; Mar 22, 1924, 1; Apr 7, 1924, 2; May 22, 1924, 1; Jun 3, 1924, 1; Jul 14, 1924, 1; Jul 15, 1924, 1.
http://www.cemeteryguide.com/gotw-hopeschool.html.

[13] *LAT,* Sep 22, 1924, 9.

[14] *LAT,* Oct 11, 1924, 2.

[15] *LAT,* Aug 20, 1924; Sep 13, 1924; Oct 3, 1924; Oct 11, 1924; Oct 12, 1924.

THE PLOT AGAINST AMERICA'S SWEETHEART

[1] *LAR,* Jun 1, 1925.

[2] *El Paso Herald,* Aug 22, 1912. *LAT,* Aug 22, 1912. *LAR,* Jul 31, 1925; Aug 12, 1925.

[3] *SBCS,* May 31, 1925.

[4] *LAT,* Jul 23, 1925, 20.

[5] *LAT,* Jul 29, 1925, ii, 2.

[6] *LAT,* Jul 29, 1925, ii, 2.

[7] *LAT,* Aug 8, 1925, ii, 7.

[8] *LAT,* Jun 3, 1925; Aug 3, 1925; Aug 6-8, 1925. *LAE,* May 31, 1925. *SBCS,* Aug 7, 1925; Aug 12, 1925.

[9] *LAT,* Jul 30, 1925.

[10] *LAT,* Aug 14, 1925, 1-2.

NINETEEN TWENTY-SEVEN

[11] Much has been imagined about the failings of the LAPD in the pre-war years. The LAPD's troubled culture would soon become a staple of the contemporary noir novels of Raymond Chandler, who projected most of the department's corruption onto the fictional "Bay City," an obvious stand-in for Santa Monica. Later writers, such as James Ellroy, continued to explore the venality and sloth of LAPD officers and detectives. Non-fictional accounts were scarce, however. Despite occasional expose's by ex-cops, such as Charles Stoker's *Thicker'n Thieves* and magazine articles, more analytical chronicles, such as John

Buntin's *LA Noir*, did not appear until the 1990s and early years of the twenty-first century.

The proto-source for much of the later work was a doctoral dissertation written in 1973 by Gerald Woods entitled, *The Progressives and the Police: Urban Reform and the Professionalization of the Los Angeles Police.* Using contemporary newspaper accounts as his primary sources, most notably the *LA Record,* Woods traced the LAPD's long, sordid history, describing various schemes of enterprising cops in the early twentieth century to supplement their low salaries. Police officers extorted "license fees" from pickpockets and bunko operators who fleeced tourists, accepted kickbacks from lawyers and bail bondsmen for steering arrestees their way, and took bribes from defendants to reduce felony charges to misdemeanors. Some profited from assignments as "policeman-in-residence" at disreputable hotels. There they worked with young girls to lure unsuspecting men into violating the rooming house or resorting ordinance, a puritanical bit of local legislation that made it illegal for two unmarried people of the opposite sex to occupy a rented room furnished with a bed. After arresting the men, they would blackmail them in exchange for dropping the charges. Others cops extorted money from unprotected bootleggers and gamblers or citizens caught in traffic violations. A few entered the bootlegging trade themselves by posing as prohibition agents to hijack the wares of rumrunners. One group of detectives even opened funeral parlors, paying commissions to officers who sent cadavers to their establishments.

[12] *Kansas City Star,* Jul 10, 1920, 2; *LAT,* Apr 29, 1927, ii, 2. *LA Daily News,* Apr 30, 1927, 1. *U.S., World War I Draft Registration Cards, 1917-1918,* Kansas City, MO.

[13] *LAT,* Jul 20, 1926, ii, 5; Aug 22, 1926, ii, 6-7.

[14] *LAT,* Apr 22, 1927, ii, 2; Apr 23, ii, 2.

[15] *LAT,* Apr 27, 1927, ii, 3.

[16] *LAT,* Apr 26, 1927, ii, 3, 4; Apr 27, 1927, ii, 2. *OAKT,* Apr 28, 1927, 20. *Arizona Republic,* Apr 23, 1927, 1.

[17] *LAT,* Apr 23, 1927, ii, 3.

[18] *LAT,* May 25, 1938, 6.

[19] H. A. Anderson, *The Whitehall News Banner,* Aug 2, 1923. Social Security Applications and Claims, 1936-2007. *Los Angeles City Directory,* 1910, 386; 1924, 1262.

[20] *OAKT,* Aug 21, 1925. *LAT,* Aug 21, 1925; Oct 16, 1925; Oct 23, 1925.

[21] *LAT,* Sep 15, 1925.

[22] In late 1925, LA's attention focused on Governor Friend Richardson's claims that local law enforcement authorities protected vice operations in many California cities. Richardson reminded reporters that the 1920 Grand Jury claimed that eight confidence rings had operated in the city for two years, bilking unsuspecting citizens of millions of dollars while paying "15 to 25 percent to certain officials for protection." "Most of the crooks escaped punishment," Richardson declared. "The corrupt officials also escaped punishment." Richardson claimed that organized vice depended on corrupt officials in Los Angeles, including corrupt cops. His information came mainly from former LAPD Chief August Vollmer, a highly respected police reformer who had tried to rid the Police Department of inefficiency and corruption but ended exhausted by its toxic environment by the time his one-year contract expired in August 1924. Vollmer agreed to return to

Los Angeles to testify before the grand jury, which had begun another investigation of Los Angeles vice conditions, particularly bunko operations, in response to Richardson's comments on paroling Hutchings.

Richardson's allegations came as he revoked the parole of a confidence man, Everett Alvin Hutchings, nicknamed "Big Hutch," who had served three years of a one-to-ten-year sentence for fraud. Hutchings, an Iowa native, had come to Los Angeles from Seattle, where he had run a roadhouse in the suburb of Georgetown. There he had been a notorious bully, known for beating debtors. He had almost killed Georgetown's mayor in a dispute over a city ordinance to limit drinking hours. In Los Angeles, he specialized in confidence games. According to the 1920 Los Angeles County Grand Jury, bunko rings had fleeced over $1,000,000 from their victims. The "crimes could not have been committed without the knowledge and protection of certain police detectives detailed to suppress this particular form of crime," the Grand Jury noted.

Charged with defrauding an Illinois farmer of his life savings, Hutchings was arrested in New York City in March 1920. For six months, Los Angeles County DA Thomas Woolwine fought to extradite him. In the meantime, Big Hutch, out on bail, enjoyed the horseracing season. After his was returned to Los Angeles in October, he was convicted of fraud and sent to San Quentin.

After Woolwine's resignation in 1923, his successor, Asa Keyes asked that Hutchings be paroled so that he could appoint him as an investigator for the DA's office. Press and political figures, including members of the Los Angeles Crime Commission, reacted to Keyes' recommendation with indignation. The protest was strong enough to prevent the parole, but less than two years later the California State Prison Board released him quietly. News of Hutchings' parole was met with outrage. By that time, he was back in New York City and working for a press organization.

Richardson had previously declined to intervene in Prison Board parole decisions and claimed that the furor over Big Hutch's parole was a political vendetta directed by his opponents, but anger over Hutchings' release forced him to act. On November 27, 1925, he revoked Hutchings' parole. Hutchings fought off extradition from New York until March 1927, at which time the New York Supreme Court having decided to honor California's extradition request, he fled to Havana and afterward disappeared. .

[23] I am indebted to J. H. Graham for this account of Marco's early career in Los Angeles. www.jhgraham.com. *LAT,* Sep 11, 1916, ii, 5.

[24] *U.S., World War II Draft Registration Cards,* 1942. *United States Federal Census,* 1880 (Arlington, Middlesex County, Massachusetts) 37. Mary O'Hara, *Flicka's Friend,* G. Putnam's Sons, New York, 1982, 48-49, 57.

[25] *General Catalogue of the Officers and Students of The Philips Exeter Academy 1783-1903,* The News-Letter Press, Exeter, New Hampshire, 1903, 140, 161, 191, 233. *The Paen,* Vol 18, Exeter, New Hampshire, 1902. J C Bates, *History of Bench and Bar of California,* Bench and Bar Publishing Company, San Francisco, 1912, 457. *The Standard, A Weekly Insurance Newspaper,* Boston, MA, Jun 10, 1904, 559. *Times-Picayune* (New Orleans), Dec 9, 1902, 13. *Montgomery Advertiser,* Dec 27, 1903, 4.

[26] *O'Hara,* 59.

[27] *Brooklyn Life,* May 19, 1906. *O'Hara,* 66-67.

[28] *Stare Decisis,* University of Southern California School of Law, 1909, 76.

[29] *Stare Decisis,* University of Southern California School of Law, 1911.

[30] Morgan and Parrot were allies of Edwin T. Earl, publisher of the *Los Angeles Express* and the *Los Angeles Tribune.* Morgan was serving as a police commissioner, having been appointed by Mayor Henry Rose. Although some City Council members had reservations about Morgan, he soon was known for his strong stances in favor of enforcement of public morals statutes. In September 1913, he and then Police Chief Charles Sebastian proposed restrictions on cabaret singers to prevent the "unwholesome mingling of entertainers with patrons." During his campaign for DA, Morgan charged that plans were afoot to open up the city to prostitution and gambling once again. Rose responded angrily, blaming Parrot for airing the false charges. He also blasted both Morgan and Parrot as amateur vice investigators. It is hard to view this vice probe as legitimate in light of Parrot's future activities. While he and Morgan broke openly with Rose and his followers, the probe did not last past Morgan's unsuccessful DA campaign.

[31] *LAT,* Jun 20, 1911; Aug 21, 1913; Sep 3, 5, 9, 12, 1913; Oct 25, 1913; Dec 13, 1913; Feb 20, 1914; Sep 9-10, 1914; Dec 24, 1914; Feb 15, 1915; Apr 8, 24, 1915; Jun 27, 1915; Jul 1-2, 4, 25, 1915; Sep 9-10, 12, 1915; Nov 2, 28, 1915. *Los Angeles City Directory, 1914,* 1772. *O'Hara,* 107-108, 122.

[32] *SAR,* Jul 30, 1915. *LAT,* Dec 6, 1915.

[33] In the spring of 1918, Parrot remarried. His new wife was Pasadena socialite, Virginia Pierce. Virginia was the granddaughter of Major Edward R. Prickett, a wealthy Illinois banker. It was her second marriage as well. In 1912, she had eloped with her stepbrother, Roy Ellsworth Pierce, son of St. Louis oilman Henry Clay Pierce. Her stepfather objected to the marriage, but he did not try to have it annulled, as he did when Roy had married a showgirl, Bessie Faulkner Chapman a few years before, arguing that his son was a drunkard and drug addict and thus incompetent to marry. However, Virginia soon found the old man was right about Roy. After four years, she divorced him for drunkenness and desertion.

[34] *LAT,* Aug 11, 1921; Dec 7, 1921; Jan 10, 18, 1922; May 6, 1922; Jul 16, 1924.

[35] *LAT,* Jul 29, 1923; Jan 16, 1926; April 16, 1927; May 5, 1927.

[36] *LAT,* Apr 22, 23, 1925.

[37] *LAT,* Apr 23, 1925.

[38] *LAT,* Apr 23, 1925.

[39] Charles H. Garrigues, *You're Paying for It: A Guide to Graft,* Funk & Wagnalls Company, New York and London, 1936, 130-31.

[40] *LAT,* Jul 29, 1927; Aug 3, 1927.

[41] *LAT,* Jul 16, 1927, ii, 1.

[42] *LAT,* Jul 15, 1927, ii, 2.

[43] *LAT,* Feb 6-16, 1927. *LAR,* Feb 6, 1927.

[44] *LAT,* Aug 8, 13, 15 20, 31, 1927. *Hollywood Citizen,* Aug 8, 1927, 12; Aug 15, 1927, 10; Aug 20, 1927, 1, Aug 8, 1927, 12; Aug 15, 1927, 10; Aug 20, 1927, 14; Aug 27, 1927, 16; Aug 23, 1927, 12; Aug 24, 1927, 2; Aug 25, 1927, 2; Aug 26, 1927, 2; Sep 2, 1927, 12; Sep 9, 1927, 12; Dec 20, 1927, 16. *LAR,* Aug 6, 1927, 1.

[45] *LAT,* Sep 9, 1927; Sep 20, 1927.

46 *LAT*, Sep 11, 1927, ii, 13.

47 *LAT*, Sep 23, 1927; Sep 24, 1927; Oct 18, 1927.

48 *LAT*, Aug 20, 1927; Oct 8, 1927; Oct 23, 1927; Aug 9, 1928; Aug 11, 1928.

AFTER THE FOX

49 Arthur L. Marek, INS New Service, *Journal Gazette* (Matton, Illinois), Feb 2, 1928.

50 Hickman and newspapers repeatedly misspelled Marion Parker's first name as "Marian." The author has chosen to correct the spelling in many cases for clarity but maintain the incorrect spelling in editorials and Hickman's writings.

51 *Modesto News-Express*, Dec 16, 1927. Hickman Trial Transcript, testimony of Perry Parker.

52 *CT*, Dec 18, 1927.

53 *Statesman Journal* (Salem, Oregon), Sep 5, 1928.

54 *LAT*, Dec 23, 1927. Hickman Trial Transcript Vol 2, 650-56.

55 *Woodland Daily Democrat*, Dec 23, 1927, 4.

56 *Woodland Daily Democrat*, Dec 23, 1927, 4.

57 *Woodland Daily Democrat*, Dec 23, 1927, 4.

58 In the evening of Tuesday, December 20, King picked Hickman out of a "rogues' gallery" of photographs. [Woodland Daily Democrat, Dec 23, 1927, 4.]

59 *Spokesman-Review* (Spokane, Washington), Dec 23, 1927, 1.

60 *OAKT*, Feb 28, 1928, 2.

61 *Sacramento Bee,* Dec 28, 1927, 2; Dec 23, 1927, 12.

62 *Philadelphia Inquirer*, Dec 29, 1927. *LAT*, Dec 24, 1927.

63 *LAT*, Dec 24, 1927. *Des Moines Register*, Dec 29, 1927. *OSE*, Dec 24, 1927, 6.

64 *Indianapolis Star*, Dec 24, 1927. *Minneapolis Star*, Dec 24, 1927.

65 *Miami News* (Miami, Florida), Dec 25, 1927. *LAT*, Dec 24, 1927.

66 *Sedalia Democrat* (Sedalia, Missouri), Dec 25, 1927. *Lincoln Star* (Lincoln, Nebraska), Dec 25, 1927. *Hickman Trial Transcript*, Testimony of H. H. Cline.

67 *Lincoln Star* (Lincoln, Nebraska), Dec 25, 1927.

68 *LAT*, Dec 26, 1927. Scranton Republican (Scranton, Pennsylvania), Dec 26, 1927. Arizona Republic, Dec 26, 1927.

69 *LAT*, Dec 26, 1927. United Press, Lincoln Star (Lincoln, Nebraska), Dec 26, 1927. Bennet, Carle R, United Press, SBCS, Dec 26, 1927. https://mirc.sc.edu/islandora/object/usc:25129.

70 *El Paso Herald*, Dec 27, 1927.

71 Naughton, Walter, Universal Service, *Palm Beach Post*, Dec 28, 1927.

72 *Pittsburgh Post-Gazette*, Dec 28, 1927.

73 *Richmond Item* (Richmond, Indiana), Dec 28, 1927. Cline testimony at Hickman trial, Transcript 2 626-27.

74 Cited by Michael Newton, *Stolen Away*, 74.

75 *OSE*, Dec 23, 1927.

76 http://population.us/ca/dunsmuir/. *LAT*, Dec 27, 1927. Detroit Free Press, Dec 27, 1927.

77 *El Paso Herald*, Dec 27, 1927. Detroit Free Press, Dec 27, 1927.

[78] Nancy Barr Mavity, *OAKT*, Dec 27, 1927.

[79] *OAKT*, Dec 27, 1927. *SAR*, Dec 27, 1927. Evening News (Harrisburg, Pennsylvania), Dec 27, 1927.

[80] Arthur L. Marek, International News Service, *Journal Gazette* (Mattoon, Illinois), Feb 2, 1928.

[81] *Sedalia Democrat* (Sedalia, Missouri), Dec 30, 1927. Richmond Item (Richmond, Indiana), Dec 29, 1927.

[82] *The Palm Beach Post*, (West Palm Beach, Florida), Dec 28, 1927.

[83] *Minneapolis Morning Tribune*, Dec 21, 1927.

[84] Hunt would get a pardon, but he would have to wait twenty-four years for it. He seems to have kept a positive attitude about his future, despite his sentence to life imprisonment. His mother moved her family to San Rafael to be near her imprisoned son. Welby made the best of prison life, becoming a skilled chess player, and kept out of trouble. On March 18, 1939, he was paroled into his mother's custody and found a job at Ross Hospital as an x-ray technician. The following year, he married Luella Page in San Rafael. The marriage did not last long; in 1944, Page married George Kenney, a Sausalito city councilman. Hunt remained single until 1950, when he married Betty Jean Hickman of San Rafael. His wife was unrelated to his former partner in crime, but her name must have caused some consternation among those who knew of Hunt's past. That past did not come up often in newspapers. Hunt became a success, the chief medical technician at Marin Medical Laboratories, a member of the Golden Gate Yacht Club, and an investor with his mother in real estate properties. Local newspapers featured his home, which he built for his young socialite wife in the Kent Woodlands. His name even appeared on the list of endorsers for a candidate for Sheriff.

Hunt's wife bore a daughter in 1957, but their marriage lasted only to 1964. In 1968, he again married, this time to Emily Seebach, the girlfriend of his first wife. The couple lived in Arroyo Grande, California. She passed away in 1974, after which he tried marriage again with the former Luella Page. This marriage ended even quicker than their first one, as they filed for divorce two months later. Hunt married a final time in 1976 to Donna Buell. In 1995, he died at his home in the upscale desert community of Rancho Mirage.

As for the third of the three Kansas City Library youths who embarked on careers in crime in the fall of 1926, Frank Bernoudy would face no punishment, as Kansas City police decided they did not have enough to prosecute him despite his confession. In 1935, he died from a self-inflicted gunshot wound to his chest.

THE JACOBSON BUST REDUX

[1] *LAT*, Dec 14, 1927. SCEE, Dec 14, 1927. IDN, Dec 27, 1927, 12; May 25, 1938, 20; Sep 23, 1928, 8.

[2] *LAH*, Dec 31, 1894.

[3] *LAT*, Jan 26, 1895.

[4] *LAT*, Jan 1, 1886.

[5] Many other areas and cities across the nation embraced the term to describe their business prosperity in years to come. While later writers suggested the term had racial

undertones, no such allusion was made in these days when the "white spot" metaphor was popular.

[6] *LAEE,* Jul 19, 1928, 1, 4; Jul 26, 1928, 1.

[7] *LAT,* Jul 10, 1928.

[8] *LAT,* Nov 16, 1928, ii, 3; Dec 12-13, 1928. *The Evening Times* (Klamath, Oregon), Nov 16, 1928, 7.

[9] *LAT,* Nov 15, 1928, 27. *Arizona Republic,* Nov 15, 1928, 1.

[10] *LAT,* Jan 17, 1929.

[11] *Seattle Republican,* Dec 9, 1910.

[12] Burton J. Hendrick, "The Recall in Seattle", *McClure's Magazine,* vol 37, 1911 647-63.

[13] *The Smart Set Magazine,* March 1913.

[14] *LAH,* Jul 29, 1919; Oct 25, 1919; July 10, 1920. *LAT,* Jun 19, 1918; Jul 25, 1919. *National Advocate,* New York, January 1918 3.

[15] Robert (Bob) Shuler, *The Strange Death of Charlie Crawford,* J. R. Spencer, Publisher, Los Angeles 1931.

[16] *LAT,* Mar 23, 1929, 18.

[17] *LAT,* Mar 27, 1929, 23.

[18] *LAT,* Mar 26, 1929, 19; Apr 6, 1929, 21; Apr 9, 1929, 23; Apr 10, 1929, 23-4. *SAR,* Mar 27, 1929, 1.

[19] Anderson testified that,

About September 1, 1928, she came to my office and introduced herself. She said she had been double-crossed and wanted to tell me what happened in the Jacobson case, since I had represented the Councilman at his Municipal Court trail. She said she had met Jacobson at the City Hall on an assessment matter and he later came to her house, where he made advances to her and tried to make love to her. She said she told Cox, her brother-in-law, about her experience with Jacobson and later met Marco and Crawford at Cox's home where she agreed to try and get Jacobson in a position where he would be arrested but they did not agree on plans for the compromise. At another meeting at Cox's home she said she met Marco again and agreed to try to get Jacobson to her house on the understanding that she was to get $1000 and $100 a month as long as she lived. She said Marco drove her to her home, brought the whisky and gave instructions. She said there was a criminal attorney in on the affair, but she would not give me his name. She was very bitter toward Jacobson and said he was as much to blame in the affair as she was.

[20] *LAT,* Apr 6, 1929, 21.

[21] While the second trial against the Jacobson defendants was mainly a repeat of the first, there was one key difference. In the first trial, Judge Woods disallowed the grand jury testimony of Callie Grimes which had restarted the Jacobson case in fall of 1928; this time, Superior Court Judge Emmett H. Wilson ruled that her testimony was admissible. Had Woods allowed the testimony in the first trial, the case against Marco and Crawford may well have reached to the jury. Since he had dismissed the charges, neither of the vice leaders could be tried a second time. The legal activity was not over, however; while

testifying, Grimes's sister, Ida Russell, declared that Jacobson offered her money to persuade Grimes to tell the 1928 Grand Jury that she helped frame Jacobson. Before the 1929 Grand Jury, however, Russell took the Fifth, as did Grimes. Her attorney, Leo Daze, refused to testify, asserting attorney/client privilege. Only Jacobson spoke to the grand jury, and he denied everything. The grand jury took no action. Although Fitts considered charging Russell with perjury and referring Daze to the Bar Association for discipline, in the end, he did nothing.

[22] *LAT,* May 27, 1938, 6; Sep 4, 1929, ii, 2.

[23] *LAT,* Oct 29, 1929, ii, 1, 7. *OAKT,* Sep 4, 1929, 3.

RELIGION AND VICE

[24] *LAT,* Feb 26, 1929, ii, 1. *LAT,* Jun 3, 1929, ii, 1.

[25] *St. Louis Post-Dispatch,* Jun 27, 1929, 24.

[26] Robert Shuler, *"Fighting Bob" Shuler of Los Angeles,* Dog Ear Publishing, Indianapolis, Indiana, 2011, 84.

[27] *LAT,* Oct 10, 1922, ii, 1.

[28] *LAT,* Apr 3, 1922, ii, 6.

[29] *LAT,* Dec 10, 1923, 19-20; Dec 29, 1923, 25. *LAH,* Jun 25, 1910, 3

[30] Robert "Bob" Shuler, *Bob Shuler's Magazine,* J. R. Spencer, Los Angeles, September 1927, 148.

[31] *Wilson,* 237-8.

[32] Kansas State Historical Society, Topeka, Kansas, *1885 Kansas Territory Census,* Roll: KS1885_35, Line: *13. Abilene Weekly Reflector,* Oct 15, 1885, 5; Jul 8, 1886, 5. *Chapman Star,* Oct 14, 1885, 4. *Abilene Weekly Chronicle,* Jun 26, 1885, 5; Oct 16, 1885, 3; Mar 05, 1886, 3. *Hope Dispatch* (Hope, Kansas), Apr 22, 1886, 2; Aug 1, 1907, 4. *Kansas State Census, 1885,* Prairie Dog, Decatur County. *Arkansas City Daily Traveler,* Jan 14, 1887, 5; Jan 15, 1887, 5; Jan 19, 1887, 3. *Arkansas Valley Traveler,* Feb 11, 1887, 3. *Weekly Republican-Traveler* (Arkansas City, Kansas), Apr 2, 1887, 5. *Abilene Daily Chronicle,* Jan 3, 1902, 4. *The Daily Tribune* (Winfield, Kansas), Mar 28, 1887, 2; Mar 30, 1887, 4. *Solomon Sentinel* (Solomon, Kansas), Jun 24, 1885, 1.

[33] *Winfield Daily Courier* (Winfield, Kansas), Jul 5, 1887, 4. *Abilene Weekly Reflector,* Aug 11, 1887, 1; Aug 25, 1887, 1. *SDU,* Jul 15, 1887, 3; Sep 1, 1887, 2; Sep 6, 1887, 2. *San Diego Daily Bee,* Jan 13, 1888, 10. *The Evening Reflector* (Abilene, Kansas), Aug 1, 1887, 1.

[34] *LAR,* Nov 14, 15, 18, 21, 30, 1914. *LAH,* Oct 21, 31, 1914; Nov 30, 1914; Dec 1, 1914, 1; Dec 19, 1914, 1-2; Dec 21, 1914, 1; Jan 15, 1915 2.

[35] A Los Angeles native, Page was nicknamed Farmer because of his "shambling gait," his somewhat disheveled appearance in his younger days when he and his brothers had sold papers at Second and Spring Streets, and his fondness for a wide-brim hat favored by farmers.

As youngsters, Page and his brothers gambled with other newsies, serving as the bank in card and dice games. While Milton had managed to avoid jail, his two brothers ran afoul of the law as juveniles. Stanley was pinched for shooting craps in September 1907 and got away with a $5 fine, a sum that did not deter the well-heeled young newsie, whose financial acumen had already been noted in the press. In December 1908, in a scene reminiscent of future Dead End Kids films, Ross and a group of boys fled over a high board fence into neighboring backyards after police blocked both exits of an alley where they were rolling dice. A woman tried to block their escape, but the boys knocked her down. Ross made it to his home at 715 Wall Street, but he was arrested after the angry woman gave his name to police.

As a young man, he played baseball, but he was not good enough to make it professionally. His youngest brother, Stanley became a leading jockey of the pre-WW1 era, riding throughout the West Coast and finishing third aboard Dr. Barkley in the 1909 Kentucky Derby and third again on Fighting Bob in the 1910 Derby. Milton tagged along until Stanley's jockey career ended in 1915. The brothers then turned to gambling. In 1916, they were arrested for gambling-related offenses for the first time. One or more of the brothers landed in jail a half-dozen times between 1917 and 1921.

After Cryer's election in 1921, Kent Parrot and Charley Crawford convinced Page to accept their protection for his gambling parlors in exchange for a split in the profits. Despite the protection, Page was arrested repeatedly for bookmaking and other gambling activities, but he was rarely convicted of any of his crimes. He also had a bad knack for getting himself in trouble and drawing unwanted publicity. In October 1924, he was running a gambling parlor at 120 West Third Street when he shot a man who pulled a pistol after losing $1100 at a card game. Claiming self-defense, Page was free to kill rival gambler Al Josephs at the Sorrento Club at 1348 West Sixth Street few months later. Page again claimed self-defense, asserting that Josephs threatened him, knocked him down and tried to draw a gun on him.

Although the court dismissed murder charges against him, Page was too toxic for organized gambling within city limits after the incident, so he switched to illegal liquor. Posing as federal agents, Page's men raided rum-running ships belonging to Tony Cornero, a leading bootlegger of Southern California, and hijacked several of his trucks after they had been loaded with booze. Cornero responded by luring the hijackers to an ambush at Long Beach and opening fire with machine guns. The police afterward ran both gangsters out of town, but both returned when the heat was off to resume their battle.

The gang war made Page a noisy liability for the Parrot/Crawford syndicate. With each death, he slipped more from his former standing.

[36] Shuler's criticism of Briegleb touched off a heated battle between the two fun-hating ministers. Both had made excellent use of the radio waves over the last decade to get out their messages, particularly Shuler, who preached on the *Los Angeles Times* Radio station, KHJ since 1922. Shuler's caustic attacks on governmental officials brought retribution, however, and, in 1930, he was fighting to keep the license for his own radio station, KGEF. Briegleb testified against him in a hearing held by the Radio Station Examiner, claiming that his old friend uttered "unjust, false, and misleading" comments against him over the air. While Shuler lost his license, Briegleb continued to use the radio to promote his causes, with funds furnished by Crawford.

On May 17, 1931, Briegleb presided over the dedication of the new home of St. Paul's Presbyterian Church at the corner of Jefferson Boulevard and Third Avenue. The educational building of the Parish House was dedicated to Amelia Crawford, Charles

Crawford's mother, in recognition of the funds he contributed towards the building. This crowning achievement of his religious life was marred somewhat by rumors circulating that he was seeking to have one of his associates named as grand jury foreman. The "Gray Wolf" had not completely left the game.

[37] *LAT,* May 21, 1931, 1. *SCEE,* May 21, 1931, 1. *St. Cloud,* Part 4 (June 22, 1938), 25. *LAR,* May 21, 1931, 2.

[38] *LAT,* Oct 27, 1929, ii, 8. *LAEE,* Sep 2, 1929, 3; Nov 24, 1928, 3. *San Pedro News-Pilot,* Nov 28, 1928, 11.

[39] *SBCS,* Jun 3, 1931, 1. *LAT,* Jun 4, 1931, 20.

[40] *SBCS,* Aug 20, 1931, 1.

[41] *LAEE,* Aug 1, 1931, 2. Richard Rayner, *A Bright and Guilty Place,* Doubleday, 2009, 17-18. *LAR,* Apr 12, 1922, 5.

[42] Perhaps the testimony of Walter Lee, a janitor who worked at an automobile agency across the street from 6665 Sunset, gave the jurors of the second trial reason to believe Crawford and Spencer were armed. Lee claimed he spotted Lucille Fisher sitting in a car outside the murder scene with a gun partially hidden in a towel next to her on the car seat. Two men entered the car after a few minutes, Lee explained. As they did, Fisher shifted the towel and gun onto her lap before the three of them drove away.

Only one juror, a 73-year-old-man named William E. Weller voted to convict, hanging the first jury. A few days after his jury was dismissed his wife found a makeshift bomb on the walk leading to their front porch.

[43] Robert Shuler, *The Strange Death of Charlie Crawford,* 15. *LAT,* May 24, 1931, 2.

RAYMOND UNBOUND

[1] *LAT,* Oct 18, 1930, 26 (office at 139 No Broadway, Suite 514); Nov 19, 1931, 26 (office at 127 S Broadway, suite 203-5); May 3, 1931 48 (office 205 So Broadway); Jan 16, 1933, 28 (offices at Broadway and 1st); Feb 9, 1933, 25 (offices 238 W 1st).

[2] *Nebraska State Journal,* Mar 21, 1928, 1. *Morning News* (Wilmington, Delaware), Mar 21, 1928, 9. *Allentown Morning Call,* Mar 21, 1928, 1. *The Amarillo Globe-Times,* Apr 3, 1928, 6. *Sing Sing Prison Admission Registers,* prisoner #81744.

[3] Born Nina Pearl Jones in 1882, the daughter of a prosperous Ames, Iowa merchant, Nina had already tried marriage four times, beginning in September 1899 with husband Fred Steele Gilbert. Her first marriage does not seem to have lasted more than a few months. The 1900 US Census shows Fred living with his parents in Waterloo while Nina was back with her parents in Ames. Fred, a strapping young railroad worker, met death in 1901 after slipping between railroad cars and being dragged five hundred feet along the tracks. Assuming the couple did not have time to finalize the divorce, Nina was a widow, a distinction she maintained publicly for most of her life. Nina, neé Jones now Gilbert, then married Arthur G. Oudkirk in Ames on Oct 4, 1904. This marriage did not last either. By June 1906, she was ready to wed Thomas Mark Sayman, the disinherited son of a wealthy soap manufacturer. It is not clear how long the couple stuck together, but both remarried in 1910, Sayman eloping with the daughter of a prominent Iowa auctioneer.

Nina had studied the piano for years and become an accomplished musician and music teacher, so it is probable she met the chocolate magnate heir at some musical event in the city. It is also possible she met him through her father, a wealthy confectioner. When she met Ghirardelli in 1910, Nina was a small pretty blonde who looked "like a girl scarcely out of her teens." Young Ghirardelli, who was known for his love of musical entertainment, was just coming off a broken relationship with a vaudeville actress, Marion Murray. His mother had ended the romance by cutting his allowance to a mere $125/month. Although this was a good sum in 1909, the actress abandoned him, remarking it was not even enough to "pay her laundry bills."

Facing opposition from his mother to his proposal to Nina, Ghirardelli and Nina eloped. They were married at the Sea Beach Hotel in Santa Cruz in July 1910. This marriage lasted longer than the rest of Nina's but less than five years. The couple separated in April 1915 and divorced in September of the same year. Nina complained that her husband loved nightlife, drinking to excess, and cavorting with female nightclub entertainers. Worse yet, he made fun of her talents as a classical pianist. Three nights a week in roadhouses around the Bay Area exhausted her to the point of nervous prostration. She received her divorce and an alimony of $100 per month.

[4] http://history.house.gov/HistoricalHighlight/Detail/35509.

[5] *SDET,* May 21, 1923, 5.

[6] https://allaroundnevada.com/impossible-railroad/. https://www.desertusa.com/mccain/oct_sdazrr.html. *SDU,* Apr 9, 1908, 7; Feb 8, 1907, 7; Nov 20, 1919, 3. *SDET,* Dec 21, 1906, 3; Dec 17, 1906, 1.

[7] Douglas L. Lowell, "The California Southern Railroad and the Growth of San Diego", *Journal of San Diego History,* San Diego Historical Society Quarterly, Fall, 1985, Volume 31, Number 4. *SDET,* Jul 9, 1920, 4.

[8] *SDET,* Jun 5, 1933, 1; Jun 6, 1933, 1, 6.

[9] *SDS,* Jun 7, 1933, 20.

[10] *SDU,* Jun 11, 1933, 1, 10. *CT,* Mar 4, 1915, 1. *OAKT Magazine, OAKT,* Nov 19, 1922, 2.

[11] *SDU,* Jun 11, 1933, 1, 10

[12] Elizabeth C. McPhail, "Shady Ladies in the 'Stingaree District' When The Red Lights Went out in San", *Journal of San Diego History,* San Diego Historical Society Quarterly, San Diego Historical Society, Volume 2, Number 2, Winter, 1973; SDU, Jan 23, 1921, 7.

[13]

While our chief of police, unquestionably a clever detective, was dashing with his detective chief up to Los Angeles to arrest a man who is accused of committing a hold-up in New York, or own latest murder case remains unsolved and virtually ignored by the police.

Unfortunately the man arrested in Los Angeles by our chief can not be tried here. He must be tried in Los Angeles where the stolen bonds were transported or in New York where the crime occurred. But it is nice to be neighborly and if the Los Angeles police are not qualified to arrest and bring to trail their criminals, or if New York isn't, it is a splendid gesture for us to aid them.

. . . .

Certainly, the sheriff of San Diego county would be as glad to have the assistance in solving local murders as the police of Los Angeles would be to have help in catching New York suspects.

Or then again, maybe our astute chief might devote some of his unquestioned talent to running down the perpetrators of recent theater robberies here. [*SDS,* Jul 4, 1933, 4.]

[14] *SDU,* Jul 25, 1933, 1. *SDET,* Jul 25, 1933, 1, 6.

[15] *SDU,* Jul 26, 1933, 1, 3; Jul 27, 1933, 1. *SDS,* Jul 26, 1933, 1, 2.

[16] After cautioning the aroused citizenry to maintain "cool heads" and avoid "hysterical mobilizing which might result in the invasion of rights of persons and property," The *Sun* lashed out at local law enforcement and the police chief:

Out deep regret is that we cannot depend upon our law enforcement agencies normally, that we have to have some such crime as the fiendish mutilation of a child to jerk them from their lethargy and push them into the path of duty. As long as the murder of this innocent child remains unpunished it will be to the shame of every man charged with the responsibility of keeping our city safe and clean.

Officials with a civic conscience would either hunt down the slayer of the Aposhian boy and drive criminals from the city or resign forthwith.

Horrible as it is the Aposhian murder is not the sole reason for public resentment. It has been a series of crimes with this, the dramatic denouement. The same police department under other chiefs was able to prevent wholesale crime here. Why isn't it done now? [*SDS,* Jul 26, 1933, 16.]

[17] "A Rationale of the Law of Kidnapping." *Columbia Law Review,* vol. 53, no. 4, 1953, 540–558. www.jstor.org/stable/1119084;

Daniels, Bebe and Ben Lyon, *Life with the Lyons: the Autobiography of Bebe Daniels and Ben Lyon* London: Odhams Press Ltd., 1953, 194-5. LeRoy, Mervyn and Dick Kleimer *Mervyn LeRoy: Take One,* New York: Hawthorne Books, Inc., 1974. *SDS,* Jul 6, 1933, 1, 15.

[1818] *SDS,* Jul 27, 1933, 1. *SDU,* Jul 27, 1933, 2; Jul 28, 1933, 1. *SDET,* Jul 29, 1933, 1.

[19] *SDS,* Jul 27, 1933, 1.

[20] *SDET,* Aug 4, 1933, 1, 6; Aug 5, 1933, 1, 2. *SDU,* Aug 5, 1933, 1.

[21] *SDET,* Aug 7, 1933, 1, 6.

[22] *SDET,* Aug 7, 1933, 1.

[23] *SDU,* Jul 25, 1933, 4.

[24] *SDET,* Aug 8, 1933, 1, 6. *SDU,* Aug 8, 1933, 1, 3.

[25] Although the boy's skin was white and bloodless, Wagner argued this condition was a natural result of the body's immersion in seawater for several days and not necessarily evidence that blood was lost before he entered the water. As for the mutilations observed in the first autopsy, they were too irregular for a knife, even a dull one, and Wagner found no evidence of knife cuts around the mouth. Although the child's gums had been eaten away, their disfigurement, like other damage to the corpse-the missing ears, lips, nose, and genitalia-was consistent with similar damage Wagner had observed on bodies found

in the ocean in his work in Los Angeles County. He noted further that the absence of water in the lungs noted in the initial autopsy was not definitive evidence that the child had not drowned. Lungs of drowning victims rarely contain water, merely a "whitish or partially blood-stained froth [is] found in the trachea in bronchi." The Autopsy Surgeon also observed that children who fall into water often die "by reason of a laryngeal spasm, caused by an intense reaction of this sensitive organ to the irritation of water." Sometimes, they die from shock.

Wagner was not allowed to examine the microscopic slides from the child's intestine containing spermatozoa. However, he noted the "allegedly human cells in reality could have been vegetable or yeast cells so commonly found in this location."

Wagner's report was restrained and sympathetic to the San Diego officials. "I hope my efforts will not be misinterpreted as an unwarranted intrusion, but correctly interpreted as an attempt to arrive at the true facts so far as I could be of assistance," he remarked.

[26] *SDU*, Aug 13, 1933, 4.

[27] *SDU*, Aug 7, 1933, 1, 6.

[28] *SDS*, Jul 6, 1933, 1, 15; Jul 15, 1933, 1; Jul 17, 1, 3, 4, 12; Aug 23, 1933, 1.

[29] *SDS*, Sep 2, 1933, 1.

[30] *SDS*, Jul 21, 1933, 12.

LA ON THE SPOT

[1] *LAT*, Jun 3, 1925, 2; May 2, 1927, ii, 10; May 1, 1927, ii, 1; May 5, 1927, ii, 1.

[2] *LAT*, May 3, 1933, 1; Aug 9, 1933, ii, 1.

[3] *LAT*, Sep 10, 1933, 11.

[4] *Wilmington* [California] *Press,* Sep 12, 1933, 2.

[5] *LAT*, Apr 19, 1934, ii, 1.

[6] *LAT*, 4-22-34. *Hallberg*, 38-39. *Finney*, 40-41.

[7] Arnold B. Larson, *Newspaper Reporting in the Twenties: Reflections* Oral History Program, UCLA 1970, 140. Garrigues, 102

[8] Some secular reformers were even willing to consider legalizing some forms of vice in order to eliminate corruption within law enforcement. They attacked commercialized vice-whether gambling or prostitution-not for its immorality, but because its campaign contributions and payoffs to law enforcement corrupted civic government. Those among the citizenry who regarded gambling dens with either indifference or approval eventually agreed that such illegal enterprises cost taxpayers and ratepayers money.

[9] *Finney*, 37.

[10] *Finney*, 46.

[11] *IDN*, Jan 19, 1934 through May 31, 1934, (Garrigues column).

[12] *IDN*, Jun 30, 1934.

[13] *IDN*, Jan 8, 1935.

[14] *LAT*, Feb 6, 1936, 2.

THE CORNER POCKET

[15] Briggs, Arthur E., *Southern California Renaissance Man*, UCLA Oral History, 1970, interviewed by Elizabeth Dixon; Lawler, Oscar, *Oscar Lawler, Los Angeles*

Attorney, UCLA Oral History, 1962, interviewed by Doyce Nunis, 624-626; Harold H. Story, *Memoirs of Harold H. Story*, UCLA Oral History, UCLA, 1967, interviewed by Elizabeth I. Dixon. *Finney*, 99-100; *McKinney and Allhoff*, iii, 22. *LAT*, Nov 22, 1933, ii, 16.

[16] *IDN*, Mar 26, 1952; *LAT*, Aug 4, 1928, ii, 9.

[17] Kynette testified in the trial of Fred Keaton, who, despondent over his losses in the Julian Petroleum stock swindle, had murdered banker Motley Flint in Superior Court. Kynette claimed he found a copy Shuler's pamphlet, *The Julian Thieves,* in Flint' possession when he and other cops apprehended the killer.

[18] *Miami Daily News,* Feb 17, 1936, 4. *LAT*, Mar 31, 1931, ii, 1; Jan 29, 1938, 5. *McKinney and Allhoff*, Nov 25, 1939, 29. *Reno Gazette,* Jan 28, 1938, 1.

[19] *LAT*, Feb 11, 1939, Part ii, 16. Colin B. Burke, *America's Information Wars*, Roman and Littlefield, Lanham, Maryland, 2018.

[20] *Hollywood Citizen-News*, Dec 19, 1935, 1.

[21] *Allentown Morning Call*, Jul 9, 1922, 23.

[22] One newspaper reporter, calling her a "Vamp Evangelist," described her,

. . . going after her audiences with all the acrobatics of Billy Sunday plus her own tricks of expression. She shouts and sings, stamps her feet, whirls her arms, windmill fashion, stands on one foot, leans against a wall. Sometimes when she feels that the thought she is trying to get across is too big and explosive for words or gestures she will stop abruptly in the middle of a sentence and turn to the cornet player.

"Quick! Quick! A song, she will shout. And before he can get the instrument to his lips will start singing. [*Montgomery Advertiser* (Montgomery, Alabama), Jun 9, 1922, 26.]

[23] Carol M. Hultin, "Whatever happened to 'The Angel of Broadway'?" http://sahpa.blogspot.com/2012/05/whatever-happened-to-angel-of-broadway.html. *Atlanta Constitution*, Oct 17, 1922, 10. New York Tribune, Oct 17, 1922, 3.

[24] *El Paso Times*, Apr 27, 1924, 32. *Muncie Evening Press,* Aug 31, 1928, 1, 7. *Tampa Tribune*, Aug 26, 1928, Part IV, 3; Feb 19, 1930, 7. *OAKT*, Aug 20, 1927, 7. *Brooklyn Daily Eagle,* Feb 19, 1930, 1. *The Ottawa Citizen,* Feb 25, 1930, 12. *Fox Movietone News Story 5-472*, Moving Image Research Collections, University of South Carolina.

[25] Crawford had a checkered record as the state relief administrator. The Department's budget was insufficient for the suffering in the state brought on by the depression, and the state legislature threatened to lower or eliminate it each year. Besides the problems caused by the depression, the Long Beach earthquake of March 1933 and the flooding of the Los Angeles River in 1934 dealt severe blows to the state's relief efforts. Crawford personally helped lead the recovery efforts, but there was widespread dissatisfaction with her management skills. The *Santa Ana Register* wrote that, "her personality is . . . a great handicapped upon the needs of the hour" and that while "She appears strong as an evangelist, but as an administrator and a diplomat, her success has not been marked."

After the 1934 state legislature cut her department's budget, Crawford offered to resign in exchange for the restoration of the funds. Governor Rolph rejected her offer and defended her against her critics, but his death in June 1934 presaged the end of her tenure. After the new governor, Frank Merriam, stated he intended to make personnel changes, newspapers reported that Crawford would be asked to resign. She was ready to go; she had been filling in for Aimee Semple McPherson at the latter's Angelus Temple in Los Angeles while McPherson traveled in Europe. Crawford wanted to play a larger role in the Temple's management.

Merriam did not accept her offer to resign, however. She continued in her position until December, when she became an associate pastor of the Angelus Temple.

[26] *LAT,* Jan 26, 1935, ii, 3; Feb 4, 1935, ii, 5; Feb 14, 1935, 7. *SCEE,* Feb 15, 1935, 1. *Wilmington Daily Press Journal,* Mar 27, 1935, 8.

[27] *Buffalo Times,* Feb 11, 1923, 17. *Tampa Bay Times,* Jan 15, 1925, 10. *LAT,* Mar 26, 1935, 18; Apr 1, 1935, 1; Apr 20, 1935, ii, 3; Apr 27, 1935, ii, 2; Jun 20, 1935, 10. *SCEE,* Apr 4, 1935, 3. *Woodland Democrat* (Woodland, CA), Apr 5, 1935, 14. *SFE,* Apr 6, 1935, 5. *Chicago Daily Tribune,* Jun 15, 1935, 23. *Jefferson City Post Tribune* (Jefferson City, Missouri), Jul 12, 1935, 12. *SBCS,* Jul 12, 1935, 2.

[28] *LAT,* Apr 9, 1935, 9; Aug 31, 1935, ii, 2; Aug 24, 1935, ii, 4. *SMT,* Aug 7, 1935, 4. *Wilmington Daily Journal,* Aug 22, 1935, 1; Aug 28, 1935, 1. *Nevada State Journal,* Aug 19, 1935, 2. *OAKT,* Aug 19, 1935, 9.

[29] *LAT,* Apr 9, 1935, 9; Aug 31, 1935, ii, 2; Aug 24, 1935, ii, 4. *SMT,* Aug 7, 1935, 4. *Wilmington Daily Journal,* Aug 22, 1935, 1; Aug 28, 1935, 1. *Nevada State Journal,* Aug 19, 1935, 2. *OAKT,* Aug 19, 1935, 9.

[30] *IDN,* Sep 5, 1935, 3

[31] *LAT,* Aug 28, 1935, ii, 5; Sep 22, 1952, ii, 9.

[32] *LAT,* Jan 6, 1934, 11; Mar 23, 1934, 17; Mar 24, 1931, 1. Lewis A Lapham, "'Jinx Ship' Bobs Into News Again", SFE, Jan 7, 1934, Part 2, 18. *Wilmington Daily Press Journal,* Feb 15, 1934, 8.

[33] *St. Cloud,* Part 6, 44-45. Confidential Report Orville Thomas Forrestor. *SCEE,* Mar 25, 1935, 2. *LAT,* Aug 26, 1935, 1, 17; Dec 9, 1936, 3. *SMT,* Sep 4, 1935, 4. *Fresno Bee,* Aug 28, 1937, 1; Dec 2, 1936, 4. *Minneapolis Star-Tribune,* Dec 6, 1936, 10.

[34] *St. Cloud,* Part 6, 44-45. Confidential Report Orville Thomas Forrestor. *SCEE,* Mar 25, 1935, 2. *LAT,* Aug 26, 1935, 1, 17; Dec 9, 1936, 3. *SMT,* Sep 4, 1935, 4. *Fresno Bee,* Aug 28, 1937, 1; Dec 2, 1936, 4. *Minneapolis Star-Tribune,* Dec 6, 1936, 10.

THE ACORN

[1] *IDN,* Nov 15, 1929.

[2] Earl Warren, *The Memoirs of Earl Warren,* Doubleday, Garden City, New York, 1975. A. Brigham Rose, "Personnel of the Syndicate," Radio Talk July 1, 1938. Interview with Grant Cooper, conducted by Marshall Croddy, May 1989.

[3] Toretsky and the other staff members held firm to their contention that the Mr. Quinn who called Massey to issue instructions was Parrot. Toretsky testified that Massey also frequently directed her to call Parrot. On one call, she claimed, "His secretary answered and I asked if Mr. Parrot was there. She asked, 'Who's calling?' I replied, 'Mr.

Massey.' A voice answered shortly, and I said, 'Is this Mr. Quinn?' The voice replied, 'Yes.' I said, 'Mr. Massey is out just now and hung up."

Although Massey claimed that Jim Dierke, a police officer on special duty with the Liquor Board, used the alias Quinn, Toretsky insisted Parrot, not Dierke, was the mysterious caller. "The voice of Dierke, known to us as Jim Dierke, was positively not Quinn. Quinn was very profane and gave his orders in a clipped voice. Dierke was always polite and used his own name."

[4] Although a deputy district attorney from Los Angeles monitored the hearings, no charges were filed against Parrot or Massey despite a resolution from the State Senate Committee declaring that the two men had perjured themselves. However, the head of the State Board of Equalization fired Massey, who resumed his position with the LAPD.

Parrot was in the clear, but the issue came back a year later. This time, interest in Parrot was aroused by statements of Helen Werner and her husband, former City Attorney Edwin Werner. Called before the Alameda County Grand Jury, which was investigating statewide corruption in liquor license awards, Werner denied allegations that he and his wife Helen exercised undue influence in appointments to liquor boards and charged that Parrot and Guy McAfee controlled liquor in Los Angeles County. "This town and county are run by Parrot and McAfee. They have a stranglehold on the chief of police, mayor and sheriff. Their influence is stronger than ever before, in their control of city and county and liquor administration." Despite the charges, Parrot escaped once more without as much as a subpoena.

[5] *LAT,* Apr 25, 1932, ii, 4; Feb 25, 1938, 3. *People vs. Kynette,* Vol. 13, 847.

BATTLE IN THE GRAND JURY

[1] *LAT,* Apr 24, 1937, 13; Apr 26, 1937, ii, 12; May 2, 1937, ii, 1; May 6, 1937, 1, 9. *Woods,* 347-50. *Reuben Borough and California Reform Movements,* 203-4.

[2] After his acquittal for the Crawford and Spencer deaths, Clark served as attorney for Southern California gambling figures, including Guy McAfee, with whom he and his wife traveled, along with McAfee's fiancée, actress June Brewster (nee Kathleen Anderson) to Italy in 1936. His foray into gambling operations became public in January 1937, after he disappeared after taking a train to San Francisco. His disappearance touched off rumors that he had fled out of fear for his safety. Clark had recently obtained a passport and was carrying $5,000 in bills. A worldwide search by local, state, and federal investigators found no trace of him. As is usual in such events, false sightings filled the papers for weeks. Two months later, Clark resurfaced in Nice in the south of France, explaining that he "just went crazy." He had spent all his money and left his baggage in a hotel on Lake Como, Italy as collateral for $350 room charges. His wife, who had already moved to a small bungalow and sold all the furnishings from their large home on South Rossmore, could not raise the funds for his return, but some of his "Spring Street" friends wired $700. A few weeks later, Clark was back in Los Angeles. He and his wife separated soon afterward.

[3] *Fresno Bee,* July 20, 1937, 1. *LAT,* Jul 21, 1937, 1, 3; Jul 22, 1937, 1-2.

[4] *LAT,* Jul 24, 1937, 1; July 25, 1937, 1; Jul 27, 1937, 3; Jul 28, 1937, 1-2. *Reno Gazette-Journal,* Jul 21, 1937, 5.

[5] *LAT*, Jul 5, 1931, Part V, 4; Nov 25, 1931, 4. . Jun 22, 1933, ii, 8; Jun 26, 1933, ii, 2; Jul 9, 1933, 18; Aug 21, 1933, ii, 2. Chris Nichols, "Charting the 127-Year History of Clifton's, Downtown's Most Glorious Resurrected Building," *LAmag.com,* Aug 19, 2015.

[6] *Chamberlain*, 8. *LAT*, Jan 29, 1937, ii, 2, 5; Feb 7, 1937, ii, 5; Feb 13, 1937, 1; Feb 17, 1937, 2.

[7] Edmond J. Clinton iii, *Clifton's and Clifford Clinton: A Cafeteria and a Crusader,* Angel City Press, Los Angeles, 2015, 85-6. *LAT*, May 21, 1938, 2; Jul 21, 1937, ii, 2; Jul 9, 1937, ii, 1. Jul 29, 1937, 1, 2; Aug 5, 1937, ii, 1.

[8] *LAT*, Aug 8, 1937, 1.

[9] *Clinton iii*, 87

[10] Rose was a New York native and a former aide-de-camp to the Persian consul in that city. He had moved to Los Angeles in the late 1920s with his young wife, a former actress and dancer. He had played a small part in the unsuccessful 1932 recall of Mayor Porter, associating with Harry Raymond's attorney, Joseph Fainer.

In 1936, Rose had defended Orville Forrester, a conspirator in the California Republicans' shakedown scheme and one of Rheba Crawford's sources for details about the Shaw administration's involvement in LA vice payoffs. After Crawford switched her support to Shaw, Forrester continued working against the mayor, furnishing another reform pamphleteer with the names and addresses of gaming and prostitution sites. Soon afterward, acting on an anonymous tip, a "flying squad" of narcotics officers raided his apartment on North Normandie Avenue and found opium in the bathroom behind a toilet paper roll holder. Arrested along with Forrester was his wife, Mabel Rodgers, a prostitute with a lengthy arrest record. Forrester claimed that he was the victim of a frame-up and the opium was planted. Police had already nosed around what he described as his "bread and butter," a bordello at 814½ South Central, where Rodgers worked. Rose convinced enough jurors that his client had been framed to hang the jury. After the DA admitted that the case was unwinnable, the judge threw it out. However, Kynette's Intelligence Squad continued to hound Forrester, bugging his apartment to get evidence that could put him away. Eventually, he left town.

The following year, Rose and Joseph Fainer represented Rheba Crawford in a $1 million slander suit against Aimee Semple McPherson. Crawford alleged that McPherson had publicly called her a Jezebel and embezzler after the two clashed over the leadership of the Angelus Temple. Rose did his best to besmirch McPherson. To prove that she had lied when she claimed in court that she never used obscene language, he forced her to read aloud intimate passages from love letters to her husband. Afterward, he implied she was observed intoxicated in downtown Los Angeles. Finally, he questioned her about reports that she and another woman associate had pitched pennies to decide who would sleep with her male secretary during a holiday on Catalina Island. When McPherson countered with a claim that Crawford extorted payoffs from Los Angeles vice leaders, it must have been clear to both women that neither would emerge unbloodied from a full trial. They decided to settle out-of-court, their reputations already having been tarnished enough.

[*St. Cloud*, Part 6, 44-45. "Confidential Report/Orville Thomas Forrestor," Joseph Shaw Collection, UCLA Special Collections. "Confidential Report, Conversation in office of Clinton Baxter 908 Chapman bldg." Joseph Shaw Collection, UCLA Special Collections.]

[11] *LAT,* Jun 9, 1936, ii, 20; *Santa Ana Register,* May 18, 1936, 3; *Van Nuys News,* May 11, 1936, 1.

[12] *LAT,* Sep 9, 1937,

[13] *LAT,* Sep 9, 1937, 1; Sep 10, 1937, ii, 4.

[14] *LAT,* Jun 16, 1936, ii, 3; Jun 18, 1936, 14; Jun 19, 1936, 17; ii, 2; Jun 23, 1936, ii, 1-2; *Bakersfield Californian,* Jun 23, 1936, 8; Jun 29, 1936, 7; *Press-Democrat* (Santa Rosa, CA), Jun 23, 1936, 1; *Billboard Magazine,* Aug 8, 1936, 42.

[15] Coyne, a Hollywood real estate broker and friend of Wilkinson, was subpoenaed by the grand jury in its investigation of reform shakedowns. Coyne, identified as "Harry L Coyne" in the original subpoena, was a Kentucky native who had first arrived in Los Angeles in 1895 under the name "Jack Coyne." A powerful young man with boxing experience, he claimed to have worked for the Thiel Detective Agency of St. Louis for seven years in various cities, including a stint in Coffeyville, Kansas, in 1892 when the Dalton brothers made their ill-fated attempt to rob a local bank. A local Los Angeles private detective named George T. Insley hired him to work on a case connected to the Tenderloin district, the assassination of Lou Suey, a popular former court interpreter and current leader of Chinatown's Hop Sing Tong.

Afterward, Coyne hung around Los Angeles. His skills as a former boxer came into play first when he beat up a couple of tenderloin saloon bouncers who tried to eject him from their establishment and later when he quarreled with his former partner in a private detective business over the ownership of some office furniture. In the latter case, Coyne supplemented his fists with the butt of a revolver that he brought down on his ex-partner's skull. Toward the end of the year, he landed a bodyguard job with the son of a millionaire named T. D. Stimson, accompanying the young man to Mexico City and back. The assignment gave him an idea. In early January 1896, he told Stimson that he had somehow learned of a plot against Stimson's life and property that was to be carried out by a crook that had just arrived in Los Angeles from Mexico. Almost daily, Coyne repeated and embellished the tale, adding details that implied an intimate knowledge of the plotter. However, Stimson, a shrewd man who had made his fortune in the lumber business, figured that Coyne was just angling for an easy payday and dismissed his warnings.

On February 6, 1896, around 10:30 in the evening, a neighbor of noticed a figure prowling around Stimson's mansion with a torch. Believing the man an arsonist, the neighbor rushed out, pistol in hand, just as a terrific explosion rocked the neighborhood. He fired several shots at the fleeing figure, who rushed down Figueroa, avoiding several men on the streets, and vanished aboard a trolley car. As a crowd gathered at the mansion, T. D. Stimson came outside, looked at the hole in the ground the explosion had left, glanced at the undamaged solid Arizona sandstone walls and laughed quietly. As the police arrived, he returned to his mansion, closed the heavy doors, turned out the lights, and went back to sleep.

A week later, police detectives arrested Harry Coyne, whose detailed knowledge of the plot against Stimson and inability to produce any other plotter but himself was incriminating. Before the summer began, the bold, presumptuous young man was convicted of extortion and sentenced to five years in Folsom prison, where he gained additional notoriety when he was caught counterfeiting coins produced from metal stripped from the prison's rock-hauling machines. After his release, he returned east to St. Louis, where he joined his brothers in establishing a large plumbing and gas fitting business named the Coyne Brothers. The business failed in April 1905 after other large plumbing supply business, allied with plumber unions, refused to supply it with plumbing materials. He and his brothers then founded training schools for young men wanting to become plumbers. Eventually the school had four locations, St. Louis, Cincinnati, Chicago and New York, with 2,500 students. When this business failed a few years later, Coyne, taking advantage of experience he had gained working with the Tammany organization while he ran the New York City campus, returned to St. Louis to become a "legislative agent." What this entailed became clear in late October 1907 when he was charged with perjury after he told a grand jury that he did not remember trying to bribe members of the state legislature. While his attorney made a brave defense, arguing that Coyne should not be tried for perjury simply because he did not recall having attempted the bribes, which others remembered quite well–Coyne claimed he had sustained a head injury in New York City a year before–he was convicted and sentenced to two years in prison. His lawyer filed an appeal. Coyne continued to be active in local ward politics in St. Louis, and by summer, ads for his trade school showed up in newspapers across the country. Finally, in late 1908, the Missouri Supreme Court reversed his conviction and remanded the case for a new trial. In 1910, he was found innocent after his attorney argued that his injury, and not an intent to deceive, caused him to deny his bribery attempt.

After the trial, Coyne remained in St. Louis for a decade. For most of the decade, he was in the automobile sales and storage business but by 1918, he had shifted to selling farm tractors. Sometime between September 1918 and November 1919, he returned with his wife and son to Los Angeles and set himself up as a homebuilder and real estate agent. He made a success of it but the adventurist spirit in him was not completely satisfied. In May 1924, he vacated his home in West Hollywood and headed north to Klamath Valley, Oregon, intent on raising polo ponies. He quickly morphed into a promoter and seller of Oregon ranch properties, becoming one of the areas' most enthusiastic boosters.

While Coyne continued to raise polo ponies and promote the Klamath Valley, he returned to Hollywood in the late twenties and continued his real estate business. His interests expanded again in the early thirties, when he backed mining operations in Arizona and Bakersfield, California. How he got into the reform business is a bit of a mystery. Coyne compiled the list of vice establishments Wendell Miller delivered to Mayor Shaw.

In September, the grand jury indicted Coyne for extorting $1,000 from two Huntington Beach café operators by threatening to expose their illegal gambling operations. He was also indicted for two counts of attempted bribery in connection with a scheme to open bookmaking establishments in Santa Monica. In November, after several months of posturing and accusations against prosecutors for framing him, Coyne abruptly changed his plea to guilty. It developed that the vice-reformer, who had blasted gambling and political leaders from a sound truck he drove around Los Angeles neighborhood streets, feared that his shady past would land him in state prison should he be found guilty after a trial. His guilty plea reduced his sentence down to a $500 fine and a short sentence in county jail.

[16] *LAT,* Sep 17, 1937, ii, 3; Sep 22, 1937, 1; Mar 20, 1941, 30.

[17] *LAT,* Sep 29, 1937, ii, 1; Sep 30, 1937, ii, 1; Oct 12, 1937, ii, 1; Oct 23, 1937, ii, 1.

[18] *Salinas Index-Journal,* Oct 25, 1937, 1.

[19] *LAT,* Oct 26, 1937, ii, 4.

[20] The first suspect named in the Bruneman murder was in fact former eastern hoodlum Johnny Rosselli. Rosselli, a onetime member of the Capone organization of Chicago, was working as the bodyguard of a studio executive. Rosselli dutifully reported to police when he heard they were looking for him. He declared that he had no idea why police wanted him but that he would help the investigation in any way that he could. He was released without charges. [*LAT,* Oct 27, 1937, 2.]

[21] *LAT,* Oct 30, 1937, 1. *BAK,* Oct 29, 1937, 1. *SCEE,* Oct 29, 1937, 1. *Wilmington Press Journal,* Oct 29, 1937, 1. *SFE,* Oct 30, 1937, 11.

[22] *LAT,* Oct 30, 1937, 1.

[23] From the report of the 1937 Grand Jury:

The publicity given to rank hearsay and unfounded rumors concerning our Judges, District Attorney, Sheriff, Chief of Police, Board of Supervisors, Mayor and other public officials is not only grossly unfair to those involved but is a disgrace to our citizenry who revel in another's discomfort. . . . . Public Enemy #1 in this county is not the gun-toting racketeer, not the oily-tongued confidence man–not the Shylocks of business–Public Enemy #1 in Los Angeles County–an enemy whom no legal weapon is provided–is malicious, unbridled reputation-smearing gossip!
. . . .

Grand Juror Clinton, aided and abetted by incompetent, legal and political advice, sought to have the Grand Jury listen to a number of witnesses who were supposed to have some knowledge of vice and corruption in the ranks of public officials. After hearing one of the so-called key witnesses in this matter the Jury quickly realized that the testimony of this witness was largely made up of rank hearsay and suggested a course of procedure which would provide for a thorough investigation of the matters suggested by Juror Clinton and prepare the evidence, if any legal evidence was developed, for proper presentation to the Jury as a whole. After some discussion, criminations and re-criminations, the entire matter was referred to a special Deputy District Attorney, approved by the Grand Jury and Juror Clinton for investigation and report.

After an investigation, based upon Juror Clinton's allegations and those of Juror Clinton's private legal counsel, a report was made to the Grand Jury to the effect that no legal evidence had been discovered which would in any way tend to establish the commission of the criminal offenses suspicioned by Juror Clinton. [Final Report of the 1937 L. A. County Grand Jury, December 31, 1937.]

[24] John Bogue, Harry L. Ferguson, Clifford E. Clinton, "To the Superior Court of the County of Los Angeles."

EXPLOSION

[25] *LAH,* Apr 29, 1938, A-10.

[26] *People vs. Kynette,* Vol. 49, 2891-2. *LAT,* Nov 6, 1937, 1; Oct 9, 1937, ii, 1; Oct 23, 1937, 1; Nov 7, 1937, ii, 1; Jan 29, 1938, 5; Aug 1, 1940, ii, 3. *SBCS,* Mar 4, 1938, 14.

[27] *People vs. Kynette,* Vol. 47, 2800-07; Vol. 49, 2900; Vol. 49, 2911-2914.

[28] *LAH&E,* Apr 29, 1938, A-11. *LA Daily News,* Apr 29, 1938, 3. *People vs. Kynette,* 368-374.

[29] *People vs. Kynette,* Vol. 10, 681. *LAT,* Apr 30, 1938, 7.

[30] *People vs. Kynette,* Vol. 4, 229; Vol. 5, 256; Vol. 47, 2800-2814. *LAT,* Jul 1, 1935, 7; Apr 28, 1938, 1; May 24, 1938, ii, 1, 3; May 25, 1938, 7; Apr 30, 1938, 7. *Fresno Bee,* Apr 28, 1938, 9. *SFE,* Apr 28, 1938, 8.

[31] *LAT,* Jan 15, 1938, 1, 2. *People vs. Kynette,* Vol. 27-8, 1694-1787.

[32] *LAT,* Dec 1, 1937, ii, 1; Jan 15, 1938, 1. *IDN,* Jan 15, 1938, 3. *LAE,* Jan 15, 1938, A-10.

[33] *LA Daily News,* Jan 15, 1938, 1.

[34] *Officers Report* 305 864, Jan 24, 1938, 1. *People vs. Kynette,* Vol. 49, 2928.

[35] *LAT,* Sep 19, 1932, ii, 4.

[36] *People vs. Kynette,* Vol. 16, 970. *LAT,* Apr 29, 1929, ii, 4; May 28, 1930, ii, 10; Jun 7, 1930, ii, 1; Nov 30, 1930, ii, 1; Dec 2, 1930, ii, 1; May 8, 1931, ii, 5; Jun 25, 1931, ii, 5; Jun 27, 1931, ii, 1; Sep 19, 1932, ii, 4; Jul 3, 1931, ii, 1; Dec 21, 1931, ii, 4. *LAR,* Oct 15, 1931, 5.

[37] *Officers Report* 305 864, Jan 24, 1938, 2-4.

[38] *People vs. Kynette,* Vol. 17, 1055-60; Vol. 16, 971-76.

[39] *People vs. Kynette,* Vol. 17, 1061-1063; Vol. 16, 992-3.

[40] *LAT,* Jan 16, 1938, 1-2. *LAE,* Jan 16, 1938, 2.

[41] *LAT,* Jan 21, 1938, 8. *LAPD Officers Report* 305 864, Jan 24, 1938, 6.

[42] *LAT,* Jan 20, 1938, 2.

[43] *IDN,* Jan 21, 1938, 1, 3.

[44] *El Paso Times,* Jan 20, 1938, 3. *LAT,* Jan 24, 1938, 1.

[45] *Montana Standard, (AP)* Jan 27, 1938, 7. *LAT,* Jan 27, 1938, 1, 6.

[46] *IDN,* Jan 26, 1938, 3.

[47] *LAT,* Feb 26, 1938, 1.

[48] *IDN,* Manchester Boddy, "Views of the News, Jan 17, 1938, 1, 2; Jan 26, 1938, 1, 3. *GJ/Raymond Bombing,* 563-567.

[49] *LAT,* Jan 31, 1938, 2; Feb 6, 1938, 1.

[50] *LAT,* Jan 29, 1938, 5.

[51] GJ/Raymond Bombing, 372-3.

[52] *LAT,* Jan 23, 1938, 1; Jan 7, 1938, 6; Feb 1, 1938, 6. *SMT,* Jan 24, 1938, 1.

[53] *LAT,* Feb 8, 1938, 6.

THE TRIAL AND RECALL

[54] https://latimesblogs.latimes.com/thedailymirror/page/533/. *LAT,* Feb 9, 1938, 9; Mar 3, 1938, ii, 2. The specific action of the district attorney that impressed body was the

arrest of a shadowy figure named T. Ray Costerisan, a close associate of Kynette who reputedly was connected to the LAPD hierarchy and underworld figures. Charges against him were dropped.

[55] *People vs. Kynette,* Vol. 21, 1287-89; Vol. 22, 1363-1403; Vol. 23, 1407-37; Vol. 21, 1296-98. *LAT,* Feb 3, 1938, 1, 8; Feb 4, 1938, 3.

[56] *LAT,* Apr 30, 1938, 1.

[57] *People vs. Kynette,* Vol. 49, 2905. *Santa Monica Times,* June 2, 1938, 2. *BAK,* May 28, 1938, 1. *LAT,* May 26, 27, 28, *ad passim.*

[58] *SCEE,* Apr 26, 1938, 2; Apr 27, 1938, 2. *Fresno Bee,* Apr 28, 1938, 2. *Santa Cruz Sentinel,* Apr 27, 1938, 1. *SMT,* Apr 27, 1938, 2. *LAH&E,* Apr 27, 1938, 7.

[59] *LAT,* Jun 17, 1938, 1, 9.

[60] *Clinton iii,* 115.
http://cliffordclintonandlosangelesreform.blogspot.com/2012/03/bombing-of-harry-raymond.html.

[61] *LAT,* Mar 9, 1938, part ii, 1; Jul 15, 1938, 4.

[62] *LAT,* Aug 9, 1938, 7.

[63] *LAT,* Sep 18, 1938, 1; ii, 1; Sep 28, 1938, 1; Sep 30, 1938, 1; Oct 7, 1938, 1; Oct 8, 1938, 2; Oct 21, 1938, 1; Nov 17, 1938, 1; Mar 4, 1939, 1.

[64] *LAT,* Mar 6, 1939, Part ii, 4.

DYING FALLS

[65] *LA H&E,* Sep 18, 1938. *LAT,* Jun 1, 1939, 2. *IDN,* Mar 26, 1952.

[66] *Frederick News* (Frederick, Kansas), Feb 4, 1895, 5. *Indianapolis Journal,* Dec 12, 1900, 5. *SFCALL,* Jun 15, 1900, 14.

[67] *Las Vegas Age,* Dec 13, 1919, 1; Apr 17, 1920, 1; Mar 4, 1922, 1; Apr 1, 1922, 1; Nov 18, 1922, 1; Feb 2, 1924, 8. Eric N. Moody, "Nevada's Legalization of Casino Gambling in 1931/Purely a Business Proposition", *Nevada Historical Society Quarterly,* Summer 1994, 79-100. *Nevada State Journal,* May 13, 1930, 6.

[68] Map of Kent K. Parrot Property, Santa Barbara Estates, Hope Ranch Park, 1926, santabarbaravintagemaps.com. *Santa Barbara Morning Press,* Feb 18, 1926, 9; Feb 20, 1926, 11; Mar 21, 1927, 7; Aug 05, 1928, 1; Feb 12, 1929, 13; Feb 21, 1929, 10; May 24, 1929, 15; Jan 26, 1930, 6; May 01, 1930, 10. *LAE,* May 9, 1940, *LA Herald Express,* May 10, 1943. *LAT,* Aug 22, 1937, Part V, 1. *SFC,* Aug 26, 1954, 10.

[69] *LAT,* Jan 30, 1965, Part iii, 9; Aug 24, 1940, Part ii, 1,3; Jan 30, 1949, Part ii, 1; Apr 6, 1949, 1; Jun 7, 1949, 1-2; Oct 27, 1950, 1-2; Nov 8, 1950, 1.

[70] *OAKT,* Dec 1, 1943, 14.

[71] *LAT,* Feb 9, 1946, Part ii, 1.

[72] *SFE,* Sep 5, 1945, 3. *LAT,* Oct 11, 1945, Part ii, 3. World War II Draft Registration Card, U3859, Earl E. Kynette. *Pittsburg, Ca, City Directory, 1947,* 117.

[73] *IDN,* Jun 20, 1951, 5.

[74] *OAKT,* Jul 2, 1955, 3; Jul 9, 1955, E1; Sep 15, 1955, 2; Sep 16, 1955, 2. *SBCS,* Jul 9, 1955, 3. *LAT,* Sep 17, 1955, 9. *Sacramento Bee,* Jul 14, 1955, 8. *SFE,* Jul 15, 1955, 31.

[75] *LAT,* Feb 15, 1939, 8; Apr 2, 1939, Part ii, 6; Apr 6, 1939, 11.

[76] Harry Raymond to Fletcher Bowron, May 28, 1953, courtesy of Jim Raymond.
[77] Interview with Jim Raymond, 2018.

BY THE SAME AUTHOR:

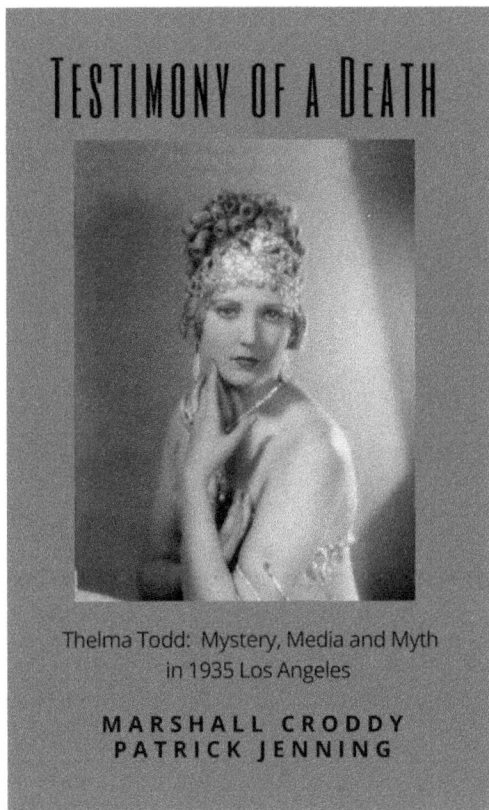

TESTIMONY OF A DEATH

Thelma Todd: Mystery, Media and Myth
in 1935 Los Angeles

MARSHALL CRODDY
PATRICK JENNING

THE COMPLETE ACCOUNT OF HOLLYWOOD'S

MOST PERPLEXING MYSTERY

www.ingramcontent.com/pod-product-compliance
Lightning Source LLC
LaVergne TN
LVHW011343080426
835511LV00005B/109